Keeping Adolescence Healthy

Exploring the Issues Facing Today's
Kids and Communities

Aaron White, PhD

Keeping Adolescence Healthy

Exploring the Issues Facing Today's
Kids and Communities

ISBN: 1-4196-8997-5
ISBN-13: 978-1-4196-8997-0

Library of Congress Control Number: 2008901561
Publisher: BookSurge Publishing
North Charleston, South Carolina

All books printed in the U.S.A.

For Avery and Skyler, two amazing kids who have taught me more about human development than I could ever learn from science.

Table of Contents

What is adolescence and why should we care?

Adolescence is the transition from childhood dependence to adult independence; the stage of life during which we form complex social identities and learn to function outside of our families. If all goes well, kids should leave adolescence heading into a healthy and productive young adulthood. In the current book, we will take a tour of a variety of issues that can influence the paths that kids take through life and the nature of the adults they become, and explore what research suggests about how best to deal with them. In this chapter, we will set the stage for those discussions by examining adolescence, what it is, what it tends to look like, and why it happens.

Looking good at any cost – The pressure kids are under to attain aesthetic perfection

Today's teens are held to standards of physical perfection unattainable by most and unhealthy for most that attain them. In this chapter, we will explore the pressure adolescents, and the rest of us, are under to attain perfection, aesthetically, and examine the impact that factors like marketing and depictions of beauty in the media can have on self-image and body satisfaction. The recent trend toward plastic surgery at younger ages will be discussed, as well as ways in which adults can help deflect the pressure kids are under to meet lofty and unreasonable cultural expectations of beauty.

Diet, exercise and relaxation – What does it mean to be a fit teen?

One key message from the last chapter is that looking good and actually being healthy are often two very different things. In this chapter, we will explore what it means to be physically healthy during adolescence, focusing on diet and exercise. We will discuss the issue of teaching kids to make healthy food choices, the impact of vending machines in public schools on adolescent health, eating disorders, the Body Mass Index, nutrition and other topics. We will also discuss research suggesting that focused and intentional relaxation, like meditation, is beneficial to adolescent health, well-being and brain functioning.

The toxic effects of videogame violence on kids and communities

In this chapter, we will continue our exploration of how cultural forces shape and mold our kids, this time focusing on digital violence. Store shelves are filled with an array of ultra-violent videogames from household names. The case will be made that the supply and demand of games that make graphic, first-person murder fun for kids of all ages points to problems in the culture and ultimately contributes to them. We will examine the data to assess the impact that such violence has on our kids and communities, explore ways to help kids make healthy decisions around gaming, and discuss how to make healthy decisions on their behalf.

School violence – Bullying, shootings and what can be done about it

Increasing rates of violence in public schools serves as a prime example of how pro-violence messages in the culture influence the real lives of our kids. In this chapter, we will take a close look at two categories of hostility that occur in schools – bullying and murder. While both include aggression, the acts are often perpetrated by very different types of kids. Is it possible to predict which kids are likely to become bullies or killers? What happens to kids who are bullied, and communities struck by the tragedy of homicides in school? Can metal detectors and guards solve the problems?

Exploration, experimentation and teen drug use – Putting things in perspective

Adolescents are built to explore and take some chances. For many kids, these tendencies are expressed through sports, the arts, or various healthy social outlets. For others, these tendencies lead to experimentation with, and sometimes chronic use of, substances that alter how the brain works. In this chapter, we will look at drug use from a developmental standpoint. We will examine how kids get started down pathways involving drug use, discuss how adults can help keep them from going too far, and lay out concrete steps for what to do once a kid begins sliding down the pathway toward dependence and addiction.

Rethinking underage drinking – What science says about the risks and how to minimize them

Alcohol is the most widely used and abused drug among both adolescents and adults in the United States. Rates have slowly declined but remain far too high. Many adults still cling to the myth that allowing kids to drink at home will somehow protect them from harm. In this chapter, we will examine patterns of alcohol use among teens and explore strategies for keeping them from damaging their lives, and the lives of others, through misuse of this highly toxic drug.

Protecting kids from disease – The immune system, how it works, and how to keep it healthy

Each year several media stories break about teens dying from drug-resistant strains of bacteria. Fortunately, such cases are rare, and we all carry around the means to protect ourselves from most infections. It's called the immune system. Like other systems in the body, the immune system undergoes poorly understood developmental changes during adolescence. In this chapter, we will explore the immune system and its role in psychological well-being, discuss how vaccines work, and examine ways in which the immune system can be optimized to help keep adolescence disease free.

Puberty and "raging hormones" – What do they have to do with adolescence?

During the second decade of life, our bodies undergo widespread changes in height, weight and hairiness. Males start generating sperm and females start releasing eggs and having periods. These changes are related to puberty, the physical metamorphosis that prepares us to have children and protect them. The physical changes of puberty and the social and psychological changes of adolescence combine to prepare kids for their adult roles. In this chapter, we will discuss puberty, what it is, how and why it happens, and how it relates to the social and psychological metamorphosis of adolescence.

Birds, bees and adolescents – The facts about teens and sex

Changes during puberty and adolescence trigger a sexual awakening. This process can be unsettling for both parents and teens. Cultural forces influence the types of behaviors that emerge at this time. How are today's kids coping and how can adults help? In this chapter, we will examine rates of sex, contraceptive use, teen pregnancy, and sexually transmitted infections, as well as the association between sex and violence in teen relationships. The aim is to help adults prepare themselves for goal-directed discussions with teens about the risks and responsibilities that go with sex and sexuality. Few deep discussions will be found here, just the nuts and bolts of the issues.

What happens when the road gets too bumpy? An introduction to adolescent psychological disorders

In previous chapters, we explored some aspects of normal adolescent behavior that can be downright troubling. Many kids experiment with drugs, drink alcohol, break household rules and the law, and end up doing just fine. But what happens when the troubling behaviors don't seem to be temporary and transient? When does moodiness cross the line into depression? When does difficulty focusing on schoolwork become ADHD? When does an argumentative attitude become a conduct disorder? In this chapter, we will examine the issue of normal vs. abnormal behavior, discuss how to spot problems and explore what can be done to help kids deal with them.

Adolescents and the Internet – Keeping kids safe on the digital frontier

There is perhaps no better example of a generation gap than the ubiquity of the World Wide Web in the lives of current adolescents. Anything can be found, or lost, online. Issues like identity theft and sexual predation will be discussed, and tips will be provided for keeping kids safe in an increasingly virtual world.

Introduction

We humans move through three basic stages of change as we mature – childhood, adolescence and adulthood.[1] During childhood, we are dependent upon the adults in our lives to provide us with what we need to survive. As adults, we should be capable of taking care of ourselves, and perhaps raising kids of our own. Adolescence represents the transitional stage between the developmental bookends of childhood and adulthood. It is the time in our lives when we aim ourselves toward independence and work to get ourselves there.

Adolescent behavior is geared toward making the transition to independence happen. Tendencies to argue with parents, clash with siblings, take some chances, keep one's life more private, and explore the world all serve the purpose of motivating teens to become more independent and start making their way toward the door. Without this process, adolescents would probably never leave home, and the species would eventually die out after years of swimming around in the shallow end of the gene pool.

At the core of the behavioral changes that take place during adolescence is the human body, particularly the brain. The brain enters a very unique phase of malleability during the adolescent years. This window of enhanced brain plasticity allows adolescents to absorb experiences with ease and learn quickly. When we enter adolescence, emotions rule the day. By the time we exit, control over our behaviors will be shifted to brain areas involved in planning, decision-making and controlling our short-term urges in exchange for long-term benefits.

One need only think of high school memories, good or bad, to recognize the powerful impact that adolescent experiences have on how we think and feel throughout our lives. Memories of the people we meet in our 30s and 40s can fade quickly, but memories of people from high school seem to remain deeply engrained in people's brain circuits for the duration.

During adolescence, the brain and all of the emotions and behaviors that arise from it are customized to fit the demands of the environment. This allows us to prepare for independence in the current world and make good use of it. Kids raised in environments that provide a healthy balance of support and discipline, and an undercurrent of unconditional love, will likely grow up to become healthy, well-rounded citizens. Those that spend their teenage years in the basement playing ultra-violent videogames while their parents silently watch ultra-violent prime time TV programs in the other room could grow up to have serious difficulties functioning in an increasingly complex global society.

The task of raising healthy adolescents has never been more difficult. The world is a very different place than it was a few decades ago, and both the opportunities and pitfalls afforded by these changes seem endless. In this book, we will explore a variety of issues that affect the well-being of adolescents, the paths they take through life, and the contributions they make to their communities. The aim is to help adults understand how the interplay between adolescents and the surrounding culture influences their emotional and mental development, and how to tweak the environment to unlock the full potential inherent in each kid.

The experiences we have during adolescence shape the nature of our adult lives. Adolescence is usually completed by one's early 20s. On average, the typical American citizen will live into their late 70s or beyond. This means that we can expect each person to be around for another 50 or 60 years after adolescence and the window of malleability it provides ends. If for no other reason than fiscal, it is crucial that we do what we can to point kids in the right direction and give them the skills they need to thrive in the modern world. The attitudes, skills and behaviors of a single adolescent might not add up to much in the grand scheme. However, collectively, the attitudes, skills and behaviors of today's kids will strongly influence the nature of the future for all of us.

It is generally impossible to find simple cause-and-effect explanations for how kids develop, regardless of how comfortable such explanations can feel and how logical they can seem. Violent videogames alone do not cause kids to become killers, but can contribute if the circumstances line up. Not all adolescents that drink will become alcoholics, but a family history can increase the odds. Magazine covers displaying skinny models do not, by themselves, cause eating disorders, but can make it much harder for girls to develop healthy body images. During actual development, an unknown number of variables constantly interact with one another, at odd angles and with varying degrees of force, to influence moment to moment changes in biology and behavior and shape kids over long periods of time. Only in movies on the *Lifetime* network do otherwise healthy kids get mad at their moms and suddenly join motorcycle gangs. This is good news. Except in cases of real trauma or true organic health issues, most kids can be made to be okay given the appropriate influences and resources.

This book represents an effort to take readers on a linear walk through the heart of several issues, sticking close to research in the social and neural sciences when possible. In practice, this is a little like plotting a straight line through a sea of scattered data points. It tells a story that makes sense, but cannot capture the true complexity of the situation. While the book is divided into chapters, savvy readers will quickly recognize that these topics are not necessarily separate in kids' lives. Sexual activity and drinking overlap and interact, as do immune system health and exercise. Drugs and psychological disorders often go hand-in-hand for many kids, and the Internet seems to play roles in all of these issues nowadays. Cyberbullying and teen suicide show up in several different chapters and could be included in several more. With that said, the chapter approach is convenient and the material can be made to obey this format. Let's take a look at each of the chapters and what is covered within them.

In Chapter 1, we will take a brief tour of adolescence, beginning with discussions of what it is and why it happens, and then exploring the behavioral patterns one ought to expect from kids during this stage of life. The aim is to provide a context within which we can explore the various issues facing today's adolescents and the adults trying to raise them.

There is an interesting duality in modern American culture. Obesity has become endemic, yet our kids are constantly bombarded with images of slender starlets and TV programs suggesting that physical attractiveness is directly tied to satisfaction in life. In Chapter 2, we will discuss the pressure kids are under to look perfect, including the alarming trend toward plastic surgery at younger and younger ages. We will examine ways to help immunize kids against the toxic psychological effects of the cultural pressure to attain physical perfection and help them find satisfaction through internal means.

We Americans are less healthy now than we ever have been. By doing a better job of teaching today's kids how to make healthy food choices and get sufficient exercise, we can reverse the trend toward nationwide obesity in just a few generations. In Chapter 3, we will discuss diet and exercise and explore what needs to be done to help our kids, and ourselves, become physically healthy.

For decades now, psychologists have debated the impact that violent media content can have on childhood and adolescent development. As those debates have played themselves out, the magnitude and realism of violence in TV programs, videogames and movies have reached alarming levels. In Chapter 4, we will review evidence that violent media content is toxic to adolescent development and discuss the limitations of such data. The case will be made that saturating ourselves and our kids with virtual violence has led to a reduction in our reactions to, and concerns about, real violence. The myth that violent media somehow produce catharsis, or a purging of violent urges, will be debunked.

Many kids are exposed to real acts of aggression during adolescence, often during the course of a typical school day. In Chapter 5, we will explore two types of hostility that take place within the relative security of school walls – bullying and shootings. We will examine evidence regarding the causes and consequences of these acts and evaluate the effectiveness of strategies put in place to deal with them. Environmental forces increase the odds that some adolescents will bully other kids or become murderers. The case will be made that, by identifying and mitigating these environmental forces, rather than profiling kids themselves, we can decrease the odds that adolescents fall into the trap of using violence to express their inner troubles, and increase the odds that all kids reach young adulthood intact.

Life can be extremely challenging and confusing for adolescents. Their bodies and internal psychological states are in a bizarre state of flux, parents pressure them to fall in line with expectations, and friends often tug them toward engaging in activities that violate family policies and the law. For many teens, drug use serves as an unofficial rite of passage, a means of exploring the world and themselves, and a way to cope with the pressures of life. Fortunately, most adolescents emerge from this phase without incident. For many others, however, drug use places them on a slippery slope that culminates in serious short- and long-term consequences. In Chapter 6, we will discuss drug use during adolescence from a developmental perspective, examining what motivates teens to use drugs, how we adults can help keep them safe, and what to do if an adolescent has already developed a problem.

Without question, alcohol is the drug of choice for both adolescents and adults in the U.S. and most of the industrialized world. In the U.S., Federal law mandates that only people 21 years or older can drink alcohol. Despite the laws, a large percentage of adolescents end up using it. Somewhere between 10-20% will go on to develop a serious problem with this particular drug, and starting early seems to push the odds higher. In Chapter 7, we will explore the issue of underage drinking in great detail, examining the causes, consequences and potential solutions. We will discuss how to spot an adolescent with an alcohol problem and what to do about it. We will also examine the role that culture plays in drinking habits and behaviors, and explore differences between adolescent drinking here in the U.S. and in Europe. Many parents believe that allowing kids to drink at home is developmentally healthy in some way. The pros and cons of doing so will be examined.

Each of us carries around an army of cells, called the immune system, devoted to protecting us from infections. Like other systems, the immune system is in flux during adolescence. In Chapter 8, we will explore the immune system, how it protects us from disease, and what happens when things go wrong. We will discuss, briefly, the purported link between vaccines and developmental disorders like autism. Keeping the immune system healthy increases the chances that an adolescent will make it to adulthood in good shape. The roles of stress, diet and even laughter in immune system health will be explored.

There was a time, not too long ago, when books on adolescence included confident explanations about how the hormones surging through our kids' bodies drive them to act in unpredictable and volatile ways. While hormones certainly make their contributions to behavior, their primary role during the second decade of life is in driving puberty, the physical and sexual maturation that overlaps with the social and psychological maturation of adolescence. In Chapter 9, we will take a tour of puberty and the changes that go along with it, such as increases in muscle mass in boys and the onset of the menstrual cycle in girls. As we will see, puberty is starting earlier and earlier, while adolescence is being completed later and later, creating a unique window of vulnerability between the attainment of physical maturation and adult-like decision-making skills.

As our kids exit childhood, the hormonal and neurological changes of puberty and adolescence give rise to a sexual awakening. This newfound awareness of sexuality brings with it a level of responsibility that is unfamiliar to most kids. Conflicts over how best to teach kids about sex have essentially created a void in that aspect of formal education. It is critical that parents discuss the birds and the bees with their adolescents, lest they form their attitudes and opinions based solely on movies, commercials, magazines and friends. In Chapter 10, we will take a brief tour of the data regarding teens and sex in the new millennium. The aim is to arm adults with the facts they need to help kids make wise-choices for themselves around the issue of sex, thus avoiding both pregnancies and the spread of sexually transmitted infections.

Normal adolescent behavior can be downright troubling. Sometimes, adolescent behavior leaves the realm of normalcy and enters the domain of pathology. Knowing when a particular kid crosses that line can be extremely difficult, and truly unhealthy psychological troubles are often only recognized in retrospect. In Chapter 11, we will explore the topic of recognizing, labeling and treating psychological disorders during adolescence. Depression, ADHD, anxiety disorders, conduct disorders, schizophrenia and suicide will be explored. Rather than attempting to provide readers with details regarding every disorder a kid could develop, the focus is on the bigger picture of distinguishing normal from abnormal adolescent behavior and knowing when to be concerned.

Since the dawn of the Internet age a few decades ago, the line between real and virtual worlds has continued to blur. Everything from shopping to dating can be done via computers, or even cell phones, these days. The World Wide Web remains unexplored by many of today's adults, yet most modern adolescents feel quite comfortable on the digital frontier. The generation gap that results can lead to a lack of supervision and guidance while kids are online. In Chapter 12, we will examine some of the real risks that await kids in the virtual world and discuss strategies for keeping them safe.

The resolution to the nature versus nurture debate rests in the fact that both are vital for healthy human development. Our kids are shaped by dynamic interactions between their internal states and the environments around them. By using research and a large dose of common sense as our guide, we can create healthier environments for our kids and help them make the transition from dependence to responsible independence successfully. It is the author's sincere hope that this book will be of help to those interested in improving the health and well-being of today's developing adolescents. Their job is to adapt to the world we create for them. Our job is to ensure that the world we create for them is a good one!

Chapter 1

What is adolescence and why should we care?

Adolescence is the transitional stage between childhood and adulthood. During childhood, we depend on adults to take care of us. By the end of adolescence, we should be able to function on our own. The ride from point A to point B can be extremely bumpy. Conflicts with parents help compel us to explore the world and establish independent identities. Changes in our bodies, including our brains, prepare us to fend for ourselves and have kids of our own. During adolescence, we are molded and shaped by interactions between our own unique personalities and the world around us, ensuring a customized fit for each of us. Until adolescents attain full autonomy, it is up to the adults in their lives to ensure that the environments with which they interact are healthy. By understanding what adolescence is, and what adolescents need, we can begin tackling some of the tough issues facing today's kids and explore how best to handle them.

If adolescence were a play, it would be performed in two acts. In act one, a thespian in the midst of his own physical and psychological metamorphosis would explain in a cracking voice that his rights were being trampled on. His parents don't trust him, and he longs for the day when he doesn't have to ask for the keys to the minivan every time he wants to go somewhere. In act two, his parents would explain that they love their son, but he is changing so fast it's scary to them – he is taller, hairier and much moodier than he was just a few years ago. They want him to be happy, but they can't just give him the keys to the minivan whenever he feels like driving around. Until he's 18, he is their responsibility, and he simply must follow the rules if he wants to enjoy any privileges at all.

Adolescence is the stage of human development sandwiched between childhood and adulthood.[1] It represents the part of the interactive developmental assembly line where knowledge and skills needed to succeed in the adult world are added to the foundational emotional and cognitive abilities acquired during childhood. All humans must pass through adolescence on the road to relative autonomy, and we come hardwired to make it happen. Tickets for the ride are provided when genes intermingle at conception, but the nature of the ride itself will depend on the world into which one is born. Neither the child nor the parent can choose to skip the moodiness and bickering that often come with adolescence, and the sudden urge to move as far from home as possible seems to come naturally for most teenagers. At the same time, because the social and employment skills required to succeed can vary greatly from culture to culture, and across generations, one's adolescent experiences will vary accordingly.

> "By adolescence, individuals have matured beyond the frailties of childhood, but have not yet begun any of the declines of adult aging. Compared to young children, adolescents are stronger, bigger, and faster, and are achieving maturational improvements in reaction time, reasoning abilities, immune function, and the capacity to withstand cold, heat, injury, and physical stress. In almost every measurable domain, this is a developmental period of strength and resilience."
> - Dr. Ron Dahl

Adolescence is inherently challenging for both kids and adults, but it is critical that the challenges are dealt with appropriately if one is to succeed in the world at large. Rebellion, conflict and odd-behaviors are to be expected from every generation of developing adolescents as they begin to wiggle free from under our wings. The trick is to recognize the underlying developmental rumblings that give rise to such behaviors, keep our egos out of it as much as possible, and do our best to prepare adolescents for their eventual independence. Kids who don't acquire the tools necessary to function in the adult world become burdens for more than just themselves, and human life expectancy has nearly doubled in the last century. We all have a vested interest in getting adolescence right.

Adolescence is boot camp for life

Not all animals require the long period of handholding that we humans need before we are able to fly solo. Some are born basically ready to take care of themselves. The human equivalent of this might be emerging from the womb wearing a suit, carrying a briefcase, and heading to the office to meet with clients! Should we be envious? Probably not. Being born prepared for independence has its pluses and minuses. On the plus side, such creatures don't have to sit through years of tedious life-skills training and can immediately go out and earn a living for themselves. They don't have to compete with brothers and sisters for attention and can survive without adult help. And think of all the money their parents must save on diapers!

On the negative side, and there are some big negatives, essentially all of the instructions the animal is going to get come with it into the world. While it might be able to learn a new trick or two, it will not be able to roll with major changes in the environment. Let's take frogs, for instance. Frogs are born prepared to dart their tongues out at black specs. Hopefully for them, the black specs are bugs. That's about all they get, at least when it comes to vision. If all of the black specs disappear, frogs are going to be in big trouble!

The long childhood and adolescent periods preceding independence in humans reflects one of our specie's major strengths – behavioral flexibility. We humans are born with an impressive ability to roll with changes in the demands of the environment. If black specs disappeared, humans would just find something else to eat. No oxygen in space? We'll just take our own. Some would argue that this kind of flexibility is exactly what has allowed us, for better or worse, to populate so much of the planet in such a short period of time. The number of humans on earth has grown from 2 billion in 1950 to 6 billion in 2000! We can all rest easy knowing that frogs don't have the brain power or mental flexibility necessary to challenge us for the top spot. We're all alone up here.

During the first ten years or so of life, roughly corresponding to childhood, an amazing amount of learning takes place as we explore the world using our families and other caregivers as home bases. If it weren't for the fact that we eventually have to venture out away from the family, out into the deeper end of the gene pool, and create families of our own, we could just stay children. But that's not how it works. At some point, we need to take what we have learned with us into the vast world beyond our front doors and begin applying it to our own independent lives. Adolescence represents the complex social and psychological metamorphosis that eventually gets us out of our parents' homes so that we can master our own destinies, buy our own minivans, and one day deal with our own difficult teens!

What does adolescence tend to look like?

Behaviorally and emotionally, adolescents are moving targets. One day they love spending time with us and the next day we don't exist to them. On Monday they have a new best friend at school and by Friday they might vow to destroy that person. For parents, the changes exhibited by children entering adolescence can be troubling. Changes in sleep, diet, mood, weight, attitudes, clothing styles and the list goes on. A glance at the DSM IV, the American Psychiatric Association guidebook for diagnosing psychological disorders, would reveal that even normal adolescents exhibit behaviors that would be considered symptoms worthy of serious concern if exhibited by adults. If an adult mentioned changes in sleep, moodiness, increased conflict with family members and weight loss during a routine checkup, there's a good chance they would leave with a referral to a psychiatrist!

Let's take a look at some of the things that happen during adolescence and discuss the purposes these changes might serve.

Anywhere but home

Given total freedom, most teenagers wouldn't choose to stay at home with their families, at least not for very long or often! Simply being seen with one's family in public can make a kid wish their life was over. Most adolescents would prefer to hang out with friends, send instant messages to friends, talk on their cell phones with friends, page their friends, etcetera. It has probably always been this way for humans. It is just far easier now to communicate around the clock than it ever has been.

By the end of adolescence we should be able to survive on our own. Living on our own requires learning the social rules of the generation to which we belong. In order to learn these rules – like how to jockey for position in the popularity hierarchy, find mates, learn how to compete with peers, form alliances with friends, etcetera – it is very important to spend time around kids one's age. Sports and other competitive play, parties, and even just hanging out in the basement can all be viewed as training for the social demands of adolescence and, eventually, adulthood.

For current adults, the challenge is to figure out how to give kids enough room to grow, socially, while keeping them safe at the same time. Kids need longer leashes and increasing amounts of privacy during the adolescent years, but they also need guidance, love, support and discipline to keep things from going awry. Regardless of what teens say, they need adults in their lives and they actually do listen and learn from them.

Pushing envelopes and taking chances

For humans, as for many other species, adolescence

brings with it an increased desire to explore the world and take some chances. This makes perfect sense given the nature of adolescence as the transitional stage that it is. If we humans became less interested in exploring the world and trying new things when we entered

> "Increased risk-taking in adolescence is normative, biologically driven and inevitable."
>
> – Dr. Laurence Steinberg

adolescence, we would never leave home! The desire to see what's out there, and to see what happens if we don't always heed the advice of adults, helps nudge kids out of the door where the real training for independence begins.

Each generation of adolescents takes risks and seeks novelty in different ways, and each generation of adults seems to think that the current generation of adolescents has gone too far. Elvis' pelvis crossed the line in the 1950s for some parents. In the 1960s, kids grew too much hair. Driving too fast has always been a source of concern for parents, and drugs offer plenty of options for thrill seeking teens. No number of laws could prevent curious adolescents from finding ways to test the waters and we shouldn't seek to prevent them from doing so. But, we should do our best to keep them from testing

> "I was cruisin' in my Stingray late one night
> When an XKE pulled up on the right
> And rolled down the window of his shiny new Jag
> And challenged me then and there to a drag
> I said, you're on, buddy, my mill's runnin' fine
> Let's come off the line, now, at Sunset and Vine
> But I'll go you one better if you've got the nerve
> Let's race all the way
> To Dead Man's Curve"
>
> - *Dead Man's Curve*
>   Jan and Dean (1964)

waters in which they could easily drown.

Pushing the boundaries – socially, athletically, artistically, or in less healthy ways – is part of what makes adolescence work as a stage of human development. As we will discuss throughout the book, creating opportunities for kids to explore and challenge themselves in activities that involve calculated risks can minimize the likelihood that they will choose less healthy, more dangerous options to satisfy their urges to explore and take some chances.

Which way to the rebellion?

Public nudity is technically legal in Vermont, so it's up to individual communities to decide how to handle the issue. In the town of Battleboro, the issue had been a non-issue until the summer of 2006, when young people in the town began shedding their clothes in the downtown area. The catalyst seems to have been a young woman who decided to sit on a park bench naked. Others followed suit – birthday suit, that is – and, suddenly, walking around nude in Battleboro was in vogue. Teenagers began taking off their clothes on the sidewalks near restaurants, bookstores, galleries, and other businesses.

According to a CNN report on the matter, "A music festival promoting nudity and rebellious-ness set up in May in a downtown parking lot attracted nude hula hoopers." That must have been an interesting spectacle. When asked by CNN why young people in Battleboro are compelled to take off their clothes in public, a 19 year old male stated, "It's just an act of freedom. We're just doing so because we can." It's unclear whether he was clothed at the time of the interview.

> Kathie: "Hey, Johnny, what are you rebelling against?"
>
> Johnny (Marlon Brando): "What have you got?"
>
> -The Wild One (1954)

Human development brings with it a bag of tricks that help move us along from stage to stage. During adolescence, exploration and risk-taking compel us to leave our homes on forays into the world beyond. The urge to rebel, to push away from adults, serves an overlapping purpose. History is replete with examples of youth rebellion, including riots and protests. Kent State comes to mind for many people, as do recent riots in Paris over employment and wages. Friction between established and emerging waves of adults can reach a boiling point, spill over, and lead to serious conflicts. Let's take a look at Kent State, followed by a more recent example. Both cases offer insights into the making of youth rebellions and reveal what happens when the views of young people are out of synch with the views of the established authority and the tendency to rebel takes center stage.

In late April, 1970, President Nixon ordered the military to attack North Vietnamese troops inside of the Cambodian border. The decision led to widespread protests at universities throughout the U.S. On the evening of May 1, violent confrontations broke out between students and local police near the Kent State University campus in Kent, Ohio. Bon fires were built, police cars were pelted with rocks and bottles, and private property was damaged. The Mayor declared an unofficial state of emergency and ordered all of the bars to be closed. The move only added fuel to the angry riots. The National Guard was called in to aid Kent police and to deter further protests and rioting. On Monday, May 4, nearly 3000 people gathered on the University Commons. Across from them, near the Kent State ROTC building, which had been burned down a few days earlier, stood an estimated 100 National Guardsmen armed with rifles. When told to disperse, the students refused. Tear gas was fired into the crowd and the Guardsmen marched across the Commons in an effort to force students to leave the scene. Protestors retreated down a hill and into a nearby parking lot and field but would not stand down. The Guardsmen followed and found themselves trapped at the bottom of the hill and under assault by rock-throwing students. They retraced their steps to the top of the hill above the crowd, turned, and opened fire. Between 60 and 70 shots were fired during a 13 second period. The volley of gun fire resulted in the death of four students and the wounding of nine more. The University was

> "There's battle lines being drawn
> Nobody's right if everybody's wrong
> Young people speaking their minds,
> Getting so much resistance from behind"
>
> - *For What It's Worth*
>   Buffalo Springfield (1967)

closed until the summer.

Fast forward to April, 1997. Angry students at Ohio University in Athens, Ohio, jumped up and down on cars, lit fires in trash cans, and pelted police with rocks and bottles. Refusing to disperse, more than 30 students were arrested. One officer was injured in the clash. The issue that caused this social upheaval and revolt? A war gone wrong? Taxation without representation? Nope, Daylight Savings Time. When the clocks struck 2AM and the hands of time sprung forward one hour to 3AM, bar owners were legally bound to stop serving thirty minutes earlier than normal. This perceived infringement on the personal rights of the students was too much for them to handle. Left with no other alternative, they protested Daylight Savings Time. Similar riots occurred on the same campus during Daylight Savings Time for the next several years, becoming a tradition of sorts.

Fortunately, most incidents of youth rebellion do not involve riots of any sort. In fact, asserting one's rights, perceived or legitimate, during adolescence doesn't always require breaking the laws at all. On an individual level, teen rebellion usually plays itself out in living rooms and manifests itself in power struggles over the perceived rights of the teen and the rules of the parents. The arguing, bad attitudes and ornery behavior of many teens, no matter what form it takes, can be enough to drive some parents crazy. The good news is that the metamorphosis from clingy children to obstinate teens is healthy in the long run. Adolescents must push away from their parents, and parents must push back, in order to slowly jettison the kid from the nest.

Intense emotions and swinging moods

The mere mention of Shakespeare's *Romeo and Juliet* is enough to remind most of us how intense and volatile emotions can be during adolescence. But such works rarely capture the flip-side of things; the boredom we feel while waiting for the ship carrying our independence to come in.

Emotional development during adolescence is, in many ways, paradoxical. Boredom and blah-ness are normal. But so are intense emotions. These two poles work together to achieve similar purposes. Being bored helps motivate us to get out of the basement and explore the world. Intense feelings, whether in the form of anger at parents or puppy love for a classmate, can give us the drive we need to actually get off of the couch and head for the door.

When healthy outlets exist for intense adolescent emotions, and proper guidance is provided, these rumblings can be a wonderful asset; fueling productivity and leading kids to find creative ways to identify and express their internal states. Many adolescents channel their intense emotions into healthy activities that help them get through the teen years and could serve them well in their adult lives. Joining drama club, playing sports, painting, writing, or any number of artistic activities serve as examples. Riding skateboards, doing gymnastics or volunteering in various organizations provide additional outlets.

> "I cried a tear for nobody but you.
> And I'll be the lonely one,
> If you should say we're through.
> Well, if you want to make me cry,
> that won't be so hard to do.
> And if you should say goodbye,
> I'll still go on loving you.
> Each night I ask the stars up above,
> Why must I be a teenager in love?"
>
> - *Teenager in Love*
>   Dion and the Belmonts (1959)

Unfortunately, left unchecked and unguided, these new and intense feelings can be confusing and quickly turn toxic. Fighting, vandalism, stealing, promiscuous sex, immersion in violent videogames, and even murder can stem from unvented or unsatisfied emotional drives.

Who am I?

Adolescence is an awkward time, socially, for many kids. Trying to figure out whom one is, and how one fits, is a taxing task that dominates much of our inner lives during the teen years. The objective is to formulate an identity distinct from our childhood selves and independent of how our families view and treat us. This challenge must be accomplished against the backdrop of changing voices,

"And these children that you spit on
As they try to change their worlds
Are immune to your consultations
They're quite aware of what they're going through"

- *Changes*
  David Bowie (1971)

braces, acne and other clear indications that one is in the midst of a physical metamorphosis. A mild sense of paranoia about adults helps kids push away but also makes it hard for them to trust help offered by those that love them. For healthy teens in healthy, supportive environments, identities take shape quickly and this turbulent phase eventually ends. For troubled kids in troubled, confusing environments, identity formation can be tortuous and often incomplete.

At a social level, identity formation during adolescence is reflected in shifting alliances with various "in-groups" and the shunning of various "out-groups." Smoker or non-smoker? Democrat or republican? Rap or pop? Drinker or teetotaler? Crip or Blood? It is common for kids to move in and out of such groups as they try to find personas that seem to fit. Without guidance, love, support and boundary setting by parents, weaving one's way through various social groups can quickly go awry and impede healthy development rather than helping kids figure out who they are and how they fit.

Development continues long after adolescence ends, meaning that kids don't have to know *exactly* who they are before they leave the teenage years. However, finding ways to help developing adolescents explore their emotions, their abilities and their beliefs can provide them with a strong sense of self and give them the confidence they need to continue heading in the right direction once they reach young adulthood.

Sliding into the driver's seat of life

Identity formation is central to the transition from dependent children to autonomous young adults. As this process unfolds, kids must meet yet another challenge – internalizing what psychologists call "locus of control." As children, it is natural for the outside world to serve as the source, or locus, of control over our behaviors. We follow our parents around, climb into our car seats when they tell us, and ask them about our plans for the day. By the time we reach adulthood, our sense of control should emanate from within. We should make our own plans for the day, plot our own courses into the future, make our own minivan payments, and take full responsibility for our actions.

The locus of control issue is captured by this simple and familiar interaction with a normal, healthy kid who makes a mistake – Kid, "It's not my fault!"; Adult, "Well, whose fault is it?"

If all goes well, one's locus of control should become strongly internal by the end of adolescence. When combined with their newfound independent identities, an internal locus of control should provide kids in late adolescence with the courage necessary to strike out on their own. That is, if all goes well. Unfortunately, over the years, a decreasing number of kids have successfully undergone this shift from external to internal locus of control by the time they graduate from high school. This is a bad thing, as an external locus of control is associated with a long list of negative outcomes, including increased rates of disease, heightened stress levels, anxiety, and apathy – all of which can degrade the general quality of a person's life and impede further development.

Failure to help kids internalize their sense of control during adolescence could affect them, and those around them, negatively long after adolescence is over. Fortunately, when kids are raised in environments that value empathy and personal responsibility, locus of control should become increasingly internal as a matter of course. Activities and discussions that highlight delaying gratification, reinforce goal setting, and require kids to take others' points of view, can help kids climb into the driver's seat of their own lives.

Oops! Decision-making during adolescence

Just before midnight early one summer, two friends, both 16, were racing home to beat their curfews. The silver Jeep they were riding in turned down an isolated country road that was straight as an arrow and several miles long. There was no reason for the driver to be driving, really. He had not intended to do so. The idea of using his newfound driving privileges to go meet with friends was just too good to pass up once he had had several cans of beer.

"Hey man, there's a stop sign," the passenger noted in a calm voice as the road approached its end. His comments were met with a mumbled response from the drunken driver. "Hey man, there's a stop sign!!" the passenger exclaimed. Last second braking did little to slow the vehicle. The Jeep careened through the intersection and slammed into a tree. The car spun, flipped, slid across the grass, and eventually came to rest on its side in front of a small house. Rain splattered against the metallic paint as the two boys made their way out through the passenger door above them. Shaken, but somehow okay.

The driver pounded on the front door of the home until an elderly man in his bathrobe answered. The boy announced to the homeowner that he had knocked over one of his trees with his car. The man's poor hearing required several repetitions of the slurred explanation. It turns out the tree belonged to the man's neighbor. It also turns out the man's neighbor was a patient of the boy's father – a well-known doctor in the area.

The elderly man and his wife were kind enough to call the boy's dad and explain the situation. "Dr. White, now don't worry, but your son seems to have knocked over one of our trees with his car." The gruff response from the receiver was sufficient to tell the boy something he hadn't yet fully grasped – that he was in very deep trouble! He had just received his license 11 days earlier and had been skating on disciplinary thin ice since he was in single digits.

By now, a crowd had gathered around the capsized Jeep. This was a small town. Several of the boy's friends and even a teacher were there. Luckily for him, the police and half of the local fire department arrived on the scene before his father. Otherwise, the punishment would have been worse than the night he eventually spent in juvenile detention.

The repercussions of the boy's poor decision-making affected his life for years to come. He wrecked his car, lost his driver's license, really shook up some elderly people, became distrusted by parents of friends, was grounded indefinitely, and could have killed his best friend. His father drove him by the scene regularly for the few weeks it took to repair the couple's yard, just to remind him that bad decisions often lead to bad outcomes.

Often, when adolescents screw up, it's while doing something for fun without appreciating how statistics work. Adolescents have a tendency to believe that things will more than likely go their way. Research suggests that, when we are adolescents, we often see the risks but minimize the likelihood that they will apply to us. We then find out the hard way that this isn't how things work. Yes, it probably *is* possible to jump your garage on a moped. It's just unlikely you are in the small minority of people that can actually do it!

In short, while teens might be capable of logically deducing that bad things can happen to a person if they do a particular drug, attempt to skateboard down a railing, have unprotected sex, drive too fast, or engage in other risky acts, the allure of the perceived gains is often enough to draw them down these tempting pathways, and the sense that they can skirt the odds gives them the confidence to keep going.

It's all in their heads

As we enter the second decade of life, begin to test drive adult behaviors and inch our way toward autonomy, our bodies, including our brains, enter a very unique and tumultuous period of flux that culminates in physical maturation and the development of brain circuits capable of governing responsible adult behaviors.[2]

The adolescent brain is a true learning machine. The ups and downs of the teen years would be wasted unless the brain were capable of recording those experiences and modifying our behavior accordingly. The author of this book and a colleague from Duke University Medical Center are currently working on a book specifically about the adolescent brain for a different publisher. It should be available in the fall of 2009.

In brief, the changes that take place in the brain during adolescence shift control over behavior toward those areas involved in thinking about the future, controlling impulses, making plans, weighing options and other critical cognitive skills necessary to function like adults. The difficulty teens have with some of these capabilities points to the tumultuous changes taking place inside of their skulls. Their brains are trying to figure out how to do the things we demand of them. Until that happens, the kids within those brains and the adults that love them are in for a bumpy ride.

The strategy that nature uses to create a window of neurological moldability concurrent with adolescence is remarkable and worth mentioning here. During the first decade of life, the amount of tissue in brain areas subserving higher cognitive skills like those mentioned above increases. Brain cells branch out and communicate with each other and essentially make too many friends. For a moldable brain, these extra connections are like extra clay. Early in the second decade of life, the trend toward increasing amounts of stuff in those areas reverses and widespread sculpting takes place, driven by a kid's experiences. Brain cells drop connections that aren't exercised and focus their resources on nurturing circuits that serve the skills required by the culture. Whatever a kid does with his or her time during adolescence is what the brain acquires. This kind of malleability allows each successive wave of adolescents to adapt to an increasingly complex world. The brain takes the demands placed on it in stride, makes the necessary changes in circuitry, and imbues the brain owner with the requisite abilities.

Appropriate experiences make capable kids but the garbage-in garbage-out rule definitely applies here. No matter how sophisticated the three pound squishy brain is, it isn't in the business of discerning whether the experiences we have when we are very young will be advantageous or detrimental down the road. It usually isn't until we reach late adolescence or young adulthood and reflect that we recognize the errors we made, or the errors that were made for us. It is crucial that adults recognize that kids have to be taught how to make wise decisions and respect the reality that each interaction with a developing adolescent could leave indelible imprints on their brain circuits. By promoting and reinforcing experiences that will benefit a child in the long run, and staying engaged in a kid's life, it is possible to help adolescents craft brains that will allow them to thrive in the adult world.

Each kid gets one brain and one chance to go through adolescence. It is critical that we do our part to ensure the sculpting that occurs contributes to a kid's future and the greater good of our communities if we want them to lead fruitful adult lives.

Boys ⟶ men, girls ⟶ women

The words "sex" and "gender" are often used interchangeably, though they are not the same. Differences between the two offer a good example of the different contributions that puberty and adolescence, biology and experience, make to development during the second decade of life.

When it comes to differences in males and females, sex refers to the biological side of things while gender refers to the development of culturally prescribed behavioral patterns for the different sexes. Some cultures nudge their genetically male kids down social pathways that place a high value on physical strength while others primarily nurture strength of character. Some cultures view successful women as assertive and independent while others expect or even legally require subservience.

With regard to sexual development during adolescence, both physically and psychologically, the initial nudge comes when a sperm cell shows up with either an X or Y sex chromosome to compliment the egg's X chromosome. This will determine initial changes in the sex organs and set up the appropriate chemical milieu in the womb to route development down a particular pathway. This generally leads to boys who are boys and girls who are girls, but not always. The presence or absence of key hormones in the womb, at key times, can create several permutations of sexual anatomy and orientation.

For the first ten years or so after birth, hormones play more subtle roles in behavior, and experience driven brain development allows for the sculpting of gender specific behavior patterns. At about the age of 10, hormones make a grand re-entry and things really start changing as puberty kicks in. As we will see in a subsequent chapter, puberty and adolescence are not the same thing, but are so inter-related they really seem to be. The onset of puberty brings with it the ability to reproduce, lots of new body hair, and a general growth spurt. It's like an upgrade package.

The hormone changes of puberty also usher in a new stage with regard to brain development. This is where adolescence begins in earnest and both physical and gender differences really begin to emerge. The brain changes allow developing kids to absorb information with ease and give them more conscious control over their behavior. The process of brain development during adolescence is fairly different for males and females. Some of this has to do with culture, but a lot of it has to do with momentum created by earlier changes in the brain and reproductive organs. Differences in their bodies, sexual orientation, and patterns of brain growth all ensure that adolescence will be a different experience for kids based on sex and gender, biology and learning.

Rites of passage

Picture this. A teenager arrives at the mall with his mom. He gets out of the car, posture slightly hunched. He checks to make sure there are no other teens around and schleps toward the entrance side-by-side with his mom as she puts the keys in her purse and runs down the list of stores she needs to visit.

Now imagine the same teen the day after he receives full driving privileges. He arrives at the mall alone and locates a prime spot. Perhaps he even backs the family van into a parking space for added effect. The door opens and, slowly, a sunglasses-clad warrior emerges proudly from the vehicle. With perfect, erect posture he scans for other teens, nodding at those that make eye contact. With an air of invincibility he shuts the door and begins to stroll effortlessly toward the entrance. Clicking the red button on the key fob over his shoulder as he walks away locks the doors, sets the alarm, and symbolically marks his crossing from boy to… well, still boy, but one much closer to becoming an adult.

Receiving a license to drive is a rite of passage for teens – one of the few official legal markers of the transition toward independence during adolescence. It's certainly not the end of adolescence, but a sign that one is moving in the right direction. Most coming of age films dealing with adolescence involve cars in one way or another. *American Graffiti* centers around cars and the freedom they bring us when we are young. *Risky Business* includes a scene where our coming of age protagonist accidentally allows his father's pristine sports car to roll into a lake. James Dean just wouldn't seem so rebellious if he walked everywhere in his movies. All of those songs from the 50s and 60s about driving fast, wiping out on dangerous curves, driving to the beach. Cars and driving are central to the mainstream American adolescent experience.

Sex, methamphetamines, cigarettes, drunkenness, and bonnets. No, it's not another Washington political scandal. It's not even spring break in Cancun. It's Rumspringa, a little known right of passage for adolescents in Amish communities. Adolescence is a developmental stage shared by all humans. However, the ways in which various cultures view and handle adolescence can differ in profound ways. In the mainstream U.S. culture, getting a driver's license, having a Bar Mitzvah, graduating from high school, reaching the voting age and being able to buy alcohol serve as markers of maturity and increasing autonomy. But this isn't the case for everyone.

The Amish in the U.S. live in a parallel culture that shares the recognition of adolescence as a critical transitional stage, but marks the transition to autonomy quite differently. When Amish adolescents turn 16, adults encourage them to leave the communities, if they are so inclined, to explore the larger culture and decide for themselves whether to stay for good or leave for good. It's a true rite of passage.

There are plenty of Amish adolescents who take a responsible approach to exploring the world beyond the wooden doors of their farm houses. For others, Rumspringa is like an extended Prom Night with lots of drugs, sex, and all the rest. This is beautifully captured in the documentary, "The Devil's Playground." As is the case with teenagers in mainstream America, most Amish kids turn out just fine.

In most modern cultures, markers of the transition from childhood to adulthood are usually painless, at least physically. Having a Bar Mitzvah or sitting through driver's education classes can be stressful – but the tears that are cried are usually tears of joy or perhaps boredom. In other cultures, pain is an integral part of the adolescent transition. Anyone with basic cable television probably knows this already. According to the World Health Organization, forced female circumcision, also known as genital mutilation, remains a rite of passage for many young females in Africa, southeast Asia and some parts of the

Middle East. Three variants of the procedure are performed, all of which involve destruction of the clitoris. At the most extreme end, the clitoris and labia are completely removed and the vagina is sewn shut. Anesthesia is rarely used. Tell your kids that story if they ever complain about how long it takes to get a driver's permit in your state!

Resilience – The hallmark of healthy kids

All of the molding and shaping we do to build healthy children hopefully translates into resilience during adolescence. Resilience refers to the ability of an individual to bounce back from adversity and keep moving forward. Resilient people are not defeated by failure. They learn from it and use the disappointment to fuel the hard work needed to improve. A resilient child faced with tough challenges from the environment will hold onto hope for a better future and will keep striving to overcome the obstacles.

The brain is highly customizable when we are young. The more we do to build resilient kids, the more resilient they will become. Over time resilience can become the brain's default way of approaching difficult situations in life. Resilient adolescents stand out from their peers in several ways. Here are some of the factors associated with resilience:

1. Internal locus of control
2. Autonomy
3. Androgyny (i.e., many resilient kids are not overly masculine or feminine)
4. Spend more time on homework than peers
5. Cooperate with teachers

Resilient adolescents are less likely to get into trouble, in general. This includes lower levels of substance use and, for females, a lower likelihood of becoming pregnant. As can be seen from the list above, resilience and locus of control are related concepts. Adolescents that recognize they are responsible for how they perform in their classes are more likely to work hard to succeed, and to bounce back if they fail. The same applies to resilient kids when they are in sports, drama, you name it.

Resilient kids also contribute to resilient communities, the kind that bounce back from tragedy and perhaps become stronger in the process. Resilience in kids can be strengthened by encouraging them to succeed and then encouraging them to keep trying if they fail. No matter where their paths take them, resilience will help them get there!

What do adolescents need?

Regardless of where we are in life, when we have needs we try to meet them. Depending on your particular circumstances, that could mean finding a bathroom, waiting for an organ transplant, or buying a new Mercedes. In general, we tend to do what we can to move ourselves from a point of less happiness to a point of more happiness. It's how we do that that matters, particularly to psychologists!

Let's say, presently, you're hovering around a 2 on a 10 point "happiness with life" scale. In fact, you're doctor might even consider you depressed. Perhaps you need medication to adjust your internal happiness thermostat in the right direction? Perhaps you need a vacation to get away from your toxic work environment and give your naturally happy self some time to shine? Perhaps your diet and exercise plan has consisted of curling French fries for a bit too long and could use some tweaking to help bring back your old self? The point is that there are lots of ways to try to meet a particular need.

Adolescence is a stage of life full of shifting needs. Some are driven by the culture, like what kind of clothing a person ought to wear in public, while others seem driven by the biological rollercoaster ride of puberty, like the need to buy tampons! Here are just a few of the things that adolescents seem to need:

- Security within the family but some distance from it
- Opportunities to make important decisions
- Structure, guidance, reinforcement and discipline
- Approval from the same sex
- Approval from the opposite sex
- Healthy diet and regular exercise
- Genuine intentional relaxation
- Goals – both short- and long-term
- Unconditional love and conditional support
- Mentoring and positive peer influences
- A sense of purpose in life
- Adventure and fun

Clearly, there is a great deal that we adults can do to help adolescents figure out how to get their needs met in the best possible ways. Helping others meet their needs is a far different task than meeting our own. Let's look at an example that involves two adults, one of whom is struggling in some way, to get a general sense of how this works and how complicated it can be.

Over lunch with a coworker, she explains to you that she just doesn't feel like herself lately. When she looks in the mirror, the person she sees seems to change from week to week. She isn't sure who she is anymore, and doesn't know where she fits, socially. She's moody and, no matter how hard she tries, she just can't seem to get along with her family. She sometimes says things that she doesn't really mean and then feels terrible about it, but her emotions get the best of her. On top of that, she can't sleep, is gaining weight and breaking out. The whole thing is like a confusing physical and emotional rollercoaster ride.

What would you do for your friend? Stealthily pay the tab and sneak out before things get really weird? Presumably, you would offer her support and understanding, tell her she'll be just fine, encourage her to hang in there, and do what you can to guide her. You would probably explain that you know how it feels to be lost, socially, and to question who you are and why you exist. If you were really concerned, you would recommend that she seek expert attention and perhaps help her find it. In short, you would do whatever you could to help your friend get through it. You wouldn't abandon her, chastise her, or persecute her for the difficulties she's having.

The situation with adolescents is similar in many ways. In addition to support and encouragement, adolescents need discipline, guidance and a clear understanding that they are loved no matter what. Adolescents are in the midst of moving from childhood to adulthood. It is the job of an adolescent to push the boundaries of the rules and sometimes defy authority. It is the job of parents and other adults to hold the line and keep kids on track. Left to their own devices, most teens (and plenty of adults!) would choose fast food over vegetables and videogames instead of homework. Until they break free and begin to function autonomously, the job of keeping their priorities in order and motivating them to move forward rests partially with the adults who love them.

The emotional turmoil that many adolescents experience as a result of the changes taking place in their bodies and in their lives can be difficult to handle. Time moves more slowly when we are young. Being grounded for a week can seem like a death sentence and the rejection felt at the end of a relationship can make life seem like it's over. Teens shouldn't be given free passes because they feel strong emotions. Most adults have to go to work regardless of whether their current emotional state is good or bad. However, it is crucial to remember that adolescence is a time when children cease to be and young adults slowly come into being. Strong emotions serve their roles in the process. As such, we must give adolescents outlets for their internal emotional drives. If not, behavioral problems of some type should be expected. Throughout the book, we will examine healthy and unhealthy options for helping kids cope with the emotional whirlwind of adolescence.

Not surprisingly, many adults are unsettled by the behavioral, and physical, transformation kids go through during the adolescent years. As teens try on new looks and habits, there could be long stretches of time when they seem unfamiliar to the adults that love them. Patience is important here, and it helps to try hard to avoid letting egos get in the way. This is difficult when the child a parent works hard to nurture and protect says things like, "I hate you!" If this sounds familiar, just know that you're not alone and that, if all goes right, this phase should be temporary.

Helping adolescents develop is an active process that requires regular interactions between adults and kids. Kids reflect their environments and what takes place within them. There is no way around that part. Providing a comfortable environment for kids should be the beginning, not the end, of what we do. If parents do not stay connected to their kids, it is far too easy to slide into the role of chauffeur and maid, where only the basic psychological needs of the kid are met, despite the physical comfort within which the child develops. On the flipside are so-called "helicopter" parents, those that hover over kids, micro-manage their lives and make the lives of school administrators and college professors difficult! One extreme is too distant, while the other is too close in the wrong ways. Something in the middle – creating an emotional safety net for kids while giving them room to learn from their own successes and failures – makes more sense.

It is important to keep in mind that the lack of overt signs of unhealthy development does not necessarily mean that healthy development is taking place. Plenty of well-dressed teenagers commit suicide each year leaving parents completely clueless about what just happened. In many cases they had everything they could have needed in a physical sense, but their unmet emotional needs proved disastrous over time. This disconnect between many modern parents and their kids is captured poignantly in the 2005 movie, "The Chumscrubber." It is also captured in the following anecdote.

While giving a talk at a private school, a parent from the audience asked the author for some suggestions. Her adolescent daughter had a friend that had just started smoking marijuana. The daughter was having difficulty figuring out how to handle the friendship. The parent asked if there was some kind of a phone number that her daughter could call for support and guidance. After a pause, the author responded, "Yes. The number is 1-800-YOU." It is our role, as parents and members of communities, to provide guidance to kids as their identities take shape. Without such guidance, we lose control of the forces that shape our kids and the odds go down that they will grow into the healthy young adults we want them to become.

In short, adolescence is a wild ride for everyone involved. Rather than shying away from teens or trying to prevent adolescence from happening, they need us to participate in this process and try to make it a positive one. Naturally, adolescents want more freedoms, but it is the job of adults to establish the parameters within which those freedoms are exercised. Yes, you can go to the mall with your friends, but no you can not just disappear for the day with the family minivan! Given the right balance of love, support, encouragement and discipline, most kids make it through the adolescent years physically and psychologically intact.

By doing what we can to help meet the basic emotional and psychological needs of a typical teen in healthy ways, we can diminish the odds that they will choose ultimately unhealthy ways of doing so.

What does it all mean?

Adolescence is the stage of human development sandwiched between childhood and adulthood. It is the transition between dependence and independence, and adolescents come equipped with the tendencies and urges needed to make the transition happen. By recognizing the unique and natural needs of adolescents, and the ultimate purpose of this stage of development, it is possible for us to approach any issue facing teens with the best interest of the kid in mind. Using science and common sense as our guides, we can construct parameters that genuinely prepare adolescents for the adult tasks ahead.

Adolescence is the time when the cellular circuits that allow us to put a spotlight on the future and aim our behavior accordingly develop. The changes in the brain involve areas that influence how kids think, feel and act. This makes sense, as adolescence is a stage full of changes in how kids think, feel and act!

In the remaining chapters of the current book, we will explore a variety of issues facing today's adolescence, their families and their communities. It is the author's sincere hope that the material will help the reader understand the issues and how best to handle them.

Quick Facts:

- Adolescence is the transition out of childhood and the dependence it requires, into young adulthood and the relative autonomy it brings.
- The body, including the brain, enters a very unique period of flux during the second decade of life, roughly corresponding to the adolescent years.
- Many aspects of physical and psychological development during the second decade of life are driven by the hormonal changes of puberty.
- Adolescence reflects the social, psychological and neurological aspects of development accompanying the changes associated with puberty.
- Puberty prepares an individual to *be able* to function in the adult world. Adolescence prepares an individual to

function in the adult world *as it is now*. Puberty and adolescence are highly interconnected but not the same.

- As our kids enter adolescence and their internal worlds begin to change, their external behaviors change, too. Taking chances, breaking some rules, pushing boundaries, bickering, and bad attitudes are just a few common characteristics of normal adolescent behavior.
- The job of an adolescent is to push away from parents and adapt to the environmental influences that impinge upon them so that they can one day function autonomously. This is true regardless of whether the environmental influences are ultimately healthy or unhealthy.
- The job of adults is to ensure that the environmental influences impinging on developing adolescents are healthy!

Chapter 2

Looking good at any cost – The pressure kids are under to attain aesthetic perfection

During adolescence, both males and females begin to look at themselves and those around them differently. Concerns about popularity and attractiveness take on greater importance. Messages from peers, commercials, movies, pictures in store windows, music videos, etcetera, remind teens that modern America places enormous value on physical beauty, particularly for females. Deep concerns about physical appearance can reach obsessive levels, driving otherwise healthy children into pathological states. In this chapter, we will examine several issues related to body image and body satisfaction during adolescence, and explore ways to help shield kids, and ourselves, from such unhealthy pressures.

Long before the agricultural revolution and the dawn of Internet dating services, we humans have had to compete with each other to attract mates. Sitting back and waiting until all of the good ones are taken can seriously jeopardize the future health of one's family tree. Competing for mates, specifically those that seem to be healthy and have good genes, makes much more sense. Fortunately, we come equipped with plenty of natural tendencies geared toward ensuring that we aren't picked last. Like peacocks, we strut our feathers and engage in all kinds of odd and culturally influenced rituals aimed at proving our worthiness to potential mates.

The complicating factor for modern humans is that we don't just have to compete for mates with those in our own little geographical areas; a task that can be hard enough. In an increasingly disconnected and virtual social world, an extremely high premium has been placed on the physical aspects of attractiveness. Via media, we are constantly being bombarded with images of people who have reached the pinnacle of desirability by current cultural standards. The physical parameters that define beauty have changed over the years, and will certainly continue to do so. But no matter what aspects of appearance are emphasized – breast size, nose size, waist size, hair color, eye shape – odds are that there will always be someone out there who is closer to perfection than we are, even before the makeup and digital editing. The media will continue to show these people to us, and advertisers will continue to make promises that they can make us look, smell and act more like those people – even if it takes surgery. The pressure this places on young people, and adults, to look perfect is staggering and leads many of us to spend ridiculous amounts of time obsessing about our appearances.

Because the information age has vastly enlarged the pool of people with which we compete, socially, the characteristics associated with perfection are often far out of reach for all but a small percentage of the population. A common example has to do with the proportions of the female body emphasized in advertisements. When young females approach reproductive age, legs lengthen, breasts enlarge and the hip to waist ratio increases. Perhaps for these reasons, the prototypical attractive female form included in many ads these days tends to highlight such attributes, often in near caricature-like proportions.

For several decades running, immense emphasis has been placed on thinness, particularly for girls. This is ironic and cruel, as it comes at a time when we westernized humans have never been fatter. This is also bad news for healthy development, as female bodies, more so than male bodies, are designed to store resources for later use. Being rail thin is inconsistent with the predisposition of the female body to store fat. In reality, uber-thin super models would not last very long in the wild, and some of them do not outlive their modeling contracts. Continually inundating young females with such unrealistic and unhealthy ideals of attractiveness promotes self-dissatisfaction and improper eating habits at an already difficult time in development. Presumably, super models are called "super models" because they stand out even in rooms full of models! In order for young women with healthy bodies to meet such unreasonable expectations of beauty, they often have to trade in their health, and emotional well-being, to do so.

This situation applies to males, too, but in a slightly different way. Imagine, if you will, a small enclave of humans in which one guy in particular is highly desirable. The other guys see this guy and try to be more like him in order to compete for the attention of females. Suddenly, someone turns on a television and reveals the existence of a man in a completely different state, or country, that obviously hit the genetic jackpot. No love handles, a full head of hair, and even his teeth are straight. Plus, he has confidence and social influence to boot. The name "Brad Pitt" comes to mind. Chicks dig him. True, he doesn't live in your particular little enclave, but now that everyone knows he exists, men in enclaves around the planet will have to compete with him, even if that competition is solely internal and psychological. Information traveling at the speed of light makes it possible to turn the entire planet into one big competitive social hierarchy. No one's ego is safe under such circumstances.

Let's take a closer look at the role that media play in shaping expectations about how one should look and influencing one's personal satisfaction with their current appearance. It is certainly possible for adolescents to reach physical maturity in the modern age without developing significant concerns about their physical appearances. However, it definitely isn't easy and requires consistent support from adults and a large dose of media literacy to inoculate kids from the ego lashings that await them in advertisements, TV shows, movies, magazines and even videogames.

Body satisfaction and the media

It is estimated that more than ½ of American girls are dissatisfied with their bodies by the age of 13. By the time they reach 17, nearly 4 out of 5 will be unhappy with how they look.[1] That's scary, and tells us that a large percentage of today's kids struggle with being comfortable in their own skin.

Various types of media play roles in fueling body dissatisfaction among kids. This includes advertisements. Most ads are designed to make us feel like something is missing. Something that only the manufacturer sponsoring the ad can provide. Because most of us are acculturated to question constantly how our appearances stack up next to the people around us, it is far too easy for companies to create ads that evoke a sense of longing to be different, presumably better, than we are currently. Once we are primed in this way, it becomes easier to get us to part with our money. The truth is, if advertisements made us feel good about ourselves, we wouldn't buy diet pills, fancy clothes, or flashy cars. If a deodorant commercial started out with, "We're sure you already smell great, but…," there would be no reason to purchase the product.

How do advertisements help create unrealistic expectations of beauty? Let's look at an example. A teenage girl of normal body size and height reads a magazine in which the beauty of a particular actress or model is highlighted in an ad or article. The airbrushed looks and body type of this woman become an ideal, even though she's thousands of miles away and of no realistic threat to the teenager's local social life. Indeed, the odds are good that the woman in the ad is no happier than those who view it! Each time the girl looks in the mirror, she will be acutely aware of the differences between her body, style of dress, etcetera, and the idealized image internalized from the magazine. If the person in the ad were average, the distance between actual and ideal images would be small, and the girl would feel less pressure and disappointment with her appearance. Instead, the women portrayed in magazines are either those with all of the appropriate genes, or their images are distorted so that they perfectly fit the current standards of attractiveness. If compelled to compete with such women, it is likely that the young girls reading the magazines will always be disappointed, extremely unhealthy, or both. For many teens, that is the situation.

Over the years, we Americans have retreated deeper and deeper into the safety of our own homes. The number of social engagements that we engage in has decreased, and the diameters of our friendship circles have shrunk. For many of us, television has become our primary source of connection with the outside world. In fact, we really don't even have to live interesting lives anymore at all. We can live lives vicariously through wacky, attractive, and super-tough television characters. Some of us have honestly come to view reality television as though it really represents reality!

In addition to entertaining us and making our lives seem more interesting, television provides a sense that we are all connected somehow. Yeah, sure, we don't know our neighbors' names, but it's a safe bet we could strike up conversations with them about one primetime show or another, or perhaps a sporting event, at the mailbox. Indeed, most conversations

---

SideNotes

Do magazine articles about dieting help teens maintain healthy weights?

No. Researchers at the University of Minnesota's Project EAT (Eating Among Teens) recently reported that reading magazine articles about dieting is associated with increased rates of unhealthy eating and dieting among teenage girls. This includes bingeing, vomiting, smoking cigarettes to lose weight, using laxatives, and skipping meals. Magazine articles seem to increase the pressure that many kids already feel to look perfect. The topic of weight as it relates to diet and health will be covered in more detail in the next chapter.

---

between men that meet for the first time seem to start with, "Did you watch the game?" Now more than ever, television serves as a window on the world for American adults and kids. Unfortunately, the view from this window is often entirely inaccurate!

Characters on television shows do not represent the populace. Reality television? Have you ever watched an episode of *Survivor*? Pick a season, any season, and you will not see the population accurately reflected in those little tribes that they assemble. The population in Venice Beach, California, maybe – but definitely not the population in Durham, North Carolina. If one took a random sample of Americans and placed them on a deserted island, most of us could live for quite some time on stored resources before we really found ourselves in danger of starving to death!

The inaccurate reflection of American body shapes and sizes is one of the most obvious distortions of reality on television. For example, one study examined the weights of 1018 characters in 10 top-rated prime time shows from six networks during the 1999-2000 television season.[2] They estimated that only 14% of females and 24% of males were overweight. The percentages of overweight (but not necessarily obese) people in the U.S. population are more like 62% for females and 67% for males! Granted, television-land is fantasyland. However, such huge disparities between depictions of reality and actual reality can create the false expectation that everyone out there is skinnier and/or more attractive than we are. This puts tremendous pressure on people, particularly adolescents trying to figure out how to fit in, to conform with unrealistic expectations of physical beauty. It also places undue emphasis on the physical aspects of who we are as individuals.

Misrepresentations of normal weight on television are likely to create internal conflicts for some viewers – particularly young and impressionable ones. If you are of normal weight, yet the television shows you enjoy make it seem like everyone is 50 pounds lighter than you, this could certainly have a negative impact on how you feel about yourself. Several studies suggest that the amount of time adolescent females, including college undergraduates, spend watching television is inversely related to how happy they are with their bodies. Indeed, having 10 year old boys and girls watch music videos and clips from television shows leads them to feel less satisfied with their bodies. Depictions of acceptable body types in the media can place developing adolescents, particularly females, in a very tenuous spot. At a time when they are becoming concerned about social acceptance and attractiveness, they can easily be made to feel as though everyone else in the world is more attractive than they are. Take away the perfect lighting, makeup, professional hair stylists, and unrepresentative casts, and it turns out those concerns are unwarranted. Further, the notion that physical attractiveness and emotional happiness overlap significantly is just plain wrong. This is readily apparent in each and every season of *America's Next Top Model*, a reality show in which young and attractive women compete to win a big modeling contract.

Side*Notes*
Popularity and body weight

Those of us who are not at the pinnacle of social popularity feel pressure to climb the ladder somehow. As such, one might expect that, over time, those who view themselves as low on the ladder of popularity might show signs of the effort to climb – new clothes, new hairdos and perhaps weight loss. In a cruel twist, it appears this isn't how it works, at least with regard to body weight. Researchers studied more than 4000 girls, with an average age of 15, over a two year period. All of the girls gained some weight over the two year period, as would be expected given their ages. However, those who viewed themselves as lower on the social hierarchy when the study began gained more weight over the two year period than those who perceived themselves as popular. The reasons for this are entirely unclear, but the findings do not bode well for kids struggling to fit in.

Television programs not only create expectations about body weight, they also set up expectations about how people at different body weights are supposed to feel and act. Overweight characters on television tend to be less romantic, eat more food, and generally appear less confident than thinner characters.

These are issues worth discussing with teens, as well as being a good reason to closely monitor what kids watch. Despite their vulnerability to these images, teens are savvy and they hate feeling manipulated. A good conversation about the distortions that occur in the media can go a long way toward limiting the disappointment and self-deprecation that can occur when teens compare themselves with these unrealistic images of attractiveness. Indeed, efforts to help teens make healthy dietary choices in general can be furthered by discussing issues of body weight and health in the context of the distorted images of perfection portrayed in the media. We will explore this issue in detail in the next chapter. Teens should be motivated to be healthy for the sake of good health, not to make them look more like today's popular stars and starlets, many of whom remain entirely dissatisfied with their appearances despite all of the accolades, and financial compensation, they receive for how they look.

Clothes, self-image and the purchasing power of today's teens

Today's teens wield a lot of financial power and are vulnerable to messages suggesting that they could be better than they are by purchasing products. This is a bad combination for kids and a good combination for major corporations.

In order for a company to survive, it helps if they sell products that need to be replaced over time. Whether due to planned obsolescence or the physics of normal wear and tear, products from microwaves to automobiles have life expectancies. Smart marketers have managed to convince most of us that clothing needs to be replaced on a yearly, or perhaps even seasonal, basis whether they show signs of damage or not. We are all familiar with the media frenzy that occurs when a celebrity is caught wearing the same outfit twice in the same eon. Clearly, clothing doesn't have an expiration date and doesn't need to be replaced on a yearly or seasonal basis. We do that because we can, and because we're afraid of being ostracized if we don't. Wearing up-to-date fashion items tells the world that we are tuned-in, active in the culture, not completely broke, and must be closer to ideal beauty than those that can't afford a revolving wardrobe.

Rapidly changing styles are driven by consumer interest and the need for corporate profits. How can a company post record profits next year if people keep wearing the clothes they bought this year? Like a siphon, once this process gets started, it just keeps going. Kids are raised in a culture where clothing is considered an important index of success and overall hip-ness. The styles offered by companies and purchased by consumers change regularly, and advertisements send the message that failure to keep up with the pace of change can cost kids socially. Marketers understand very well the motivation teens feel to climb social ladders, and they milk that motivation for every dollar it is worth. Even students at the very top of the social hierarchies at their schools could quickly fall out of favor if they started dressing in ways inappropriate for the year or season. There was a time in the 1970s when tight polyester pants and rainbow colors were cool. Dressing this way in the early 21st century would probably have the opposite effect on one's social standing.

The financial might of mainstream American teens helps drive the consumer clothing industry. According to Teenage Research Unlimited (TRU), a company that polls 2000 or so teenagers each year to get a sense of their habits, here's how much money American teenagers spend each year on products and services, including clothing:

2001 – $172 billion
2002 – $170 billion
2003 – $175 billion
2004 – $169 billion

2005 – $159 billion

Their estimates suggest that the spending power of teenagers is decreasing, yet anything approaching $160 billion per year is still a lot of money! This is almost three times the amount of money that Americans spend on illegal drugs each year and is enough to fund a foreign war for a little while. It is impor- tant that we adults help them make wise choices about how to spend their money, lest it simply feed industries built on the premise of planned obsolescence.

> "It's as though the question 'Who am I?' has been replaced with 'What image do I want to project?' "
>
> - Psychologist Ann Kearney Cooke

Many affluent parents think they are doing their kids favors by keeping them dressed in the very latest clothing and making sure they carry the newest handbags. This is usually driven by concern that their kids will be marginalized and unpopular if they don't keep up with the latest fashion trends. Unfortunately, by doing so, parents teach their kids to put a high premium on material appearances. This must make major retailers very happy! Ultimately, such an approach might do more to satisfy the social needs of adults than to promote truly healthy adolescent psychological development.

Plastic surgery – When nature refuses to cooperate!

It used to be that changing one's body weight, getting a hair cut, or buying new clothes and new makeup, were the primary ingredients of a teenage makeover. Not so in the modern world. Plastic surgery, once available only to the elite, and often looked down upon by the general populace, is now accessible to, and accepted by, people from all walks of life. Indeed, there are several television programs on a variety of channels dedicated to showing people before and after plastic surgery. In many of these shows, the person's plastic changes are unveiled at the end of the program and are met with rounds of supportive applause. That sends a pretty powerful message about the importance of physical appearance and almost trivializes the often dangerous procedures that take place in order to change the way a person looks. At a deep level, such spectacles suggest to viewers that well-being is directly linked to appearance and that both can be easily improved through plastic surgery.

The American Society for Aesthetic Plastic Surgery[3] estimates that, in 2005, Americans spent $12.4 billion on 11.5 million cosmetic procedures, both surgical and non-surgical. This marks a 444% increase in cosmetic procedures since 1997. Of the 11.5 million procedures performed, 2.1 million were surgical. The number of breast augmentations and breast lifts increased 9% and 23%, respectively, between 2004 and 2005. Most cosmetic surgeries (91%) were performed on female patients. Liposuction accounted for the majority of procedures, with breast augmentation coming in second. Roughly half of all women receiving alterations were between the ages of 35-40. Only 2% of all procedures were performed on kids under the age of 18, with rhinoplasty (nose jobs) being the most commonly performed procedure in that age group.

While the rates of surgery among kids are relatively low, rates among adults continue to grow. As such, today's kids will soon be entering an adult world where surgically altering one's body in order to approach an ideal image is even more widely accepted. And there are no signs that interest in plastic surgery will diminish anytime soon. The BBC News reported that, among 2,000 girls surveyed for a *Bliss* magazine story, 4 out of 10 desired plastic surgery.[4] According to a report in the Washington Post, televised media only add fuel to the fire by setting up unrealistic expectations for girls, as well as for the boys pursuing them. The article also highlights the role that parents play in enabling decisions about plastic surgery.[5]

"The enormous popularity of reality TV shows such as 'Extreme Makeover,' 'The Swan' and MTV's 'I Want a Famous Face,' as well as an explosion of Web sites that extol the virtues of cosmetic medicine, has fueled the desire of adolescent girls to alter their bodies permanently, and they are finding more surgeons willing to oblige them. Breast implants and liposuction are now bestowed by parents as graduation or birthday gifts. Some doctors say they have performed breast augmentations on baby-boomer mothers and their teenage daughters."

One of the truly frightening aspects of the surge of interest in plastic surgery among kids, and the constant stream of television programs touting the wonders of plastic surgery, is the fact that such surgeries do not always go well. It is highly unlikely that you will ever see an episode of *Extreme Makeover* or *Dr. 90201* in which a surgery goes poorly, the patient suffers from serious infections or pain, they are truly dissatisfied with the outcome, they are disfigured or they die. Yet these things happen day in and day out, as the tragic death in 2007 of musician Kanye West's mother after plastic surgery attests. It is not a minor procedure to stuff a saline-filled sack into the breast pocket. Muscle tissue is cut, nerves can be damaged, and chronic

SideNotes

What "A Girl Like Me" tells us

In the 1940s, husband and wife research team Kenneth and Maimie Clark conducted a series of studies revealing that young black children come to view white dolls and white skin as pretty and good, but view black dolls and black skin as ugly and bad. In 2005, 16 year old film maker, Kiri Davis, created a short documentary, "A Girl Like Me," in which she replicated the basic findings of the Clarks' work 65 years later, demonstrating that young African American children in the U.S. still come to associate their own skin with ugly and bad, while white skin is perceived as pretty and good. While all kids are placed under intense pressure to conform with cultural standards of beauty, this pressure must be far greater for those who are taught to view basic properties of their appearances, like skin color, in a negative light.

pain can result. It is also not a minor procedure to jam a metal tube under the skin and suck out fat cells. Both are far more invasive than root canals, and nobody wants those. There are risks involved in cosmetic surgical procedures and the outcomes can be truly disastrous.

A 2003 study published in the journal, *Annals of Plastic Surgery*, suggests that some women seek breast implants as a means to cope with underlying psychological dysfunction. The authors examined suicide rates among more than 2,000 breast implant recipients in Finland and found the rate of suicide among this group was three times as high as among the general population. Such findings highlight the fact that decisions regarding plastic surgery must be made very carefully, and underlying psychological pathologies should be ruled out before the procedures are performed. At the very least, the decision to seek plastic surgery for purely aesthetic reasons is suggestive of a strongly external locus of control. As discussed in the first chapter, an external locus of control is often indicative of other problems, meaning that all patients seeking unnecessary plastic surgery should be carefully evaluated before the green light for surgery is given. Given the popularity of plastic surgery and its high cost, it seems that most plastic surgery centers should be able to afford to keep at least one trained psychologist on staff if it helps ensure the well-being of potential patients.

Common sense suggests that plastic surgery is inappropriate for adolescents in all but exceptional cases, and the American Society for Aesthetic Plastic Surgery seems to agree. Body dissatisfaction isn't something that simply goes away with age and is unlikely to be rectified by a single surgery. Indeed, the fact that some patients keep going back for more reflects this and suggests that something like a plastic surgery gateway effect might occur in some people. Learning to become comfortable with one's body is one of the main challenges of adolescent psychological development. Plastic surgery involves changing one's body to more closely fit an internalized image of attractiveness. It can be quite difficult for teens to think through the long-term repercussions of their decision to surgically alter their appearances to fit current trends in beauty. If things go right, the social reinforcement they receive only serves to reinforce the decision to seek external means of improving one's internal state. If things go wrong, one's adolescent years could be spent trying to get the botched job fixed.

Every effort should be made to help teens who are dissatisfied with their bodies find satisfaction through healthy diet and exercise, as well as through putting more effort into activities that make them feel validated and in control. Playing sports or music, for instance. Urge them to wait until adulthood to revisit the issue of plastic surgery. It is unlikely the field of plastic surgery will shrink and disappear anytime soon, and the procedures should become safer over time, so the option should still be available to them in a few years after their bodies have had a chance to finish developing.

Regardless of the risks, cosmetic plastic surgery is a choice, and one that can be beneficial for some people in some cases. If one were considering plastic surgery – or considering allowing their teen to have it – here are some things to consider:

- Carefully research the potential surgeon.
- Ask for before and after photos of previous patients receiving similar modifications.
- Pick a doctor who performs procedures in a hospital or an actual surgical suite of some kind – not in their office or at your home!
- If anesthetics will be used, make certain that a licensed anesthesiologist will be present and responsible for this part of the procedure.
- Make certain that your surgeon will be on call after the procedure in the event of complications.

- If you allow your child to have plastic surgery, recognize that they will probably be given a prescription for pain medications. These need to be used as prescribed and only under your supervision.
- Be prepared to spend some time black, blue and sore and recognize that the end results might not be observable for some time after the procedure.
- Consult information from the American Society for Aesthetic Plastic Surgery. This is the professional organization that monitors trends and risks in these procedures. They have generally taken an assertive stance *against* purely cosmetic plastic surgery in minors.
- Prepare yourself, or your teen, for the very real possibility that the surgery will not yield the desired results and remember that death is always a possibility.

In America, breast implants and liposuction top the list of favorite procedures. What about elsewhere? As the following passage from a 2002 *Time* magazine article on plastic surgery suggests, there are real cultural differences involved in plastic surgery choices.[6]

"As in the rest of Asia, South Korea's primary cosmetic obsession is with the eyes. Having bigger eyes is every girl's dream, and it can now be realized through a simple $800 operation, in which a small incision or suture is made above the eye to create an artificial double lid. Teenagers as young as 14 are doing it, and eye jobs have become a favorite high school graduation gift from proud parents."

At the moment, plastic surgery appears to be a cultural mainstay, both in the U.S. and abroad. However, like parachute pants and leggings, there's a chance that such procedures could fall out of fashion at some point. Let's hope!

Modern culture as body dysmorphia factory

For many of us, looking at ourselves in the mirror is not the highlight of our days. We are aware of the imperfections on our faces, the extra deposits of fat in various places, and the fact that we just don't look like people on magazine covers. For most kids, the inordinate pressure to look a certain way can cause significant anxiety. For some, such anxiety becomes truly dysfunctional and can culminate in entirely inaccurate perceptions of one's physical characteristics and proportions. A diagnosis of Body Dysmorphic Disorder (BDD) is given in cases where the individual's preoccupation with their flaws reaches obsessive levels and threatens their overall well-being. When we look at kids with BDD, we might see healthy bodies. When they look at themselves, they see imperfections, and can become obsessed with them. Something similar happens in the eating disorder anorexia, as we will discuss in the next chapter. The individual's perception of reality becomes faulty. We see skin and bones, they see bulges of fat.

It is difficult to imagine how a normal kid raised in modern America could escape a small amount of body dysmorphia. Indeed, as we have discussed, it is normative for kids to be deeply dissatisfied with at least some aspects of their appearances. However, in cases of true BDD, the obsession with one's flaws goes way beyond normal dissatisfaction with looks, and can involve warped perceptions of reality. Here is a description of BDD provided by the Mayo Clinic:

> "Body dysmorphic disorder (BDD) is characterized by an excessive preoccupation with a real or imagined defect in physical appearance. People with body dysmorphic disorder have a distorted or exaggerated view of how they look and are obsessed

with actual physical characteristics or perceived flaws, such as a certain facial feature or imperfections of the skin. They often think of themselves as ugly or disfigured. People with body dysmorphic disorder often have problems controlling negative thoughts about their appearance, even when reassured by others that they look fine and that the minor or perceived flaws aren't noticeable or excessive."

Figuring out how to treat something like BDD is complicated. Significant anxiety is a hallmark feature. Anxiety about the flaws is often followed by checking to see if the flaws are still there, locking the person in a terrible cycle. The pattern makes the condition akin to Obsessive Compulsive Disorder (OCD), in which intense anxiety is followed by a behavioral pattern aimed at keeping the anxiety in check. Anxiety about germs followed by handwashing, for instance. Indeed, the treatments that work for BDD are similar to those that work for OCD. Medications can be used to reduce anxiety, and cognitive behavioral therapies can be used to break the repetitive cycle of intense anxiety followed by checking for the flaws. Again, from the Mayo Clinic:

"Treatment for body dysmorphic disorder may involve a combined approach involving medication and talk therapy (psychotherapy). Antidepressant medications used along with cognitive behavior therapy can help people with body dysmorphic disorder manage the obsession and anxiety about their appearance, increase confidence in how they look, and obtain normalcy in their social and work lives."

It can be comforting to know that one is not alone, and actually belongs to a group of people with similar symptoms. However, it is crucial to remember that labels are just short descriptions of a condition and do not represent cures. The label is just the beginning. In all likelihood, BDD emerges when a particular type of kid interacts with a particular type of culture. The condition could take years to create. Recovery could take an equal amount of time. The combination of medications and/or anxiety reduction techniques like meditation, along with therapy to help break the cycle of obsession and compulsion, can definitely help.

What does it all mean?

As our children enter puberty and begin to undergo the complex physical changes that will enable them to procreate and take care of their families in the adult world, they also begin the awkward social and sexual awakenings that most of us go through and become increasingly concerned about how they look. Like previous generations, today's adolescents are struggling to become comfortable inside of their physical bodies.

Beginning at young ages, kids in the U.S. and elsewhere are exposed to advertisements promising to bring about instantaneous increases in attractiveness and make life better. Before using the fancy new shampoo, your hair is dull and drab. After using it, colorful flowers will spring from your scalp whenever you flip your head from side to side. Advertisements for all sorts of products promise to help us close the gap between cultural ideals of beauty and what we perceive to be our lackluster selves. Sadly, obsession with our physical appearances has become the norm. Rates of plastic surgery among both adults and kids are on the rise. Nearly half of all young females have considered plastic surgery, and many thousands have actually done it.

Given the current cultural climate, it is easy to understand why so many young people, as well as many adults, are uncomfortable with their appearances. The desire to ascend to the top of social hierarchies and attract attractive mates is probably inherent. However, the intensity of these drives and the ways in which we attempt to satisfy them is culturally mitigated. Through honest science-based education and discussions around the dinner table, we can teach kids to understand the motives behind television and magazine ads, and the risks, both physical and psychological, involved in trying to attain images of beauty piped into our homes from around the world. It is critical that we all do what we can to help buffer the pressure kids feel to be physically perfect, as the stress and anxiety it causes can easily spill over into other aspects of their lives and impede healthy development.

Quick Facts:

- We humans are built to compete with members of the same sex for resources and potential mates.
- Because we raise teens in a culture where external appearances, including body features and clothing, are highly valued, our kids naturally strive to become pictures of perfection, often at a great cost.
- By the age of 13, more than 50% of adolescent females in the U.S. are dissatisfied with their bodies. That percentage swells to 80% by the age of 17.
- Such dissatisfaction is driven by a constant stream of airbrushed pictures of supermodels, TV shows in which people are applauded for going from ugly to beautiful with the aid of plastic surgery, and non-stop advertisements for beauty products and new clothes.
- The pressure that adolescents feel to look perfect is reflected in the increasing numbers of teens turning to plastic surgery to improve their appearances.
- We adults must do more to inoculate children and young adolescents from these pressures by stressing the importance of internal states over external appearances.

Chapter 3

Diet, exercise and relaxation – What does it mean to be a fit teen?

In the 1960s, President Kennedy initiated the Presidential Fitness Plan, aimed at getting American school kids to exercise more. In the nearly five decades since, we Americans and our kids have become decreasingly fit. A decade ago, not a single state had a rate of obesity greater than 20%. Now, there is only a single state without a rate that high. Food choices play a big role in America's weight problem, but so do sedentary activities like TV viewing and web surfing. A growing number of schools no longer offer physical education classes, while others have moved their physical education classes online! Elevators, escalators and people movers help us conserve energy for later use. Unfortunately, we store such energy as fat, and carrying too much fat can shorten our life expectancies. In this chapter, we will explore what it means to be healthy, beginning with body weight, and then discuss ways in which the health of our kids can be improved through encouraging, and modeling, exercise and wise food choices.

Readers who came of age prior to the 1990s might recall the commercial for Kellogg's *Special K* cereal in which the actress asks viewers if they can "pinch an inch." Few people would be happy with Kellogg if they ran that particular commercial now, as most of us can pinch some serious inches these days. America has undergone a collective growth spurt, perhaps more aptly called a girth spurt, over the last few decades. Obesity is a bigger problem than ever, and one that costs the country more than $75 billion just for the healthcare side of things alone. The trend has trickled down to our kids, who now represent the fattest generation of adolescents in the history of the planet.

Few people talk about how many inches they can pinch, but many of today's adults and teens are obsessed with how much they weigh, and are reminded constantly by cereal commercials, magazine covers and the like that they could weigh less. Kellogg's promises people will lose 6 pounds in two weeks on their *Special K* diet plan. A billion other companies make similar promises to help consumers shed their extra weight. Let's explore diet, exercise and adolescent health, beginning with a discussion of body weight and the Body Mass Index.

How much do you weigh?

Many of us treat stepping on a scale like it's a trip to the doctor's office. We wait with baited breath for the shaky little hand or digital readout to stabilize so that we can decide whether we are healthy or unhealthy, whether the future looks good or bleak, whether dessert will consist of bananas or banana-splits.

It turns out that body weight, by itself, is far from a reliable reflection of one's health regardless of how much time we might spend obsessing about it. Body weight is essentially nothing more than the amount of pressure our bodies exert on a scale as a result of our mass and the earth's gravity. For those of us woefully under- or over-weight, the number of pounds we carry can have real and urgent meaning. For the rest of us, body weight can be a useful but imperfect index of health. Despite this fact, concerns about the specific number of pounds we total are central for many of us.

These days, rather than just using weight, the Centers for Disease Control (CDC) recommend using a measure called Body Mass Index, or BMI, as the preferred index of health. The BMI equation takes a person's height into consideration along with weight. Age and sex can also be factored in. In fact, in other countries, BMI is even adjusted according to a person's race. Here's the basic calculation for American adults.

$$BMI = \text{Weight in pounds} \div \text{Height in inches} \div \text{Height in inches} \times 703$$

The formula for children and adolescents is a bit more complicated and is adjusted for age and sex. According to the CDC, the age-adjusted-BMI correlates nicely with measures of body fat, immediately making BMI more valuable than body weight per se as an index of

SideNotes

The magic of family meals

There is compelling evidence that family meals are extremely valuable for the psychological well-being of teenagers. Researchers at Project EAT report that, even after controlling for other factors, kids who frequently eat dinner with their families are less likely to drink and do other drugs, commit suicide, or have low grade point averages.

health. If you want to know whether your teen's BMI is within the normal range, the CDC offers a calculator for children and teens. Just search for "BMI kids" at www.cdc.gov.

Using the age-adjusted-BMI, those scoring in the upper 5% for their age group are considered overweight. Researchers at the Harvard School of Public Health recently reported that, for women, being overweight according to BMI at age 18 is associated with an increased likelihood of death during early- and middle-adulthood. This is frightening, as rates of overweight and obesity among teens are steeply on the rise. At present, the CDC estimates that around 15% of kids 10-17 years of age in America are overweight according to BMI. These rates are higher among kids in single parent homes and among those of a lower socioeconomic standing.

Despite its superiority over body weight alone as an index of health, BMI is not a perfect measure, either, and there are several caveats that should be considered when interpreting one's placement in the BMI spectrum. Kids and adults who run long distances everyday might weigh less than they should for their height and age. On the flip side, muscle is heavier than fat, making the charts less informative for the muscle-bound among us.

It appears that teens are carrying their extra weight with them into adulthood, fueling the growing adult obesity epidemic. According to the CDC, in 1995, there wasn't a single state in the country with more than 20% of its citizens in the obese category defined by height and weight (30 pounds overweight for a person 5'4"). Fast forward to 2006, and every state but one, Colorado, had an obesity rate greater than 20%! In fact, 32 states now have rates of obesity greater than 25%.

Let's explore the relationship between body weight and health more closely, beginning with the basic question – why do we eat? By understanding the reasons why we eat, and the reasons why we gain weight, we can make informed decisions about how to help our kids, and ourselves, stay healthy and begin to shift America's overall BMI in the right direction.

Why do we eat?

Quite simply, we eat to provide our bodies with energy. Imagine you're at a backyard barbecue munching potato chips off of a paper plate. The molecules in the potato chips contain energy. After you eat one, your digestive machinery goes to work, breaking the food down and mashing it to a pulp. Small molecules from the food are absorbed out of your intestines into your blood and distributed throughout your body. These molecules are torn apart and the energy contained in them is used to generate the body's preferred energy currency – called ATP (adenosine triphosphate). Every cell in the body uses ATP to keep itself running.

The secret to ATP's utility resides in its third phosphate molecule, the *tri*-phosphate part. It snaps off easily, releasing energy like a spark and turning ATP into something like a spot welder. The third phosphate can be replaced over and over again, making ATP the ultimate, natural rechargeable energy source. If a muscle cell wants to twitch or a brain cell wants to send a signal to its neighbors, ATP is cashed in.

Let's look at an example. While munching your chips at the barbecue you are momentarily distracted by a large mosquito that has just touched down on your arm. You spring into action, stealthily swatting it with your free hand. Your response required several major muscle groups and even some brain activity. Without ATP to spare, your only option would have been to watch helplessly as the mosquito plunged its proboscis into your arm. From potato chip to dead mosquito, the body uses the chemical energy stored in food molecules to keep the machinery running.

When it comes to using energy, the body's strategy is waste-not want-not. When the amount of energy taken into the body during a given day exceeds the amount of energy needed to get through that day, the body stores the excess fuel for later use as fat and chains of sugar. As a result of this process, we gain weight. We will return to the topic of weight gain in a few sections. How much food energy does it take to create enough ATP to keep the body running and how do we know if we are getting enough or too much? For that, we will need to turn our attention toward Calories.

How many Calories in that?

A calorie is a measure of the amount of energy contained in food molecules. Here in the U.S. at least, when the number

SideNotes

Understanding Food Product Labels

Want to know how to decipher all of that information on food nutrition labels? Here is a link to an extremely helpful website put together by the FDA: www.cfsan.fda.gov/~dms/foodlab.html

of calories per serving is given on a food container, the word "calorie" actually means "kilocalorie," or 1000 calories. For this reason, we will use a capital "C" to differentiate between the little calorie and the big Calorie.

Foods with higher Calorie counts contain more energy. For instance, one of the potato chips mentioned above probably has around 10 Calories in it. Depending upon how much a person weighs, how much they exercise, what medications they're on, and other factors, somewhere around 2000-3000 Calories are usually sufficient to keep the body running for a typical day. That is, without a change in weight.

Metabolism – The Calorie furnace

Metabolism refers to how quickly one's body burns energy. Metabolism can be measured in different ways. For our purposes, it is sufficient to view metabolism in terms of how many Calories it takes to run the body for a day. It is a little like asking how much gas your car needs each day, which depends on factors like how much you drive, how fast you drive, whether you're driving uphill, etcetera. Same with metabolism. If you are active, get exercise, and happen to be 16, you probably have a high metabolism and burn through plenty of Calories. If you are 37 and lay on your floor writing books every day, there is a good chance your metabolism has slowed to a crawl and you are getting pudgy.

People's metabolisms vary greatly. In fact, people's metabolisms vary significantly during their own lifetimes. Metabolism is quite high during childhood and adolescence - much higher than during adulthood. For example, the brain uses more energy than any other organ in the body, and brain metabolism drops by about half between childhood and adulthood, its peak coming during early adolescence.

As we age, our metabolism slows. This means that we burn through less energy on a daily basis, and thus will start gaining weight even if our diets don't change. Let's take a look at the relationship between Calorie intake, metabolism and weight change, tying together the material we have covered so far.

Why we gain and lose weight

Quite simply, when the number of Calories taken in during a day equals the number expended through metabolism, body weight remains stable. If a person doesn't take in enough Calories during a particular day, the body releases stored fuel into the blood stream, temporarily covering the Calorie debt until more food is eaten. If this keeps happening over a sufficient number of days, weight loss results from the burning of stored fuel. If too many Calories are taken in, they are stored for later use, mostly in the form of fat, resulting in weight gain.

SideNotes

How many fast food meals do you eat as a family each week?

A study published by researchers Project EAT suggests that the number of fast-food family meals consumed each week predicts several other important health related variables. Parents who purchase fast food for family meals three or more times per week are more likely to have teens that are overweight, exercise too little, and eat other kinds of junk food.

Small changes in Calorie intake might not add up to much in the short-term, but such changes can reveal themselves over time. Allowing for individual variability, the sources of the Calories and in the absence of concurrent changes in activity, each time you add an extra 3500-4000 Calories to your diet, whether it's over a week or a month, you will probably gain a pound. Each time you decrease your intake by that much, whether over a week or years, you will lose a pound.

For most of us, when we go on diets we hope to see changes fast. It is tempting to slash our Calorie intake during the week before a vacation in the hope that our bodies will gobble up our bellies and double chins. When we do things this way, the results are usually favorable early on, but progress quickly grinds to a halt. This could be due, in part, to the fact that the body has lost weight and now requires fewer Calories to function, so the pace of weight loss begins to slow. However, it might also be that the body has lowered its basal (normal) metabolic rate in order to stave off what it perceives to be a drought of food. By slowing basal metabolism, the body can make stored energy last longer. Though it might be annoying to us, it is a protective strategy aimed at keeping us from starving to death.

This adaptive process is the source of the familiar yo-yo dieting effect. Slashing Calorie intake leads to weight loss and slowing of metabolism. Going off the diet leads to weight gain due to the slowed metabolism. Let's take a look at how this cycle plays itself out:

- Decreased food intake causes rapid weight loss as the body burns stored fuel
- Rapid weight loss causes a compensatory slowing of metabolism
- Metabolism slows until energy output is matched to the new energy input – leading to a settling of weight at a new level
- Weight loss grinds to a halt
- When the diet ends, food intake increases again
- Increased food intake coupled with slowed metabolism leads to quick weight gain

Although there are many specific diets one can follow, success rates are not all that different. For example, while Atkins dieters (low carbohydrates) tend to lose weight faster, Weight Watchers participants (balanced, reduced Calorie diet) tend to boast better long term success. Regardless of the specific details of these diets, what matters most is that Calorie intake is decreased, and perhaps metabolism is increased, without compromising the health and balance of the foods one consumes. If a person already eats a healthy diet but is not losing weight, simply reducing the serving sizes would eventually lead to weight loss.

Under all but extraordinary circumstances, there is never a need for adults or teens to starve themselves, unless the orders come straight from a doctor. Small reductions in food intake coupled with modest increases in energy output usually lead to the desired results over a healthy period of time, without forcing the body to go into crisis mode to deal with rapid fluctuations in Calorie intake and energy storage.

SideNotes

Do scales make teenagers fat?

We all know people who swear that weighing themselves everyday helps keep them motivated to lose weight. While it might work for them, a recent study suggests that daily weigh-ins are unhealthy for teenage girls. Researchers at the University of Minnesota School of Public Health tracked the eating habits and body weights of over 2000 adolescents across a five year period. Girls who weighed themselves frequently gained nearly twice as much as other girls in the study. They were also more likely to engage in binge-eating, vomit after eating, skip meals, and even smoke cigarettes. The real question is whether the scale does it or if frequent weighing is just another sign, along with the unhealthy eating behaviors, of some underlying problems.

Exercise burns Calories and boosts metabolism

Exercise is essential to health and is the capstone to any sensible diet plan. Exercise promotes weight loss in several ways. First, exercising requires muscle movement, muscle movement requires energy in the form of ATP, and the creation of ATP requires Calories. So, exercise can help us negate the affects of the donuts we ate for lunch simply by burning up Calories in order to fuel our muscles.

How many Calories can you burn by exercising? That depends on what you do and for how long. People who climb Mount Everest are estimated to burn between 10-15,000 Calories on summit day. Walking back and forth from the couch to the kitchen every hour, the author's favorite exercise routine, probably doesn't negate more than about two spoonfuls of ice cream in a 24 hour period.

The table below lists the number of Calories burned per hour while performing various forms of exercise. Values are calculated for a 154 lb person needing around 2000 Calories per day. To give the numbers in the table some relevance, a medium order of McDonald's French fries contains 380 Calories. A Big Mac contains 570.

Calories burned during various exercises

Moderate Physical Activity	Calories burned per hour
Hiking	370
Light gardening/yard work	330
Dancing	330
Golf (walking and carrying clubs)	330
Bicycling (<10 mph)	290
Walking (3.5 mph)	280
Weight lifting (general light workout)	220
Stretching	180
Vigorous Physical Activity	**Calories burned per hour**
Running/jogging (5 mph)	590
Bicycling (>10 mph)	590
Swimming (slow freestyle laps)	510
Aerobics	480
Walking (4.5 mph)	460
Heavy yard work (chopping wood)	440
Weight lifting (vigorous effort)	440
Basketball (vigorous)	440

During a typical diet that does not include exercise, the goal is to keep the metabolic rate constant and decrease the number of Calories consumed. An alternative is to raise basal metabolic rate through exercise in addition to, or instead of, reducing Calorie intake. Exercising infrequently will burn some Calories. Exercising regularly is more effective for weight loss, as it teaches the body that energy will be expended on a regular basis. The body adapts by raising basal metabolism to keep the machine prepared for exertion. On a day-to-day basis, this could tilt the balance of Calories-in and Calories-out in favor of weight loss.

Diet pills

If it's January and you want to look good in your bathing suit for a spring break trip planned for March, the thought of losing four pounds per month by shaving 500 Calories from your daily diet might seem like too slow a process. For this reason, many people turn to diet pills, prescribed or over-the-counter, and other weight loss short-cuts. Americans spend an estimated $46 billion per year on diet pills and diet self-help books, $22 billion of which is spent on over-the-counter diet aids.[1] Research suggests that nearly 15% of teenage girls have used such products in an effort to lose weight.

The aim of most, but certainly not all, diet pills is to increase one's metabolism and thus cause one's body to burn more Calories than normal. Most over the counter products do this through the use of stimulants like caffeine, often from exotic sounding supplements like guarana, the seeds of which contain about three times as much caffeine as coffee beans. Do they work? Those with stimulants can work, but at a cost, and they are completely unnecessary if one is willing to adjust their eating and exercise habits and be patient. As we discussed above, losing weight quickly rarely leads to lasting changes in body weight. Further, the added strain than many diet drugs place on the cardiovascular system could put one's health at risk if they truly do have a weight problem. Indeed, the Chinese herb ephedra, once found in many diet supplements, was banned after several healthy young people died from its effects on the cardiovascular system. For otherwise healthy adolescents and adults, diet pills should be viewed as a low priority. Weight loss can be achieved in healthy ways through a reduced Calorie diet and increased levels of physical activity.

Some diet pills promise a more intriguing effect than a boost in metabolism. What if you could eat whatever you wanted, but the fat in the products never made it into your body? That's what some companies promise. The truth is that clinical data are lacking for the vast majority of these products. They might work in a test tube, but the body is far more complicated.

Diet pill advertisements often contain outlandish claims. In November of 2004, the Federal Trade Commission (FTC), the organization responsible for monitoring the veracity of claims made by advertisers, launched Operation Big Fat Lie. The FTC went after six major companies making wildly unsubstantiated claims in their advertisements and began educating the public about the nature of the claims. One of the companies, Natural Products, makes and sells a diet aid called *Bio Trim*. According to the FTC:[2]

> Bio Trim advertisements made "false and unsubstantiated claims that Bio Trim: (1) causes users to lose substantial weight, while eating unlimited amounts of food; (2) causes substantial weight loss by blocking the absorption of fat or Calories; (3) works for all overweight users; and (4) is clinically proven to cause rapid and substantial weight loss without reducing Calories."

In the world of weight-loss products, as in the world of dietary supplements in general, there is little regulation and often less research. Buyer beware!

Making the body run more smoothly

In this chapter, we have examined the relationships between food intake, metabolism and weight change from the standpoint that the body is like a car that requires a certain number of Calories to function on a daily basis without ending up in Calorie poverty or Calorie gluttony. Just as it is possible to fine tune a car so that it runs more smoothly and efficiently on the fuel it gets, it is possible to do the same with the body. This is the holy grail of physical well-being.

Nutrition is about more than healthy hair and skin. When the cellular machinery that makes ATP works effortlessly, the body always has plenty of potential energy to spend on building things, rebuilding things, making new brain circuits, cleaning out waste, and so forth. When the body has all of the building blocks it needs to repair cell walls, stock up on chemical transmitters and beef up muscle fibers, it can get by on fewer Calories than an inefficient body and the person can begin to benefit from real health. When the body runs more efficiently, the brain works better, people feel better, think more clearly, and are generally more efficient and productive.

Giving the body what it needs to function at a high level is important. Many of us, and our kids, eat the right number of

SideNotes

Sleeping the pounds away

Sleep seems like a completely passive process, but it's not. There are plenty of things going on in the body, and particularly in the brain. In fact, it seems that sleep plays an important role in maintaining a healthy weight. For one thing, you can't eat if you're sleeping soundly in bed, so it keeps us out of the refrigerator during the wee hours. Researchers tracked 68,000 women over a 16 year period to assess the relationship between sleep and weight, and observed that women who slept 5 hours per night were 32% more likely to gain significant amounts of weight during the study period compared to women who slept 8 hours per night.

Calories per day, but might not necessarily get all of the essentials. We will revisit the issue of healthy daily food intake in a few sections.

Exercise and relaxation both improve health

Exercise helps the body run more smoothly by delivering oxygen to muscles and discharging many of the toxic effects of the day's stress, whether caused by math class or a board meeting. It also promotes weight loss via the involvement of the sympathetic nervous system, the system that controls the "fight or flight" response. A trip to the gym to work out amounts to purposeful activation of the sympathetic nervous system, and it feels good.

Like any process in the body that can go up, there is a compliment to the sympathetic nervous system that does the opposite and, in the process, brings sympathetic nervous system activity back down. It's called the parasympathetic nervous system. Rather than promoting the burning of fuel, it promotes the rebuilding of cells and tissues. Rather than moving blood away from the gut and slowing digestion, it promotes digestion. Rather than increasing heart rate and blood pressure it calms it. While exercise-induced sympathetic nervous system activity is good for us, activating the parapsympathetic nervous system is proving equally important for the health of kids and adults.

The parasympathetic nervous system can be activated by doing anything that promotes natural relaxation, meaning not the kind of relaxation that comes with a few glasses of wine or from watching a crime drama like *CSI: Special Victims Unit*. Formal meditation, deep breathing exercises, Yoga, slow stretching, biofeedback and probably just lying in the sun promote parasympathetic nervous system activity and the many ways it helps the body to keep itself healthy.

Activating the parasympathetic nervous system leads to weight loss. It does so in several interrelated ways, many psychological. In a well-written piece about meditation and weight loss,

Brooke Brassell[3] captures the intersection between parasympathetic nervous activity and psychological well-being:

> "Because of the stress relief and relaxation effects that meditation provides, it can be quite beneficial to emotional eaters. Emotional eaters are those who tend to eat not so much out of hunger, but rather out of a need to fill some sort of void. That 'void' may exist due to an intense day on the job, an argument with a spouse, disappointment in a child, fear of the future, or anything that sparks one to feel an onset of powerful emotions. Contrary to what many believe, emotional eating can also be caused by intense happiness as well."

It turns out that people who go to gyms and spend their hour doing Yoga or meditating rather than pumping up their muscles might really be on to something!

Teaching kids to choose foods wisely

As we discussed, one's body weight results from a blend of Calorie intake and metabolism, which can be adjusted up or down by modulating physical activity levels or taking often risky stimulants. Given the influence of Calorie intake on body weight and the role of nutrition in health, a big part of the obesity problem in the U.S. could be dealt with by teaching kids, and adults, to make healthier food choices.

We humans come into the world with a hankering for breast milk, which is mildly sweet and high in fat and Calories. From those basic leanings, food preferences are modified by experience. American food preferences are quite different from those in many other countries. Just ask residents of Afghanistan who tried to eat the MREs (Meals Ready to Eat) that U.S. forces airdropped to them during the early stages of the war there.

Wherever there is learning there are changes in the brain. Fascinating research has begun to shed light on the brain mechanisms underlying our food choices, and how those mechanisms develop during childhood and adolescence.

Drs. William Kilgore and Deborah Yurgelun-Todd at Harvard Medical Center[4] recently conducted brain imaging while female subjects aged 9-15 viewed pictures of various foods, including some that were particularly high-Calorie (e.g., cheeseburgers, French-fries, ice cream sundaes). They then compared those data to data from a previous sample of adults that performed the same task. The amount of activation in brain structures involved in memory and emotion, particularly the hippocampus and areas related to it, remained relatively constant regardless of age. However, the amount of activation in the frontal lobes increased with age. The frontal lobes, located behind the forehead, are involved in conscious thought and decision-making. The findings suggest that, as our brains develop during adolescence, we begin to *think* more about the foods we see rather than simply reacting to them emotionally. This provides a developmental window of opportunity for training kids to choose foods wisely, a task made more difficult by easy around-the-clock access to tasty junk food.

SideNotes

Could eating a lot during pregnancy teach babies to eat a lot after they're born?

Researchers in Australia suggest that the amount of food a baby is exposed to in the womb sets up brain circuits that influence eating habits after birth. Children born to heavier moms are more likely to be born heavy, grow up heavy, and become heavy adults. It appears that perhaps children are born with an appetite consistent with how much food the mother was taking in during the period of pregnancy.

Research suggests that kids tend to eat what is around them. If healthy foods are added to kids' diets at young ages, preferably before adolescence, the tendency to eat healthy things can stick. Coercing kids to eat healthy things can often backfire and breed resentment, so it is best to just keep putting vegetables on their plates and suggesting they eat them until they start doing so. As with other behavioral patterns we want kids to exhibit, modeling the right way to do things is critical when it comes to teaching kids how to make wise choices around food. This includes when foods are eaten and for what reasons in addition to the types of foods involved. Kids whose parents tend to eat to satisfy hunger rather than provide comfort or kill time are more likely to view food as a means to an end rather than the end itself.

Vending machines in schools

In 7th grade, the author had the opportunity to help take care of animals and clean glassware in the school science lab. At the end of the class period, his teacher, Mr. Runkle, would always buy a bottle of soda for each of the students cleaning the lab. There was one vending machine in the school, and it was reserved for teachers. Things have changed!

Vending machines are now ubiquitous in public schools throughout the country. A recent audit of school vending machine revenues in the state of Utah revealed that vending machines were present in secondary schools in all but two of the state's 40 school districts.[4] The machines bring in big money for Utah schools, generating estimated revenues of $3.25 to $3.75 million in 2005. Around 70% of that income was generated by the sale

Side*Notes*

Should teens take multivitamins?

Adolescents are in the midst of major changes in the size and shape of their bodies, the health of their immune systems, and the organization of their brains. All of this construction and remodeling requires building materials. Adding a multivitamin can increase the odds that the building materials will be there when needed. One recent study suggests that teens who take multivitamins live healthier lifestyles than those who do not. They exercise more, are less likely to smoke, less likely to be overweight, more likely to eat healthy foods, watch less TV and drink less soda. This is yet another chicken and egg question. In this case, while multivitamins probably contribute to the health of those who take them, those who take them are probably more likely to live in homes where healthy lifestyles are already considered important.

of products from Coca-Cola and Pepsi. The rest came from the sale of a variety of snack foods and, occasionally, milk or refrigerated food items.

How do schools make money from vending machines? Most schools enter into contractual relationships with vendors who bring in the machines, keep them stocked, and pay the school their share of the profits made from students. According to the Utah audit, payment generally comes in three forms.

- Commissions – A set percentage of sales revenues per month
- Signing bonuses or lump sum bonus payments made on a yearly basis during the term of the contract
- Non-monetary compensation, including things like branded sports drinks and coolers for school athletic teams, free beverages for students, restaurant gift certificates for teacher appreciation awards, scoreboards, bleachers, and even school surveillance systems

Where does the money go? In general, funding is directed to unbudgeted items, like unanticipated supply needs, and/or to augment funding for budgeted items, like transportation for athletic teams.

Auditors in Utah list the following as the main foci of spending there:

- Awards, parties, meals for students
- Classroom supplies and equipment
- Athletic supplies and equipment
- Assemblies (speaker fees, for example)
- Cell phone bills
- Staff appreciation items, meals, and treats
- Facility improvement

A recent Gallup poll of roughly 800 kids aged 13-17 across the U.S. found that 67% eat junk food or drink sugary sodas from vending machines at school.[6] Additional research suggests that students who eat or drink sugary products from vending machines are also more likely to eat fast food.

The potential problems are nicely captured in this statement from the Center for Science in the Public Interest:

> "Soda and low-nutrition snack foods are a key source of excess Calories in children's diets, contribute to overweight and obesity, and displace more nutritious foods. Obesity rates have doubled in children and tripled in adolescents over the last two decades. Studies show that children's soft drink intake has increased, and children who drink more soft drinks consume more Calories and are more likely to be overweight than kids who drink fewer soft drinks."

The good news is that the tide seems to be turning. Former President Bill Clinton's foundation, the William J. Clinton Foundation, paired up with the American Heart Association to convince beverage distributors to stop selling most empty Calorie, high sugar drinks in school vending machines. According to the Mayo Clinic:

> "Under the new guidelines, only lower Calorie and nutritious beverages will be sold to schools. Cadbury Schweppes, Coca-Cola and PepsiCo have agreed to sell only water, unsweetened juice, and flavored and unflavored low-fat and fat-free milk to elementary and middle schools. In addition to these beverages, diet sodas, diet and unsweetened teas, flavored water and low-Calorie sports drinks will be

sold to high schools. Whole milk and regular soda will not be offered to any schools."

The changes will occur gradually and not all companies have agreed to change the products they provide. However, by 2010, students in public schools should have a much healthier array of foods from which to choose. At present, the easy access to junk food provided by school vending machines contributes to the epidemic of obesity we currently face. However, it is quite possible that school vending machines could one day provide an opportunity for kids to practice making healthy food choices when away from home. While some companies do stock school vending machines with healthy snacks, the variety is typically small and simply can't compete with the allure and low cost of tasty junk foods. When bottled water costs more than bottled water with a whole bunch of sugar and flavoring in it, it's hard to pass up the soda!

When weight loss strategies become pathological

There is a strange duality in American culture – food all over the place but intense pressure to be thin. No wonder so many teens (and adults!) are displeased with their bodies. The desire to look different does not necessarily indicate a problem, but it can. Distinguishing normal adolescent urges to fit in from the early signs of potentially dangerous eating disorders can be tricky. The following details should help.

Two well-known eating disorders are anorexia nervosa and bulimia nervosa. While not considered an eating disorder, obesity certainly passes for one in most cases, as it is generally caused by maladaptive and unhealthy eating habits. Type II diabetes also qualifies as an eating disorder in cases where it is triggered by over-intake of sugar. Let's take a look at these conditions, beginning with anorexia nervosa and bulimia.

Anorexia nervosa is a disorder characterized by excessive weight loss leading to unhealthy thinness. It typically begins during the teen years and is much more common in females than males, though it certainly does occur in males. A few years back, the young lead singer from an Australian rock band acknowledged his own battles with anorexia. Symptoms of anorexia include:

- Refusal to maintain body weight above minimally normal weight for age and height
- Intense fear of gaining weight, even though underweight
- Distorted body perception
- Tremendous influence of weight or body shape on self-evaluation
- Denial of the seriousness of their current low weight
- Amenorrhea (no menstruation) in females due to lack of nutrition

The malnutrition that accompanies anorexia can cause significant, potentially permanent damage to the brain at a time when the brain is supposed to be thriving. Unlike other organs in the body, which can use alternatives to glucose (sugar) for fuel if no glucose is available, the brain is largely dependent on glucose to function. In a pinch, it can use alternatives, but not unless it is desperate. Choking the brain off from adequate supplies of glucose impedes its functioning and can lead to cell death. Over time, the brain shrinks in size and the psychological health of the starving person suffers immensely. The body literally devours itself in an effort to keep fuel going to the brain. It can be difficult for a healthy person to concentrate after skipping just one meal. Imagine the toll it would take on the brain, performance, and emotional well-being if one continued to skip meals for days and weeks on end.

Treating anorexia can be extremely difficult. As is the case with other, seemingly unrelated disorders like drug addiction, the individual can be in complete denial about the problem.

When we look at them, we see ribs. When they look at themselves, they see disgusting bulges of fat. Only by strictly controlling their eating patterns can they cope with the uncomfortable emotions involved. How and why this happens is unknown, but it's a safe bet there are both social and inherent biological reasons for it.

SideNotes

Maladaptive learning and disordered eating

In March of 2007, CBSnews.com ran an article detailing the struggles of Allegra Versace, daughter of fashion designer Donatella Versace. The article quotes Donatella Versace as saying the following:

> "Our daughter, Allegra, has been battling anorexia, a very serious disease, for many years...She is receiving the best medical care possible to help overcome this illness and is responding well."

In the image accompanying the article, a dangerously wafer thin Allegra stands along side her cosmetically enhanced and buxom mother.

Is it possible there is some maladaptive learning involved here? Like many other conditions, typically there is a strong learned component somewhere in a person's disordered eating patterns. If thinness is praised as beautiful in a young girl's world, it makes sense she would strive for thinness, perhaps to the point of death. Anorexia is a very real condition rooted in brain development. Brain development is guided by the environment, whether healthy or toxic.

One of the more common treatment approaches these days for anorexia and other eating disorders involves the use of antidepressants, and such medications appear to be of benefit for many people with the condition. Why this is the case is not known for certain. It is largely a myth that antidepressants trigger weight gain, but some people do find themselves eating more while on the drugs. More likely, the meds help enable individuals to feel a little better about themselves in general, including with their bodies. They also work well to calm anxiety, which is often present at dysfunctional levels in those with eating disorders. As small changes in thoughts and behaviors occur, and are reinforced, further positive changes should result.

Bulimia nervosa is a different disorder, though it has unrealistic expectations of body weight in common with anorexia. Unlike those with anorexia, in which body weight can be grotesquely sub-normal, bulimics often have normal body weights. Rather than refusing to eat, sufferers of bulimia often binge on food and then make themselves vomit or take large doses of laxatives to avoid absorbing all of the Calories from the food they consume. As with anorexia, bulimia is much more common in females than males, though it does happen in males.

One of the major risks associated with the repeated bingeing and purging of bulimia comes from bathing the mouth and throat in highly toxic stomach acids. These acids can eat away at the enamel on one's teeth and can produce ulcers in the esophagus. When laxatives are used, healthy bacterial flora in the gut are swept away, negatively affecting digestion and the absorption of important nutrients. Further, medications, like food, fail to absorb if time for digestion is not allowed.

In recent clinical studies, antidepressants were found to cut bingeing and purging associated with bulimia by more than 50%. The effectiveness of antidepressants for bulimia is roughly equivalent to the benefits of cognitive behavioral therapy. So, it makes sense that a combination of the two approaches would be wise if one is considering the use of medications.

Therapy, by the way, is no picnic for those who need it and eventually benefit from it. People often say that they sought treatment, or were forced to go through it, only after they "hit rock bottom." For those with underlying issues that need to be dealt with, rock bottom can seem like a day in the park compared to the pain of processing long-buried emotions. This point is captured nicely in the following quote from the treatment guide, *Cognitive Behavioral Therapy for Eating Disorders*, by Waller and colleagues:

> "Successfully negotiating change always involves tolerating short-term discomfort in order to reach longer-term chosen goals. Such change not only requires an ability to withstand a certain level of distress, but also the capacity to keep those longer-term goals in mind. This task of change is more complex for patients with eating disorders. Not only must they tolerate the short-term distress of developing a regular pattern of eating and weight stabilization/gain, but (in order to initiate this process and as a result of it) they are exposed to their thoughts and feelings. These are the very aspects of themselves that they have been trying so hard to avoid through their eating behaviors."

Just as eating too little can be a problem, so can eating too much. Many people in the U.S. are overweight or obese and the numbers are not yet improving. Sadly, as rates of obesity have climbed, so have rates of Type II diabetes, a condition that can be triggered in susceptible people by months and years of over-eating sugar. Normally, as sugar enters the blood, the body releases a hormone called insulin. Insulin then sweeps the sugar from the blood and gets it into cells in the body so that the sugar can be converted to ATP and used for energy. When a person eats too much sugar, and insulin levels remain too high for too long, cells in the body learn to ignore the insulin. As a result, the person must eat more and more sugar just to get enough energy into the cells. This process just keeps going until the insulin becomes basically ineffective regardless of how much sugar the person eats.

It is becoming quite clear that over-eating sugar when we are young not only predisposes us to conditions like Type II diabetes, but also to conditions like Alzheimer's. People with Type II diabetes are more likely than other people to develop Alzheimer's. The culprit appears to be an enzyme called Insulin Degrading Enzyme (IDE). Normally, IDE is released in order to break down insulin after the insulin does its job. IDE also plays a role in breaking down proteins that contribute to Alzheimer's. As insulin receptors become less sensitive during the course of Type II diabetes, less IDE is released. Less IDE means that the protein that contributes to Alzheimer's isn't broken down as well, thus making it harder for the body to stave off Alzheimer's and the cognitive decline it represents.

Thus, teaching kids to make healthy food choices not only produces healthy benefits while they are young, but could also help them avoid, or delay, the onset of cognitive dementia related to aging.

What does a healthy teen diet, exercise and relaxation plan look like?

So far in this chapter, we have taken a tour of eating, the reasons why we do it, the reasons why we gain and lose weight, the role of exercise in maintaining a healthy level of stored fat, the parasympathetic nervous system and a few disorders that can emerge from unhealthy eating habits. What can be gleaned from this material to help establish and maintain the dietary, exercise and relaxation needs of adolescents? What might a satisfactory diet and exercise regimen look like for statistically normal adolescent males and females?

Dietary needs depend on one's current health, age, sex, and exercise level. The U.S. Department of Agriculture (USDA) suggests that teen girls need around 2200 Calories per day to maintain adequate functioning of their bodies, while teen boys, particularly highly active ones, need somewhere around 2800

Calories per day. Those who burn through lots of Calories due to high levels of exercise or very fast basal metabolic rates will need more, while those who don't exercise or have inherently low metabolic rates need less and could actually gain weight at recommended levels of Calorie intake.

How many servings of each food group per day per teen?		
	Teen girls (2,200 Calories)	**Teen boys** (2,800 Calories)
Grains Group • 1 slice of bread • 1 cup cereal • 1/2 cup cooked cereal, rice or pasta	**6**	**11**
Vegetable Group • 1 cup raw leafy vegetables • 1/2 cup other vegetables cooked or raw • 3/4 cup vegetable juice	**3**	**5**
Fruit Group • 1 medium apple, banana, orange, pear • 1/2 cup chopped, cooked, or canned fruit • 3/4 cup fruit juice	**2**	**4**
Milk, Yogurt, Cheese Group • 1 cup milk or yogurt • 1.5 oz natural cheese (like Cheddar) • 2 oz processed cheese (like American)	**3**	**3**
Meat and Beans Group • 2-3 oz cooked lean meat, fish, poultry • 1/2 cup cooked dry beans or tofu • 2.5 oz soyburger • 1 egg • 2 tablespoons peanut butter • 1/3 cup nuts	**2**	**3**
From the USDA Dietary Guidelines for America, 2002		

Calorie intake, by itself, says nothing about the quality of the foods that one puts in their bodies, only about the amount of potential energy taken in during meals. In a pinch, Calories from junk food are better than nothing, but getting one's Calories through inherently unhealthy and highly processed snack foods can trigger a wide variety of health problems even if one's weight remains in the normal range. Plenty of skinny people die from heart attacks and strokes following decades of unhealthy eating.

The USDA recommends sex-specific dietary guidelines for adolescent males and females. Recommendations are included in the table on the previous page. Your pediatrician should be able to help craft a dietary strategy specific to your adolescent, taking into consideration medications, exercise level, existing illnesses, and so forth. There are also plenty of very well trained nutritionists these days that can provide the family with assessments of how well they are doing and how to improve.

In 2004, researchers in California reported in the *Archives of Pediatric and Adolescent Medicine* that exercise and time spent lounging around, more so than food choices, were the key differences between normal weight and overweight male and female adolescents. How much exercise do typical teens need? According to the USDA, preferably 60 minutes per day, most days of the week. But there are caveats. Research suggests that regular exercise during adolescence can diminish the likelihood of developing bone diseases, like osteoporosis, later in life. It also provides an outlet for pent up stress, can strengthen the immune system, and can be a lot of fun. Overdoing it, however, can cause injuries and influence changes that take place during puberty. Females who are seriously competitive athletes during adolescence, and train hard continually, are prone to something called "athletic amenorrhea," which basically means exercise-induced suppression of the menstrual cycle. This could be bad, but it certainly is good in some ways. As we will discuss in a subsequent chapter, menarche, the onset of the menstrual cycle, has been coming earlier and earlier for U.S. females due primarily to kids' weights. Early onset of menarche increases the risk of cancers and ushers in the ability to reproduce at an age when kids can't possibly be ready for the responsibility that goes with it. The amenorrhea is probably an adaptive strategy on the part of the body to prevent pregnancy at a time when the individual is burning through resources too fast to support a developing fetus. The long-term consequences aren't known. In general, whenever possible, it's best not to mess with the normal changes in hormones and development underlying puberty. However, it certainly negates the risks that go with a body-weight-triggered early onset of menstruation.

What about weight training exercises for adolescents? Should weight lifting wait until adulthood? According to the American Academy of Pediatrics,

SideNotes

The gamble of anabolic steroids

Many athletes looking for shortcuts to building muscle or enhancing performance have fallen into the trap of using synthetic steroids aimed at mimicking the anabolic (muscle building) effects of hormones like testosterone. As recent scandals involving the Olympic athlete Marion Jones and an array of baseball players attest, steroids are banned from competitive athletics for good reason. The short-term gains in muscle mass and performance come at a great price, particularly during adolescence. Statistically, somewhere between 1-3% of high school seniors report using anabolic steroids each year. This strategy triggers rapid muscle growth and can give users a feeling of strength and power. Unfortunately, synthetic steroids can also interfere with the normal changes in hormones that occur during adolescence, triggering bones to stop growing too early, deepening voices in females, causing breast development and a shrinking of testicles in males, causing baldness, producing acne and giving users bad breath. In short, this strategy just isn't worth it. While not addictive like other drugs that teens use, the damage caused by anabolic steroids can be far greater and might not materialize for years after use stops. Finally, steroids can cause unpredictable mood swings. In Chapter 11, we will discuss the suicide of Taylor Hooten, a promising young baseball player who took his life at the age of 16 after abusing and then abruptly quitting steroids.

weight lifting can be okay during adolescence, even at 11 or 12 years of age, with some important caveats. They recommend using low levels of weights and more repetitions rather than high levels of weight, particularly during early adolescence. In part, this is because the weight can put undue pressure on growth plates, cartilage at the ends of bones that will eventually turn to bone once elongated enough. This could affect bone growth.

Also, lots of warm up exercises prior to weight lifting are recommended. During adolescence, the bones grow faster than muscles, meaning that the muscles become increasingly stretched, leading to a reduction in flexibility as we age and an increase in injury risk. That's why most young kids can tie themselves up like pretzels but most adults have a hard time touching their toes! If injuries do occur during adolescence, adequate time to heal absolutely must be given, or the adolescent could end up with an injury that plagues them throughout their adult years. Finally, research suggests that the value of strength training declines precipitously after 2-3 workouts per week, meaning that there is no need for adolescents interested in gaining strength to do weight training more than three times per week, no matter how motivated they might be to work out constantly.

Side*Notes*

The value of sports

There is little doubt that organized sports can play important, positive roles in development. The trick is to use the opportunities correctly. Not only do kids get much needed exercise by participating in everything from YMCA soccer leagues to high school football, they also learn valuable lessons about teamwork, dedication, and how to handle both victory and loss. Some parents fail to grasp the value of these exercises, and instead simply drive their kids to victory at any cost, often while being obnoxious from the bleachers. When used correctly – as opportunities for exercise, self-discipline, and building of teamwork skills – sports can promote healthy physical and psychological development in kids.

Parents interested in getting their kids to exercise more do not have to sign them up for expensive classes or turn their garages into home gyms. The data say that kids, as well as adults, who have access to skateboard parks, walking trails, basketball courts, and bike lanes, use them. Identifying, and perhaps advocating for, such opportunities for kids in one's community could improve the health of adolescents and reduce the odds that they turn to less healthy options to cope with stress and pass time.

It is becoming clear that relaxation is also important for healthy physical development, and can reduce the tendency to eat for comfort rather than hunger. True relaxation cannot be accomplished by watching TV, surfing the internet or playing videogames. Those activities can increase blood pressure and heart rate in kids. True relaxation, like that provided via meditation, which tends to involve focused breathing, reduces heart rate and blood pressure and confers other benefits.

One recent study found that 20 minutes of meditation per day (10 minutes at school and 10 minutes at home) for three months reduced blood pressure and heart rate in healthy middle school kids.[8]   In another study, adolescents aged 11 to 16 attending a yoga camp developed better memory skills , while no change was observed in kids attending a fine arts camp for a similar period of time.[9] In adults, meditation increases blood flow to the brain and is speculated to actually promote the development of circuits in the frontal lobes.[10]   Indeed, people who meditate regularly have been shown to have more brain tissue in the frontal lobes than controls.[11] Training subjects to meditate leads to a 40-50% reduction in how strongly their brains respond to painful stimuli,[12] potentially minimizing the disruptive effects that pain can have on psychological well-being. Meditation dampens the response of the brain to emotionally aversive movie clips, further suggesting that meditation helps the brain cope with stress and negative stimuli in the environment.[13]

And so, a balance of healthy eating, regular exercise and intentional relaxation is necessary to promote optimal development during the adolescent years.

What does it all mean?

As a whole, we Americans have never been heavier. While genes certainly play a role in how much fat our bodies tend to store and where our bodies tend to store it, most of the increase in weight can be attributed to poor habits. Quite simply, we eat too much and exercise too little. Not surprisingly, so do our kids! Today's teens need more exercise than they currently get and the value of focused relaxation cannot be overstated. They also need to eat less unhealthy food, a task made more difficult by the presence of soda and snack vending machines in many schools.

By modeling healthy eating and exercise habits, we can teach kids the importance of making healthy food choices and being physically fit. Research suggests that meditation and other activities that promote parasympathetic nervous system functioning can help mitigate the effects of stress, help take emotions out of our relationships with food and help us maintain healthy weights.

Quick Facts:

- Being overweight has become the norm for adolescents and adults in America, contributing to increased rates of diseases from cancer to diabetes.
- For adolescents and adults, the solution to being overweight is altering eating habits and increasing exercise time. Taking time to relax the body can also help, in part by improving mood and reducing the urge to eat for pleasure or comfort.
- In general, teenage females need about 2200 Calories per day to maintain current weight, while teenage males need around 2800 Calories. Anything over will probably lead to weight gain while anything under will probably lead to weight loss.
- To stay healthy, teenagers need between 30-60 minutes of exercise per day everyday.
- Studies show that simply turning off the family TV leads to increases in exercise and decreases in weight.

- Kids from homes where the family eats meals together tend to weigh less.
- By modeling and reinforcing healthy eating, exercise and relaxation habits, we can spare current and subsequent generations of adolescents from the deleterious physical and psychological effects of obesity.

Chapter 4

The toxic effects of videogame violence on kids and communities

Technology allows for easy access to all kinds of media, including some containing gratuitous levels of violence. Whether in the form of videogames or television programs, many of us, our kids included, are exposed to images of violence and gore on a regular basis. As adults, we like to think that kids can tell the difference between reality and the fantasy worlds of television and videogames. Is this true? And does it matter? With regard to videogames specifically, kids are actually committing acts of violence rather than passively observing them. The visceral response is both measurable and unhealthy. What kind of an impact does exposure to violence have on adolescent psychological development, and what are some ways in which we can protect our kids, and our communities, from the deleterious effects of interactive media violence? We will answer those questions in this chapter.

Before the early 1970's, most people interested in playing videogames would have been out of luck. They did not exist, at least not in forms accessible to the mainstream public. That all changed in 1972 when a videogame system developed by German-born American engineer Ralph Baer was marketed by Magnavox as the *Odyssey*. Today, people wear watches that are more complicated than the *Odyssey*, but the concept was revolutionary at the time. Between the spring of 1972 and fall of 1975, Magnavox sold 350,000 *Odyssey* units. An additional 80,000 "rifle packs" were sold, which allowed users to play basic shooting games. By the mid-70's the videogame revolution was in full swing.

In 1975, Atari – which means something roughly equivalent to "check" in a chess match – released *Pong*, a table tennis game for TV. It was sold exclusively through Sears department stores and was the hottest selling Christmas item that year.

In 1977, the *Atari 2600* game system was released and everything changed. The author was seven at the time and still gets a little excited at the mere mention of it. At a retail price of $249, the unit was not cheap, but that didn't hinder sales. Because they were on display at retail stores, boring trips to the mall with one's mom suddenly became an exciting opportunity to test drive new videogame technology.

Over the years, access to games and game systems, the array of games from which to choose and the amount of time people spend playing games have all expanded greatly. As of this writing, there four primary types of gaming consoles on the market, in addition to the personal computer – Sony's *Playstation*, Microsoft's *Xbox*, Nintendo's *Game Cube*, and Nintendo's *Wii* – and thousands of games from which to choose. In 2004, sales of game consoles and game cartridges raked in roughly $10 billion annually in the U.S. and about $30 billion worldwide. These numbers don't include computer based games. In 2006, Neilson Media Research estimated that 41.1 percent of U.S. households (45.7 million homes) had a videogame console. This is an increase of 7 million homes from two years earlier. No doubt these numbers will continue to grow.

The violent game niche

As technology has advanced, game play has become incredibly realistic. As competition for market share has grown, games have increasingly targeted the things that interest those who buy them. In America at least, that includes a high degree of violence. A growing percentage of videogames in all rating categories (ratings will be discussed in a subsequent section) contain significant levels of violence.

In some games with violent content, the violence is minimal, like hitting pedestrians with a car. In others, the violence is graphic and approximates physical reality as closely as the technology allows. Whereas the *Odyssey*'s rifle pack allowed users to shoot simple objects on the screen, some new games allow users to shoot realistic characters, often controlled by other users in the room or over the Internet. The end result can be gory. The level of realism allowed by newer gaming systems is impressive, meaning that the realism of death and destruction in violent games is becoming increasingly intense. The closer the games get to real life, the more likely they are to affect kids like real life experiences.

Concerns that violent games could affect kids negatively

Whenever new technology comes onto the scene, or a new use is identified for it, it is normal for concerned adults to wonder about its ultimate safety. This has certainly been the case with the use of videogame technology to allow for interactive violence. Over the years, parents have become increasingly concerned that the violent content of some videogames could be toxic to development. Let's look at some examples that have provided fuel for such concerns.

One of the most popular videogames during the 2004 Christmas season was *Grand Theft Auto: San Andreas.* Douglas Gentile, a psychologist at Iowa State University and research director for the National Institute on Media and the Family, describes the game as follows:[1]

> "In this game, you play the part of a psycho-path, basically. You run around the street, you can run down pedestrians with the car, you can

do carjackings, you can do drive-by shootings, you can run down to the red-light district, pick up a prostitute, have sex with her in your car, and then kill her to get your money back. Most parents are unaware that this most popular game in the country has such very adult themes in it."

More recent games make *Grand Theft Auto: San Andreas* seem as harmless as an episode of Sesame Street. Below is a description of the 2007 shocker, *Manhunt 2*, also from Rockstar Games, the maker of *Grand Theft Auto: San Andreas*. In the game, you assume the persona of Dr. Daniel Craig, an institutionalized scientist who must torture and kill his way out of the insane asylum if he ever wants to find out what happened in his life to land him there in the first place. From GamesRadar.com:[2]

"Like in the first Manhunt, each of the weapons you'll find have three distinct levels of brutality, depending on how long you can lurk behind your intended victim. You're free to administer a quick, instant kill, but if you wait a few seconds before attacking, you'll get to see something a little more unsettling - like your victim getting his trachea ripped out by wire cutters (again, not quite as gruesome as it sounds). Wait even longer, and you'll pull off a brutal torture-kill, like the [castration] we described earlier."

As might be expected, there is an ongoing, spirited debate over whether such games affect players, and thus the culture, negatively. In his book, *Stop Teaching Our Kids to Kill*, Lieutenant Colonel Dave Grossman argues that videogames teach kids to become killers, desensitize them to violence, and reinforce aggressive tendencies. The culprits, he argues, are the corporations providing violent media, including violent video-games, to kids.

With regard to the teaching part, there is no doubt that games are capable of teaching us things and shaping our behavior. In fact, some researchers argue that many violent games utilize all of the best-practice techniques for teaching and instruction. These include the following:

- Steady progress in mastering knowledge and skills in the curriculum
- Multiple ways of solving problems which increases flexible use and generalization of the skills to other settings
- Students can over-learn the skills and knowledge thus making them automatic
- Activities provide an adrenaline rush that excites the user
- Rewards for achieving success include opportunities to use higher level skills and more advanced tools to tackle even more difficult material
- Popularity is gained by success leading students to aspire to be the best
- Success is available to all regardless of past academic record, standardized test score, or socio-economic status

If such games do use effective teaching methods to shape game play, and the game play involves violent thoughts and actions, then it seems reasonable that kids might carry these rewarded violent thoughts and actions with them into their daily lives. If so, one might expect to see obvious increases in violent conduct among kids who play violent games. Unfortunately, this issue is much more complex than it might seem at first glance. Correlations between exposure to violence and tendencies toward violence abound, but evidence of a direct cause-and-effect link between violent games and violent acts does not exist.

This should not be surprising, as very few issues pertaining to development follow simple "this causes that" relationships. The lack of clear evidence of a causal relationship between videogame violence and real-world violence has led some researchers to argue that people have unfairly blamed violent media for society's ills. According to Guy Cumberbatch, a psychologist and author of several publications on the topic of media violence:[2]

> "The real puzzle is that anyone looking at the research evidence in this field could draw any conclusions about the pattern, let alone argue with such confidence and even passion that it demonstrates the harm of violence on television, in film and in video games. While tests of statistical significance are a vital tool of the social sciences, they seem to have been more often used in this field as instruments of torture on the data until it confesses something which could justify publication in a scientific journal. If one conclusion is possible, it is that the jury is not still out. It's never been in. Media violence has been subjected to lynch mob mentality with almost any evidence used to prove guilt."

Dr. Cumberbatch is not alone. Several influential media researchers in the United States have sided with the gaming industry – even in legal battles. In 2002, led by Marjorie Heins at NYU Law School, 33 experts on the topic of media violence filed a legal brief with the U.S. Court of Appeals for the Eighth Circuit arguing against a law barring minors from gaining access to violent videogames.[2] Why? In their collective view, data linking the games to actual acts of violence, or even to increased aggression in laboratory studies, is too weak.

In the absence of cause-and-effect data linking games to violence, are we to conclude that violent games pose no risk?

No. The available data give plenty of reasons to pause and carefully consider the issues. As is the case with videogames and violence, there currently are no cause-and-effect data linking specific beer commercials to the recruitment of new drinkers. This doesn't necessarily mean that the ads are benign; it could be that their negative impact is broad and subtle rather than focused on a relationship with a single outcome. The same is likely the case with exposure to violence through videogames. Like beer commercials, at the very least the games reinforce attitudes and beliefs that we could do without – in this case the attitudes and beliefs that violence, including torture and murder, can be fun and that the use of force and brutality is the proper approach to problem solving.

It is also important to think about the ripple effect that violent video games could have on a culture. Klaus Mathiak and Rene Weber, researchers who have studied brain functioning during violent games, state the following:[3]

> "The cumulative dose of video games in modern societies is immense: about 10 million hours are played daily by US adolescents... Thus, even a small effect in terms of increased aggressiveness or decreased pro-social behavior would be influential across the society."

In brief, there remains no proven *causal* link between videogame violence and actual violence. If it were that simple, we would expect to see rashes of violence in the suburbs during the weeks after Christmas, and that doesn't happen. However, as we will see, there is compelling evidence that the games stoke feelings of aggression in children and adolescents and reinforce violent tendencies in those who have them. Even if the games don't trigger kids to attack their neighbors and go on crime sprees, reinforcing thoughts of aggression and violence can't possibly be good for kids and the communities in which they live. We will review some of the arguments and evidence for minimizing kids' exposure to violent videogames, and other violent media, below.

Violent videogames reinforce violent behavior

One of the very obvious problems with violence in videogames is that, in the balance of reward and punishment, the games are tilted decisively toward the reward side. In videogames that include committing acts of violence against virtual human enemies, reinforcement is provided for such violence in the form of points, more weapons, etcetera. Doing well at the game requires efficient killing. Efficient killing is rewarded. As the cycle repeats, it seems reasonable to expect that the individual's attitude toward violence will become less negative – if not positive!

One recent study examined the relationship between rewarded violence in video games and levels of aggression in game players.[4] The researchers had subjects, comprised of male and female undergraduates, play one of three versions of a car racing game for 20 minutes. In one version, players received points for destroying opponents' cars and running over pedestrians. In another version, they lost points for doing so. In a third condition, there was no violence, just racing. After game play, subjects were asked to complete the State Hostility Scale, which asks them to indicate how much they agree or disagree with statements like, "I feel aggravated" or "I feel angry." In the first experiment, subjects in the two conditions containing violence, regardless of whether the violence was rewarded or punished, exhibited an increase in hostile feelings.

In a subsequent experiment, hostility was assessed via a word completion task that allowed subjects to complete the first few letters of a word. Half of the word fragments could be completed to make aggressive words. For instance, if presented with "KI_ _", subjects could complete the word in multiple ways, such as "KITE" or "KILL." In this task, researchers found that subjects in the rewarded violence condition were more likely than other subjects to complete the word stems with words associated with violence and aggression.

Playing violent games also seems to change kids' attitudes toward other risky behaviors.[5] In a fascinating study, researchers at the University of Pittsburgh selected 100 males, aged 18-21, from the college population and then assigned them to one of two conditions – playing *Simpsons: Hit and Run* (low violence) or *Grand Theft Auto III* (high violence). Those randomly assigned to the high violence game exhibited greater changes in blood pressure, greater negative emotions in general, were less coopera- tive and expressed more permissive attitudes toward drug use than those playing the low violence game.

Violent video games are unlikely to cause a mild man- nered, well-adjusted kid to open fire on classmates. However, a predilection for violent games is common among school shoot- ers. Indeed, a news story released in September, 2006, yields insight into the personal life of a gunman that opened fire on students at a college in Montreal. The assailant was a 25 year old man who called himself "The Angel of Death." It appears he spent considerable time playing an online game based on the school shootings in Colum- bine, Colorado, that left 13 students dead. Playing a war game is one thing, playing a game based on the real-life massacre of innocent adolescent boys and girls might be quite another.

> "Work sucks ... school sucks ... life sucks ... what else can I say? ... Life is a video game you've got to die sometime."
>
> These are some of the last words written by Kimveer Gill, a gunman that opened fire on students at Dawson College in Montreal. The man killed at least one person and injured 19 others before being shot and killed by police.

If videogames can train soldiers they can train kids

While videogames cannot capture the true experience of war, the military seems to think they can get close enough to be useful in training. For decades, the military has used simulators to train pilots how to fly multimillion dollar planes, drive tanks, and kill. According to Nina Hunteman, a videogame researcher:[6]

> "The U.S. Marine Corps has used the very popular video game *Dune* in its training of soldiers in tactical combat. They have taken the game's basic design and modified it for training soldiers. They find some value in using video games as training devices, which is significant when we think about those same games, slightly modified, being played in the culture at large, outside of a military organization."

In addition to using games to train soldiers, the military also uses games to attract new recruits. In 2002, the military released its own videogame called *America's Army*. Within a few years, the game became one of the most popular on the Internet. It can be downloaded free, purchased for some home gaming systems, or obtained on disc by visiting your local Army recruiter. The game was the topic of an informative article entitled, "Like the video game? Join the Army. 'America's Army' brings combat to a messy teen's bedroom near you," in the Christian Science Monitor on September 19, 2006. In it, a military Colonel and member of the game's development team was quoted as saying:

> "The idea was to create a game to get the word out about the Army, and we would make it fun because the Army is fun, and we'll get it right in their living rooms where they're already operating every day."

In defense of the game, it does not contain the over-the-top hyper-glorified violence found in many war games. Players must complete a virtual boot camp and learn how to operate their weapons effectively before being sent out to kill the enemy.

While not as violent as other games, the violence in it is rewarded, and this has many parents steaming. The military used taxpayer money (more than $6 million) to develop a violent shooting game that can be downloaded for free and played by kids. As a recruiting tool, it paints a positive picture of military service without providing an honest depiction of the risks. Winslow Wheeler, a military expert at the Center for Defense Information in D.C., was quoted by the Christian Science Monitor as saying:

> "It's the 21st-century version of a John Wayne movie... Because they don't show people's best friends getting their arms blown off ... these kinds of games can be very deceptive."

In short, the military routinely uses games and game-like virtual simulators to train soldiers to fight and pilots to fly. In combat situations, training can make the difference between life and death. It is unlikely the military would rely on such technology if it did not shape and mold behavior to make soldiers and pilots more effective in war. While most teenagers do not have access to combat and flight simulators, they do have access to an array of interactive games in which killing is rewarded. Even in the absence of a direct causal relationship between virtual violence and actual violence, the repetitive reinforcement of violent thoughts and actions provided by videogames must influence how kids interact with the world and view their roles in it.

Do videogames influence kids' worldviews?

The companies behind today's games do a truly remarkable job of establishing the context in which game play occurs. This includes more than just realistic graphics – it includes compelling plots that motivate players to succeed for specific reasons. Obviously, these plots are designed primarily to sell games and not to teach morals or shape one's view of self and others. Nonetheless, it appears that games are capable of doing just that. Below is an abstract from a paper on sexism in video-games published in the 1990s.

"Using content analysis, this research examines the portrayal of women and the use of violent themes in a sample of 33 popular Nintendo and Sega Genesis videogames. It is proposed that video games, like other media forms, impact the identity of children. This analysis reveals that traditional gender roles and violence are central to many games in the sample. There were no female characters in 41% of the games with characters. In 28% of these, women were portrayed as sex objects. Nearly 80% of the games included aggression or violence as part of the strategy or object. While 27% of the games contained socially acceptable aggression, nearly half included violence directed specifically at others and 21% depicted violence directed at women. Most of the characters in the games were Anglo."

In defense of the companies creating these games, there is no reason to expect them to do anything other than focus on producing games that sell. They are in business to make money, and their shareholders expect them to do so. It would do them no good to edit, filter and screen their games using focus groups consisting of religious leaders, representatives of the feminist movement and grandparents. Their target market primarily consists of adolescent boys and young adult men looking for games that are bigger, badder and better. As we will discuss in an upcoming section, it is up to parents to screen what kind of games their kids play. With that said, when lax parenting meets plots designed to sell games and generate profits, kids can become entangled in virtual games that inadvertently teach them about ethics, morals, how to view and treat others, and how to view and treat themselves.

People that like to play videogames often find themselves trapped between the desire to play games that are technically good – excellent graphics, compelling plots, realistic and challenging game play – but are ethically questionable. The following online article by Ren Reynolds of the International Game Developers Association captures the complexity of the situation perfectly.[8]

"Generally speaking good games are those that have strong gameplay, impressive graphics or simply are just plain fun; whereas bad games are ones that have poor graphics, are too simple or are just not enjoyable. However when a politician or pressure group says a game is bad they mean something very different. In this context they are charging a game with being corrupting, immoral or even evil. But can a mere game be bad in a moral sense? I believe that they can. And I believe that there is a solid philosophical argument to back this view... To illustrate my points I will examine Grand Theft Auto III (GTA3) from Rock Star Games / Take-2 Interactive... Game players and the game industry alike are crazy about it. GTA3 is ground breaking in its use of the PlayStation 2 platform and has pushed back the boundaries of interactivity. What's more, just about everyone in the games world agrees that it's a great game. On the other hand for the mass media and a number of pressure groups, GTA3 represents all that is wrong with computer games, games culture generally and possibly the whole of modern society. According to these groups GTA3 is sexist, corrupting, violent, offensive and immoral. In short GTA3 represents what is supposedly the best and worst in current computer games and sits at the centre of the debate over the morality of games and game play."

We certainly cannot expect the values of videogames to *reflect* the values of our communities, but we have every reason to be concerned that the values of videogames could *influence* the values of our communities.

Lessons from research on TV violence

Videogames are not the only means by which kids are exposed to violent media content. Television is another. With the number of TVs in American homes (2.73 TV sets on average) now outnumbering the number of people in American homes (2.55 people on average), and the presence of TVs in everything from buses to elevators, we can now quench our thirst for televised entertainment just about anywhere. Below is an excerpt from a September 21, 2006, Associated Press (AP) story about the ubiquity of television sets:

> "David and Teresa Leon of Schenectady, New York and their four-year-old twins have seven sets, plus an eighth they haven't set up yet. They include TVs in both the parents' and kids' bedrooms, the family and living rooms and one in the kitchen that is usually turned to a news station. 'No one ever sits down for more than a few seconds in this house,' said Teresa, a stenographer. 'This way you can watch TV while you're moving from room to room, folding laundry or taking care of the kids."

The AP article sites Nielsen Media Research for data indicating that television sets are on for an average of 8 hours and 14 minutes per day in a typical American household. That's roughly one-third of each day, every day! It also represents an increase of about 1 hour per day in the past decade.

Television came onto the scene long before videogames, providing several additional decades of research into its potential impact on behavior. If the interactive violence afforded by videogames is bad for kids, shouldn't the passive stream of violence provided by TV programs produce at least a detectable impact on society's psyche?

Yes. Beyond contributing to the sedentary lifestyles that many Americans have adopted, television influences how we think, feel, and view the world. When the content is violent, the impact on development appears to be negative. In 2000, a Senate Commerce Committee heard expert testimony from Dr. Craig Anderson about the impact of media violence on children. He began by laying out the following four facts concerning TV and movie violence:[10]

> "**Fact 1**. Exposure to violent TV and movies causes increases in aggression and violence.
>
> **Fact 2**. These effects are of two kinds: short term and long term. The short term effect is that aggression increases immediately after viewing a violent TV show or movie, and lasts for at least 20 minutes. The long term effect is that repeated exposure to violent TV and movies increase the violence-proneness of the person watching such shows. In essence, children who watch a lot of violent shows become more violent as adults than they would have become had they not been exposed to so much TV and movie violence.
>
> **Fact 3**. Both the long term and the short term effects occur to both boys and girls.

Fact 4. The effects of TV and movie violence on aggression are not small. Indeed, the media violence effect on aggression is bigger than the effect of exposure to lead on IQ scores in children, the effect of calcium intake on bone mass, the effect of homework on academic achievement, or the effect of asbestos exposure on cancer"

These facts might be arguable in the strictest scientific sense, but the message is clear – violent TV content has a powerful influence on attitudes and behavior.

Is there actually a relationship between viewing television violence during childhood and committing acts of aggression later in life? Addressing this question requires longitudinal studies in which the same group of subjects is assessed multiple times over a long period. One study, published in 2003, did just this and found that subjects who watched more TV violence as children (at 6 to 10 years of age) were more likely to exhibit aggressive behaviors 15 years later.[11] This was true for both boys and girls and was particularly strong when subjects identified with aggressive TV characters and/or perceived the violence as having a high degree of realism.

Most parents, if they had their way, would probably prefer that their kids never witness acts of violence, but the numbers show that we're failing. Estimates are that, by the time an American adolescent turns 18 years-of-age, he or she will have witnessed 200,000 acts of televised violence, including 40,000 murders. That's a lot of violence and death, and the numbers are not decreasing. The Parents Television Council recently assessed rates of violence in prime time television programs during the first two weeks of November in 1998, 2000, and 2002. They observed that overall rates of violence in primetime programs airing between 8-9PM, so-called family hour, increased by 41% between 1998 and 2002. For programs airing between 9-10PM, rates of violence increased 134%, while for programs airing between 10-11PM, rates increased 63%. Not only did rates of violence increase, but the acts of violence depicted in programs shifted from less violent acts (fist fights or martial arts fights) to more violent acts (use of guns or other weapons).

Does TV violence really desensitize kids to real violence?

Humans come into the world primed to react with fear to just a few stimuli – like spiders and snakes. Presentation of those stimuli evokes an emotional response aimed at getting us to fight or run. As we go through life, we learn to associate natural fear-inducing stimuli with other things and eventually come to fear them, too. If you're afraid of snakes and every time you pass by a particular pet store you see a huge snake in the window, odds are you won't like that place very much! Getting the flu right after visiting that new Chinese restaurant could permanently kill your interest in going back. This type of associative learning is generally beyond our control and can have powerful effects on behavior. Pairing new stimuli with others that already evoke emotional responses is the underlying basis for advertising. Pairing products with attractive people makes consumers want the products more. It's not clear why clowns sell food, but that seems to be a popular strategy, too. Odors are also a common means of selling things – a good idea given the direct influence smell has on the emotional centers in the brain.

In the same way that we can learn to react with more fear to stimuli, we can learn to react with less fear to stimuli. If one is repeatedly exposed to something that once caused fear (say, the clowns in those hamburger commercials), and there are no negative repercussions accompanying the stimuli, one will eventually learn to react with less and less fear to the stimuli. It's simple, and can be very beneficial. For instance, it can allow kids to persevere and learn to do things that scare them at first.

Sometimes the things that kids like to do are downright frightening until they get the hang of it. The ability to keep going until some of the fear subsides is highly adaptive for them.

The natural tendency to react with decreasing amounts of fear to scary things can also be detrimental. With regard to media violence, many wonder if repeated exposure to death and carnage desensitizes kids, and adults, to those horrors. The logical answer, and one supported by decades of research, is yes. Early studies showed that the physiological arousal evoked by violent television diminished over time with repeated viewing, and that brief exposure to media violence reduced one's reactions to real-life violence. Just recently, studies have shown that once kids become desensitized to violence, they will experience far less internal conflict than other kids when considering aggression as a means to solve problems. Absent that internal conflict, violence might be viewed as a more viable solution to social problems.

In short, it is a plausible hypothesis that repeated exposure to violence in the media desensitizes kids to violence in general and creates a culture more tolerant of the use of violence to solve problems. If unconvinced by the limited review of the data in this chapter, a little introspection should suffice. One need only think about the sheer amounts of violence and gore in many current prime time shows relative to prime time shows of the 70s, 80s, and even 90s. Mr. T never took any bullets. Most episodes of the various *CSI* prime-time crime dramas contain dismemberment, corpses, graphic murder, and sometimes all of the above. It is difficult to find an explanation other than desensitization to explain how such shifts in tolerance for televised violence have occurred.

Assuming people do become more tolerant of violent media the more they're exposed to it, who cares? Does it really do anything negative to the culture, or does it just shift people's threshold for thinking things are gross? If violent media don't influence behavior then maybe this issue isn't really a big one after all. Let's look at how the relationship between violent media and behavior might work, and the evidence for it.

Is there any logical reason to think that violent media content could alter thoughts, feeling and behaviors?

There are a variety of ways in which we humans learn about the world and how to engage in it. One of the primary ways is via observational learning. Quite simply, we learn by watching what other people do. Indeed, our brains routinely and automatically conduct the computations necessary to figure out how to mimic another's behavior whether we end up doing so or not. If someone else knows how to do something, why not copy them rather than trying to reinvent the wheel?

One of the best, and oft cited, sources of evidence for the tendency kids have to mimic the violent behavior they see is a classic study performed by psychologist Albert Bandura in the 1960s. Dr. Bandura observed that children who watch adults physically assault an inflatable doll (one of the types that you punch and it keeps coming back up for more) are more likely to assault it themselves, and to do so by mimicking what they observed the adults do.

A recent tragedy, in which a seven year old girl was killed by her sister and her sister's boyfriend, both teenagers, highlights the role that observational learning could play in the violence-promoting effects of videogames. According to statements from the murdered girl's sister, the two alleged killers were acting out moves learned by playing the videogame *Mortal Kombat*. Thankfully, such incidents are not common, despite the intense press coverage they receive.

In addition to learning by seeing, we also learn by doing. When we behave, we receive feedback – positive, negative or neutral. If one receives positive feedback for a behavior, the likelihood that the behavior will be exhibited again increases. If you're hungry and someone feeds you every time you hop on one foot, you'll probably find yourself hopping on one foot quite a bit when you're hungry! In this same way, if one commits an act of aggression and is rewarded, then the likelihood of committing another act of aggression will go up.

What about catharsis? Doesn't watching violence help us vent aggression?

From a historical perspective, one of the more interesting debates in psychology centers on whether viewing violence, or even engaging in it, reduces aggression or contributes to it. Many advocates of the right to choose violent media argue that viewing violent media causes a cathartic reaction, leading viewers to actually become *less* hostile rather than more so. The word catharsis is rooted in Greek and essentially means "to cleanse or purge." Its use in psychology dates back to Sigmund Freud in the late 1800's. When applied to the issue of violence, use of the word implies that, somehow, witnessing violence cleanses a person of their violent impulses, leading to a reduction in aggression.

Does science support the catharsis hypothesis? No. More than 40 years of research on the topic has failed to provide compelling evidence of catharsis when it comes to violent media. A 1975 study by Geen and colleagues is representative of the literature.[12] In that study, the researchers enrolled 90 male subjects, some of which were aggravated and insulted at the beginning of the experiment by a confederate (a person who acts like a subject but actually works for the researcher). Some subjects then watched as the experimenter delivered what appeared to be real shocks to the confederate. Next, the subjects themselves were allowed to shock the confederate. From the perspective of catharsis, watching shocks being delivered to the confederate should cleanse one of their anger and diminish the amount of shock they deliver to the confederate. Nope. Data from a litany of other studies compel similar conclusions.

One need not look to laboratory studies for evidence that the catharsis hypothesis is fatally flawed with regard to violence. If catharsis occurred, kids that witness abuse in their homes would be less likely to become abusers themselves, not more. Kids who grow up in neighborhoods where they routinely witness acts of violence would be less likely to become violent themselves, not more. In both such examples, the likelihood of becoming aggressive goes up, not down.

It is worth noting that the failure to find evidence of catharsis extends beyond witnessing aggression and even applies to hearing about it. In 2003, researchers at Iowa State University reported that subjects who listened to songs with violent lyrics exhibited an increase in aggressive thoughts and feelings.[13] Those who listened to similar songs without lyrics about violence did not exhibit such an increase.

In short, while some argue that viewing violence should actually pacify people, research suggests that the opposite is true. When it comes to violence, witnessing it, or even hearing about it, stokes the coals rather than extinguishes them.

How can we minimize the impact of violent media on kids?

If violent TV programs and video games promote aggression in some way, then limiting kids' access to such media should reduce aggression. Indeed, that's what researchers at Stanford recently reported.[14] The study included all of the third and fourth graders at two elementary schools in San Jose, California. The purpose was to evaluate the effectiveness of an intervention designed to reduce TV time and video game play. The program consisted of 18 classroom lectures taught by regular teachers who were trained by the researchers. The program began by having kids monitor and report their own TV and video game use. This was followed by a *TV Turnoff* challenge in which kids were challenged to keep their TVs and game consoles turned off for 10 days.

To assess the impact of turning off TVs and game consoles on behavioral patterns and internal psychological variables, the researchers measured peer ratings of the treated subjects' aggressiveness, monitored playground behaviors for aggressiveness, and assessed how mean and scary the world seemed to the kids in the study. Relative to control subjects, children in the TV Turnoff group were rated as less aggressive by peers and exhibited reduced levels of verbal aggression on the playground – all from watching less TV and spending less time playing videogames.

Such findings suggest that one easy way to minimize the potentially negative impact of violent media on kids is to keep them from watching TV or playing videogames. With young children, this approach makes perfect sense. However, when raising older children and adolescents, this approach is impractical and can make kids feel like they are being punished if their friends engage in such activities but they cannot. It can also promote underground TV viewing and game playing while at friends' houses, and thus create opportunities for deception and distrust. A more practical approach is to monitor the content of the TV programs kids watch and the games they play and to limit the amount of time they spend doing so. There are plenty of harmless and entertaining programs on TV and lots of really entertaining and nonthreatening games. It is entirely possible to find a balance here in which time is monitored and limited but kids still get watch some shows and play some games.

With regard to TV in particular, here are some simple suggestions to help protect kids from the negative effects of violent programming:

- Know what your kids watch. What is your family policy regarding appropriate programs for your kids?

- Limit the number of hours kids watch TV. The American Academy of Pediatrics recommends no more than 2 hrs per day. It can be helpful to give your kids freedom to choose when to utilize their allotted time and what they watch within the range of agreed upon programs
- Know and approve of the games your children play.

Remember, no matter how mature a particular adolescent is, it remains the responsibility of adults to create healthy environments for them, even if the adolescent fails to immediately grasp the wisdom of the decisions made on their behalf. Hopefully, their future selves will thank you even if their current selves curse you!

Fortunately, technology has simplified the task of screening videogames and TV programs for violence and other content inappropriate for kids. For televisions, technology referred to as the *V-chip* has been standard on all sets with 13" screens or larger since 2001. The V-chip allows parents to filter out programs that they would prefer their children not see. Parents can set the V-chip to filter content based on the rating system created by the television industry, which includes six age-based ratings and some modifiers. The age ratings are:

TV-Y: Appropriate for all children
TV-Y7: Appropriate for children aged 7 and older
G: General audience
TV-PG: Parental guidance suggested
TV-14: Parents strongly cautioned
TV-MA: Mature audiences only

Descriptors that can be used to characterize the specific content included in shows in various age ratings consist of the following:

FV: Fantasy violence
L: Language
V: Violence
S: Sexual situation
D: Sexual dialogue

And so, a rating system for TV programs exists and essentially all TV sets contain a special chip that allows parents to filter out programs with ratings that are inappropriate for the viewer's age. Consult your TV manual for specific instructions for controlling the V-chip on your particular television set. If you threw out the manual the day that you bought the TV, check the manufacturer's website for a replacement and more details about the chip.

With regard to protecting kids from violent videogame content, a rating system for videogames also exists and is intended to help parents make decisions about which games their kids can play. The system, created by the Entertainment Software Rating Board (ESRB) consists of the following ratings:

E: Everyone
T: Teen
M: Mature (17 and over)
AO: Adults only (18 and over)

Unfortunately, the rating system is far from perfect. According to the National Institute on Media and the Family:

> "The ESRB video game rating system, like its cousins in the movie and television industries, is owned and operated by the industry it is supposed to monitor. This obvious conflict of interest is why only eighteen games out of ten thousand have ever been rated Adults Only (AO)."

They go on to argue that games labeled **M** for mature continue to get more violent, use more profanity and include more sex as the years go by. Yet, such games continue to receive the **M** rating rather than the **AO** rating. In June of 2005, researchers discovered that players of Rockstar Games' *Grand Theft Auto: San Andreas* could gain access to a hidden mini-game (game within a game) in which the main character could engage in sex with various girlfriends. The mini-game has come to be known as the "Hot coffee mod," as the sexual encounters begin when the girlfriend invites the character in for coffee. It took the company a few weeks to publicly acknowledge that the hidden mini-game had somehow made it on there. Simulated interactive sex is considered pornography. Obviously, pornography constitutes "Adult Only" content, and the failure of the ESRB to change the game's rating seems to support the arguments made by concerned advocates. Remember, only one year separates the recommended cut point for **M** and **AO** games. The big difference is commercial. Major retailers have so far tended to stay away from selling games with **AO** ratings. It is quite likely this concern over the marketability of a game with an **AO** rating is what drove the following series of events.

As discussed earlier in the chapter, the game *Manhunt 2* involves acts of torture and mutilation beyond anything thus far seen in videogames. Even seasoned gamers seem to concur that it is the most violent game to date. The game initially earned a rare **AO** rating from the ESRB. This would have hampered sales, as many mainstream retailers do not carry games rated **AO**. Fortunately for Rockstar Games, after removing a scene involving castration and making some other minor tweaks, the ESRB lowered the rating to **M** before its release in the fall of 2007. Defending their decision to let the game go forward with the **M** rating, the ESRB released the following statement:[15]

> "This is a very clear and firm warning to parents that the game is in no way intended for children."

It is worth noting that both versions of the game, modified and unmodified, have been banned in Britain by the British Board of Film Classifications. The changes simply did not go far enough for them, as captured by the following statement:[15]

"The impact of the revisions on the bleakness and callousness of tone or the essential nature of the gameplay, is clearly insufficient. There has been a reduction in the visual detail in some of the 'execution kills', but in others they retain their original visceral and casually sadistic nature."

Rules are only useful if they make sense and are enforced. The presence of a videogame rating system suggests that only age-appropriate games will be sold to children. Most of us are accustomed to the movie rating system introduced 30 years ago by the Motion Picture Association of America (MPAA), in which an **R** rating is not just a warning to parents, but an indication that the turnstile will only click if you are 17 or older, or have parental permission. Ratings of **G** (general audience), **PG** (parental guidance suggested), **PG-13** (parents strongly cautioned), and **NC-17** (no one under 17) round out the system. Clearly, these age restrictions are not always enforced. However, it's a safe bet that the enforcement of age restrictions for videogame sales is even worse.

A study by the National Institute on Media and the Family found that, about half of the time, young children can walk out of stores with games rated **M** for mature. It is worth noting that the Institute praises the company Best Buy for their enforcement efforts and suggests that they should serve as a model for other companies.

The Institute conducts research on minors' buying and playing habits, and assesses parental awareness of their children's behaviors. In a survey of 657 students aged 8-17 years, seven out of ten, mostly boys, reported playing **M**-rated games.

Seventy-eight percent of boys said they owned their own **M**-rated games. Only ¼ said their parents ever stopped them from buying a game due to its content and rating. Only 40% of the parents surveyed reported that they understand the video game rating symbols.

The ESRB website includes a warning that games played online might not have a rating, particularly in cases where the players themselves can create and insert their own content. In these cases, the players pick up where the programmers left off and are often free to create what they want. Many current games are geared toward online play, making this issue more important than it might seem at first glance.

It can be very difficult for parents to decide what kinds of games to allow kids to play, particularly when glitzy advertisements for ultra-violent games suggest they are harmless. The website, What They Play (www.whattheyplay.com), is a great source for reviews and recommendations regarding games for kids of different ages.

With regard to so called "first person shooter games" in general, here is some logic worth considering. In these games, the player has a killer's-eye-view of the action. For some games, the killer's-eye-view includes views of torture, dismemberment and disembowelment. It is unlikely that most parents would allow their children to watch TV shows – even animated ones – in which, from a first person perspective, the character runs around killing people with grotesque results for the duration. If that's the case, then allowing one's kid to be the character in the animated show running around killing and dismembering people seems like an illogical choice. It is also unlikely that many parents would allow their kids to play first person games in which they run around raping virtual characters. Is murder somehow less of a concern here?

ESRB Videogame Rating Symbols*

EARLY CHILDHOOD

Titles rated **EC (Early Childhood)** have content that may be suitable for ages 3 and older. Contains no material that parents would find inappropriate.

EVERYONE

Titles rated **E (Everyone)** have content that may be suitable for ages 6 and older. Titles in this category may contain minimal cartoon, fantasy or mild violence and/or infrequent use of mild language.

EVERYONE 10+

Titles rated **E10+ (Everyone 10 and older)** have content that may be suitable for ages 10 and older. Titles in this category may contain more cartoon, fantasy or mild violence, mild language and/or minimal suggestive themes.

TEEN

Titles rated **T (Teen)** have content that may be suitable for ages 13 and older. Titles in this category may contain violence, suggestive themes, crude humor, minimal blood, simulated gambling, and/or infrequent use of strong language.

MATURE

Titles rated **M (Mature)** have content that may be suitable for persons ages 17 and older. Titles in this category may contain intense violence, blood and gore, sexual content and/or strong language.

ADULTS ONLY

Titles rated **AO (Adults Only)** have content that should only be played by persons 18 years and older. Titles in this category may include prolonged scenes of intense violence and/or graphic sexual content and nudity.

*Content in the table above is directly from the ESRB website (www.esrb.com)

In defense of the technology – It's all about content

It is important to remember that, at the core, videogames are games. They are interactive, they involve rules and strategies, players can win or lose. Most people like to play games of one sort or another – whether it's bingo, polo, or *Halo*. There is nothing wrong with playing games. In fact, for a variety of reasons, playing games can be extremely good for us! In the end, it is the nature of the games, the content involved, and the reasons for playing them that matter.

In a fascinating study, young burn victims (aged 5-16) played a virtual reality game during burn treatments in an effort to reduce subjective pain beyond the relief provided by pain medications alone.[9] The game was adapted from the popular first-person shooter game called *Quake*. In it, the player runs around shooting monsters. Pain scores while playing the game were roughly 1/3 as high as pain scores during analgesia alone. In other words, the distraction provided by the game was sufficient to reduce the pain felt by these kids. Other studies have shown similar effects of watching television.

Nina Hunteman makes the case that games can be simultaneously beneficial and harmful to individuals and communities.[6] Regarding the benefits of playing games:

> "Clearly, post 9/11 we're living in a much more fearful world. We carry more fear with us than we did 2 years ago, and one of the things these games allow people to do is, even if just for 45 minutes, sit and play a game – it gives you a sense of getting back the control of that fear. It's fantastical, it's temporary, but if you can play a game where you are neutralizing a terrorist threat – for 45 minutes you can pretend you have some sense of agency, some

control, or at the very least, some part in trying to make the world a safer place."

Regarding the downside of playing games:

"Of course, the downside of that is if the only place where you address the fear is in your fantasy world, is in your entertainment, is in a game for 45 minutes, then that leaves the rest of you really wanting for another way of addressing that. Talking to other people, becoming part of a community effort to make your neighborhoods safer, learning more about your fears, and so forth, are things to think about. If you get your relief from that fear via a temporary and fantastical scenario, it could take away from addressing it in a realistic, long-term, and healthy way."

The importance of game content in evaluating whether a particular game has the potential to be healthy or unhealthy for kids, or adults for that matter, cannot be overstated. The key issue here is not whether videogames are *always* good or *always* bad, it's whether the violence in videogames *can be* bad for kids. And the answer seems to be yes. Violent games reward and reinforce

Side*Notes*

WILL Interactive – Games that let you "Play it out before you live it out"

WILL Interactive is a Maryland based company that started making educational games for kids aged 12-18 in 1998. The pioneers behind WILL interactive created what they call "Virtual Experience Immersive Learning Simulators." This technology allows teenagers to live the lives of other teens in interactive full-motion movies. They get to make choices and control the direction that the characters take in life. Players must make decisions about drugs, sex and other challenging issues. The hope is that, by allowing real kids to live out virtual lives, they will learn about the repercussions of both good and bad choices, and will be better prepared to make wise decisions when confronted with similar situations in their own lives. This sure beats games with rewarded disembowelment!

violent attitudes and violent approaches to dealing with problems, desensitize kids to violence in general, and paint disparaging pictures of women, law enforcement, and, increasingly, those in middle-eastern countries.

To understand the varied impact that games could have on kids, it is critical to recognize that not all games contain violent content. Many games are purely educational in nature and can help children master the types of skills valued in schools. Some games require kids to expend lots of energy. Research suggests that the game *Dance Dance Revolution*, which requires players to actually dance and do so fast, is an effective adjunct to weight loss programs for kids. New games for Nintendo's *Wii* console promise similar benefits. The *Wii* requires players to engage in simulated real world movements in order to play games like shuffle board, bowling, baseball, and others. This is wonderful for purposes of physical therapy and can allow the aging and really lazy among us to play the games we like without leaving home. Sure, it's not real golf, but at least you still get to swing. In addition, once one moves away from standalone game consoles and enters

Side*Notes*

What about sports? Don't they promote violence, too?

Many parents struggle with the distinction between the violence that kids are exposed to in videogames and the aggression inherent in many sports, such as football and mixed martial arts. If kids should be shielded from game violence, shouldn't they be shielded from sports, too? One of the key differences between aggression in videogames and in sports rests in the purpose of the aggressive acts. In videogames, the purpose is often to maim or kill. In athletics, the purpose is to compete and win, hopefully without killing someone on the other side. In games, killing is rewarded. In sports, killing is frowned upon. In games, acts of violence are often carried out while the game player sits on a couch. Being aggressive in sports requires a high degree of physical preparedness and actual movement. Finally, while the word "aggression" applies to both game play and sports, words like "violence" and "hostility" fit best in discussions of games rather than sports. The evidence suggests that violent game play can impede healthy adolescent development. In contrast, playing sports is typically beneficial to health, even if the off-field antics of some players are not.

the world of computer based games, the opportunities for safe and educational entertainment expand greatly.

In the end, the impact of violent media content on kids, regardless of its actual scope, can be minimized or negated through proper screening for content on the part of parents and other caregivers. When wise choices are made on behalf of game-playing kids, the outcomes can be entirely positive rather than potentially negative.

What does it all mean?

Today's adolescents are being raised in an increasingly violent world. The violence comes from multiple sources – some of them outside of the home and some inside. Exposure to violence through television and videogames is not benign, and considerable research suggests that exposure to such violence can have long-lasting, deleterious effects on the quality of a kid's life. Watching or engaging in violence, real or pretend, increases aggression among kids and decreases the strength of their reactions to seeing violence.

In a world that values corporate responsibility with regard to social issues, the large companies that create and fill the pipeline pumping violent media into our stores and homes would recognize the potential damage they are doing and police themselves better. One day perhaps, but not today. Regardless, in the end, parents and other guardians are responsible for protecting kids from over-exposure to violence. Only they have the ability to filter and screen the content that comes into their homes through cable lines, satellite dishes, the Internet, or videogames. Rating systems can help, particularly if they are used by parents in the decision-making process, but are too often ignored or glossed over.

In the next chapter, we will move from discussions of virtual acts of violence committed by kids to actual acts of violence committed by kids. Media violence cannot be blamed for such acts, but it certainly contributes to the hostile and emotionally disconnected environments that create kids capable of committing them.

Quick Facts:

- The sheer level of violence in TV programs, movies and videogames has grown to outlandish proportions in the U.S. and other countries.

- The trend toward ultra-violence reflects the rapidity with which we become desensitized to violent imagery over time.

- We Americans have become hooked on violence, including sexualized violence, like crack. It is no surprise that our kids are following in our footsteps.

- Videogames in which players slaughter virtual people not only occupy our kids' minds with thoughts and images of gore and mutilation, they trigger changes in vital signs like heart rate and blood pressure and teach our kids that guns and death are no big deal.

- The fact that so many games contain fun and rewarded acts of brutality, maiming and torture trivializes very real suffering in the world and points to a culture making poor use of its kids' time.

- Rating systems exist for TV programs and videogames, but the rating systems were created by the industries themselves, and many parents are unaware they exist.

- Parents and community leaders, not kids or videogame makers, should determine what content is appropriate for kids and how much time they should be allowed to spend viewing or interacting with it.

- In the end, violence in the media only serves to elevate the level of hostility and lack of interpersonal connectedness we are experiencing in modern America.

Chapter 5

School violence – Bullying, shootings and what can be done about it

Fortunately for most adolescents, the violence they are exposed to tends to be virtual. However, for many other kids, violence and aggression strike close to home, and can occur within the confines of school walls. Most kids learn how to tame their anger and channel it appropriately. For others, violent urges cross the threshold between thoughts and actions, leading them to injure or oppress the kids around them. Kid-on-kid violence takes many forms and includes bullying and sometimes murder. In this chapter, we will dive into the data and discuss ways in which parents and educators can help reduce the likelihood that kids will either commit or experience acts of violence, particularly within school walls.

Brenda Spencer didn't like Mondays. Or at least that's the reason she gave a reporter for killing the Principal and custodian at San Diego's Grover Cleveland Elementary School, across the street from her family home. Eight students and a police officer were hit with bullets but survived. During the siege on her home that followed, the 16 year old stated, "I just started shooting, that's it. I just did it for the fun of it. I just don't like Mondays. I just did it because it's a way to cheer the day up. Nobody likes Mondays."

The year was 1979, and this was the first high profile case in which a teenager shot other school kids in what has become a long 30 year period. The .22 caliber rifle she used was a Christmas present from her father, whom she would later claim was abusive. In the case of Brenda Spencer, the students she

shot survived. As we will see later in this chapter, the outcomes of many school shootings since have not been so comforting.

Over the last few decades, America has become an increasingly violent place. Homicide is now the second leading cause of death for adolescents overall in the U.S. Car crashes rank first and suicide third. Among African-Americans, homicide ranks as the leading cause of death for those aged 10-24. In some parts of cities like Philadelphia, kids report that even having an attractive girlfriend or wearing nice clothes can get you killed these days. According to the Federal Bureau of Investigation (FBI) Crime Clock, a violent crime was committed in America once every 22.7 seconds in 2005. A forcible rape occurred once every 5.6 minutes and someone was murdered once every 31.5 minutes.

The sheer level of violence, particularly gun-related violence, in the U.S. is most apparent when juxtaposed to levels of violence in other countries. Researchers at the Centers for Disease Control and Prevention examined rates of gun-related deaths in the U.S. and 35 other countries. The differences are frightening. In 1993, guns killed an estimated 14.24 citizens per 100,000 in the U.S. This rate is 35 times higher than the rate in England and 285 times higher than the rate in Japan. In the U.S., a child or teenagers is killed with a gun once every three hours or so. According to recent data from the Centers for Disease Control and Prevention summarized by the National Education Association Health Information Network (www.neahin.org),

"American kids are 16 times more likely to be murdered with a gun, 11 times more likely to commit suicide with a gun, and nine times more likely to die from a firearm accident than children in 25 other industrialized countries combined."

Adults in America have huge appetites for acts of violence and aggression. We watch it, commit it, read about it, grieve over it, and glorify it. Unfortunately, the trickle down impact of our lust for violence can threaten the well-being of our kids and the future of our communities.[1] Violence has become an ever present facet of life for a large swath of young Americans. A 2001 study of 7 year olds in urban Philadelphia observed the following:[2]

- 75% had heard gun shots
- 18% had seen a dead body outside
- 10% had seen a shooting or stabbing in the home

Fear of being killed was a daily part of life in three out of five of these kids. Higher exposure to violence was associated with more symptoms of anxiety and depression, poorer school performance, a greater number of missed school days, and lower self-esteem. A 2005 study from Boston University found that simply witnessing violence can cause, or at least contribute to, the following symptoms in teens:[3]

- Sleep difficulties
- Poorer performance in school
- Somatic symptoms (headaches, upset stomach, other physical complaints)
- Anxiety about separation from caregivers
- Increased anger and aggression

- Depression, social withdrawal, apathy
- Intrusive thoughts, memory, and worries
- Increased delinquent or anti-social behavior

In addition to affecting the psychological lives of kids, exposure to violence increases the odds that kids will go on to become violent, themselves. A study published in 2001 indicates that children who view real violence and/or are victims of violence are more likely to become violent adolescents.[4] The researchers surveyed students from schools in Cleveland, Ohio, and Denver, Colorado. From a sample of 3725 students, 484 were identified as dangerously violent (DV) – meaning that they had stabbed or shot at someone in the previous year. These students, both male and female, shared several common traits that separated them from kids in the control group. Chief among the predictors of becoming a DV teen were exposure to violence in the home or neighborhood and being victims of violence in the home or neighborhood.

In their wonderful review of best practices for school-based violence prevention programming, Iris Boworsky and her colleagues at the University of Minnesota provide the following list of risk and protective factors related to becoming a violent youth. The list, on the next page, highlights the critical role that early environmental influences have on a kid's penchant for violence.

Given the nature of the current culture, many of the risk factors noted by Boworsky and colleagues are common in the lives of kids. As such, it is not surprising that many kids do, in fact, turn to violence to express their emotions, feel in control of their lives, and settle arguments. Based upon media coverage, it might seem that most violent acts involving kids occur within our schools. While that's not true, schools have become hostile places for many kids. Let's look at the numbers.

Risk and protective factors related to becoming a violent kid	
Risk	**Protective**
Prenatal/perinatal stress	Caring and support
Ineffective parenting	Good communication
Family violence	Family-connectedness
Learning problems	High expectations
Substance abuse	Emotional health
Involvement in anti-social groups	Opportunities to participate
Media violence	School achievement
Culture and history of violence	School-connectedness
Availability and legal access to firearms	Connectedness to an adult in the
Economic deprivation	community
Overcrowding	
Prejudice and discrimination	

From: Smith, A., Kahn, J., & Borowsky, I. (1999). "Best practices in school-based violence prevention." Minneapolis, MN: University of Minnesota Extension Service. Online: http://www.allaboutkids.umn.edu/cfahad/7286-01.html

The FBI collects data regarding criminal incidents from the nation's law enforcement agencies. Over a five year period from 2000-2004, with 33% of all law enforcement agencies reporting, a total of 17,065,074 crimes were logged. Rates of crime inside and outside of school increased by roughly 65% during that five year period. On average, only 3.3% of the crimes that occurred each year took place in schools (including colleges). While that is a small percentage of all crimes, it adds up to 558,219 incidents over the five years span, and 96% of those crimes fell into the assault category. Most incidents involved males (77%) and most assaults were committed by Caucasian students (71%). Importantly, these numbers only reflect documented crimes and do not include incidences of aggression not reaching the criminal level.

Acts of violence and hostility in schools can run the gamut from one-time fist fights to calculated hazing and even premeditated murder. In this chapter, we will explore two categories of school related hostility, bullying and school shootings, both of which have drawn intense interest over the years from concerned parents, school administrators and the media.

As we will see, though bullying and murder might seem to differ only in the quantity of anger involved, they are actually qualitatively different acts committed by very different types of kids. Fortunately, both are also solvable problems.

Bullying

Bullying involves the imposition of one's will on another person with the aim of repressing or subjugating them. Many kids are exposed to acts of aggression via bullying. Conversely, many kids commit acts of aggression via bullying. How bad is the problem? What causes kids to bully? What can be done about it? Those and other questions will be addressed below.

In this chapter, the word "bully" is used to refer to kids that engage in bullying practices. It is inaccurate to assume that an entire subgroup of kids exists that can be *permanently* identified as "bullies." We all know people that carry the tendency to bully with them into adulthood. But, it is quite possible that kids who bully today will not do so tomorrow. Indeed, research suggests that many kids on the receiving end of bullying often go on to bully other kids.

Let's take a look at some of the things we know about bullying:

- Bullying, the verb, takes many forms, including physical aggression, threats, teasing, harassment, and manipulation of relationships.
- Bullying is quite common among kids with around 30% being bullies or bullied at any given time.
- Physical bullying peaks during middle school but verbal bullying continues throughout the school years.
- Girls and boys bully differently. Boys' acts of bullying are usually overt, such as physical acts. Girls' acts of bullying are more often covert and involve spreading rumors, sabotaging relationships and the like.

- Bullying is bad for both the bullied and the bully. Both have poorer health outcomes than the non-bullied and the non-bullies.
- The presence of bullying behavior is likely indicative of other problems, and possibly predictive of future problems.

In short, both bullying and being bullied are toxic for kids and can have dire consequences for development. The prognosis is poorer for kids on both sides of the equation than for kids who manage to avoid using such tactics or having them used on them. For these reasons, it is paramount that we figure out how to keep kids from becoming bullies and protect potential targets from the threats posed by kids who do. After exploring what is known about the problem, we will examine what we can do about it.

Why do some kids bully and others get bullied?

Adolescence requires a level of social competence not needed during childhood. We begin to look at each other differently. Members of the opposite sex, or sometimes the same sex, stop seeming gross to us and we start competing for their attention. Finding a place in the social hierarchy, preferably as high up as possible, becomes a major concern for most kids. How we choose to climb through the ranks will depend on several factors – including the sum total of our experiences in life and the biological tendencies that we each bring to our interactions with others. For some kids, life experiences – including TV and movies, interactions with parents and other relatives, interactions with children in the neighborhood and at schools, siblings, etcetera – have taught them that the best way to handle social interactions is to treat everyone as an equal. Others have learned to be submissive and avoid conflict. Still others have learned that might makes right and that it is okay to use coercion and other forms of aggression to dominate others.

In broad terms, kids that learn to submit to others tend to be bullied. Kids that learn to dominate others tend to do the bullying. Only those kids who can keep their use of power, both physical and social, and responses to it, in balance stand a good chance of keeping out of the fray.

Bullying provides young bullies with a sense of power and control during a tumultuous stage of life. If the actions help the bully-er achieve their objectives, then the behavioral tendencies will be reinforced and the likelihood of using those tactics again increases. As we will see, the common tactic of ignoring bullies only emboldens them to bully more, as it inadvertently rewards their actions and can make them feel untouchable.

Bullies are often portrayed as kids on the fringes; the ones that don't really fit in or get the positive attention they need. While there are kids like that, it isn't just kids on the fringes that bully. Sometimes the acts are committed by popular kids – those at the highest rungs of the social ladder, not the lowest. In a fascinating study, researchers Anotonius Cillessen and Lara Mayeux at the University of Connecticut identified two categories of popular students.[5] One category includes students who are genuinely well-liked by their peers. The other consists of students that are quite popular but not necessarily well-liked. Popular kids liked by their peers tend to be kind, trustworthy and sociable. Kids perceived to be popular but not well-liked by their peers can embody pro-social traits, too, but they also tend to be dominant, arrogant, and aggressive in both physical (e.g., hitting) and relational (e.g., coercing) ways. Their social status is maintained by the fear they induce in other kids. Crossing them could have dire consequences, so they are allowed a free pass to the top of the hierarchy, at least for a while. Adult life works this way sometimes, too.

While bullies themselves aren't always on the fringes, their targets tend to be. Statistically, kids are more likely to be targets of bullying if:

- They are isolated with few if any good friends
- They do not fit in socially
- They are physically weaker than their peers
- They are insecure, passive and unlikely to retaliate
- They are in need of positive feedback and nurturing – the opposite of bullying
- They are dealing with sexual orientation issues
- They have disabilities or other characteristics that make them stand out

Recognizing risk factors for being victimized can help parents and educators identify kids to keep an eye on. Bullying is best dealt with quickly in order to protect those being bullied from further persecution and to re-route development for the bully before the tendency to oppress others becomes a stable trait.

How does bullying affect a kid's future?

As mentioned above, kids who are bullied fair more poorly than their peers. According to the U.S. Department of Health and Human Services, bullied kids are more likely than other kids to:[6]

- Get into fights
- Steal or vandalize property
- Drink alcohol
- Smoke cigarettes
- Be truant and/or drop out of school
- Suffer academically

- Dislike school
- Carry weapons

Kids who engage in bullying behavior suffer, too. They are more likely than their peers to be convicted of crimes by the age of 24, and exhibit increased risks of all kinds of health conditions. To understand why, from a developmental perspective, bullying is so toxic, let's take a look at what life might be like for adolescent bullies and those they bully.

Imagine that you are a teenager who uses bullying tactics to get your own way. Your peers are afraid of you and do not attempt to prevent you from bullying others. Their main concern is staying off of your radar screen. Teachers don't intervene or do so with no consequence to you. What lesson would be learned from this? Probably that bullying is an effective means of getting what you want, and that you are somehow above the rules.

If teachers and other adults cowered in the face of your bullying tactics, you would become emboldened to intensify your misguided use of power. Given the purpose of adolescence, to prepare you to function in the world on our own, you will likely carry your reinforced bullying tendencies with you into adulthood. While this might prepare you for a career in politics, to be a trader in the stock market, or to be a professional diva, it will not prepare you to have healthy adult relationships or to raise children to be kind, empathetic and caring.

What if you were the person being bullied instead of the one doing the bullying? You are made to feel weak and out of control so that the bully can feel strong and in control. If people on the sidelines stay on the sidelines and don't come to your aid, the sheer amount of social rejection you feel could be difficult to bear. Inaction on the part of your peers, and perhaps even teachers and parents, could make you feel truly helpless and perhaps hopeless. If you fit the general profile of a bullied kid, you might already be socially awkward and unsure of yourself. The whole experience would only reinforce the voice of uncertainty in your head. This is your adolescence – the time when your interactions with the world mold and shape you and determine the trajectory you will be on when you enter young adulthood. If you have learned that there is no use in trying to fight those who seek to oppress you, it will be harder to stand up for yourself and your family in times of conflict. Indeed, you might even turn to bullying tactics yourself in the hope of regaining a sense of control.

When not dealt with by adults, bullying is reinforced and begets more bullying. Those who get bullied are made to feel flawed and powerless. The prognosis for kids in both groups is poor, but perhaps more poor for kids that get bullied than for those doing the actually bullying. As we will see later in this chapter, being bullied is one of the few things – other than being male and Caucasian – that school shooters seem to have in common.

Kids aren't the only people who suffer when bullying happens in school. Parents who love the kids involved often struggle to figure out how best to handle the situation. In Chapter 11, we will discuss the tragic case of Ryan Halligan, an adorable boy who took his own life after years of being tormented by a bully and struggling with depression and learning difficulties. His father, John, writes eloquently about how he and Ryan's mother wrestled with how best to handle the bullying in the years leading to Ryan's death. Adolescence is a time when we want to give kids more freedom to handle their stressors, but we want to keep them safe, too. This is a difficult balance to establish and maintain. Later in this chapter we will examine some steps that might help those for whom this situation sounds familiar.

Virtual bullying causes actual harm

When done on the Internet, bullying is often referred to as *cyberbullying*. In many ways, cyberbullying can be more damaging, psychologically, to the victim than face-to-face bullying. When face-to-face, the source of the aggression and insensitivity can be identified. There is hope that the bully can be sidelined somehow. It is not that easy on the Internet, where bullies can hide. The anonymity emboldens many bullies to say things that are more venomous and hateful than the things they might say in person. Death threats, for instance. Even worse, kids who might normally stand on the sidelines in cases of face-to-face bullying often add their voices to virtual bullying, siding with the bully-er in order to feed off of their power. Thus, rather than contending with a single bully and throngs of bystanders, children bullied online often have to contend with a chorus of hatred and vituperation and, potentially, tens-of-thousands of virtual bystanders around the world.

The world of cyberbullying is a shadowy one. Many parents are not even aware that such a world exists, or that it affects their kids. In one recent study, only 15% of parents were aware that cyberbullying occurs while 42% of kids reported having been bullied online and 35% reported receiving some form of direct threat against them. Half of all middle school students in one study had visited websites created by bullies to torment classmates.

The tragic story of Jeff Johnston, a Florida youth who died by suicide after years of unrelenting bullying, reveals how devastating cyberbullying can be. Jeff was a student at Trafalgar Middle School in Cape Coral, Florida. His mother was a teacher at the school. Sadly, her presence did not prevent her son from becoming the target of a malicious student. It wasn't enough for the bully to torment Jeff on school property. He eventually began tormenting him via the Internet, as well. After years of constant bullying, Jeff gave up. His parents found him hanging in his closet. He was only 15 years old. In a note that he left behind for his friends, he said "I give up." Years later, the parents of the bully continued to proclaim their son's innocence, providing an informative glimpse into the world that created him.

The equally tragic story of Megan Meier offers another example of the traumatic impact that cyberbullying can have on kids. Like most 13 year olds, Megan Meier, from Dardenne Prairie, Missouri, was struggling to find herself and fit in with other kids her age. Also like many kids her age, Megan suffered from depression and Attention Deficit Disorder, further complicating her efforts to feel good about herself and find friends.

A brief reprieve from her struggles came in the fall of 2006 in the form of a boy named "Josh Evans," whom she met via the social network, *MySpace*. After a month of corresponding, Josh abruptly ended their online friendship, telling her he had heard bad things about Megan, including that she was mean to her friends. The incident crushed Megan, and culminated in her suicide the following day, October 16, 2006. As was the case with Jeff Johnston and Ryan Haligan, Megan hung herself in her room.

Soon after the suicide, Megan's grieving family was dealt another blow. Megan's Internet friend, Josh Evans, never existed. In fact, the person claiming to be Josh Evans wasn't even an adolescent boy. He was a character contrived by one of the Meier's neighbors, the mother of one of Megan's former friends. According to the woman, she created the character of Josh Evans to win the confidence of Megan so that she could monitor what Megan was saying about her own daughter. The woman, her daughter, and another person had typed the correspondences with Megan.

The neighbor was not charged, as no crimes were technically committed. However, the community of Darden Prairie has since passed a new ordinance making Internet harassment a crime. Hopefully, the ordinance will prevent further tragedies like the one that befell the Meier's.

Preventing bullying and stopping it once it starts

Bullying is a much bigger problem than most adults recognize. As we have seen, it is bad for everyone involved – including the bully, the bullied, the kids on the sidelines, parents and teachers. It is both a causable problem and a solvable one. We have taken a brief tour of the causes. Now let's look at the ingredients of the solution.

- Schools should allot time each year to teaching parents and students about bullying, including cyberbullying, and the consequences that could follow.
- Bullying must be taken very seriously by both parents and schools. A clear message should be sent to all students and parents at the beginning of every school year that kids who bully, and their parents if the situation is not dealt with at home, will suffer consequences.
- Social services should be contacted in instances where it is suspected that the bullying might stem from abuse or neglect in the home.
- When threats move online, law enforcement should be contacted and legal action, perhaps including civil action against the parents of the bully, should be pursued when possible.
- Students should be urged not to stand on the sidelines. They should help each other – either by informing parents or talking to teachers and staff. Adults should reinforce their actions and respond responsibly.
- Words often speak louder than actions. Supporting a fellow classmate who has experienced bullying can make them feel better about the situation.
- Actions often speak louder than words. Confronting the bully as a group, with sufficient support from the

populace of students, can force the bully to avert. There is safety in numbers. This strategy should only be used when the adults involved have failed to effectively deal with the situation.

From a parenting standpoint, here are some suggestions from the non-profit group, Mental Health America:

- From a very young age, instill self-confidence in your child – teach them to be assertive and to stand up for themselves.
- Teach your child to say "no" in situations that make them uncomfortable.
- Explain to them why some kids bully.
- Teach them to take action if they see someone being bullied – either by speaking out directly against the bully or by informing teachers and parents.
- Start early to teach kids about bullying and how to deal with it.

Here are a few other things to consider:

- If you are the highly motivated type, and your child is struggling with a bully, organize a meeting of parents to discuss how to handle it. There is safety in numbers with these things.
- Don't beat yourself up if you can't figure out what to do here. If there were a perfect way to handle it, we would all know about it and this chapter wouldn't need to be written.

The U.S. Department of Health and Human Services provides a helpful list of things *not to do* when it comes to helping a bullied child.[8] For instance, parents should not:

- Ask children to solve a bullying problem between themselves—because of the differences in power, the child who has been bullied will suffer further.
- Advise the bullied child to fight the bully—fighting is in violation of the school conduct code and the child might be seriously injured.
- Try to mediate a bullying situation. Bringing together children who are bullied and those who do the bullying, to "work out" the problems between them, generally is not a good idea. It may further victimize a child who is being bullied and it sends the wrong message to both parties.
- Blame either the victim or the bully. Instead, gather as much information as possible. Look at your own child's behavior and style of interaction and consider how you might help him/her handle these types of situations in the future. Contact the school for assistance.

Beyond dealing with the consequences of bullying when they emerge, much more needs to be done by parents and schools to route kids down developmental pathways that make bullying less likely. A recent report[9] by Melissa DeRosier and Sara Marcus, both at the Institute for Social Development at the University of North Carolina at Chapel Hill, suggests that school-based programming can be effective at building resilience against the nefarious effects of bullying.

The program, called Social Skills Group Intervention, or S.S. GRIN, aims to help kids learn to fit in and build relationships with peers. It also aims to help kids cope better with teasing and bullying. Toward this end, students are taught pro-social skills like cooperation, compromise, negotiation, initiation and communication. They are taught how to manage their emotions, question their assumptions about the world, and control their impulses. Kids in the treatment group participated in one group session per week, during school hours, for eight weeks. Training sessions included role playing, positive reinforcement for good decision-making, and cognitive reframing (helping kids learn to think about situations differently). By helping kids learn to function at a higher level, socially, the hope is that the program will improve the well-being of kids in general, beyond the bullying issue.

The findings reported by DeRosia and Marcus suggest that the program achieves its objectives. The children enrolled in the study could be divided into three groups based upon the nature of their social difficulties. Students were either peer rejected, victimized (being picked on) or socially anxious. Outcomes of the program were similar across these three groups – all showed improvements in peer acceptance and social behavior, based upon both self-report and comments from peers themselves. In the words of the researchers:

> "Children who received the intervention left the program feeling better about themselves (higher self-esteem and self-efficacy) and about their ability to be successful in social situations (lower social anxiety) and made better choices about friendships (lower antisocial affiliations)."

In stark contrast, those in the control group showed a worsening of social abilities during the year following the treatment.

It seems the S.S. GRIN approach was able to nudge the kids enrolled in the right developmental direction. By doing so, it seems likely that the benefits of the program would extend beyond decreased vulnerability to the nefarious actions of bullies. By increasing social comfort and competency, it seems reasonable to expect decreased odds of engaging in a range of delinquent and dangerous activities, from risky sex practices to substance use, particularly in cases when pressure from ones peers is involved.

School killings

The psychological wounds caused by bullying can be traumatic and, in some cases, fatal. Fortunately, those involved usually live to tell about it and most make full recoveries. School killings are a different story. In typical cases, pent up anger is expressed in a single burst of violence that ends lives, shatters communities and creates life long difficulties for those closest to the events.

Historically, the most deadly atrocity involving the murder of school-aged children in the U.S. occurred in Bath Township, Michigan, in 1927. A farmer and school board member named Andrew Kehoe blamed a new school tax for his own financial hardship. After killing his wife, Mr. Kehoe set fire to his barn, apparently to draw police and fire crews out of the town. He then detonated explosives at the Bath School; the reason for the tax hike. The explosion destroyed one wing of the building. Fortunately, 500 pounds of explosives in another wing of the building did not detonate as planned. When rescuers arrived, Kehoe drove his truck, which was filled with shrapnel and explosives, up to the school and detonated it. By the end of the well-planned rampage, 45 adults and children were killed and 58 more wounded.

The Bath School attack was carried out by an adult. In the 80 years since, America has witnessed a growing list of such atrocities, most orchestrated by students themselves. The mere mention of the word "Columbine" is sufficient to give many adults chills. On April 20, 1999, two teenage students at Columbine High School in Columbine, Colorado, opened fire, killing 12 students and a teacher before turning the guns on themselves. Twenty-seven other students were injured during the 45 minute massacre, three of them while trying to escape the school amidst the gunfire. The two shooters, Dylan Klebold (age 17) and Eric Harris (age 18), were both seniors at the school.

The Columbine massacre remains one of the worst violence-related tragedies to occur at a school in the U.S. For those who keep tabs on these things, Columbine ranks third among all school shootings committed by students behind two shooting rampages on college campuses. In 1966, a troubled student at the University of Texas opened fire from the top of a bell tower, leaving 13 dead and more than 30 wounded. In April, 2007, Virginia Tech student, Seung-Hui Cho, woke up like normal, killed several people on campus, took a break for a while, and then continued killing. Twenty-seven students and five faculty members died.

Several things make the Columbine incident stand out as particularly unsettling. In both of the college shootings mentioned above, the killers were troubled individuals. Charles Whitman, the University of Texas shooter, had a history of psychological difficulties and, during the autopsy performed after the shootings, was found to have a cancerous tumor in the hypothalamus. Many neuroscientists joke that the hypothalamus is involved in the four "F's" – "Feeding," "Fleeing," "Fighting," and "Sex." It is quite possible that the tumor played a role in the murders, but we will never know. Seung-Hui Cho, the Virginia Tech student who murdered his teachers and classmates, had a long history of stalking and mental illness. Photocopies of two plays Cho had written were later posted by AOL News. One in particular was truly disturbing. His troubled psychological state brings some comfort to those not directly affected by the killings, because it seems to provide at least a cursory explanation for his behaviors.

Columbine is different. The two shooters were kids from apparently normal families. Both had histories of theft and antisocial behaviors, but so did many of their peers. Both spent copious amounts of time playing violent video games, but so did many of their peers. Unlike their peers, these two kids opened fire on classmates.

Is it possible to predict which kids might become school shooters?

The fact that the two shooters in the Columbine case did not stand out as obvious threats, at least not obvious enough for adults to intervene beforehand, caused a lot of confusion among concerned parents across the country. We would all rest easier if it were possible to "profile" potential school shooters, but it's just not that simple. The signs and symptoms of the deep psychic turmoil that must precipitate such acts of violence do not always rise above the din of normal adolescent rebellion, risk-taking, mood swings and conflict with authority. As with kids who commit suicide, the magnitude of the emotional turmoil experienced by school shooters in the making isn't usually recognized until it's too late.

As mentioned earlier, one of the few characteristics that school shooters and a percentage of bullies seem to share is that many were persecuted, bullied or ostracized before turning their hostility on other kids. According to an investigation conducted by the U.S. Secret Service, which included interviews with 10 school shooters and in-depth reviews of 27 other cases, three-quarters of school shooters felt persecuted, bullied, threatened and/or were physically attacked prior to the shootings. The school shooters had one other thing in common – they were all boys.

> "At home
> Drawing pictures
> Of mountain tops
> With him on top
> Lemon yellow sun
> Arms raised in a V
> The dead lay in pools of maroon below
> Daddy didn't give attention
> To the fact that mommy didn't care
> King Jeremy the wicked
> Ruled his world
> Jeremy spoke in class today"
>
> - *Jeremy*
>   Pearl Jam (1991)

Variables like those listed above are helpful for identifying the basic characteristics of kids who kill. However, in most cases, the events leading up to school killings paint complicated portraits of young males turned into killers by interactions between themselves and their environments over long periods of time. Both diamonds and charcoal briquettes contain carbon. Interactions with the world determine the shape the carbon takes.

The unique life experiences that mold particular kids into killers are poignantly captured by the story of Jeff Weise. In 1997, when Jeff was eight, his father committed suicide after a long standoff with police. Jeff's grandfather, an officer on the Ojibwa reservation in Minneapolis, tried to intervene in the standoff but was unsuccessful. In 1999, when Jeff was 10, his mother, with whom he lived, suffered permanent brain damage following an alcohol-related car crash. Jeff was eventually forced to move back to the Ojibwa reservation. An overweight kid who donned a black trench coat year round, Jeff was an easy target for classmates. Behavioral problems in school led to the start of a home schooling program in 2004, followed by a suicide attempt.

Internet postings during those years capture the struggles of a young, articulate, very troubled boy trying to figure out who he was and how he fit. As he worked to cobble together a sense of self, his social views drifted toward Nazi-ism and he began leaving tell-tale signs of the murders to come, including comments about opening fire at the school, and the creation of clever computerized (flash) animations depicting murder and carnage.

What exactly happened that broke the last twig is unclear. What is clear is that, on the afternoon of March 21, 2005, Jeff Weise shot and killed his grandfather and then his grandfather's girlfriend. He drove his grandfather's patrol car to the high school, shot and killed a guard, barged into the school, and then opened fire on students and teachers, reportedly smiling as he did so. When police stormed the school, Jeff placed a gun to his head and pulled the trigger, ending his tormented life as his father had several years earlier. When the dust settled that day, four adults and five students were killed, and more than a dozen others wounded.

Jeff Weise's story includes familiar predisposing factors: Family history of substance abuse, suicide by a family member, an attempt to take his own like, history of violence in the community, problems at school, bullying and social persecution, and an unhealthy interest in death and gore. Like many other school killers, he was also taking prescription antidepressants, which are acknowledged to increase aggression and cause agitation in susceptible people. The combination of increased aggression *and* agitation is a particularly bad one! Ultimately, it was the dynamic interplay between lots of predisposing factors over lots of years, and not one *single* factor at a *single* point in time, that led Jeff Weise to become a killer.

It is worth noting here that several recent rampage-style killings have been perpetrated by young people in the process of going *off* of psychiatric medications rather than going on them. This appears to be the case in a shooting rampage at Northern Illinois University on Valentine's Day, 2008. Steven Kazmierczak, by all accounts a good student who was highly respected by the faculty, shot 21 people in a geology class before turning the gun on himself. Five students died in addition to the shooter. No notes were left and no motive has been found. His family claims his behavior had become erratic after stopping his medications, which included the antidepressant Prozac. It appears he had developed a keen interest in guns in the months leading up to the shooting and suicide, suggesting that the massacre was not a spur of the moment decision.

Not all soon-to-be killers drop hints about their plans, but most do. Jeff Weise, for instance, dropped hints that such an attack was imminent. On the Internet, he talked about opening fire on classmates, even claiming that he had been blamed for a threat the school received sometime earlier. After the murders, it became quite clear that a fairly long list of students were aware of what Jeff Weise planned to do, but said nothing to adults.

Dropped hints about the impending murders is one of the most obvious threads winding through these tragedies. Following their investigation into school murders, the U.S. Secret Service shared their findings with the Chicago Sun Times, which published a piece about it on October 15, 2000.[10] It turns out that most school shooters told peers about their intentions. Unfortunately, as in the case of Jeff Weise, the peers rarely passed that information on to adults. Indeed, several of the school shooters interviewed by the agents revealed that they would have told adults what they planned to do if one of them had asked.

Below is an excerpt from the Chicago Sun Times article. It is based upon an interview between Secret Service agents and Luke Woodham, a boy who killed his mom and two students in Pearl, Mississippi, on February 19, 1997. Luke was 16 at the time of the murders, making him near 20 by the time of the interview.

" **Q.** Did any grown-up know how much hate you had in you?

A. No.

Q. What would it have taken for a grown-up to know?

A. Pay attention. Just sit down and talk with me.

Q. What advice do you have for adults?

A. I think they should try to bond more with their students. . . . Talk to them. . . . It doesn't have to be about anything. Just have some kind of relationship with them.

Q. And how would you have responded?

A. Well, it would have took some time before I'd opened up. If we kept talking . . . I would have . . . said everything that was going on. "

It is hard to find more valuable insight into how to prevent school violence than from the reflections of a kid who perpetrated such an act. A little communication between parents and kids could go a long way toward detecting potential attacks before they happen.

With regard to profiling kids to spot potential killers, this has proven nearly impossible. Profiling individuals makes more sense when the individuals are adults with relatively stable characteristics. Kids are moving targets. As such, no profile has a chance of being accurate unless it takes the environments in which kids live and learn into consideration. Indeed, profiling environments to spot breeding grounds for potential killers makes much more sense than focusing on the rapidly changing characteristics of the kids themselves.

In summary, it is not possible to determine, based on profiles, which individual child is at risk of becoming a school shooter or even a school bully. In most cases, the problems do not seem to stem from inherent flaws in the kids. In the same way that increasing rates of obesity reflect flaws in the messages that we send kids about regulating their urges to eat, increasing rates of violence among kids reflect flaws in the messages we send them about regulating their urges to solve problems with aggression and violence.

What can schools and parents do to prevent violence?

In general, it sure seems that schools do their best to protect students. Limitations in funding, combined with the fact that we don't know for certain how to prevent all acts of violence committed by students, makes it difficult for schools to completely rid their buildings of violence and crime. Further, schools receive students from the outside society. They don't give birth to them, and they are not designed to function as surrogate parents or daycares, and nor should we want them to do so. As such, even the most well-funded and well-equipped schools cannot prevent all acts of crime. With that said, what exactly are schools doing to minimize violence and crime? The table below contains a summary of statistics provided by the National Center for Education Statistics.

Violence prevention methods used by public schools	
Method	% using It
Violence prevention curriculum	87
Behavior modification intervention	91
Counseling or other therapeutic activities	93
Individual mentoring, tutoring, coaching by students or adults	92
Recreational or leisure activities for students	83
Including students in attempts to deal with conduct problems	57
Programs that promote a sense of community among students	82
Hotline or tipline where students can report problems	31

SOURCE: Crime, Violence, Discipline and Safety in U.S. Public Schools: Findings from the School Survey on Crime and Safety: 2003-04. US Department of Education, National Center on Education Statistics.

In addition to student-focused strategies for combating violence and aggression in schools, many schools have used creative means for screening and monitoring student activities. The following statistics were provided by the National Center for Education Statistics and refer to the 2003-2004 school year:

- 29% of elementary schools, 42% of middle schools and 60 percent of high schools used security cameras to monitor activity at the school
- 6% required students to use clear book bags or banned book bags
- 83% controlled access to school buildings by locking or monitoring doors during school hours
- 48% required faculty and staff to wear badges of some sort

- 6% of schools required students wear badges of some sort
- 13% of high schools performed random metal detector tests on students
- 58% of high schools reported using dogs to sniff for drugs
- 28% of high schools reported random sweeps that did not involve dogs

Iris Boworsky, a pediatrician at the University of Minnesota, provides a tremendously informative review of best practices for violence prevention in schools. Her review, and a wealth of additional information related to adolescent well-being, can be found at the website, www.allaboutkids.mnu.edu. The table below lists some of the approaches that appear to work for schools and some that don't.

Dr. Boworsky and others stress how important it is for students to feel connected to others, particularly teachers, in their schools. This provides students with a sense of belonging and a sense of support, both of which are critical if students are to make it through school successfully and without incident.

Effective and ineffective school-based violence prevention strategies	
Effective	**Ineffective**
Perspective-taking Problem-solving Family behavior management Family problem-solving Decreasing gun access/media violence Student motivation	Scare tactics Didactic programs Programs focusing only on self-esteem Segregating aggressive/antisocial students Programs focusing only on anger-management Individual counseling/intensive casework
From: Smith, A., Kahn, J., & Borowsky, I. (1999). "Best practices in school-based violence prevention." Minneapolis, MN: University of Minnesota Extension Service. Online: http://www.allaboutkids.umn.edu/cfahad/7286-01.html	

Despite the perceived ubiquity of metal detectors in public schools, they are actually used quite sparingly. During 2003-2004, only 3.7% of public high schools required students to pass through metal detectors on their way into school. There is a general dislike of metal detectors among school officials and parents, as they create a climate of fear and make school feel like punishment for good kids. This is not to say that metal detectors don't work at deterring kids from bringing weapons to school, because there is some evidence that they do. In discussing the use of metal detectors in a school system in New York City, researchers at the University of Minnesota report that,[11]

"In addition to confiscating over 2,000 weapons, all weapon-related incidents decreased, attendance increased, and anecdotal evidence indicates that students reported feeling safer at school. Of note, this intervention was implemented concurrently with several other interventions including violence prevention curricula, peer mediation programs, and crisis intervention teams."

The researchers go on to report some of the limitations of using metal detectors in schools, stating the following:

"In addition to being extremely costly, a funda-mental drawback to environmental changes, such as metal detectors, is that it can send a message to children that they are not to be trusted, which threatens their sense of school-connectedness and self-worth. Hence, not only are metal detectors unlikely to reduce violent behavior, they may actu-ally encourage it, by lowering student morale."

To understand the emotions surrounding the use of metal detectors in public schools, let's turn to New Haven, Connecticut for an example. Between the spring of 2005 and the fall of 2006, metal detectors – either walk through portals, wands, or both – were installed at all 13

> "Tell me: If you were a crazed teenager who hated the world, had been pushed around, had a history of making death threats, and wanted to go out in a blaze of glory, would you really go through the security checkpoint before you pulled out your .45s?"
>
> - Nick Evans, junior at Hill Career Regional High School in New Haven, Connecticut (The Yale Herald, October 6, 2006)

of New Haven's public high schools. The decision set off a firestorm of debate and protest among students and community members. Some students complained that the long lines pushed back the start time of school. Others pointed out several different ways that a motivated student could still smuggle weapons into school despite the metal detectors. Others reported that they liked the idea of the metal detectors because they made them feel safer.

The Chicago Sun Times articles about school shootings included the following interchange between the Secret Service and school shooter Luke Woodham:

"**Q.** Would metal detectors have stopped you?
A. I wouldn't have cared. What's it going to do? I ran in there holding the gun out. I mean, people saw it. It wasn't like I was hiding it. I guess it could stop some things. But by the time somebody's already gotten into the school with a gun, it's usually gonna be just about too late."

As with all forms of deterrence against violence, placing metal detectors and police officers at entrances *can* dissuade kids from carrying weapons into school and, more importantly, *can* keep unwanted visitors from gaining entry. However, such tactics do not stop kids bent on violence and destruction from bringing weapons with them, and probably force many others to simply find creative ways of avoiding detection before their

"Secret Service researchers find educators' approaches to keeping students from killing may do more harm than good; they recommend simply listening to children and improving school climates."

- Bill Dedman
Chicago Sun-Times

plans are executed. Recall that Jeff Weise shot his way passed security guards to carry out his plan to kill teachers and students.

The combination of an overcrowded and ever-expanding justice system and rising rates of youth violence reveals that punitive laws only go so far at routing kids down healthier developmental pathways. This point will become clear in the next chapter. Continuing to expand punitive measures, whether in the form of more metal detectors or giving teachers licenses to carry handguns, will only add fuel to the fire rather than extinguishing it. If this were not the case, the problem would have gone away a long time ago. Those who advocate for such extreme measures might gain votes or TV viewers, but their naïveté is dangerous and reflects a mentality that has given rise to failed policy after failed policy regarding how to deal with kids, and has served to only worsen the problem of youth violence over the years. Solving the problem requires all of us to take a close look at the culture of violence in which we currently raise our kids. Policies and rules have their place, but so do efforts to alter the culture in a direction that values empathy and compassion and devalues, rather than reinforces, violence and aggression.

Devaluing violence and aggression would require responsible adults to do a much better job of controlling their own lust for violent media programming and spend more time reinforcing healthy behaviors in their kids. Listening to, and supporting, teens is central to this. A tall, but completely do-able, order. It would also require schools and communities to scale back their reliance on largely punitive measures for routing kids *away* from violent pathways and develop incentive-based approaches that move kids *toward* healthier pathways. At the end of the chapter, the reader can find an overview of one such school-based approach that seems to be effective at shifting the culture of schools in the right direction.

Dealing with the aftermath of school shootings

School killings tear deep wounds in communities. The aftermath is traumatic, regardless of whether the killings occur in wealthy suburban areas or on Native American reservations. Like a bomb, the events do an incredible amount of damage in a concentrated area. Not only are students and perhaps teachers killed and wounded, but others present during the attacks are sure to suffer at a deep psychological level. Then there are the families of the kids and teachers involved. Then there is the town or city in which the school is located. Finally, there is the national psyche.

Like school killings, war is one of those things that we all hope never happens. However, when war does occur, major advances in medicine typically result as the military develops new ways to treat and save wounded soldiers. Something similar happens with regard to treating the trauma caused by school killings. With each event, experts learn more and more about how to help students, parents and communities heal, and how to prevent such tragedies from occurring in the first place.

Crisis experts like Scott Poland, a psychology professor at Nova Southeastern University, stress that helping an individual deal with the trauma requires first identifying the needs of that individual. It helps to begin by assessing how close the individual was to the trauma. Clearly, those who witnessed the shooting or were in the school when it occurred stand to suffer the most, and thus need more intensive counseling and support. Depending upon the factors at play in an individual's life at the time, even those relatively far removed from the tragedy can still suffer greatly. Chronic illness, recent loss of a loved one, current emotional problems, and a variety of other factors can amplify the impact that such events have on a child.

Invariably, in the aftermath of a school shooting, media outlets run programs in which experts decry the use of violence by kids and adults. However, simultaneously, they indulge viewers in an orgy of details and images surrounding the events. Every network wants to be the first to pump live, breaking, shot-by-shot news about school murders into the homes of viewers. Nothing seems to boost ratings more than images of blood and gore, even if the injured and dead are merely children. The end result is a national phenomenon something akin to the rubber-necking that occurs on highways after traffic accidents. We all want to catch a glimpse. Unfortunately, there are several un-wanted consequences of this, particularly for kids.

Night and day media coverage of school homicides sends the message that such events are more prevalent than they really are. When kids see images of injured students and perhaps pictures of the killers, it is common for them to worry that this could be a reality for them someday. They might not know where, on a map, the events took place. Based on constant coverage in newspapers, online and on TV, they might feel as though the event occurred next door.

For those who live in communities where such events occur, media coverage serves as a constant and painful reminder of the trauma they are living through. This can make it much more difficult to cope and heal. Imagine being mugged and then having a picture of the mugger's face shown constantly in newspapers and TV programs.

Because media coverage of school shootings is so pervasive, the odds are high that most kids will learn of the events and perhaps see some of the discussions and highlights that air in the weeks afterward. It is best to minimize the amount of media material that kids are exposed to, as well as spending time talking with them about their fears and concerns. Experts suggest explaining to young children that the reason the event is garnishing so much attention in the media is precisely because these events are so rare.

School killings invariably give way to discussions about how to make schools safer. It is tempting, and understandable, for schools to consider diverting their limited funding away from other services to install metal detectors and beef up security. This is particularly true when the school at which an attack occurs comes under fire for perhaps not doing a good enough job of protecting students. Unfortunately, as we have discussed, metal detectors and armed security guards can do little to stop a student determined to cause carnage. In the end, it is the responsibility of the culture at large to raise healthy, well-balanced kids that don't kill.

Fortunately, mainstream American culture is showing early signs of slowly beginning to revalue the kinds of factors that protect kids from becoming violent or becoming victims of violence – family connectedness, personal responsibility, school achievement, access to healthy outlets for emotions, positive relationships with teachers and mentors, and others. In recent decades, violent incidences at public schools have been on the rise. With any luck, the trend will reverse itself in the decades to come.

Non-rampage-related school killings

In this chapter, we have focused on the kinds of school killings that involve volleys of gunfire radiating away from angry kids on rampages. Obviously, this isn't the only kind of murder that occurs on school grounds. Some killings are isolated events involving two students and reflecting violence in the community at large. A recent case involving a single shooter and single victim at a Memphis high school highlights this fact.

On February 11, 2008, a 17 year old sophomore at Mitchell High School in Memphis, Tennessee, walked up to another student, a senior aged 19, in the cafeteria, shot him twice, and then handed the gun to a coach standing nearby, saying, "It's over now." It appears that the victim will live. The shooting stemmed from an argument that began outside of school and reflects the significant problems that the Memphis community has with youth violence in general. Such cases reinforce the fact that schools receive kids, including violent ones, from the community and do not give birth to them.

Memphis schools like Mitchell High already employ metal detectors and use them in non-daily searches and sweeps. Certainly, many people in the community and around the country will now ask why these schools do not use their technology daily. The assumption here is that such technology, itself, can prevent events like the one discussed above. As we have seen, while it helps, technology is not the answer, and diverting significant additional resources to adding metal detectors and guards will have limited and temporary utility for schools like Mitchell High. The trick rests in diminishing violence community-wide so that Memphis schools and others receive more kids prepared to learn and fewer kids prepared to perpetrate acts of violence.

What does it all mean?

Today's teens are raised in a climate of violence and hostility, real and pretend. Such exposure can have toxic effects on psychological development. It also lends a sense of normalcy to acts of hostility, thereby reducing the gap between socially acceptable behavior and criminal conduct and making it easier to cross the line. The voracious appetite that we adults have for real and virtual violence sends a complex and ambiguous message to kids. Their job is to adapt to the demands of the culture so that they can eventually thrive in it. If violence is celebrated and enacted by the adults around them, it only makes sense that kids would emulate what they see. Indeed, perhaps more surprising than the violence committed by today's kids is the fact that we fail to see the contribution that mainstream society makes to it.

Bullying is, and probably always has been, a common source of exposure to hostility for kids. Bullying takes many forms; female bullies often focus on sabotaging social relationships while male bullies often resort to threats and physical aggression. Kids who get bullied and those that do the bullying are more likely to end up in trouble down the road. In recent years, bullying has moved online, making it easier for bullies to remain anonymous and harder for kids to escape persecution. When adults and students turn a blind eye to bullies, the situation usually goes from bad to worse. Parents, schools, and kids on the sidelines must intervene and make clear that such conduct will not be tolerated. There is safety in numbers here.

Typically, bullies are not kids on the fringes. However, students that turn to murder to express their anger tend to be. The last 30 years have witnessed a growing list of school shootings, many committed by Caucasian males from affluent families. An obsession with violence, often fed by countless hours of immersion in violent media, is one familiar denominator. Despite a short list of common characteristics, the behaviors exhibited by future killers are not usually sufficient to make them stand out to adults. However, in most cases, it appears that the killers make their intentions clear, usually to other students, before carrying out their plots. Encouraging students to come to adults with such information should be part of any strategy aimed at preventing such attacks.

Quick Facts:

- Bullying is bad for those who do the bullying and those who get bullied – both have higher rates of interpersonal, legal and health problems down the road.
- It is difficult to profile school killers but many are persecuted kids on the fringes that spend copious amounts of

time immersed in violent media, and most give warnings to other kids before they kill.

- Appropriate school policies are critical to protect students from violence, but data demonstrating that metal detectors and guards detour violent rampages are limited.
- Opening and maintaining lines of communication between parents and kids can help parents recognize what is happening in their teens' lives before their inner turmoil reaching a boiling point.

SideNotes

The Mastery Model and violence reduction in schools

Until the fall of the 2006 school year, Shoemaker school was one of Philadelphia's most troubled schools. Violence, low test scores, and a general lack of discipline were just a few of the school's problems. A novel approach to improving the school appears to be succeeding in turning Shoemaker around. In 2006, the school was revamped and renamed the Mastery Charter School – Shoemaker Campus. To reduce violence and increase motivation and discipline, the school instituted a comprehensive set of strategies known as the "Mastery Model." The model has been used successfully at several other schools in Philadelphia (for more background visit www.masterycharter.org). Below is a list of attributes of the Mastery Model and the types of changes it requires schools to make.

- Improvements in physical facilities
- Teacher development, including promotions and bonuses based on student performance
- An emphasis on teaching students to take responsibility for the quality of their school
- Requiring students to treat others with respect and courteousness
- An emphasis on order and discipline, such as walking in single file lines between classes
- Students wear name badges and carry a card for listing both merits and demerits
- Incorporation of technology into classrooms and maintenance of a 3:1 ratio of students to computers.
- Individualized attention via small classes of around 24 students and small schools with less than 600 students
- All students are required to agree to, and abide by, a code of conduct that emphasis personal responsibility for actions
- Mandatory tutoring for struggling students
- An emphasis on rewarding good behavior rather than simply punishing bad behavior

According to Scott Gordon, CEO of Mastery Charter Schools, "Our approach is not metal detectors and security guards. The approach is to build a school community that supports and polices itself. Our deans of students are really proactive - combination of disciplinarians and social workers who work with kids before problems arise and work closely with parents."

The underlying strategy of the Mastery Model – though not stated as such – is to create a safe environment in which student behavior is shaped through a balanced combination of reward and discipline. After behavior problems improve, teachers and students can get down to the real business at hand – learning!

Chapter 6

Exploration, experimentation and teen drug use – Putting things in perspective

America's drug cabinets and stash boxes are full of all sorts of chemicals that can alter the way that we think and feel. We have legal drugs with restricted access (alcohol, nicotine, ephedrine), legal drugs with unrestricted access (caffeine, St. John's Wort, aerosols), prescription drugs (Prozac, oxycodone, amphetamines) and illegal drugs (marijuana, heroin, absinthe). The topic of drugs, in one form or another, seems to dominate much of the discussion surrounding teenagers. Every parent has been told to fear drugs, yet many have used them. Kids are told to watch out for drug dealers outside of the home, yet highly addictive prescription drugs can often be found in medicine cabinets within the home. It is against this confusing backdrop that today's parents are trying to raise kids that do not fall into the trap of drug abuse. In this chapter, we will discuss teen drug use in the context of adolescent development. We will then discuss ways in which we can use teens' natural tendencies to prevent drug use and, if needed, to treat drug problems.

Jannelle Hornickel and her boyfriend, Michael Wamsley, were heading home when the truck they were driving in slid off of a snowy Nebraska road. The fierce snowstorm outside made it difficult for them to get their bearings. The crystal methamphetamine in their systems made matters much worse. During the hours that followed, Jannelle and Michael made a series of phone calls to 911 operators pleading for help. The two 20 year olds were convinced they were blocks away from their apartment in Omaha. In fact, they were in a remote, wooded area 23 miles away. Rescue workers frantically searched for them, but hallucinations brought about by the artificial surges of dopamine in the couple's young brains made it impossible for them to give useful clues to their whereabouts. Their would-be rescuers were led on one wild goose chase after another. Below is an excerpt from Jannelle's first 911 call at 12:28AM.

Dispatcher: 911, what's your emergency?

Hornickel: Hi, I'm in Omaha like in the Mandalay apartment complexes, only like right above them in the trees, the living area, and there's a lot of Mexicans and African Americans and they're all dressed up in like these cult outfits, and they're moving all the vehicles, the Mandalay ones they were above ... They blocked us all up in these trees up above Mandalay on Pacific...

Dispatcher: Whoa, whoa, your phone's breaking up for one, ma'am. I'm having trouble understanding what you're actually saying.

Hornickel:... They blocked us all in these trees above Mandalay apartments on Pacific.

Dispatcher: What's the address?

Hornickel: Right above Mandalay apartments.

Dispatcher: What is the address?

Hornickel: My address at Mandalay is 7524. The address for this is in the trees right above those complexes... (Wamsley in background: There's no power.) There's no power here (crying) ... (Wamsley in background: Get an officer here now!)
....

Dispatcher: How are they getting the cars in the trees?

Hornickel: They're ... breaking them down, taking the pieces of cars off, moving the pieces of metal around, and they're going in there.
....

Dispatcher: How many are out there?

Hornickel: I don't know. (to Wamsley: How many do you think are out here?) (To dispatcher) There's a ton of them. (Wamsley to Hornickel: There's a hundred, 200.) (To dispatcher) Oh, I have no idea there's a ton of them. I don't know...

...

Dispatcher: And they're taking the cars apart and putting them in the trees?

Hornickel: Yes. ... unless the owner is there moving the car for them. If the person is there they let them. Otherwise they do it themselves. And they they're putting them in the trees. And I can't find my car. I just have our pickup. (groan) They're very native looking - tribal ... They're in the trees and carving them... There's a lot of trails back...

Dispatcher: Is that north, south, east or west of the apartments?

Hornickel: (Asks Wamsley: Are they east or west of the apartments, would you say?) To dispatcher: Straight south. Go down 75th, go straight into them. Yeah, I think I'm just going to have to start running and get out of here. I don't know who else to call. OK, thank you.

Dispatcher: All right.

Hornickel: OK, bye.

The couple had plenty of gas – half a tank – in the truck. Waiting out the storm in the warm cab would have been the logical thing to do. Unfortunately for them, the meth removed logic from the equation. Fearing for their safety, the couple fled the truck and set off into the storm. They eventually found shelter in an abandoned shed near a gravel pit. The couple believed they were surrounded by people, some of whom were on the roof of the shack. During a call from Micheal Wamsley at 1:45AM, one of the dispatchers asked him whether he had done any drugs that evening.

Dispatcher: Have you done any kind of drugs tonight?

Wamsley: No, I haven't done (garble) drugs.

Dispatcher: We can't prove it if you have, but it would help me to know if you did.

Wamsley: I don't do 'em, seriously, ma'am, I just, I really don't.

Dispatcher: Well, how come all these 200 people that you see, how come they can't help you?

Wamsley: Ma'am, I don't think they speak any...

Dispatcher: What?

Wamsley: Ma'am, I don't (silence for several seconds).

Dispatcher: OK, but I speak all kinds of different languages. So I need for you to get one of those people that don't speak English on the phone. They understand hand signals to wave them over to come to you.

Wamsley: They couldn't, they wouldn't.

Dispatcher: That's a universal language.

Wamsley: (Yelling aside) Hello! Could you please talk to her on the phone? Can I get help? Can you talk to her? Please? Help me? Can you please help me? (garble)

The thin walls of the shed could not protect the two from the subzero wind chill. At some point during the night, perhaps feeling threatened by the people they perceived to be all around them, they set out again. Janelle was the first to die. Her frozen body would be found in a field quite some distance from Michael's. The last contact with dispatchers occurred at 4:20AM. During the conversation, Michael no longer refers to "we" and uses the first person singular, "I." Janelle was presumably dead at this point.

Dispatcher: Saunders County 911.

Wamsley: (garble) I've just escaped (garble).

Dispatcher: Where are you at?

Wamsley: (garble) front gate (garble).

Dispatcher: Front gate of what?

Wamsley: Front gate.

Dispatcher: What's your name?

Wamsley: Michael Wamsley.

Dispatcher: OK. What front gate are you at?

Wamsley: ... There's one kind of a horseshoe shaped ...

Dispatcher: We're trying to find you. You were in a shed. You're out walking again?

Wamsley: Yeah. It's OK. There's...

Dispatcher: Where you're at we can get you some help?

Wamsley: OK.

Dispatcher: Are there any houses around you?

Wamsley: No. No houses.

Dispatcher: No.

(Static).

Janelle Hornickel was a junior at Creighton College with a seemingly bright future ahead of her. She was an attractive young woman, a good student, a member of a sorority, and a former cheerleader. To those around her, she did not seem like a drug addict out of control, and probably wasn't. In fact, she might have had her first experience with methamphetamine in the days leading up to her tragic death.

Janelle's story is a perfect example of the fact that methamphetamine does not discriminate. Users are drawn to the drug for its initial effects – pleasure, confidence, energy, improved mood, and a buzz that lasts for eight or more hours. Historians believe that Hitler was treated, daily, with methamphetamine, whether he knew it or not. Methamphetamine is highly addictive, and before long, many users crave it and their lives become focused on one objective – getting more. This drug grabs hold like few others, save perhaps heroin, nicotine and smoked cocaine. Letting go of the drug, if it happens, often follows years or decades of abuse. During these years, teeth fall out, fortunes are spent, careers are lost and families are destroyed. Hardcore addicts often feel as though bugs are crawling under the skin. These psychotic symptoms eventually lead many users to pick holes in their skin in an effort to get the bugs out.

It is difficult to comprehend the toll that drugs like methamphetamine can take on a person without living that life for oneself. Perhaps for this reason, most people do not realize they're in trouble with their particular drug of choice until it's too late, no matter how many cautionary tales they've heard that parallel their own lives.

Statistically, drug use is more likely to begin during adolescence than any other stage of life. In this chapter, we will explore some potential explanations for the initiation of drug use during the teen years. The case will be made that the natural adolescent urge to explore and take risks sets them up for experimentation with drugs. Because the teen brain is so malleable, it picks up drug-related behaviors, or drug "habits," with ease. If the individual carries such habits with them into adulthood, beyond the window of enhanced brain malleability afforded by adolescence, replacing such habits with healthier ones can become extraordinarily difficult.

While we are young and measure the future in days rather than months and years, many of us are willing to risk our health (and freedom!) for the short-term enjoyment produced by commonly used and abused drugs. Once we mature enough to value the future, most of us realize the magnitude of the mistakes that we made and are no longer willing to make such trades. We could do kids a huge favor by helping them avoid the pitfalls of drug use to begin with. Substance use is a slippery slope. It's much easier to prevent kids from sliding down it than it is to hoist them back up to the top and keep them from sliding down again. For this reason, every effort should be made to dissuade kids from heading down these dead-end pathways and to debunk faulty expectations about positive outcomes resulting from drug use.

What is a drug?

Never before in human history has it been so difficult to define exactly what a drug is. It makes the standard "Just Say No to Drugs" mantra seem even sillier in light of the smeared lines between legal, presumably good drugs, and illegal, presumably bad drugs. According to the Food and Drug Administration (FDA), a drug is something that is:

> "intended for use in the diagnosis, cure, mitigation, treatment, or prevention of disease" [1]

Because of the exorbitant cost of developing a compound and getting FDA approval for it, big pharmaceutical companies are the only entities able to afford the official FDA "drug" stamp. This means that anything sold by your local health food store cannot legally be considered a drug. Fortunately, the 2007 FDA Amendments Act makes it easier for small drug companies with unique offerings to get in on the action, which should lead to faster advances in treatment. The law continues to allow the FDA to charge "user's fees," special fees that, among other things, can speed up the process of approval for a new drug or biologic, but waves those fees for small companies with global revenue under $50 million.

Interestingly, on the surface, the FDA's definition of drug seems to exclude many substances used to get high, because many such chemicals are not intended to treat or cure diseases. How can we possibly make sense of this mess? In a subsequent section, we will look at the history of laws regarding drug use. This should help clarify how we arrived at the current, confusing view of what drugs are and the equally confusing approach we use to deal with them.

For the sake of our discussion in this book, we will define the term "drug" as any non-food substance that alters the way that the human body/brain functions. That allows us to include both prescription pharmaceuticals and street chemicals. Like pornography, we all know drugs when we see them. However, when it comes down to it, it is quite difficult to find a definition that includes everything that should be included and excludes the rest.

The slippery slopes of drug use

Most alcoholics, crack addicts, methamphetamine addicts, chronic weed smokers, junkies and cigarette smokers start out using their drugs of choice recreationally. It isn't until people start sliding down the slope of abuse and addiction that they realize they're in trouble – if they ever do. How steep the slope is will depend on several factors – including the addictive potential of the drug, the intentions behind the drug use, cultural attitudes about the drug, ease of access to the drug, the individual's history of drug use, genetic predispositions, and the presence and strength of protective factors. Some drugs are far easier to become hooked on than others. Heroin and drugs related to it – painkillers like Vicodin and OxyContin, for example – have an extremely high potential for abuse and dependence. They feel good, they act fairly quickly, and a small amount of withdrawal (i.e. physical and psychological discomfort) can occur after a single dose – which can motivate the user to use more of the drug to ease discomfort.

Past year drug use by 10th graders: 2002-2006
(Source: Monitoring the Future)

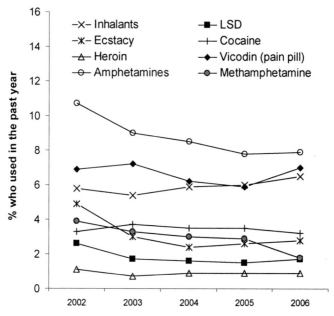

In general, levels of drug use by adolescents declined slightly in the opening years of the new millennium, though use of some drugs, such as prescription pain killers, increased. This is captured in the graph above, which displays trends in use of various drugs by 10th graders between 2002-2006.[2] Each year represents a new wave of students, suggesting that slightly fewer adolescents are picking up the baton of drug use than in years passed. Good news, though any use of some of the drugs listed could be disastrous.

Despite small declines in the use of some drugs, nonmedicinal use of prescription narcotic pain medications is on the way up and the problems they cause are here to stay for awhile. Indeed, the number of Americans age 12 or older that abuses or is dependent on prescription pain killers is now on par with the number that abuses or is

SideNotes

Heroin for kids. "Cheese" heroin in the Texas area.

One unfortunate consequence of the war in Afghanistan has been the unhindered outflow of opium from this poor country. Much of this opium is eventually converted to heroin and smuggled into the United States. Heroin also enters the United States from Mexico. The flooded heroin market has led to the development of cheap and potent forms of the drug. In the past few years, this has included a form of heroin called "cheese," presumably because the final product looks a bit like grated parmesan. Cheese heroin is made by combining Mexican black tar heroin, up to about 8% potency, with crushed up tablets of Tylenol PM. The combination is then snorted. At least 21 teenagers have died from overdoses of "cheese" in the Dallas, TX, area since 2005. At $2 per buzz, the cost makes the drug too alluring for some kids to pass up.

dependent on cocaine. Given the ubiquity of pain killers in medicine cabinets, schools and neighborhoods, it does not appear that the situation will improve anytime soon.

Let's look at a scenario that involves a kid living on the pain killer slope. We'll begin with the first pill and see how each subsequent decision influences the likelihood that an individual would find oneself in serious trouble down the road.

Let's say you are an adolescent who goes to a party and decides to take a pain pill that a friend offers. It feels good. Really good. Much better than your typical internal state as a typical teen. She gives you a few for later. You decide to take one before school. No one notices. You take one at home. Your parents don't notice and it helps make family dinner more enjoyable. You start thinking about them in class and wishing you are on one when you aren't. It isn't heroin and you aren't taking them everyday or anything. They're prescription drugs not "sketchy drugs." That makes a big difference, right? Adults take them, so how can they tell you not to take them?

You discover that your parents have an old prescription in their medicine cabinet and you grab them. Score! Dozens of pills! Taking pain pills is on your mind a lot at this point. You worry about running out. You can't wait to get more. It's just so much more enjoyable than your normal state, and you notice that you seem to feel a little extra bad when you don't take them. You begin wondering if it could become a problem for you and convince yourself that you'll cross that bridge when you come to it. As a strong willed kid, you're sure you can handle it. The die is cast.

SideNotes

Are addiction and dependence the same thing?

Nope. Colloquially, the words addiction and dependence are often used as synonyms. In reality, these phenomena are separate but overlapping. The term *addiction* refers to giving oneself over completely to something, whether it is a drug or Internet gambling. Intrusive thoughts, cravings and a compulsion to engage in the activity are all part of the addictive process. *Dependence* has a more specific physiological meaning. Following repeated exposure to a drug, the brain adjusts itself in a way that minimizes the impact that the drug has on brain function and behavior. This is called *tolerance*. If enough tolerance develops, the person can actually find themselves functioning at a subpar level during times when the drug is not onboard. This motivates drug use to get rid of withdrawal symptoms, which tend to be opposite of what the drug does for a person. The cycle simply continues from there.

It is possible for a person to be *addicted* but not *dependent*. This is probably the case with pornography or gambling problems. It is also possible to be *dependent* but not *addicted*. The author views his caffeine habit in this light. Of course, it is also possible to be both addicted *and* dependent, as is the case with cigarettes, heroin, alcohol and other abused drugs.

You started taking pain pills recreationally for pleasure and now you're going to have to experience a fair amount of pain to stop, assuming you can. After you stop, the real battle begins – not going back to them. If you can make it through the first few weeks, the physical pain will dissipate, but you may spend the rest of your life wanting another pill. Your old friends are now threats to your sobriety. You can't go to parties anymore, unless you want to risk going back to being an addict.

This scenario applies to a wide variety of drugs used by kids and adults these days, including cocaine, heroin, alcohol, ecstasy and nicotine. What goes up must come down, and because of tolerance, there is a law of diminishing returns with these drugs. Each time a user goes up, they go up a little less. Each time a user comes down, they come down a little farther. Because the rewarding effects decrease with each use, users often find themselves chasing the high and the fun. Breaking free from the gravitational pull of substance use once it has gone too far is far harder than many young drug users anticipate, and there is nothing fun about trying to learn to function again without the chemicals.

Marijuana is not quite as bad as many other drugs, and most savvy teens are aware of that fact. The drug has powerful effects on thinking and emotions, but does not seem, at least at the moment, to damage the brain in significant ways. Physical dependence is also less of an issue than with other drugs. In drug-to-drug comparisons, the science strongly suggests that drugs like alcohol and nicotine are far more hazardous and habit forming than marijuana. However, marijuana, too, can put users on a slippery slope, not to mention exacting some tolls on one's health.

The graph on the next page displays trends in marijuana use among adolescents, 10th graders in this case, during a five years period from 2002-2006. A clear trend toward decreased use is apparent, and follows a sharp increase in use during the 1990s.

Despite common misperceptions about the drug, marijuana definitely can be habit forming, and plenty of people – many of them teens – have difficulty quitting once they become accustomed to its psychological effects.[3] The drug alters the way that we think and feel. It has powerful effects on the higher cortical structures in the brain, thereby altering one's perception of the world and their place in it. This isn't all bad, but it certainly can be for kids or adults that learn to hide within those cognitive changes.

In laboratory studies, chronic marijuana users show all of the classic signs of addiction – looking forward to using the drug, worrying about running out, using the drug despite its interference with daily activities, preferring the drug state over sobriety, arranging one's life around use of the drug, and having difficulty cutting down on use.[4] Although the symptoms of addiction and dependence might be less severe with chronic marijuana use than heroin use, such symptoms do occur and reflect the difficulty that many marijuana users have functioning without the drug once it has become part of their daily routines.

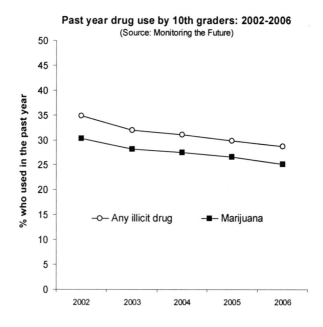

Past year drug use by 10th graders: 2002-2006
(Source: Monitoring the Future)

Recently, withdrawal symptoms from cessation of chronic marijuana use were well-characterized in a clever study [5] in which researchers brought young daily users into a laboratory and allowed them intermittent access to marijuana and placebo joints, which are quite similar to the real thing. Three days of access to marijuana were followed by three days of access to placebo. Withdrawal symptoms, including anxiety, craving and aggression were measured throughout. On days without marijuana, the subjects' levels of anxiety, craving and aggression were all elevated. These symptoms were minimized by giving subjects small amounts of THC – insufficient to produce intoxication – in pill form, strongly suggesting that the mood changes were directly related to the drop in THC levels in the brain during non-smoking days.

Like adults, teens are often drawn to drugs for the pleasure and psychological distraction they produce. Whether one chooses pain pills or marijuana, initiation of use immediately places one on a slippery slope. Dabbling in the drug a little too much can lead to physical and psychological discomfort upon cessation, and pulls kids away from the primary purpose of adolescence – to interact with the world in healthy ways and prepare oneself for the challenges of adulthood. Unless one lives in a culture that places a high value on rolling nice joints or being able to inject large amounts of heroin without dying, drug use during adolescence ultimately has a high likelihood of being a waste of time, no matter how fun it can be.

How normal adolescent development might predispose teens to experiment with drugs

Most drug use begins during adolescence, if it begins at all. Statistically, if an individual can make it through the second decade of life without developing a drug habit, the odds go down that it will ever happen. The reasons for this are complex, but the state of adolescent brain development probably contributes.

As we have discussed briefly in previous chapters, the teen brain is in flux. As the transition from childhood to adulthood ensues, the brain enters a unique period of plasticity. The changes that take place serve multiple purposes, including making us more interested in exploring the outside world, taking some chances, and trying out different personas until we find one that fits. Most kids also feel emotionally blah during early adolescence. All of these changes predispose us to experiment with drugs during this stage of life.

The frontal lobes, located behind the forehead, play central roles in thinking about the consequences of our actions and putting the brakes on to keep us from doing things that could have dire consequences. At about the age of 10, the frontal lobes enter a decade-long period during which they are molded and fine-tuned by interplay between the adolescent and the outside world.[6] The changes that take place help prepare the adolescent to make forward thinking decisions and control urges during the daily grind of adulthood. Until changes in the frontal lobes are complete, they are not working at full capacity and can make it difficult for teens to function like adults with regard to delaying gratification and planning for the future.

During the early teen years in particular, the frontal lobes are far from finished developing, and this immaturity can manifest itself in difficulties with decision-making and impulse control. As such, a teen might have difficulty inhibiting the urge to do something that sounds fun, even if she can see that negative consequences might follow. In addition, many teens have lofty, positive expectations about the good that can come from risky behaviors, like drinking and using of other drugs. This can further tilt the balance in favor of initiating drug use. Those of us who try drugs during adolescence and find that they satisfy our adolescent needs better than the environments in which we live might have real difficulty mustering the frontal lobe strength necessary to keep us from going back for more.

This is where the importance of adult mentoring and support becomes quite clear.

Dealing with teen drug use

Drug use is both a public health issue and a legal issue. Unfortunately, our national policies regarding drug use have thus far focused disproportionately on the legal side. We are now nearly a century into America's official "War on Drugs." How are we doing? There has never been a better time, from an economic standpoint, to be a drug user. With rare exception, most commonly used and abused drugs are easier to find than a few decades ago, cost less, and are more potent. If you've ever wanted to be a heroin addict but couldn't locate or afford heroin, now is a good time to live out your dream. In addition to become cheaper and more potent, the list of drugs from which to choose has become much longer and now includes a litany of prescription substances that can alter consciousness, produce pleasure and damage health.

Punitive approaches to dealing with adolescent drug use have their place. When laws are broken, some sort of punishment must follow or the laws will not be obeyed. However, the data overwhelmingly compel the conclusion that the current approach to dealing with teen substance use has generally failed and that new directions are needed.

Prevention and education programs remain the cornerstone of non-punitive efforts to dissuade kids from using substances, and the evidence indicates that they can work. Drug courts appear capable of reducing the likelihood that kids who enter the legal system due to drug use will return. We will explore such efforts in a moment. First, let's take a tour of the history of the War on Drugs and examine how and why it has failed to meet its objectives.

Anatomy of the failed War on Drugs

To understand where we are as a nation with regard to dealing with teen drug use, and to figure out how to proceed from this point, it helps to place the present situation in its historical context. Here is a brief chronological overview of drug use in America and the laws aimed at combating it. We'll begin in 1900 and quickly work our way to the present. Those not interested in the history lesson can skip ahead to the section on prevention efforts without missing anything vital.

In America at the turn of the 19th century, drug addiction was a major problem, particularly addiction to morphine. Morphine is one of the three major psychoactive components found in the sap of the opium poppy. It is a potent pain reliever for those with pain. For those without pain, it can produce temporary feelings of bliss – a state without fear or concern. That is, until the buzz wears off, at which point the fun ends. Non-medicinal, and even medicinal, use of morphine automatically puts an individual on a very slippery slope. The drug eases pain for those who need it, and produces bliss in those who use it but don't need it. Obviously, for both groups of people, there is powerful reinforcement to continue using.

Where did all of that morphine addiction come from? In the mid-1800s, morphine was widely used during the civil war to ease the pain of injuries and make operations tolerable. At least, this was the case in the North. Before getting a limb hacked off in the South, whiskey was often the only comfort available. So, soldiers represented a portion of morphine addicts. However, according to Richard Bonnie, Director of the University of Virginia Institute of Law and former Associate Director of the National Commission on Marihuana and Drug Abuse, and Charles Whitebread, Professor of Law at the University of Southern California Law School, a large percentage of morphine addicts in the early 1900s was comprised of middle-class white women. Door-to-door salesman would often come through offering elixirs to fix what ails you. Many of these contained up to 50% morphine. No matter what is wrong with you, whether it be physical or psychological, chugging morphine would probably ease your discomfort for a time! Such elixirs could also be purchased over the counter at drug stores and must have brought about plenty of untimely deaths.

The early history of the drug war in the U.S. is nicely summarized in a 2001 document prepared for The Canadian Senate Special Committee on Illegal Drugs.[7]

"From the time of the U.S. Civil War (1861-1865) to the end of the 19th century, the use and sale of opium, morphine, cocaine and other psychoactive drugs were legal and common. Opium was available with or without a prescription and was an ingredient in many patent medicines, including various pain-killers, cough mixtures and teething syrups for infants. Cocaine was also used medicinally, as well as in soft drinks and wine. Things started to change around the turn of the century. Heroin was first isolated in 1898 and was purported to convey the same benefits as opium or morphine, without the risk of addiction. The realization of heroin's addictive properties soon after its introduction coincided with racist appeals to protect American society from drugs. Initially, two drugs were targeted: Cocaine, associated mainly with blacks who were said to go on violent rampages under its influence, and opium, the smoking of which was associated with the Chinese. Alcohol temperance societies and religious groups also played key roles in lobbying for prohibition."

Passage of the Pure Food and Drugs Act of 1906 marks the beginning of Federal legislation aimed at controlling the distribution and use of drugs in the U.S. The act required that food and drugs be approved by the government before sale, distribution, and consumption. The agency we now know as the Food and Drug Administration (FDA) was created to handle this. The act required that certain drugs be sold only by prescription from a doctor, and that those that can be habit forming contain a warning to that effect. Suddenly, morphine was not easily available and thousands of citizens had to deal with the reality of addiction and withdrawal.

In 1914, the Harrison Act was passed. It was the first Federal law in America criminalizing the use of drugs for non-medicinal purposes. The act outlawed the use of morphine and related drugs (opium, codeine), as well as the use of drugs derived from the coca plant (cocaine). It did so by placing an enormous tax on the non-medical distribution of the drugs. Why a tax rather than a crime? The Constitution gives states, not the Federal government, the power to prosecute criminal activity. However, two powers that were given to the Federal government included taxation and the regulation of foreign and interstate commerce. Hence, placing a high tax on drugs and prosecuting those who did not pay the tax afforded a way for Federal control of behavior deemed criminal. Getting arrested for possession at that time would have led to a charge of tax evasion! Because the drugs were outlawed via taxation, the law was enforced by people in the Treasury Department. The act also required doctors to pay a tax every year in exchange for a stamp allowing them to prescribe the outlawed drugs.

In 1937, another tax-related drug law was passed, called the Marihuana Tax Act. By the time this Federal law was passed, 27 states had already outlawed marijuana. Several states, like Texas, were trying to deal with the influx of Mexican workers, many of whom smoked marijuana. Law professor Charles Whitebread describes the climate this way:[8]

"All you had to do to find out what motivated the marijuana laws in the Rocky mountain and southwestern states was to go to the legislative records themselves. Probably the best single statement was the statement of a proponent of Texas' first marijuana law. He said on the floor of the Texas Senate, and I quote, 'All Mexicans are crazy, and this stuff (referring to marijuana) is what makes them crazy.' Or, as the proponent of Montana's first marijuana law said, (and imagine this on the floor of the state legislature) and I quote, 'Give one of these Mexican beet field workers a couple of puffs on a marijuana cigarette and he thinks he is in the bullring at Barcelona.' "

When states in the northeast caught a whiff of the supposed problems in the southwest, many took preemptive measures to keep citizens from using marijuana in case the drug found its way up there. Alcohol was outlawed by the 18th amendment, a.k.a. "Prohibition," and the north was replete with recovering narcotic addicts following passage of the Harrison Act. It seems they were concerned that recovering addicts and those craving a drink might spiral downward into addiction if marijuana were not outlawed. Based on the hype in southwestern states, they had legitimate reasons for their concerns.

Congressional hearings leading up to the Marihuana Tax Act lasted just a few hours. The legal fate of marijuana in America was probably sealed by the testimony of Henry J. Anslinger, Commissioner of the Federal Bureau of Narcotics during more than three decades – from 1930 until 1962. Commissioner Anslinger told Congress that,[9]

"Marijuana is an addictive drug which produces in its users insanity, criminality, and death."

Anslinger believed that punishing drug users was the only way to deal with the problem. He would have his way.

In addition to Commissioner Anslinger, the Chief Counsel to the American Medical Association, a lawyer and doctor named William Woodward, testified at the hearings. Interestingly, in direct contrast to the testimony of Commissioner Anslinger, Dr. Woodward stated,[9]

"The American Medical Association knows of no evidence that marihuana is a dangerous drug."

According to transcripts of the hearing, a Congressman immediately replied,[9]

"Doctor, if you can't say something good about what we are trying to do, why don't you go home?"

The bill passed through the House and Senate with virtually no debate and was signed into law by President Roosevelt.

In the 1940s, Commissioner Anslinger learned that many musicians, particularly jazz musicians, were smoking marijuana despite the new law. He sent out letters to local law enforcement agencies instructing them to determine which musicians in their area were using the drug. The plan was to have a huge national roundup of marijuana smoking musicians during a single, undisclosed, day. This proved more difficult than the Commissioner expected. He had trouble finding law enforcement agencies that would cooperate or that could identify musicians who were breaking the law. In 1948, the Commissioner appeared before a Senate Committee and requested funding for more agents. When asked why he needed more agents, the Commissioner stated,[9]

"Because there are people out there violating the marijuana laws."

When asked who was breaking the law, the Commissioner replied,[9]

"Musicians. And I don't mean good musicians, I mean jazz musicians."

Drug use in America did not go away so, in 1951, the Boggs Act was passed. The Boggs Act increased penalties for all drug violations by four-fold. In his testimony supporting the law, Commissioner Anslinger was willing to admit that he was wrong about the addictive nature of marijuana and that it does not cause insanity and death. His new position was that it is unequivocally the first step toward heroin addiction.

The Daniel Act was passed in 1956. The impetus for the Act was organized crime and the realization that much of the money that flowed underground stemmed from drug trafficking. The Daniel Act increased penalties by another four-fold.

During the late 1950s and throughout the 1960s, many states passed their own laws increasing penalties for drug possession, sales, transport, etcetera. Criminal prosecution of drug offenses took off and punishments often exceeded those for violent crimes by a long shot. In the words of Professor Whitebread:[8]

"Just to show you where it was, in the same time period first degree murder in Virginia had a mandatory minimum sentence of fifteen years. Rape, a mandatory minimum sentence of ten years. Possession of marijuana -- not to mention sales of marijuana with its mandatory minimum of forty years -- mandatory minimum of twenty years."

In 1961, representatives from the American Medical Association and the American Bar Association worked together to assess whether drug addiction is best treated as a crime or a medical condition. They concluded that drug addiction is a disease and that criminal activity among addicts emerges from the combination of dependence on the drug and high prices due to the illegal nature of addictive substances. They also concluded that alcoholism was a much bigger problem than addiction to other drugs. They advocated for further research into treatment options and cautioned that prosecuting users as criminals could not, by itself, provide the answer to America's drug problem. Commissioner Anslinger severely criticized the report and countered that treating addicts in clinics would only increase the number of addicts, not decrease it.

Passage of the Comprehensive Drug Abuse Prevention and Control Act in 1970 led to significant changes in the way that we categorize drugs and prosecute drug offenses. The Act covered all drugs – with the exception of nicotine and alcohol. The Drug Enforcement Agency (DEA) was established in 1973 to enforce all Federal drug laws, including those in the Comprehensive Drug Abuse Prevention and Control Act. The new act repealed many of the previous drug laws, including the Harrison Act and Marihuana Tax Act, in favor of a new approach. The new approach involved sorting drugs into categories, or "schedules," based upon answers to two key questions

1. Does the drug have a medicinal use?
2. Does the drug have abuse potential?

The act proscribes that the penalties should be tied to the schedule of the drug. Below are the drug schedules, what they mean, and examples of drugs in the category.

Schedule 1. No accepted medicinal value and high potential for abuse and dependence. Pharmacies cannot sell them and doctors generally cannot prescribe them (marijuana is sometimes an exception to that rule). Marijuana, heroin, morphine, MDMA (ecstasy), LSD, gamma-hydroxybutyric acid (GHB).

Schedule 2. Limited accepted medicinal value. High potential for abuse and dependence. Some are available with prescription. Cocaine, codeine, amphetamines, methamphetamines, opium, oxycodone (OxyContin, Percocet).

Schedule 3. Accepted medical uses and less potential for abuse and dependence than the previous two. Some available with a prescription. Anabolic steroids (body building drugs), barbiturates, ketamine (Special K).

Schedule 4. Accepted medical uses and low potential for abuse and dependence. May be available with prescription. Alprazolam (Xanax), diazepam (Valium), flunitrazepam (Rohypnol), zolpidem (Ambien), modafinil (Provigil).

Schedule 5. Accepted medical uses and lowest potential for abuse and dependence. Regulated but do not require a prescription. Cough suppressants containing small amounts of codeine (e.g., Robitussin AC).

During the late 1960s and early 1970s, use of marijuana and psychedelic drugs became widespread in the youth counterculture, which included antiwar protestors and the like. Stressing the illegal nature of drug activities allowed for the easy targeting, demonizing and imprisonment of young people against the war. Nixon launched a very public war on drugs that amounted to a war on disgruntled youth and vowed to rid the nation of the problem.

In the 1980s, the War on Drugs kicked into high gear under the Reagan administration. Crack cocaine use was a major concern then and preventing drug use was a passion of the first lady, Nancy Reagan. The first national media campaigns highlighting the horrors of drug use were launched, including the classic "This is your brain, this is your brain on drugs" commercial. Several acts, including The Comprehensive Crime Control Act of 1984, the Anti-Drug Abuse Act of 1986, and the Anti-Drug Abuse Amendment Act of 1988, increased federal penalties for drug violations. They also increased funding for enforcement of the laws. The Office of National Drug Control Policy (ONDCP) was created in 1988 with the passing of The National Narcotics Leadership Act. Leaders of the ONDCP have come to be known as "Drug Czars."

In the 1980s, presumably in part due to steps taken by the Reagan administration, drug use declined relative to 1970s levels. Indeed, in the late 1980s, marijuana use reached a 20 year low. Imprisonment for drug offenses surged, particularly for offenses involving the use or sale of crack cocaine, a drug associated with African Americans in inner cities. Penalties for the use or sale of powdered cocaine, associated with Caucasian drug users, remain far less harsh. Unfairly so.

In the 1990s, drug use among adults remained relatively constant, yet drug use among adolescents aged 12-17 skyrocketed. Most of the increase in overall drug use was driven by an increase in marijuana use.

As we have seen in this chapter, the first decade of the new millennium has witnessed small decreases in use of drugs overall.

Despite the passage of laws outlawing drug use and promising to punish American citizens severely if they still choose to do illegal drugs, drug use has not gone away. The general approach that the U.S. has used to deal with drugs during the past century has failed. In fact, in some ways, we seem to be failing worse now than we were in the early 1900s. For every new drug law, it seems there is a report from a bipartisan or impartial committee concluding that users need better access to treatment services, not harsher punishments. Unfortunately, the laws are not based upon science. Indeed, the laws here often ignore science.

This is perhaps best reflected in the findings of a 1977 report by the New York Bar Association regarding the Rockefeller drug laws. The Rockefeller drug laws were the harshest in the country when passed in 1973 by the New York State government. The aim of the laws was to use severe mandatory prison sentences and harsher penalties in general to deter drug use and sales. The New York Bar Association concluded that the harsher penalties had no impact on drug abuse in the state and that mandatory sentencing didn't help. Yet, despite such reports, mandatory minimum sentences remain all the rage. Spending on the law enforcement side of the drug war has grown astronomically – from around $2 billion in 1988 to well over $10 billion in 2008. In contrast, Federal funding on education and prevention initiatives is disappearing fast, despite evidence that well structured initiatives work. On the treatment front, funding and support have remained relatively stagnant over the years and only a few percent of adolescents who need help, probably somewhere around 10%, are estimated to get it.

We now have a century's worth of data demonstrating the limited utility of a largely punitive drug war. Some cities have chosen to take a new tact regarding how they view and deal with drug offenses, particularly those involving marijuana. Cities like Denver, Seattle and Oakland have made marijuana possession a very low priority for law enforcement, though it is still technically illegal. In Denver, adults 21 or older carrying an ounce of marijuana or less for personal use can receive tickets similar to those issued for traffic citations. Time will tell whether such moves are good or bad for public health there. This kind of approach is in line with the science, but still requires intensive education efforts to ensure safe and responsible use, and only by adults. It remains to be seen how people there will respond to changes in the drug's legal status. This might not be the best approach, either.

SideNotes

Are criminally negligent drug companies and their executives exempt from the War on Drugs?

Pain medications are a godsend to those who need them, but are often abused by those who don't. In 2005, the number of Americans aged 12 and older that abused or were dependent upon prescription pain medications was on par with the number that abused or were dependent on cocaine. In the case of cocaine, billions of dollars in taxes are spent yearly tracking down and arresting dealers and users, and destroying coca fields in foreign countries. Mandatory minimum sentencing ensures that those who provide this addictive drug to kids pay for their crimes with their freedom. In 2007, the president of Stamford, Connecticut based Purdue Pharma acknowledged guilt in Federal court for intentionally misleading the country's MDs about the risks associated with its ultra-potent formulation of oxycodone, OxyContin. The company was made to pay a $634.5 million fine; a fraction of the billions it continues to make from the drug.

In a May 11, 2007, article entitled, "OxyContin maker, execs guilty of deceit," ABCNews.com quotes U.S. Attorney John Brownlee as saying:

"With its OxyContin, Purdue unleashed a highly abusable, addictive, and potentially dangerous drug on an unsuspecting and unknowing public. For these misrepresentations and crimes, Purdue and its executives have been brought to justice."

Immediately after the settlement, Purdue Pharma representatives backpedaled publicly, claiming the settlement wasn't an admission of guilt and that OxyContin is safe. Not surprisingly, the public and many MDs remain enraged by the settlement and lack of prison time for guilty Purdue Pharma executives. The plea constitutes admission of responsibility for contributing to the documented overdose deaths of more than 400 citizens, many of them kids, and to 100s of thousands of cases of OxyContin abuse and dependence. The company was allowed to pay for its crimes in cash. Do you concur with the U.S. Attorney that justice was served in this case? How would the government have handled this scourge if the drugs were sold in plastic baggies rather than plastic prescription drug containers? Is it appropriate for such companies to use the nation's MDs as prescription dispensaries for dangerous drugs? Should MDs be reimbursed for their time in cases where companies plead guilty to misleading them?

In the past few decades, data have accumulated regarding the efficacy of specific treatment modalities and prevention initiatives. While punitive approaches have proven to be less than effective, education and treatment have proven themselves to be invaluable in our efforts to keep adolescents healthy.

Prevention and education programs – Do they work?

In a perfect world, everyone would make it through adolescence with some scrapes and bruises, maybe a few minor emotional or physical scars, and that's it. Because drug use can lead to more serious and sustained problems, it is critical that we give teens and their parents the tools they need to make wise choices. Often, teens are unaware of the problems that drug use can cause, and the ease with which things can get out of hand. Because we adults tend to focus on the illegal nature of drugs, so do teens. Adolescence is a time when challenging rules and evading laws can be fun, increasing the allure of drugs for some kids. Laws reflect external control. Getting teens to make wise choices around the issue of drugs requires making it relevant to them and shifting the sense of control here to an internal one.

There are several things that adults can do to help ensure that teens either make it through the teen years without testing the waters or, if they do, they do so without drowning. Having science-based, well-conceived, well-planned, and well-executed education and prevention programs is one of them. Let's take a look at some example programs, the approaches they use and how they have fared, beginning with one that didn't work.

Drug Abuse Resistance Education (D.A.R.E.) – Learning from failures

The story behind the D.A.R.E program is an interesting one. It begins in Los Angeles in the mid 1980s. Then police chief Daryl Gates hatched a plan to get law enforcement agents into schools and, hopefully, dissuade substance use among teens at the same time. The premise of the program was simple – kids need to learn skills to resist peer pressure to use drugs. This fit perfectly with the "Just Say No" mantra offered by then First Lady, Nancy Reagan. Well-intentioned law enforcement agents administered the program to kids in 5th and 6th grade. Kids learned about the ravages of drug use and role-played scenarios in which they were approached on the school yard, in the hallways, or at parties, and offered drugs. The approach made intuitive sense, but intuition can be misleading.

During the 1980s and early 1990s, D.A.R.E. spread very rapidly, and eventually made its way into more than 70% of all schools in the U.S., as well as schools in more than 40 other countries. Communities embraced it, bumper stickers were plastered on cars everywhere, t-shirts were sold, and it seemed like D.A.R.E. was the answer. There was just one problem – it didn't work. It galvanized communities and raised awareness of some aspects of drug abuse, but it did not truly protect children from drug use. And so begins the most interesting part of the story.

In the 1990s, researchers began to point out the severe limitations of the D.A.R.E. program. These researchers had something that D.A.R.E. advocates lacked – data. The data failed to reveal any decreases in drug use among kids that had passed through the program. Overall, the only two noteworthy changes associated with the program were a short lasting increase in respect for law enforcement and a diminished likelihood that other prevention programs would increase the chances of drug use. Yes, odd as it seems, in some geographic and socioeconomic strata, kids who received school education and prevention programs were actually more likely to become drug users. For these kids, D.A.R.E. decreased the odds that further programming would contribute to drug use. However, the data revealed clearly that D.A.R.E. did not decrease the chances that children would use drugs.

According to a February 15, 2001, article in the New York Times:[10]

> "D.A.R.E. has long dismissed criticism of its approach as flawed or the work of groups that favor decriminalization of drug use. But the body of research had grown to the point that the organization could no longer ignore it. In the past two months alone, both the surgeon general and the National Academy of Sciences have issued reports saying that D.A.R.E.'s approach is ineffective; several cities, most recently Salt Lake City, have stopped using the program. D.A.R.E. is also responding to a new hardnosed mentality among federal education officials, who distribute about $500 million in drug prevention grants each year. Starting last year, the Department of Education said it would no longer let schools spend money from its office of safe and drug-free schools on D.A.R.E. because department officials did not consider it scientifically proven."

D.A.R.E. failed for several reasons. First, kids aren't as weak as the curriculum presumes and direct peer pressure is not the primary fulcrum leading kids to start using drugs. Peer pressure is usually far more subtle and implied rather than in-your-face and confrontational. Another probable reason was its administration by law enforcement agents! That strategy might be fine for white kids in the suburbs, but what about kids in inner city schools or in areas rife with police corruption and deep mistrust between cops and citizens? America's prisons are straining at the seams, particularly with non-Caucasians. The U.S. contributes about 5% to the earth's population but holds 25% of the earth's prisoners. The vast majority of those serving time for drug offenses, around 90%, are African-American or Hispanic. If your brother was arrested on a drug charge, pulled over on the basis of racial profiling, or roughed up by police, it's unlikely you'll respond well to drug-related messages from law enforcement officers in your classroom. While putting "good cops" in proximity to children might have helped build some trust with kids, it was not an effective drug education strategy.

It must be stressed that there is no doubt the program worked wonders in some highly involved communities, it simply didn't do so nationwide.

There are other, more subtle reasons for the failure of D.A.R.E. and similar well-intentioned programs. It turns out that administering programs to large groups of kids is not always the best idea. Nobody wants to be an outcast. For an individual to state, in a room full of peers, that he plans to say "No!" to drugs can make him feel like an outcast. In group settings, kids tend to glorify drug use, their own or use among others. This is why many adolescent substance abuse treatment programs forbid kids from sharing their drug use war stories in group meetings. Thus, in the context of a prevention program, the social dynamic could inadvertently reinforce pro-drug messages and increase curiosity about substances. For example, at the college level, mailing feedback to students regarding their drinking is more effective at reducing drinking than providing such feedback while the student is in a room with his or her peers. This is part of the reason that online programs like *AlcoholEdu*, from Outside the Classroom in Needham, MA, have the potential to be so effective. In group settings, many college students have a tendency to play up their levels of alcohol use rather than taking an honest look at their behavior.

When adults think about teen drinking and other drug use, we only see the potential negative consequences. Most programs, like D.A.R.E, are aimed at teaching kids about those consequences and using them to dissuade use. Research sug-

gests that kids are already aware that drugs have negative consequences, even if their knowledge of the actual facts is limited.
While parents and educators try to dissuade use by focusing on
the negatives, many kids remain attracted to the drugs because of
their perceived benefits. Research suggests that many adolescents
tend to overestimate the potential positive outcomes associated
with risky behaviors, like drug use. Even if there's a chance that a
drug can kill them, some adolescents will remain drawn to it
because it seems fun and they tend to think that the really
negative outcomes won't happen to them. Clearly, most of these
perceptions about benefits are inaccurate. Not much good
usually comes out of drug use during adolescence. Regardless,
programs that fail to address misperceptions about the positive
effects of drugs tend to fail themselves.

In the author's view, it is just as important to discuss the
perceived benefits of drug use as it is to discuss the risks. For
instance, alcohol can make it easier to be social, approach
people, talk in crowds and so forth. But it can do some bad
things, too. Taking this balanced approach has several advan-
tages. It demonstrates an awareness of what motivates adolescents to experiment with drugs. It provides an opportunity to
debunk rumors of benefits that are untrue and often circulated in
ignorance of the facts about the drug's effects. This strategy also
provides an opportunity for each teen to formulate their own
strategy for dealing with situations in which drugs are available.
A teen is far more likely to refuse the opportunity to try a drug if
she has thought through the pros and cons and made an independent decision than if she has simply been taught a list of
dangers and told to say "No!"

In response to critics, the D.A.R.E. program has been
revamped. The curriculum now extends beyond 5th and 6th
grade and includes booster programs during middle and high
school – both very good ideas. With the reach and resources
that D.A.R.E. has nationally, there is hope that the changes

could turn it into the program its creators wanted it would be. Time, and data, will tell.

Programs that work – Learning from successes

The world doesn't always cooperate with us and seemingly good ideas don't always pan out. We all wish that every treatment, whether it's a new medicine or a drug education program, could be thoroughly tested and studied before being tried. But that's not possible – so we often learn from our mistakes. Because the creators of D.A.R.E. believed in their approach and worked hard to implement it, a lot of very valuable information was gleaned from its successes and failures. The program did not accomplish its goals, but it has helped other programs to evolve. Over the years, prevention researchers have taken the lessons learned from failed programs and used them to guide the creation of successful programs. Many of these programs have only been implemented at the local level – often due to budget constraints, but also because some are not easily adaptable to national-level prevention.

One of the author's favorite initiatives, both because of its curb appeal and because of promising data, is *Project Northland*.[11] Project Northland is an alcohol prevention program that addresses alcohol use at multiple levels – from individual factors to factors in the community. Community-wide programs make sense in general. Project Northland includes programming aimed at kids from 6th grade through graduation, skipping only grade 10 – and students are not the only people involved. Parents and members of the community, including business owners, are also included. The program approaches the topic of alcohol use among adolescents from a very comprehensive perspective. You will not find any top down, authoritarian "Just Say No" slogans at use in Project Northland.

The content and strategies used in Project Northland are grade specific. Sixth grade programming focuses on parent/child communication, classroom activities related to alcohol, and the formation of community task forces that work toward altering the culture of drinking, and attitudes toward underage drinking in particular, in the larger community. During seventh grade, a combination of role-playing, group discussions, and homework assignments are used to educate young adolescents about alcohol. At this time, community task forces address city-wide ordinances and talk to business owners, while kids in a peer program help organize alcohol-free events. During eighth grade, students are urged to become active in their communities. Ninth grade includes education and activities surrounding drinking and driving, as well as teaching kids to evaluate alcohol advertisements. Programming during 11th and 12th grade builds upon the work of previous years and includes debates and discussions regarding the pros and cons of drinking, not just in terms of individual outcomes, but in terms of the health of the community.

Data indicate that the program works. Measurements taken at various stages of the program suggest that program participation leads to:

- Slower rates of increased drinking throughout high school
- Lower levels of cigarette smoking and marijuana use
- Increased communication between students and parents about alcohol
- Less permissive norms regarding adolescent drinking among parents of program participants

Not bad! So, in short, Project Northland seems to be a success. Unfortunately, its scope and complexity will make it difficult to employ at the national level. However, the early success of Project Northland demonstrates that prevention programs can work and highlights the importance of addressing issues like underage drinking in a much broader context than simply listing the negative effects of the drug and using the threat of punishment to deter use.

In contrast to in-depth, interactive programs like Project Northland, some programs aim to change attitudes and perceptions of drug use via media campaigns. One of the more promising new media campaigns is *Above the Influence*.[12] The message the campaign conveys is that drugs aren't necessarily going to hurt you, but they can take you away from experiencing life to its fullest. No program before it has succeeded in conveying this crucial point to kids. Hopefully, this one will. One commercial slot for the campaign shows a boy sitting on a friend's couch. The boy says that he smoked weed and nothing bad happened. In fact, he says, smoking weed seems to be a lot safer than going out into the world and actually doing things. For these reasons, our protagonist stands up and proclaims that he is getting off of his friend's couch and heading out into the world to experience the adventures of life.

This is a sensible approach, and one that is consistent with what we know about both drugs and adolescent development. It seems a vast improvement over recent ad campaigns from the Office of National Drug Control Policy, which have thus far relied on ineffective and sensationalistic messages. Let's see if these examples ring a bell. Shortly after September 11th, ads aired telling kids that if they purchased marijuana they could be complicit in acts of terrorism. A few years ago, a public service announcement was released in which a boy smokes marijuana and accidentally shoots his friend in the head with a loaded gun from his dad's desk drawer. Yes, these things could happen, but it's more likely that a kid will simply waste his time and blow the opportunity to grow in healthy ways than accidentally kill his friend with his father's loaded gun.

The Above the Influence website includes metered, science-based information about how marijuana affects the brain. The site includes an interactive graphic of the human brain in which users can click on various brain areas to see what marijuana does to them and how those changes affect perception and performance. A very different approach, and one that seems to hold potential.

Finally, it is worth noting that the Above the Influence message extends far beyond the topic of drug use. It is a pro-social, pro-health, pro-kid message that can be adapted to address a number of other risks facing adolescence – like bullying and sex.

Other programs deserve mention here, as well. *Life Skills Training*, the *TRUTH* campaign for smoking prevention, the *Seattle Social Development Project*, and *Big Brothers Big Sisters* are all programs that have shown successes. Many of these programs kill lots of birds with just a few stones. They recognize that risky behaviors tend to cluster. For instance, smoking cigarettes predicts higher levels of alcohol use among teens, high levels of alcohol use predict higher levels of violence, violence predicts drug use, and so on. Many of these programs promote pro-social behaviors by teaching kids how to function in the world, rather than driving home frightening messages about one specific drug or another. Logically, kids who are coping well with life will be less likely to get caught in the gravitational pull of drugs.

In addition to programs aimed at altering the culture surrounding drinking and drug use, there are several programs that target individual kids with great success. *Brief Motivational Interviewing* is an approach developed masterfully by researcher Dr. Peter Monti and colleagues at Brown University and the Providence Veterans Affairs Medical Center. It involves getting kids to take a close look at their drug use and its role in their lives. This is particularly helpful when done shortly after life changing experiences involving drugs, such as when a kid ends up in the ER after drinking too much. It is based on an effective therapeutic approach called *motivational interviewing*. One aim is to help patients resolve issues about which they are ambivalent. A kid is more likely to be ambivalent about drinking again if he just got arrested for urinating on the sidewalk! Good Brief Motivational Interviewers can seize those opportunities and help orient kids in safer directions.

What can parents do? Communicate early and often!

Parents are the first line of defense in protecting kids from the negative impact of drugs. Unfortunately, the line does not always hold up so well. In the past century, the pace of social and technological change has quickened and adolescence has lengthened, causing a widening of generation gaps and making it more difficult to know how to talk to teens, even for parents who want desperately to do so.

The Partnership for Drug-Free America estimates that more than 1/3 of parents do not talk to their kids about alcohol. They also estimate that kids whose parents do talk to them about alcohol are 42% less likely to drink than other kids. Organizations from the National Parent Teacher Association to the National Institute on Drug Abuse site communication between parents and teens as pivotal in preventing negative behaviors like drug use and nudging kids toward positive alternatives.

Many parents are uncertain how to talk with their kids about alcohol and other drugs, and often have inaccurate perceptions about the risks involved. They are also often unaware that their kids drink or do other drugs, and tend to underestimate the extent of drug use among their kid's peers. They might feel overwhelmed by the prospect of trying to become well-informed enough to talk to their kids, or they might believe that their kids actually know more than they do. Fortunately, plenty of good sources are now available that translate the science of drug actions into simple, useful, and accurate language. And the fact is that while kids have access to an immense amount of drug information on the Internet, from friends, or from health classes – much of it is wrong. Once parents recognize that, and then learn the facts for themselves, they are well on their way to having productive conversations with kids about substance use.

Here are some tips that might make the process easier and more effective:

- Do your homework first. The following National Institutes of Health (NIH) web sites - www.niaaa.nih.gov and www.nida.nih.gov - are good places to begin, but be aware that the NIH is not free of political influence. The books "Buzzed" and "Just Say Know," both written by colleagues of the author from Duke University Medical Center, are also excellent resources.

- Talk to kids as soon as you think they are capable of understanding the issues. And the first talks don't have to be about drugs. Talk to young children about their bodies – the kinds of things that keep them healthy, like good food, and the kinds of things that can harm them, like injury and illness. Help them to understand, at a very early age, that the things they put into their bodies, such as foods and medicines, all have an impact on how they feel at present and how they will ultimately develop as they grow. With these building blocks in place, when it comes time for a conversation about drugs the job will be much easier.

- When talking about drugs and drug use, be sure to focus plenty of attention on the false expectations that people have about what drugs will do for them. Research suggests that teens are aware of the general risks of drug use, but tend to have an overblown expectation of how good it will be.

- Use TV commercials, both public service announcements and drug company commercials, as opportunities to bring up the topic of drug use in general and to discuss the tactics of advertisers.

- Establish clear expectations surrounding alcohol and other drug use. What is your family policy? What consequences would follow violations?

- If you drink, model healthy drinking practices. Kids follow our lead.

- State your willingness to drive your teen home, no questions asked until the next day, if he is uncomfortable getting into a car with someone for any reason. This compromise can build trust and help keep kids safe. If teens follow through on their end of the deal, it can also save parents some serious stress!

Many parents still believe the myth that having conversations with kids about drugs will plant ideas in their heads and increase the likelihood they will end up doing them. When it comes to most unsafe behaviors – alcohol and other drug use, sexual promiscuity, violence, and so on – open, honest and respectful communication between parents and kids tends to increase the odds that adolescents will avoid the pitfalls and make healthy choices. While such conversations will plant ideas in kids' heads, such ideas should help keep them safe, not increase the odds that bad things will happen.

Reconciling your past with your adolescent's future

What goes around really does come around. If you are currently an adult, it's a safe bet you thought you were far cooler than your parents when you were a teenager. It's also a safe bet that your kids will think they're much cooler than you! Having been a cool teenager does not make the task of parenting any easier. As we have seen, adolescents are built to internalize what we teach them while pushing away at the same time. It's possible that the best stories from your teen years will be met with rolling eyeballs and sheer boredom if you try to share them with your adolescent. Every generation thinks they have figured out what the previous generation missed. Most teens think that adults are boring and out of touch. That's okay, and should not interfere with one's ability to guide a teenager down the right path. When faced with rolling eyeballs and sighs of boredom, try to keep your ego out of it, recognize that it is normal, and stay on task. Remember, the goal is not to be well-liked, it's to keep your adolescent moving in a healthy direction.

One of the challenges that parents face when trying to have forthright conversations with their kids about drugs is the fact that many current adults dabbled with drugs when they were young. Statistically, the odds are better than 50/50 that an adult who came of age in the 1970s or 80s has at least tried marijuana, and many were (or still are) regular users. This can certainly make the task of discussing drugs with kids more daunting, particularly for those who enjoyed their experiences and did not suffer any observable repercussions. How can we convince teens that drugs will ruin their lives if we, ourselves, have done some of them and survived? How can we maintain open and honest lines of communication if we are not willing to share such stories with our kids?

Fortunately, it is quite possible to talk with teens openly and honestly about the risks of substance use without obfuscating the facts or pretending to have lived the life of a saint. It's not possible to make a specific recommendation about whether, or to what degree, to be forthcoming with your teen about your own drug use history. However, it is a good idea to try hard *not* to fall into the trap of trying to convince a teen that you are as cool as you say you are by telling them your own drug stories, particularly if the stories involve you having lots of fun. It might get a teen to pay closer attention to you while you speak, but it is unlikely to help them make better decisions when it comes to drugs, and could put you in the position of looking like a hypocrite if you ever have to discipline your teen because of drug use.

When gearing up to talk with a kid about drugs, recognize that knowledge about the risks inherent in drug use during the teen years has expanded greatly since today's adults were kids. We had no clue 20 years ago that the brain was still developing during adolescence, or that drugs like alcohol can have a lasting impact on the teen brain (see the next chapter for a brief overview of that literature). Thus, regardless of one's drug use history, it is quite clear that we simply did not know then what we know now about some of the risks. This simple fact should give previous drug using parents the conviction necessary to work hard at dissuading drug use by their own kids.

Importantly, efforts to dissuade drug use by adolescents should go hand-in-hand with identifying and promoting activities that scratch the adolescent itches that often lead to experimentation with drugs in the first place. Kids who are passionate about their hobbies or busy with extracurricular activities are much less likely to turn to drugs for thrills than kids who or bored and lack healthy outlets for their needs to explore and be social. Similarly, adolescents that have a high sense of self-worth, an internal locus of control, and who are surrounded by supportive and loving adults are less likely to turn to drugs to help them cope with the pressures of life.

How can you tell when drug use has become a problem?

Most teens who experiment with drugs of various kinds do not end up developing serious problems with them, but some do. Before we can treat a substance abuse problem, it has to be spotted. Statistics suggest that, by their senior year in high school, 80% of today's teens will have consumed alcohol outside of the home, 50% will have smoked marijuana, and at least 10%

will have taken pain pills recreationally.[13] The fact that an adolescent has used a particular drug cannot, on the surface, compel the conclusion that there is a clinical problem that requires professional treatment. However, it should raise red flags.

Based on the brain science, there are no known safe levels of drug use during adolescence. This includes alcohol. Any drug use by teens should be a cause for concern, but not necessarily concern sufficient to seek treatment. So, what do you do when your teen comes home smelling of alcohol, or you find that little bag of pot in the drawer next to the school planner and the dusty old Cub Scout Badge? Situations like this are serious, and it is very important that parents react quickly, calmly, and firmly. But how do you know when to get professional help, and what kind to get? This can be a difficult decision, but there are some obvious signs that can point in the direction of pursuing formal treatment. This is true independent of the drug in question. These signs include, but are not limited to:

SideNotes

Should companies that sell habit forming drugs be allowed to do stuff like this?

During the fall of 2006, the drug company that makes Lunesta, Sepracor, began offering potential patients seven free pills. Lunesta is a prescription sleep aid with the potential for abuse and dependence. As such, the tactic of giving away free samples of the drug to lure users is eerily similar to the tactics employed by many school-yard drug dealers.

Get 7 Free LUNESTA Tablets LUNESTA® is proud to announce a new 7-Night Trial Script® Voucher Program. If you have trouble sleeping and your doctor thinks LUNESTA is right for you, take advantage of this special offer today to get your seven free tablets. After your doctor attaches the voucher to a completed and signed prescription form, go to the pharmacist of your choice and receive seven tablets, at no charge. This offer is only good through December 31, 2006.

Should such tactics be allowed? From the author's perspective, no. Glitzy ads for prescription drugs go too far as is. Using the nations MDs to pass out samples of habit forming drugs is unconscionable and inappropriate, and ought to be illegal.

- Known dishonesty about the extent of use
- Use in the morning or difficulty functioning without use in the morning
- Stealing money or selling belongings to continue use
- Greater than normal amounts of irritability on family trips lasting more than a day or two
- A drop in grades associated with the onset of, or escalation in, substance use
- Failure to meet obligations as a result of substance use
- Hanging out with kids known to use/abuse drugs

Deciding to pursue further options is the easy part. The hard part is trying to figure out which options to pursue. Because money is often the determining factor in treatment decisions, early in the process, one should place a call to one's insurance company to determine how much assistance they provide for substance abuse evaluations and treatment.

If one has a family doctor or pediatrician, it is worth placing a call to their office to seek a referral for a treatment center. Alternatively, one can look in the yellow pages under "Substance Abuse" and visit the Substance Abuse and Mental Health Services Administration (SAMSHA) website to locate a treatment provider in the area.[14]

Once the potential provider has been identified, call and ask if it will be possible to evaluate your child to assess the nature and extent of their particular problems, and to assess whether there might be underlying medical or psychosocial triggers involved. Also ask about the specific services that are offered, the cost, and whether they deal with your particular insurance company. Finally, schedule an appointment to have your teen evaluated, and hope they go peacefully!

Does treatment work?

It certainly can, but there are several factors that influence whether treatment will work initially and whether the benefits will stick over time.[15] In the author's own research, motivation to improve one's life at the onset of treatment serves as a strong predictor that an adolescent will get through a treatment program without relapsing. Other studies suggest that motivation predicts good outcomes after the treatment ends, as well. In short, when teens want to change, it is much easier to get them to change!

Treatments come in a variety of shapes and sizes, lengths and costs. Some programs are outpatient and involve the entire family. The author is particularly fond of programs like this because teen substance abuse influences, and sometimes stems from, the family dynamic. As such, the family needs to be engaged in the treatment process. It is naïve to think that a teen will stay sober after treatment if the home remains littered with liquor bottles and the fridge is packed with beer.

In addition to outpatient programs, which are the most widely used type of program for adolescent drug treatment, residential programs, in which the teen lives at the facility, are also available. The extent to which these programs involve the family varies considerably. There are also non-traditional options, like wilderness programs, boot camps, and alternative schools. The data on those programs are mixed. In general, it appears that wilderness programs can help, but not for all teens. These programs are superior to boot camps, which lack evidence of effectiveness. Alternative schools that provide intensive counseling and health promotion are a worthwhile option to consider for those with some money in the bank.

In all of the above cases, it is important to recognize that the environment in which the treatment occurs is probably quite different from the environment in which the teen uses substances, unless of course the teen lives in the woods or only does drugs while white water rafting! This makes it essential to plan carefully for re-entry once the program is finished. What safe guards will be in effect to prevent use once the teen returns home? How will the teen be shielded from triggers for craving and use, such as particular kids or contexts? Similarly, what parameters (rewards and punishments) will be in place to motivate the teen to avoid returning to their bad habits?

Treatment programs tend to focus primarily on the adolescent and perhaps the family. It will be up to parents to deal with any environmental factors that contributed to the onset of use and pose risks for triggering relapses. Counselors at the treatment program you choose should be able to help you prepare for your adolescent's reintegration into a normal life.

With regard to traditional treatment programs, it is difficult to compare outpatient to inpatient programs because they are so different from one another. One advantage of outpatient treatment is that the treatment can take place without completely disrupting the life of the teen. It is also much less expensive, does not disrupt the school year, and allows for greater family involvement. One advantage of inpatient programs is that patients can be kept under observation and should be guaranteed not to have access to drugs for a set period of time. For those with resources or adequate insurance coverage, inpatient followed by outpatient treatment is a possibility to consider.

Regardless of the treatment modality or setting, the hard work begins, not ends, with treatment. The difficulty for most kids is staying away from drugs once they return home.

Drug abuse often hides other problems

Many readers have probably seen the A&E program, *Intervention*. It's a good one. The show portrays the lives of individuals struggling with one problem or another – usually drug addiction, but sometimes eating disorders or other conditions. At the end of the program, each individual experiences an intervention. They are brought into a room with loved ones and friends and asked to get help. Those who say "yes" are promptly taken to a treatment facility specializing in their condition.

By watching these individuals live their lives, it becomes clear that, for many of them, drug abuse is only one of several problems. In some cases, the drug abuse appears to be secondary to an underlying psychological pathology (see Episode #31, "Cristy"). In other cases, the drug abuse stems from efforts to control physical pain. Episode #53, "Brooke," provides a powerful example. Here is a description from the A&E website:

> "Brooke, 26, was a beautiful teenager with a magnetic personality. An elite gymnast on the cheerleading squad, she looked forward to a successful and athletic life. But tragedy struck in her senior year when she was crippled by Still's disease, an early form of rheumatoid arthritis. Her doctors prescribed narcotics to ease her pain, but Brooke soon became addicted. Her heartbroken family has sought new treatments to help Brooke, but she denies she's an addict. Now her family has turned in desperation to their last hope--an intervention."

Until the actual intervention, Brooke's family underestimated the amount of pain she was in, and failed to appreciate the bind in which Brooke found herself – not wanting to be dependent on narcotics but not being able to cope with the pain without them. They viewed and treated her as if she were an addict by choice, which was clearly not the case here.

Helping an adolescent stay clean after treatment

Anyone who has ever wrestled with an addiction, smoking for example, is well aware that quitting can be the easy part. The trick is staying quit! Most of us know smokers who manage to go weeks without cigarettes, long beyond the length of time necessary to deal with the physical discomfort of withdrawal, which is usually over within the first week. Yet, their cravings, often in response to triggers like advertisements or even changes in the weather, can be enough to draw them back years later. Having a strong social support network and lots to do can help. Starting hobbies that are inconsistent with the drug habit, such as jogging for those trying to stay away from cigarettes, can also help. The point is that getting off the drugs initially, regardless of how painful and difficult it is, can be easier than staying away from the drugs in the days, weeks, months and years to come.

Context has a powerful influence on behavior. While sitting alone in her room, a teen in recovery might crave substances but can avoid doing them. But at a party with friends, the context in which the drug choice is made is very different. Clearly, in this context, the risk of relapse is much higher. Falling off of the wagon one time can be enough to trigger a resumption of drug use. Thus, it is paramount that kids in recovery *not* be allowed to hang out with the kids with whom they used drugs. Even if those kids quit, too, the risk of a synergistic relapse is simply too great.

Part of the recovery process must involve carefully monitoring whom the teen spends time with and where. Slowly, over time and with maturation on the part of the kid, the leash should be lengthened and they should be allowed to engage in unsupervised activities with non-drug using kids in safe environments. The incentive to stay clean should include their relative freedom along with any other agreed upon reinforcers. The consequences of screwing up should be made clear and enforced. These rules should be laid out very clearly within a reasonable number of days after the end of in-patient treatment or during the early stages of outpatient treatment. Dealing with relapses can be heart breaking and frustrating. The experience can be made less difficult if the rules regarding relapses, as well as plans for what to do next, are etched in stone early in the process of recovery.

Home drug tests can now be purchased at most local drug stores, and they are worth considering for a while after formal treatment ends. It helps to explain to the teen why the tests are being used, which is presumably to help them stay on track. Consequences of failed drug screens should be decided upon and made clear to the adolescent up front. Every effort should be made to help the teen recognize that the drug screen is being use to promote their recovery, not out of distrust or with the intent to punish or pester them.

What if the teen fails a drug screen? To be certain that the test was accurate, it is worth performing another screen to verify. After that, the agreed upon contingency plan should be enacted. If the teen completed a treatment program, hopefully a counselor is available from the program to help you through the process via phone. If the teen denies drug use, but fails multiple urine screens, probability says to trust the tests.

What about kicking a drug using teen out of the house? Failed efforts to get a kid to quit using drugs can be a gut wrenching situation. Many parents are tempted to simply kick their child out of the home. If you feel like doing so, remind yourself that state laws consider kids the full responsibility of their parents until the age of 18. This means that kicking them out might not be an option to begin with! Again, if the teen has been through a treatment program, a follow-up consultation can be arranged to re-assess the problem and help determine the most effective course of action. If they are out of control, and parents feel threatened or afraid for the child, a call to law enforcement might be in order. The same is true if the teen decides to run away from home and cannot be talked into returning.

Throughout the process, remind yourself that you love your child and want only what is best for them, even if you don't have access to those feelings at the moment! Despite their protestations, if you are truly concerned about the path they are on, the only reasonable course of action is to do your best to help them. Fortunately, the vast majority of teens make it to adulthood okay, even if the situation seems hopeless at the time. Like a bad sprain, the long-term prognosis for drug-dabbling-kids tends to be better than appearances suggest. Keep that in mind as you try to ride out the process.

Giving kids incentives not to use drugs?

Each year, an inordinate amount of money is spent trying to dissuade kids from using drugs, chasing down those who use them, and then punishing them for their actions. Recent research strongly suggests that providing incentives to recovering teen drug users helps keep them clean.[16] If this is true, then what about providing incentives, perhaps financial, to kids and families to avoid drugs *before* the drug use begins? For instance, what if kids and their families were offered the opportunity to earn free tuition or other compensation by getting through high school without using drugs? Bonuses could be added for maintaining a Body Mass Index in the healthy range, graduating from high school, scoring above the national average on standardized tests, etcetera. In this way, we could provide incentives to kids not to use and reward them for making wise choices. Should they choose to use, they would lose the incentives. It would be like a stimulus package promoting health.

Think this sounds crazy? Think about it this way. Underage drinking costs taxpayers an estimated $60 billion per year. That's just drinking, not the use of other drugs. If the population consists of 300,000,000 people with an average life expectancy of 75 years, and the population were equally divided among those 75 years (which it isn't), then there would be something like 4,000,000 eighteen year olds eligible to graduate from high school each year. Let's assume for a moment that we could spend our $60 billion in tax money on something else rather than on cleaning up the damage caused by underage drinking. We could offer $15,000 to each graduating senior who made it through high school with clean random urine screens and no alcohol or other drug violations. Perhaps free tuition or even a new car could be given as options instead of the cash.

Even if 10% of students actually made it, that's 10% of America's youth who will have protected their brains and bodies from the potentially deleterious effects of drug use and will not become a burden to society in those ways. Further, we would be reinforcing positive, healthy decision-making rather than waiting for an adolescent to screw up so that we can punish them. These kids could become positive forces for change, and the cash reward could help them start their young lives right. Unrealistic? Perhaps, but the fact remains – incentives work to keep kids from using, even as they struggle to overcome the cravings and other symptoms that linger well into recovery.

The need for substance abuse treatment for incarcerated adolescents

Under President Reagan, the drug war escalated to unprecedented levels. This led to skyrocketing rates of incarceration for drug offenders. At the Federal level, the number of inmates imprisoned for drug offenses swelled from 8,152 in 1984 (29.5% of all prisoners) to 77,867 in 2004 (54.1% of all prisoners). As hindsight now reveals, these escalating rates of incarceration have done very little, if anything, to deter drug use among either adults or juveniles. Indeed, as the number of adults incarcerated for drug offenses rose steeply in the 1990s, so did rates of drug use among teens, those next in line for the adult justice system.

The current, general approach to rehabilitation in the juvenile justice system amounts to sending kids away for a long period of time in the presence of other troubled kids, with minimal effort to deal with their underlying problems. It would be the equivalent of sending a kid to her room for a long time for being rude, only her room is full of other kids with bad manners! For an increasing number of kids, detention homes or even prisons have replaced public high schools and community wide education and prevention programs for shaping attitudes and behaviors around the issue of drugs.

The adolescent brain is very moldable.

SideNotes

The importance of grass roots groups and motivated parents

Sheboygan, Wisconsin, is a fascinating city with a tremendous amount of cooperation between grass roots groups and government-funded public health entities. Not long ago, parents in a Sheboygan community became concerned as evidence accrued that heavy drug use, and perhaps dealing, was taking place in a neighborhood home. They dealt with it in an ingenious way, by placing signs saying something like, "This Is a Drug Free Home," in the yards of homes *around* the drug house. The people in the alleged drug-house eventually moved out. The incredible cooperation between parents and organizations in Sheboygan is made possible by the dedication of people like Phil Duket at the city's Family Resource Centers. Without dedicated people, many of them volunteers, the limited amount of funding available to strengthen communities wouldn't be sufficient to effect positive change. Sheboygan should serve as a role model for other communities for how to focus their resources on the problems of underage drinking and drug use.

This means that there are unique opportunities for change, including rehabilitation, for teens. Simple incarceration is not enough to reform most kids, particularly those with substance abuse problems rooted in poverty and/or deep emotional distress. Locking them away in the midst of negative influences, and creating in them additional emotional discomfort, virtually ensures a trajectory of unhealthy development. For many, emotionally unhealthy conditions are what initially led to the behaviors for which they were arrested. The data support the assertion that we should escalate our efforts to help kids in trouble, not tuck them away and try to forget about them.

The good news for those teens with serious drug problems is that, once they're incarcerated, they are forced to quit, at least for a while. The bad news is that, at present, a large percentage return to drug use after they leave. By dealing with substance abuse issues while a teen is in the juvenile justice system, the odds decrease that they will return to the justice system after release. This is highlighted in a 2000 report from the Council on Criminal Justice in Minneapolis, Minnesota.[17] The report concludes that substance use in the six months after being released from incarceration is a key predictor of recidivism (re-entry into the juvenile justice system) during the two years that follow. Stated differently, adolescents who did not use in the six months post-release were less likely to find themselves back in the justice system within a two year period. As such, addressing substance abuse problems while kids are in the system could increase the odds that they leave detention heading in the right direction and decrease the odds that they come back.

Several reports suggest that a comprehensive approach for dealing with adolescent substance use and delinquency increases the odds that a teen will integrate back into society successfully rather than ending up back in the judicial system. Juvenile drug courts have emerged across the country to meet the rising demand for effective rehabilitation for young offenders. Originating in Dade County, Florida, in the 1980s, these courts represent alternatives to the ineffective turnstile that characterizes so much of the American justice system. Developed for adults, drug courts were adapted to the juvenile population in the mid-1990s. By 2005, a total of 1262 drug courts were active around the country, with 335 of them processing juvenile offenders.

The exact nature of individual drug courts varies considerably from community to community, but they share the common objectives of reducing the cost of incarceration, reducing levels of substance abuse, reducing recidivism, and helping teens get their lives back on track. These courts take themselves very seriously, and are engineered to try to address as many of a juvenile's needs as possible. The aim is not just to reform the individual, but to try to understand and address the environmental factors that contributed to the individual's arrival in the juvenile justice system in the first place.

A review and evaluation of the Eleventh Judicial District Juvenile Drug Court in San Juan County, New Mexico, was undertaken in 2006. The stated objectives of this particular drug court are as follows:

1. Reduce recidivism.
2. Enhance self-esteem by developing responsibility and accountability in juvenile offenders.
3. Provide intensive outpatient substance abuse counseling for youth in the community. Counseling to include individual, group and family.
4. Monitor program participants through urinalysis and regular reporting regarding treatment and academic progress.
5. Increase accountability through regular court appearances and the use of sanctions and incentives.

In order to be accepted into the program a juvenile must be free of a record of violent felonies or sex offenses. They must also be charged with something other than a first degree felony in the current case. Finally, the offense for which the individual is charged must be alcohol or other drug related.

The Court attempts to meet its stated objectives using an impressive combination of carrots and sticks. Providing incentives for improvements is a primary part of the strategy. Incentives include praise, ceremonies, movie tickets, and – for those who complete the program successfully – college scholarships! Assessments are performed at the program outset and counseling is provided while the juvenile is in the program. But does it work?

In 2006, Pitts compared outcome data from program participants to data from peers in the system who were eligible for drug court but, for whatever reasons, ended up in the mainstream system.[18] Importantly, program participants and non-participants were quite similar, including the length of time spent incarcerated, about 10 months, and average age, about 16. Recidivism rates were recorded for up to 40 months after program completion. Those individuals who were processed by the juvenile drug court rather than the mainstream court system were *significantly less likely* to return to court.

If this outcome holds true across drug courts, and regions of the U.S., we could be on the way to a far more effective means of dealing with drug offenses and young drug offenders. Drug courts bridge the gaps between the prevention, treatment, and justice communities. In fact, John Walters, current Director of the Office of National Drug Control Policy is quoted as saying that,[19]

> "drug courts are perhaps the most significant inno-
> vation in criminal justice of the past twenty years."

The promise of juvenile drug courts highlights, yet again, the importance of comprehensive, and incentive based, approaches to dealing with the overlapping problems of teen substance use and delinquency of other types. So, there is real hope for the juvenile justice system with respect to drug abuse and young offenders. As discussed previously, there have also been some advances in the prevention strategies used to help teens avoid trouble with drugs in the first place. It is entirely possible that the number of juvenile offenders being referred to drug courts could decrease in the coming years, and that those who enter the system will be less likely to return. The savings could then be reinvested in the system and further progress could me made.

Why does all of this matter, anyway?

The topic of drug use, whether during adolescence or adulthood, is a confusing one. Some dangerous drugs are legal or prescribed, while some safer compounds are outlawed and understudied. Public service announcements stoke the coals of fear surrounding illegal drugs, while beer commercials suggest that nothing will improve life more than drinking alcohol.

When trying to dissuade kids from drug use and educate them about the risks, it is quite easy to lose track of why we want to keep kids off of those slippery slopes to begin with. The motivation should be to protect kids and their brains until they are old enough to make these decisions for themselves. The motivation should not be simply to "bust" kids and punish them for breaking the rules. Drug abuse among teens, as with adults, is often a sign that something is missing in the individual's life. It is unlikely that punishment alone will fill those holes, and could just cause problematic behavior to move from substance use to something else.

There are plenty of reasons why we should do what we can to teach kids to value their bodies and their futures, and to avoid alcohol and other drugs at least until they are adults. The most compelling reasons have to do with helping them reach their full potential and find pleasure internally rather than searching for an external substance to make them feel good or cope. Recall our discussion about internal vs. external locus of control from Chapter 1. In the long run, those who seek external means to find pleasure tend to suffer in a variety of ways.

The purpose of adolescence is to create a healthy foundation for adulthood. This involves learning skills, honing cognitive functions and becoming comfortable interacting with the larger social world. Drug use, particularly repeated drug abuse, can hinder all of these objectives. As such, we adults should do our best to dissuade drug use and to nullify the allure it has for kids by creating environments that keep them busy, keep them healthy, and help them build positive momentum. Keeping these objectives in mind can provide adults with a sense of purpose when it comes to trying to prevent kids from using alcohol and other substances. At the same time, we need to be honest about levels of drug use among adults, which are particularly high among aging Baby Boomers, and address it in a way based on evidence rather than ignorance, fear and legalism.

"Which is worse for you, alcohol or marijuana?"

High school students often want to know which drug is worse for a person, alcohol or marijuana. This isn't the kind of question a speaker wants to answer in thirty seconds or less. However, it's obviously something that crosses kids' minds while wrestling with these issues. Clearly, in a perfect world, all kids would forego both. In reality many do both, often at the same time. For the sake of argument, let's examine this question, briefly, from the perspective of the drugs' effects on the brain and behavior. Only one paragraph will be given to each drug and its effects. Keep in mind there are no perfect comparisons here.

Alcohol is a simple molecule that easily crosses the blood-brain barrier and inserts itself into the membranes of brain cells. What it does then is complicated, but it tends to disrupt the ability of individual cells to work. This compromises the ability of the brain circuits these cells form to keep up with what they are supposed to be doing. Some neurological loops in the brain are sped up by alcohol while others are slowed down. Like spilling water on a laptop, the brain short circuits, initially just a little. At low doses, the parts involved in anxiety are calmed and life seems more tolerable. Some people feel a little energized here. After a few servings, alcohol produces pleasure by increasing dopamine levels in the brain's reward center. The brain reads this as reinforcement for whatever it is the person is doing, making the activity seem more enjoyable and fun. For some people, the reinforcement combined with reduced anxiety translates into instant confidence. After a few more servings, thinking is really affected. Many adults like this part as it seems to interfere with the brain's ability to worry and ruminate. This also leads to "reduced inhibitions," or reduced concerns about the consequences of one's actions. Another drink or two and alcohol begins numbing the brain from the top down, affecting cognitive abilities like decision-making and impulse control. If the level of alcohol that hits the brain is big enough early on, memory blackouts are common. As we will see in the next chapter, memory blackouts represent spans of time during which people can't record what they are doing, despite the fact that they could be doing just about anything. At high enough doses, alcohol turns the basics like walking and talking into real chores. A few shots passed that and basic life support functions can be shut off, bringing about a premature demise. Some aspects of what alcohol does are molded by the culture, like whether it's cool to keep drinking after you vomit or, perhaps even worse, do karaoke. Other effects depend mostly on gene-driven biology. For 10-20% of the population, trouble quitting will be a reality if they start drinking regularly, and the earlier one starts the closer their particular risk will be to the big number.

Marijuana is a bit different but problematic in its own ways. Its effects follow a different time course and involve qualitatively different effects on the brain. Fortunately, marijuana does not share the profound impact alcohol has on vital reflexes, like gagging and breathing. If it did, it would be common to hear reports of people choking on food while trying to satisfy the munchies or dropping dead after that last bong hit; smoke wafting from their smiling dead lips. Marijuana can bring about death via its effects on the cardiovascular system, particularly in the first half hour or so after smoking it. It can also lead to death by causing people to do stupid things that seem really smart at the moment. Like alcohol, heavy use can lead to cancers of various types. Unlike alcohol, marijuana has very selective effects on particular types of receptors in the brain, called cannabinoid receptors. Those receptors are somehow involved in the growth and development of the brain during childhood and adolescence and the continued formation of brain circuits afterward. With regard to one active component of marijuana, THC, the brain makes its own. Release of this substance might play a role in the "runner's high" that many get from exercise (endorphins might play roles, too, but probably for pain relief mostly). Whether inhaled, eaten or sprayed in the mouth, THC crosses the blood-brain barrier and alters how circuits in the brain function. Unlike alcohol, it doesn't produce the widespread numbing of the brain that leads to real problems regulating behavior. Its effects are concentrated in areas involved in thinking, memory formation, abstract reasoning, emotional reactions to environments, the perception of time and space, things like that. While alcohol reduces anxiety marijuana can exacerbate it, intensely in some people, leading to the paranoia often attributed to the drug, and causing entire rooms full of people to collectively gasp if some-one knocks on the front door. A wise neuroscientist once told the author, "Marijuana won't kill you, but it can make you feel like you're going to die." He referred to highly potent strains as "hospital pot," as many inexperienced adolescents ingest more THC than their developing psyches can handle and they struggle to cope with frightening thoughts and emotions. Indeed, accord-ing to the D.A.W.N. network, which tracks mentions of drug use recorded during visits to Emergency Rooms, marijuana-related visits have been on the rise of late, surpassing the number of Emergency Room visits attributed to heroin. The potency of marijuana has gone up considerably over the years, and the potent strains are really all that users should use, just in small quantities. In large quantities, marijuana can make doing nothing seem like the most important thing a person could be doing. It doesn't appear to permanently change kids into unmotivated kids, but it can sure unmotivate them for a time. The initial effects of the drug last for a few hours, but alterations in mood and even some cognitive functions, like memory and attention, can linger for a day or so. For this reason, daily use amounts to creating a drug state that persists round the clock. As with alcohol, there appears to be a genetic component to marijuana dependence. A recent study examined the DNA of kids with and without dependency on the drug, and found that there is a particular type of gene associated with dependence as well as another associated with use but no dependence. Around 12% of the sample had the putative dependence-risk-enhancing gene.

Despite differences between the drugs with regard to their specific effects on the brain, the behavioral output produced by them can overlap greatly, meaning that the combination of the two can spell real trouble for some people in some situations. Alcohol and marijuana both produce memory impairments and both make it dangerous to drive, though for slightly different reasons. Alcohol impairs the ability to brake quickly and engage in all but primitive evasive maneuvers. It has the paradoxical effect of impairing the ability to recognize when one is driving poorly and increasing confidence that one can drive well. Marijuana makes it easy for drivers to be distracted and research suggests that young drivers in particular are susceptible to wrecking cars when their attention is divided. Marijuana might make it less likely that a driver recognizes a crash is about to occur and that evasive maneuvers are necessary. The combination of alcohol, marijuana and driving is entirely unsafe. While many people view both drugs as truth serums of sorts, neither is. Alcohol does not make it more likely that people will express honest emotions and marijuana alone will not unlock the secrets of the universe for you.

If one had to be chosen as the riskiest for developing kids, it might just be a flip of the coin. If the issue were forced, alcohol would likely emerge as the more dangerous due to the fact that it can kill directly and has profound toxic effects on developing brains, though early research suggests that regular use of marijuana during the teen years might alter how the brain develops, too. For adults, both drugs appear to be fine when used wisely, in moderation, by healthy people, and not when important decisions have to be made or when one is responsible for the safety of others. For kids, both drugs can become sinkholes for time, attention, energy and money, and pull them away from the real task of learning to thrive in the world. As such, we should do everything we can to dissuade use of either drug until adulthood.

What does it all mean?

It seems that multiple developmental changes converge during adolescence and increase the odds that substance use will occur then. Teens are built to explore, take some chances, push away from authority, and try out different identities until they find one that fits. At some point during all of this, many teens, but not all, experiment with substances of one type or another – most commonly alcohol. Fortunately, most kids do not get hooked, arrested, or injured as a result of experimentation with drugs, and move on without any serious damage. Others and their families are not so lucky. For them, there are options.

Understanding the intra- and inter-personal factors that contribute to teen drug use can help us create better safety nets for our kids and minimize the odds that drugs will become an ever present facet of their lives. For those kids who have already crossed over the line from experimentation to regular use, a variety of out-patient and in-patient treatment options are available and can be successful in many cases.

It is critical to keep drug use during adolescence in perspective. We should all be concerned about the easy access that kids have to drugs, including many made by pharmaceutical companies. We should also be concerned about the damage that drug abuse can do to developing adolescents, their families, and the surrounding communities. But drug use is only one of many categories of risk, and focusing disproportionately on the problem of adolescent drug use can distract us from addressing other issues and from promoting activities that actually support healthy development. Drug use can be bad for kids and adults, but simply avoiding drugs does not guarantee health! That requires activities aimed at actually promoting health. In the end, the best strategy for keeping kids off of the slippery slopes of drug use might be to put resources into creating healthier environments for kids in general. It might not be possible to prevent all experimentation with drugs during adolescence, but much can be done to prevent such use from becoming problematic.

Quick Facts:

- For many teens, drug use kills several birds with one stone – exploration, attainment of social reinforcement, and escape from the stress of daily living.

- Most teens that dabble in drugs make it through adolescence unscathed. However, others aren't so lucky.

- Generally, adolescents with serious drug problems do not set out to develop them. The first use of a particular drug places them on a slippery slope. Repeated use of the drug causes them to begin sliding down. Most kids are unaware they're in trouble until it's too late.

- Once drug use has begun and is detected, and if it's a problem, there are a variety of ways in which parents can proceed, including the use of inpatient and/or outpatient treatment programs.

- As is the case with adults, quitting is often the easy part for adolescents. The tough part is staying quit.

- By keeping kids busy and reinforcing healthy decision making, it is possible to help kids build enough positive momentum that they make it out of the adolescent years with using or abusing substances.

Chapter 7

Rethinking underage drinking – What science says about the risks and how to minimize them

Alcohol use is pervasive among adolescents in the U.S. Despite a minimum legal drinking age of 21, roughly two-thirds of high school seniors report having been drunk. One-third sees no great risk in consuming 4 or 5 drinks per day, everyday. Underage drinking costs taxpayers an estimated $60 billion each year, three times the amount spent on alcohol by underage drinkers. If alcohol were a benign drug, teen drinking wouldn't be a big cause for concern, but it's not benign – particularly for teens. Alcohol plays a prominent role in the three leading causes of death among adolescents and young adults (unintentional injury, homicide, and suicide). By a margin of about 6 to 1, alcohol consumption accounts for more deaths among adolescents than all other drugs combined. The use of alcohol by teens is associated with many other risky behaviors and bad outcomes, including sexual assault, violence, unintended pregnancy, and use of other drugs. Little progress has been made toward addressing the problem on a national level, though levels of use have declined slightly in recent years. The alcohol industry has been given a long leash to target kids with both television and print advertising, simply claiming that any appeal their ads have to kids under 21 is purely accidental. The industry has been exempt from the efforts of the official War on Drugs. Where does alcohol come from and how did it get so popular? How big of a problem is it for adolescents, including college students? What ought we do about it? We will address those questions and others in this chapter.

Alcohol is the world's intoxicant of choice, and has been for thousands of years.[1] Drinking predates written history by a long shot. Clay vessels with wine residue in them were discovered recently in Northern China and date back to 7000 B.C., revealing that humans have been intentionally fermenting and bottling alcohol for at least 9000 years. The first known writing sample dates back to about 3500 B.C., meaning that our ancestors were drinking alcohol for quite some time before they could even write about it. In what is now western Iran, wine and beer were made and bottled as early as 5400 B.C. Distillation was added around 1000 B.C., giving us the categories of beer, wine, and liquor that we enjoy today.

When the European colonists set sail for the new world, they brought with them a culture of drinking and an ample supply of booze to sustain them for the long journey. Once arriving, they quickly set about the task of making more. Modern America was founded by drinkers. Sociologist Dr. David Hanson provides the following facts:[2]

- The Mayflower carried more beer than water on its voyage to the New World.
- There wasn't a single abstainer among the original signers of the Declaration of Independence.
- George Washington, Benjamin Franklin, and Thomas Jefferson made their own alcohol.
- Thomas Jefferson wrote the first draft of the Declaration of Independence in a tavern.

In the centuries since the colonists arrived, Americans have enjoyed a love-hate relationship with alcohol. Mostly love. The 18th amendment prevented citizens from drinking between the years of 1919 and 1933. During these "Prohibition" years, the only way to obtain alcohol legally was by getting a prescription for distilled spirits written by a doctor and filled at a pharmacy. For the most part, the American Medical Association opposed prohibition, primarily because, at the time, alcohol was used as a medicine for several conditions. Indeed, it was the preferred treatment for snake bites, and appears to have been the cause of death for many snake bite victims.

Prohibition caused small decreases in consumption, but generally failed to achieve its objectives.[3] The hope was that outlawing alcohol would make society safer and healthier, but it ended up doing the opposite. There was a decrease in documented liver disease, but the social costs of that health effect were staggering. Until prohibition, going to bars was primarily a male dominated activity. Now that everyone had to hide their drinking, women were invited to the bars, too. People started making their own alcohol, called bathtub booze, often with disastrous, and poisonous, consequences. Murder rates skyrocketed at the beginning of prohibition and came back down after prohibition was repealed in 1933.

In the years since prohibition, drinking levels in America have fluctuated greatly, reaching a peak of about 2.75 *gallons* of alcohol per person 14+ in the late 1970s and declining thereafter. In the present day, Americans consume more than 60 billion servings of beer, 13 billion servings of wine, and 29 billion servings of distilled spirits each year. That's still a lot of alcohol!

During the 1970s, research began to reveal that alcohol produces a litany of deleterious effects on health, including effects on the brain. Alcohol is a neurotoxin, a substance capable of injuring cells in the brain. It also blocks the ability of the brain to change with experience, often leaving holes, known as *blackouts*, in one's memory.

Alcohol is particularly bad for developing brains, as it prevents circuits from forming correctly. Any circuits forming when alcohol is present might not form at all. This can have disastrous consequences depending upon which circuits are developing when alcohol enters the brain. When the brains of unborn children are exposed to alcohol, the drug can interfere with normal brain development in the womb, leading to cognitive deficits and sometimes anatomical abnormalities. These realizations led to swift changes in how we view the relationship between alcohol and pregnancy, and led to widespread reductions in drinking while pregnant. Early indicators suggest that a similar shift is underway with regard to drinking during the teen years, given evidence that the teen brain is still developing and that alcohol could interfere with that development.

What is "underage drinking"?

After prohibition, most states adopted a minimum drinking age of 21 to restrict access to alcohol for young people. At the time that America was colonized by Europeans, the concept of underage drinking didn't exist. Everyone drank, often out of necessity due to poor water quality. That all changed during the 20th century with the growing realization of the dangers posed by alcohol and the enacting of laws preventing people under certain ages from drinking legally. In essence, such laws amount to age-related prohibition, but with good reason.

In July of 1971, the 26th amendment to the constitution lowered the voting age to 18. Based partly on the logic that, if kids are old enough to die for their country they should be old to drink, 29 states lowered their drinking ages to 18 or 19. In 1984, President Reagan signed the National Minimum Drinking Age Act, and by 1987 all 50 states had raised the legal drinking age to 21. Failure to conform would have cost states a substantial amount of Federal highway funding.

The appropriate legal drinking age remains a matter of debate to this day. As this book is being written, a movement is afoot to stimulate discussion of the legal age 21 issue. In an oped column written for the New York Times, former Middlebury College president, Dr. John McCardell, argued that problems with excessive drinking on college campuses might be ameliorated if the legal drinking age were lowered. Dr. McCardell's organization, *Choose Responsibility*,[4] is sponsoring seminars and policy forums on college campuses across the U.S. in an effort to promote a data-driven discussion of the pros and cons of a legal age of 21.

From a purely neuroscientific standpoint, the drinking age should probably be raised to 25, rather than lowered to 18. Still, not everyone bases their viewpoints on data from the field of neuropsychology, and even the most compelling scientific perspective does not necessarily carry the day in public policy or law. Dr. McCardell argues that the legal age of 21 has failed to achieve its main objectives – keeping young people safe. He points out that, while fewer people under 21 probably drink than would if the age were lower than 21, those who drink underage often go way overboard and do so more quickly than they would if they were able to drink in public. As we will see, drinking a lot of alcohol in a short period of time can be a recipe for disaster.

Dr. McCardell and his group make several compelling arguments for lowering the drinking age. Ultimately, the argument hinges on the assumption that we could do a better job of getting adolescents to make responsible choices around alcohol if we lowered the age at which they could drink, legally. If the age were lowered to 18, we could begin to have candid discussions with young people about how to drink safely and wisely.

At present, there seems to be little doubt that the movement to lower the drinking age is premature. The Choose Responsibility website includes the following statement:

"Alcohol is a reality in the lives of young Americans. It cannot be denied, ignored, or legislated away."

Yes. This is true. The presence of alcohol in young people's lives cannot be denied, ignored, or legislated away, and the statement seems to argue strongly against trying to approach the problem by messing with legislation regarding the legal age of access.

How alcohol affects the body is not culturally bound. Whether the drinking age is moved up or down, the fact remains that those who start drinking at young ages seem to be at greater risk of developing dependence. With that said, there are several alcohol-related variables that can be influenced by culture. For instance, how aggressively a person drinks, how often they drink, and how they act when they drink can all be influenced by learning.

As we will discuss throughout the current chapter, it appears that the culture here in the U.S. plays a prominent role in fueling our current problems with excessive drinking by some young people. If the culture were to change in substantial ways, and teens were raised with a greater sense of personal responsibility and restraint, perhaps the drinking age could be lowered by a few years or even removed altogether. However, at present, simply lowering the drinking age would probably prove disastrous, particularly early on, and would stand in direct opposition to the implications of recent research on alcohol and adolescent development.

The author agrees with the intentions of the Choose Responsibility movement. However, before we consider lowering the legal drinking age so that kids can *choose* responsibility, we need to make stronger efforts to *promote* responsibility. At present, there is simply no reason to expect that, in the current cultural climate, lowering the legal age would be of any real benefit. Cultural changes, and more science regarding the age-dependent effects of alcohol, should precede any further tinkering with the minimum legal drinking age.

The cost of underage drinking

Despite substantial changes in U.S. alcohol use during the past century, alcohol use by adolescents continues to cause serious problems. Teen drinking contributes to ruined relationships, pregnancies, the spread of sexually transmitted infections, wrecked cars, injuries, and death. The National Institute of Alcoholism and Alcohol Abuse (NIAAA) estimates that alcohol kills 6.5 times more kids under 21 than all other drugs combined.

The National Center on Addiction and Substance Abuse at Columbia University (CASA) estimates that roughly 1/4 of all underage drinkers (relative to 1/10 adults) meet the criteria for abuse or dependence. CASA also estimates that, in 2005, alcohol abuse and addiction among Americans, young and old, cost tax payers roughly $220 billion. They contrast this value with the yearly cost of cancer ($196 billion) and obesity ($133 billion). How much of that cost can be attributed to underage drinking? Researchers at the Pacific Institute for Research and Evaluation (PIRE) estimate that underage drinking alone costs taxpayers $62 billion annually. By their estimate, each $1 that kids spend on alcohol ends up costing the country $3. The money shelled out by taxpayers each year to clean up the damage caused by alcohol is in addition to the $120 billion or so spent on the products! Researchers at CASA and PIRE place underage alcohol sales at roughly $20 billion. That's a lot of money! Far more money than is available for alcohol abuse education and prevention efforts.

Promising signs that the situation might be improving

On a positive note, data from the most recent National Youth Risk Behavior Survey (NYRBS), conducted by the Centers for Disease Control (CDC), shows some promising trends. In a nutshell, the data suggest that the percentage of students actively drinking (one or more drinks in the previous month), as well as the percentage engaging in heavy episodic drinking (five or more drinks in a row), has declined. Data from the 2006 Monitoring the Future (MTF) study paint a similar picture, though the declines in drinking are less obvious.[5]

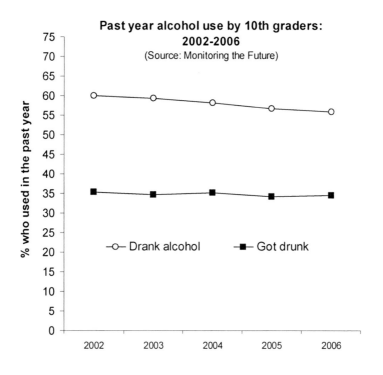

The graph above displays the percentage of 10th graders that drank in the year before the survey, as well as the percentage of 10th graders reporting that they got drunk in the year before the survey.

The topic of underage drinking is a complicated one, but the bottom line is simple – alcohol is a dangerous drug, particularly for teenagers whose brains, including the cognitive control centers that allow for good decision making, are nowhere near finished developing. There is nothing wrong with moderate, responsible drinking during adulthood, nor with the occasional overindulgence if done with a little foresight. The trick is figuring out how to convey the truth about alcohol to our teens in such a way that they recognize the importance of waiting until their brains have finished growing before deciding whether to start drinking. Doing so will require all of us to take a close look at ourselves, at the unmet needs of today's teens, at the alcohol industry, and at our policies regarding underage drinking.

Effectively dealing with the underage drinking issue requires knowing the facts. Not just facts about how many people drink and how much, but facts about what alcohol is and how it works. We will now backup a little bit and discuss these issues. After we have covered the basics about alcohol and how it works, we will return to our discussion about the impact of alcohol on adolescent health and examine strategies for using the information in this chapter to help keep kids safe.

Alcohol the drug

There are several different types of alcohol, but ethyl alcohol, the kind in beverages, is the only kind that is relatively safe to drink. All alcohols can kill you – ethyl alcohol (the beverage kind) just kills you more slowly!

Alcohol is a product of fermentation – a process by which yeast gobble up sugar and give off alcohol as a waste product. Tossing yeast into a container with wet sugar, or just waiting until spores of yeast simply land in the concoction, is all that's really necessary to make alcohol. The amount of alcohol found in the brew will vary depending on the amount of sugar and the length of time that elapses. Yeast can't live in an environment with more than about 14% alcohol, so 14% alcohol – about the concentration in many wines – is the upper limit for naturally fermented beverages.

The alcohol content of beers varies considerably, but, on average, is in the 5% range. Concentrations of alcohol in liquor, or distilled spirits, can approach 95% in some cases, but tend to average around 40% (80 proof). Distilled spirits are made by heating a fermented mash and running the steam through a length of tubing where it condenses and drips into a bottle. The basic premise is that the alcohol vaporizes at a lower temperature than water, so the condensate in the tubing contains a higher concentration of alcohol than the original fermented concoction.

SideNotes

Proof and percent – It's all about concentration

The alcohol content in liquor is either expressed as a percentage or in terms of "proof." Proof is double the percentage – so vodka with 40% alcohol can be said to be 80 proof. Why? The story goes that British soldiers would test the alcohol content of their rations by mixing the alcohol with gunpowder and setting it on fire. Alcohol has to be at least 50% in order to burn in this case. So, if it burned, that was considered proof that it was a legitimate ration. Thus, 50% alcohol conveyed 100% proof.

Alcoholic beverages come in many shapes, sizes, concentrations, and types. This can make it difficult for an individual to keep track of how much alcohol they actually consume. Other countries, like Australia, have taken the important step of requiring alcoholic beverage containers to state, specifically, how many servings of alcohol they contain. This is consistent with the ways in which foods and other beverages are labeled to describe the numbers of servings per container and other important information related to the possible health consequences of consuming them, and would be an excellent idea for alcohol-containing beverages here in the U.S.

The need for greater awareness of the alcohol content of drinks is illustrated by some research that the author and his colleagues have done showing that college students tend to over-pour their drinks. They make the largest errors when pouring liquor, but also over-pour beer and wine. This is particularly unnerving given that women tend to drink mixed drinks more often than males, and it's very easy to pour far more than one serving of liquor into a mixed drink. Other researchers have found that people in the general public also pour drinks that are larger than they think.

Below is a graphic showing standard drink equivalents. Each of the beverages is a single serving and contains the same amount of pure alcohol (0.6 oz) as the others. Please keep in mind that there is no universal "standard" drink. What matters is that a single serving of each type of drink contains equivalent amounts of alcohol so that the total number of drinks can be tracked.

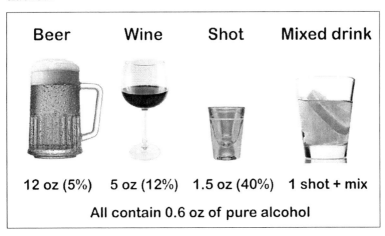

Beer	Wine	Shot	Mixed drink
12 oz (5%)	5 oz (12%)	1.5 oz (40%)	1 shot + mix

All contain 0.6 oz of pure alcohol

If you are an adult and you drink, please keep the above values in mind. It is common to hear that moderate drinking – up to one or two drinks per day (one for a woman or two for a man) – can help prevent cardiovascular disease, which is more or less true. However, for women, anything over one drink per day can increase the risk of breast cancer. So, if you have one glass of wine each night, but the glass happens to hold 32 ounces, you could be doing more harm than good!

What about those new fruity-flavored products from Skyy, Smirnoff, and other names? The ones many argue were created to draw in young female drinkers. Where do they fit? Most of them contain about 5% alcohol, on par with beer. This is no accident – they are more like Mountain Dew with alcohol added to them than actual beer. The manufacturers can put in exactly how much alcohol they want. The real difference between normal beer and so-called "malternative" beverages, beyond taste, is the calorie content. While a standard beer, such as a can of Budweiser, contains about 140 calories, sugary drinks, like Smirnoff Ice, contain well over 200 calories! That's about as much as a candy bar.

For those who are weight conscious, even moderate drinking can pack on the pounds. Let's say a person has two standard drinks, each 200 calories, every day. During a one month period, that adds up to 5600 calories, or roughly 1.5 pounds of extra body fat! Over a 12 month period, those two drinks would add up to 18 pounds of added weight. Any potential benefit a few drinks could have for heart health is quickly undone by the deleterious effects of added body weight on the cardiovascular system.

What does alcohol do to the body?

When we drink alcohol, it enters the stomach, mixes with food (if any is present), and eventually gets emptied into the small intestine. It is here, not the stomach, that most of the alcohol is absorbed into the blood. Once it gets into the blood stream it makes a pass through the liver before being pumped throughout the body.

As soon as alcohol enters the body, the liver goes to work getting rid of it. An enzyme called alcohol dehydrogenase breaks alcohol down into acetaldehyde, which is toxic. From there, acetaldehyde dehydrogenase breaks the acetaldehyde down into acetate and water. How long this takes depends on a person's liver. In general, it takes about 90 minutes to get rid of the alcohol in a single drink but, as the chart on the next page reveals, these numbers vary a lot depending on factors like sex and weight.

Interestingly, alcohol actually competes with other drugs for the attention of the liver, which means that drinking while taking other drugs can cause unexpected and undesirable consequences. For instance, those who take Tylenol or other acetaminophen-containing products while they drink are at a heightened risk of liver damage. The reason is that alcohol competes with acetaminophen for metabolism, causing levels of toxic byproducts of acetaminophen metabolism to build up and reach potentially damaging levels as the liver tries to process the alcohol.

The amount of alcohol in a person's system can be measured in a variety of ways – most commonly through blood or breath. Alcohol is a very small molecule, small enough to travel anywhere in the body that water goes. Unlike a lot of drugs, alcohol mixes easily with both water and fat. Some drugs, like Ritalin, mix most easily in water. Others, like THC (the psychoactive agent in marijuana), mix most easily in fat. The presence of both fat-loving and water-loving components allows alcohol to travel more freely throughout the body than some other drugs, and to distribute itself pretty evenly, including in and around the brain and lungs.

After a person drinks, a small amount of alcohol comes out, unchanged, in their breath. By having that person exhale a specific volume of air – a standard amount used for all breath alcohol readings on a particular device – the amount of alcohol contained in the sample can be measured and used to calculate how much alcohol there is in the person's body. This value, called a blood alcohol concentration (BAC), is important for several reasons. Laws regarding drinking and driving incorporate BAC levels. Every state in the country uses 0.08% as the legal threshold for adults and, technically, 0.00% for people under 21. It is illegal for people under 21 to drive with any detectable alcohol in their systems. To cover the error margins of the breathalyzers used to asses BACs, many states use a threshold of 0.02% for people under 21 rather than 0.00%, but the policy is still considered zero tolerance.

Blood Alcohol Concentrations (BAC) resulting from a single drink in males and females of different weights and how long it will take the body to get rid of it

Weight	Males		Females	
	BAC from one drink	Time to get rid of it (in hrs)	BAC from one drink	Time to get rid of it (in hrs)
100 lbs	0.043	2.5	0.051	3.0
125 lbs	0.034	2.0	0.041	2.4
150 lbs	0.029	1.7	0.034	2.0
175 lbs	0.025	1.4	0.029	1.7
200 lbs	0.022	1.3	0.025	1.5

BAC values also allow for educated guesses about a person's level of impairment. Certain affects on the brain and behavior tend to emerge or peak at certain BAC levels. There is quite a bit of variability in the impact of alcohol on individuals, so there are no set rules with regard to when a given person will start to stumble, slur words, vomit, etcetera. Just guidelines. The table below breaks down what to expect at increasing BAC levels.

	Drinks in one hour		The effects of alcohol at different BAC levels and the number of drinks it takes to get there

| BAC (%) | Drinks in one hour | | Effects on behavior and bodily functions |
	125lb female	150lb male	
0.02	0.5	0.75	Illegal to drive in every state if you are under 21
			Drowsiness (sleepiness) begins, attention is impaired
0.03-0.04	1.0	1.5	Driving is definitely impaired at this level
			Vision, balance, and hand-eye coordination are impaired
0.05-0.06	1.5	2	Reaction time, perception, and memory are impaired
0.07	1.75	2.5	All driving-related skills are dangerously impaired by this level
			Nausea and perhaps vomiting at this level and up
0.08	2	3	Illegal to drive in all states even if 21+
0.10	2.5	3.5	Approx 10-15X more likely to die in a car crash than when sober
0.15	3.75	5	Almost 400 times more likely to get into crash than when sober
0.30	7.25	10	Memory blackouts very common at this level and up. Many college students over the years have died with BACs between 0.30 and 0.40
0.40-0.50	10	14	Estimated that 50 out of 100 people would die from an overdose

The BAC values in the table were calculated assuming that all drinks were consumed within one hour and the BAC reading was taken at the end of the hour. In real life, a drinker's BAC level at any given time depends on several factors – including sex and weight, how much they had to eat before drinking, how quickly they consumed their drinks, whether their livers are healthy, etcetera. Women reach higher BACs than men after each drink due in part to lower levels of an enzyme that breaks some of the alcohol down before it ever gets absorbed into the blood. Women also achieve higher BACs than men because women have less available water in their bodies. The less body water a person has, the higher the concentration of alcohol there will be within it. Regardless of whether one is male or female, drinking on an empty stomach allows the alcohol to get into the body faster, raising the BAC higher than it would go if the person had a Big Mac before their Budweiser. Similarly, drinking beverages with high alcohol concentrations, like shots, allows the alcohol to be absorbed more quickly than if the person drinks a beer.

Once inside the blood stream, and distributed to various organs, alcohol has so many different effects that it is more like a shotgun blast than a precise hit. It is what we might call a "dirty" drug, because rather than bind cleanly with specific receptors to produce effects, like most drugs do, alcohol interacts with brain cells in a variety of ways and produces widespread changes throughout the brain. There are few brain areas, or brain functions, not affected in a negative way by alcohol. Indeed, at high enough levels, alcohol can actually shut off important centers in the brain necessary for keeping us alive.

The case of Rahim Bathe, a Duke student who died of an overdose in 1999, serves as an example of how hard alcohol hits the brain. Rahim returned home from a night of drinking with his friends with a belly full of alcohol. He put himself to bed.

However, at some point during the night, it seems the alcohol concentration in his brain reached a level sufficient to cause his body to vomit – a last ditch effort to purge the body of poisons. Tragically, the alcohol content was also high enough to severely inhibit the area responsible for alerting him when something like vomit was blocking his airway. As a result, he inhaled some of his own vomit and eventually contracted aspiration pneumonia, a deadly condition that occurs when bacteria enter the lungs. Rahim died a week later. His mother, Catherine Bathe, has since become a vocal proponent of education and prevention initiatives on college campuses and now serves as vice-president of a non-profit organization called *Security on Campus*. Coming from a good family, getting into a good college, being a good kid, and having a wonderful mother are not sufficient to protect one from the deadly effects of high doses of alcohol. The physiological effects of alcohol on brain activity are unrelated to the quality of one's upbringing or current environment.

The deaths of two students at Colorado schools in the fall of 2004 are hauntingly similar. Samantha Spady and Lynn Gordon "Gordie" Bailey were young, healthy students who drank too much and died after shutting down crucial centers within their brains. The tragedy involving Gordie Bailey is the focus of a documentary called *Haze*, which is due to be released in the spring of 2008.[7] His death was particularly horrendous, as the fraternity members that urged him to drink the lethal dose of alcohol he consumed that night also wrote racial slurs and other comments on his body in marker, and then tried to wipe them off after they found him dead the following morning.

In short, alcohol is a toxic drug. But it also causes brain changes that, for many, create a pleasant buzz. For this, and other reasons, alcohol has a high potential for abuse and dependence, with minimal medicinal benefits. Sounds much more like a DEA Schedule II drug than a legal and recreational compound that can be purchased at gas stations in many states. Indeed, if alcohol were not already a legally available product, it is inconceivable that it would survive as either a prescription or non-prescription drug in today's litigious climate. Even in an era of oft-cited and readily apparent corruption in the FDA, the financial power of the alcohol industry would not be sufficient to earn alcohol approval as an over-the-counter or prescription product. It would go right into the poison category.

Given the popularity of alcohol among adults, and its legal status for those over a particular age-limit, it is easy to get. The billions of dollars spent each year by beverage manufacturers to promote their products ensure that consumers, both young and old, will keep consuming them. Danger or no danger, alcohol is here to stay.

Fortunately, most young people do not die when they drink. However, it is becoming clear that alcohol produces very significant impairments in thinking, as well as memory formation, at far lower doses than those necessary to cause death. For the author, one of the most fascinating and truly frightening consequences of overindulgence is the alcohol-induced memory blackout.

Blackouts – An example of the powerful effects of alcohol on the brain

Most people know someone – maybe even you – who has woken up after a night of drinking unsure about what happened the night before. These memory lapses are called "blackouts." Blackouts are more common than many people think – particularly among young people. They are so common, in fact, that people don't really seem to make a big deal out of them unless something really bad happens. In

> **Blackout** – Inability of the brain to record memories for places a person goes or things they do while intoxicated but still conscious.

reality, blackouts are no laughing matter and actually represent a serious neurological event. To put them in context, if you fell and hit your head hard enough to induce a memory deficit, or had a seizure that caused a memory gap, your doctor would order a full neurological workup immediately, and probably an MRI scan of your brain, as well.

Blackouts are periods of amnesia during which a person actively engages in behaviors (e.g., walking, talking) but their brain is unable to create a memory trail for the events.[8] This is quite different from "passing out," which means either falling asleep from excessive drinking or literally drinking oneself unconscious. Blackouts are gray areas of consciousness in which one functions but will not later recall having done so. Blackouts are common. A study conducted by the author and colleagues in 2002 indicated that, at one selective university, 50% of all students who had ever consumed alcohol had experienced at least one blackout in their short drinking careers. Of those who drank in the year before the study, 40% experienced a blackout during that period. Finally, of those who drank in the two weeks before the study, 1 in 10 had at least once blackout. These are alarming numbers given the neurological severity of a blackout. If 1 in 10 students experienced a concussion with memory loss at least once every two weeks, there would be very serious concern for their well-being.

All blackouts are not the same, and are differentiated based on their severity. *En bloc* blackouts represent a complete inability to recall events that occurred during a given period of time. Memories for some portion of the evening's events are missing in their entirety – like film on the cutting room floor. The memories are never formed and so no amount of digging will uncover them. They don't exist. *Fragmentary blackouts* are less severe and are characterized by spotty, or fragmented, memories of events. Fragmentary blackouts are far more common than the en bloc type. More often than not, a drinker who blacks out remembers some details of events but not others, and perhaps not enough to make sense of what transpired. In the case of fragmentary blackouts, probing one's memory can often jog recall of some of the missing pieces.

From a neurological standpoint, blackouts are fascinating for several reasons. They cause an inability to form *new* memories but spare the ability to remember things that happened *before* the blackout began. Because of this, even in the midst of a blackout, a person can carry on conversations, drive a car, even tell stories about events that happened earlier while they were intoxicated but not yet in the memory vacuum. Outside observers are typically unaware that an individual is in a blackout. The person in a blackout might not even appear to be very intoxicated. They are present yet vacant at the same time, engaging in experiences that won't have staying power for them, even if they have staying power for those around them.

Anything a person can do while they're drunk and not blacked out, they can do while they're blacked out – they just won't remember it the next day. This includes anything from the mundane, like brushing one's teeth, to the insane, like murder or jumping off of an apartment complex roof into a swimming pool. The author once worked with an undergraduate, now doing his medical residency, who loved to drink but frequently experienced blackouts when he did so. Indeed, this student participated in a story about underage drinking and teen brain development written for Discover magazine in 2001. In the article, he went by the name "Chuck," which is the name he gave the alter ego that often emerged when he drank too much. The litany of things Chuck did during blackouts without getting killed or arrested was astonishing. A trip to Mardi Gras comes to mind. Our young friend recalls being in a bar buying a round of drinks. The next memory he formed was upon awaking in a car full of strangers in a different state. Upon demanding an explanation, he was told that the idea was his, and that he had somehow convinced the group to take the drive. It is easy to see how this could be very funny – if it weren't so dangerous.

Unfortunately, the events that transpire during blackouts are not always benign. During his research, the author has learned of blackouts encompassing events ranging from vandalism to sexual assaults. The number of young women who awaken to be told that they had engaged in sexual intercourse, but with no recollection of the event itself or the events leading up to the sex, is impossible to know for certain, but is high. This is one of the truly tragic aspects of alcohol misuse among students and underscores the life-altering impact of blackouts for some young drinkers. In the aforementioned 2002 study of blackouts among college students, 25% of respondents indicated that they had engaged in some type of sexual activity during a night of drinking and had to be told about it later. Sexual activity is a very memorable event, at least it should be, and to not remember something of that magnitude is a good indicator of the suppressive effects that alcohol can have on brain circuits.

From the sidelines, the author has watched several court cases unfold in which either the alleged victim or alleged perpetrator of a rape did not recall what happened. The most common scenario is as follows – A young male and female, both drinking, have intercourse. The female has no recollection, and is therefore uncertain whether the sex was apparently consensual (that is, it seemed to be consensual from the male's perspective) or if an intentional rape occurred. Charges are brought against the young male and the courts are left to decide what happened. Sometimes, the evidence suggests that rape occurred. Other times, it seems that the young male, intoxicated himself, was convinced by the female's actions that she was giving him consent. In some cases, eye witness testimony from credible sources suggests that the female involved actually initiated the interaction. In some cases, it appears the male was completely aware of the female's compromised state and knowingly committed rape.

The issue of alcohol and sex, in general, must be dealt with more aggressively and honestly through alcohol education and prevention initiatives and discussions between parents and teens. Regardless of what happens in the movies, and the fact that alcohol ads tell us that drinking and sex go together like peanut butter and jelly, it is never acceptable to take advantage of a person's intoxicated state to facilitate sex. It is also not acceptable to feed someone drinks in the hope that it will increase the odds of having sex. It is not only morally wrong, it is illegal. These are facts that are not often conveyed to young people until after they have started drinking, and many find out the hard way after making bad choices around the issue of alcohol and sex, or falling prey to someone else's bad choices.

Importantly, even at levels of intoxication sufficient to produce blackouts, alcohol does not erase knowledge of the rules of right and wrong. Thus, not remembering what one did is no excuse for doing obnoxious, dangerous or criminal things.

Over the years, the author and his colleagues have received countless e-mails from people struggling with guilt after acting out of character during a blackout. People who are told they did offensive things, yet have no memory of doing them, are often concerned that they might be losing their minds – that an alternate and devious personality might be lurking below the surface. One impetus for this guilt is the widespread misperception that alcohol makes us act more like our true selves. Clearly, this is not the case! If it were, the CIA would use vodka in interrogations and alcohol would save marriages not ruin them. Ultimately, we are still responsible for the behaviors we engage in while drunk, whether we can remember them or not, but there is no reason to expect that those behaviors are necessarily accurate representations of our true selves.

What does alcohol do to the brain to produce blackouts?

It appears that alcohol shuts down circuits in the hippocampus, a brain area that plays a very important role in making memories for what happens in our day-to-day lives. Information coming from both the outside environment and the inside environment is sent to the neocortex, a layer of tissue blanketing the top of the brain. Eventually, this information is funneled down into the hippocampus, where it enters a loop of circuitry that sends it back out to the neocortex and to several important brain areas that influence our emotional states. Somehow, this process results in a relatively choppy and selective recording of our daily lives. (As an exercise, rather than seeing how much you can remember from childhood, think about all of the events for which you really have no memory at all!)

Research suggests that a key part of the memory-making process involves the opening of pores, or passageways, that allow for a trickle of calcium atoms to enter neurons in the hippocampus. This trickle of calcium sets off a cascade of changes that leads to potentially permanent alterations in how the neurons look, work and with whom they communicate. Experiences are stored as a result and the brain uses these stored experiences to modify future behavior. Alcohol prevents the calcium pores from opening completely, thus preventing the calcium influx and, presumably, any memories that would have been made at that time are either degraded, incomplete, or completely missing.

By interfering with how these memory circuits work, alcohol creates a void into which the incoming information about what's happening simply disappears. Even if the information gets through the loop, it isn't going to be recorded without the calcium, or at least that's what the research suggests.

Several laboratory studies using rat brains suggest that alcohol blocks the opening of calcium channels in the hippocampus more effectively in adolescent brains than adult brains. As a result, smaller amounts of alcohol are needed to disrupt activity in the memory circuits of young, developing brains than adult brains.[9] Assuming this is also true in humans, it could help explain why blackouts are so incredibly common among adolescent drinkers, and would serve as yet another example of how dangerous alcohol can be for young people. If any other drug, over the

---

SideNotes

Could a person commit murder during a blackout and not know it?

Donal Sweeney is a physician with decades of experience studying blackouts in clinical practice. His interpretation of the literature is different than the author's, but his book, "The Alcohol Blackout: Walking, Talking, Unconscious & Lethal," is well worth reading. In it Dr. Sweeney discusses several fascinating anecdotes about blackouts. In one passage, he recounts his interview with a young man sitting in prison for two murders apparently committed during a blackout. The young man was drinking at a bar with friends until they decided to move on. On the way to their next destination, he crashed his car into a guardrail. His passengers headed back to the bar, but he decided to walk home. He recalls nothing else until awakening in bed, in his parents' home, naked, with no clue where his clothes were. A few days later, the news reported that a husband and wife were stabbed to death in the bedroom of their home. The young man's drunken walk would have taken him near the home, the young man and his family once lived in that home, and the slain couple slept in the young man's old room. Could he have done it? A few years later, while attending an Alcoholics Anonymous meeting, the young man told the story and disclosed his fear that he could have been the killer. Someone relayed the story to police, who discovered that his prints matched those found in dried blood in the murdered couple's room.

counter or prescription, carried even a small risk of causing amnesia, both the public and the FDA would be up in arms. So far, this has not yet been the case with alcohol.

Make it a night you won't forget, not one you can't remember

Malternative beverage advertisement circa 2004
By providing such a warning to consumers, the manufacturer acknowledged that their products can shut down memory centers in the brain and produce temporary amnesia. The ad suggests this would happen if a person had six servings rather than two. How quickly the blood alcohol level rises is key here, but six could certainly do it!

Research suggests that there are several factors that can increase one's risk of blacking out, in addition to having a young developing brain. Anything that causes a person's BAC to rise quickly and reach a high level puts one at risk. The BAC rises quickly when lots of alcohol gets into the bloodstream at once. This could mean drinking on an empty stomach, doing shots, chugging beers, or all three. Being a female is also a risk factor for several reasons, some of them cultural and some biological. In today's society, females are more likely to drink on an empty stomach than males, and they tend to drink beverages with higher concentrations of alcohol than beer, such as mixed drinks, shots and wine. From a biological standpoint, they reach higher BACs than males after each drink due to differences in critical enzyme levels and the amount of free-floating water in the body. In all cases, the best predictor that a drinker will blackout is whether they have blacked out before. Some people seem to be very susceptible to them, while others are relatively resistant to the serious effects of alcohol on memory.

Blackouts aren't necessarily a sign of a problem with alcohol, but they are always a reason for concern. In one of the author's studies of blackouts among college students, we observed that a single blackout doesn't say much about an individual. However, students who had experienced three or more blackouts in their lifetimes had lower grade point averages, had started drinking at younger ages, were more likely to have a history of alcoholism on their father's side, and were far more likely to have had friends and/or relatives voice concerns about their drinking. Blackouts should always serve as a good reason to evaluate a person's relationship with alcohol. At the very least, a history of blackouts suggests the person is susceptible to suffering acute amnesia, which is a good reason on its own to consider altering one's drinking habits!

Alcohol use at colleges and universities

Very few topics have drawn more media attention than college drinking, particularly since more than half of college students nationwide are not legally old enough to drink. Despite what it might look like on television or movies, there is no epidemic of college alcohol abuse and the problems are not new. However, heavy drinking continues to do damage night after night on college campuses around the country. In most cases, students are able to balance drinking and school work and keep out of trouble. For others, the consequences of overindulgence while at school are disastrous.

Side*Notes*

Rohypnol ("roofies") and date-rape. Is alcohol enough?

Rohypnol is a drug that is structurally similar to Valium, but much more potent. Like Valium, Rohypnol can be lethal when combined with alcohol. In recent years, rape and other forms of sexual assault involving acquaintances and alcohol have become common. For awhile, there seemed to be good reasons to think that many attackers used the drug Rohypnol to facilitate their assaults. In England, the Association of Chief Police Officers examined 120 cases of date-rape between November, 2004 and October, 2005. They found a list of other drugs involved, but did not find any sign of Rohypnol. This certainly does not mean that rape involving Rohypnol doesn't occur, it simply suggests that it might not be as common as once feared. At least not in England. According to Det Ch Supt Dave Gee, author of the report, "The most common method of spiking drinks is alcohol."

During the past decade, the overall level of alcohol use among college students has remained relatively stable. This stability has been maintained by the migration of students into two opposing categories of drinkers – abstainers and heavy drinkers. That is, more and more students are choosing not to drink at college. However, at the same time, the proportion of students who drink excessively (three or more instances per two-week period of having 4+ drinks per occasion for females or 5+ drinks per occasion for males) has also grown.

Colleges have attempted to deal with the growing number of heavy drinkers using a wide variety of approaches. Many have chosen to employ education and prevention models like *social norming* – changing how students define normal levels of drinking – which has shown some promise at reducing overall consumption among students. Recent advances in technology have allowed for the development of highly interactive online alcohol education programs, such as *AlcoholEdu*, that combine elements of a variety of programs. Many institutions now require all incoming freshmen to complete such programs either before they arrive on campus or shortly thereafter.

The Drug-Free Schools and Campuses Regulations of 1989 require all institutions of higher education receiving Federal funds to have explicit policies aimed at combating the underage possession, distribution, and consumption of alcohol, as well as the use of other drugs. The specific policies implemented by schools vary considerably. While one might expect an increase in the strength and enforcement of policies to lead to reductions in consumption and the risky behaviors that follow, this is not always the case. In recent years, there has been an increase in the number of students receiving sanctions (e.g., fines, mandatory attendance at alcohol education classes, and community service) for violation of campus alcohol policies, yet the number of heavy drinkers and the negative consequences associated with drinking have remained stable or continued to rise. Indeed, even at schools that completely ban the use of alcohol, nearly 40% of students engage in heavy episodic, or *binge*, drinking.

Such data support conjecture that dealing with underage drinking, or any risky activity that has taken root in youth culture, requires broad and comprehensive strategies, not just the use of educational initiatives or disciplinary action.

Obviously, drinking by college students is a complex problem, and college administrators have been struggling with it for years. The limited research suggests that strict enforcement of campus drinking policies by campus security might deter underage drinking for those students living on campus. However, other studies indicate that most underage drinking occurs in off-campus housing, putting many students beyond the reach of the institution. One study indicates that roughly 37% of underage students who attend off-campus parties drink 5+ drinks, whereas only about 10% of those attending parties in dorm rooms consume alcohol at that level.[10]

On the other hand, the conventional wisdom is that many underage college students drink heavily in their dorm rooms before going out for the evening so that they can get their evening's dose of alcohol before heading out onto campus where they might not be able to drink. Many college administrators feel that this type of "front loading" leads students to consume high doses of alcohol over short periods of time – thus increasing their risk of blackouts, injuries, and other adverse effects of high alcohol doses. They would argue that if a student is going to drink five drinks, it would be better to allow them to do that on campus, over the course of a five-hour evening, than to force them to pack it into one hour of front loading behind closed doors. Similar logic led to changes allowing pubs in England to stay open all night in the hope that patrons would space their drinks rather than binge. By all accounts, the move has failed to achieve its objectives and has contributed to an increase in alcohol-related problems in the country. It turns out that patrons just stay and drink longer! There is no reason to believe that colleges would have better luck by making it easier for kids to drink, at least not in the current culture, which seems to promote and glorify drunkenness.

In-bound college students bring their drinking habits with them

Heavy underage drinking is a problem that colleges often inherit rather than create. Many heavy drinking students begin doing so well before they arrived on campus. Several studies, including some or the author's own, have reported that students' drinking habits during high school predict their drinking habits at college and their likelihood of experiencing alcohol-related consequences. Students that drink heavily during high school generally continue drinking heavily during college.

Clearly, prior to arriving at college, the responsibility for establishing and enforcing rules regarding alcohol use rests on the shoulders of the students, their parents, and the communities in which they live, not the colleges that they will later attend. Quite simply, if parents are unable to control alcohol use by their college-bound high school students, it is unreasonable to assume that the administration of a college will be able to control them once they arrive on campus. Efforts to deal with the problem must consist of more than administrative decision-making and policy enforcement. Schools need to work with both parents and communities to deal with alcohol misuse on college campuses.

Nearly all college students are legal adults, even if they are under the legal drinking age. As such, students themselves are responsible for their behaviors and any consequences that follow – not their parents and certainly not the universities they attend. The role of colleges should be to create and maintain healthy environments for all students, doing their utmost to minimize problems such as underage drinking. However, colleges cannot control the lives of their adult students and they are not responsible for the decades of experience students have before arriving on campus.

The damage done by irresponsible college drinking

As the number of heavy drinkers on campuses has increased, so has the incidence of alcohol-related problems among students. As is the case with high school students, college students experience, and cause, a wide range of negative consequences as a result of alcohol misuse.[11] Alcohol increases the odds that college students will commit crimes, including vandalism and physical assault, and non-drinkers routinely suffer from other students' irresponsible drinking. The more a student drinks the lower his or her overall GPA is likely to be. More than ½ of students in one nationwide survey reported having their studying or sleep disrupted by someone else's alcohol use. In addition, as in the larger population, drinking and driving is a problem on many campuses. Traffic crashes claim more lives than any other cause among young people, and alcohol is involved in a significant proportion of these crashes.

While these statistics are stark, and clearly indicate that alcohol misuse is a problem on college campuses, it is important to recognize that not all college students misuse alcohol. Yes, some college students drink irresponsibly and do great harm to themselves and/or others. But it is unfair to assume that all college students are drunkards. Indeed, the data tell a much different story. The majority of college students either do not drink or do so without causing problems. Indeed, African American students, whether on diverse campuses or at historically black colleges and universities, tend to drink far less than their Caucasian counterparts. However, based on media reports, it is easy to understand why so many people believe that the majority of college students drink to excess. It is virtually impossible to read the paper or turn on the news these days without hearing ominous statistics about the supposed epidemic of alcohol abuse on college campuses.

The recent legal debacle involving Duke Lacrosse players highlights many of the problems with college drinking, and the fact that small groups of people misusing alcohol can do big damage to a school, its reputation, and its relationship with the surrounding community. In the spring of 2006, the players had a raucous party at their off campus house, wedged between the University and the surrounding town. This wasn't the first loud party the players had. In fact, this small group of young men – all white except for one player – was responsible for a disproportionate number of complaints filed by citizens against Duke students in off campus housing. At this particular party, the boys hired two strippers from the area, both African-American. One of the strippers emerged from the party alleging that she had been berated, humiliated, and forcibly raped in a bathroom by several players. The public outcry was tremendous. Three players, including the team captain, were eventually charged with rape and kidnapping by an overzealous District Attorney (DA). Shortly after the DA won re-election, it became clear that there was simply not enough evidence to pursue legal charges against the boys. Still, the DA stuck to his guns until, humiliated by the ineptitude of the investigation, and his own inappropriate public statements early in the case, he turned the case over to the North Carolina Attorney General. After a thorough investigation the Attorney General dropped all charges, apologized to the wrongly-accused players, and referred to the DA as a "rogue prosecutor." Ethics charges against the DA were filed and he was eventually stripped of his license to practice law in North Carolina. All of these outcomes were appropriate and the truth was a welcome relief to the University and friends of the players.

Despite the fact that the case against the lacrosse players was without merit, and they were not guilty of the charges, the situation brought several problems associated with off-campus drinking to the forefront. Underage drinking is a problem at

Duke, as it is on other campuses. The party attended by the strippers was certainly not the first obnoxious party held at the Lacrosse team's house. Hopefully, the movement toward change on Duke's campus, and in the larger Duke community, has enough momentum to make it happen.

The trouble with binge-drinking

When it comes to underage drinking issues, particularly at the college level, media reports tend to focus on "binge-drinking." When used colloquially, the term "binge" implies consuming large amounts of alcohol in a relatively short period of time. But how much alcohol, and how much time? In Europe, the term "binge" is often used synonymously with the word "bender," which means getting drunk, and staying that way for days. In the U.S. the term binge has come to mean something more specific – four or more drinks (4+) per occasion for females and five or more drinks (5+) per occasion for males. These thresholds might seem too low to some people, but that is really just a semantic argument. The thresholds were established in a rigorous, scientific way and do have some practical meaning.

In the 1980s and 90s, Henry Wechsler and his colleagues at the Harvard School of Public Health measured levels of drinking among college students as well as rates of alcohol-related consequences, like hangovers, sexual assaults, and others. They observed that the risk of experiencing alcohol-related negative consequences goes up when females hit the 4 drink mark and males hit the 5 drink mark – hence the 4+/5+ definition of a "binge." It is estimated that roughly 45% of college students nationwide meet or exceed this threshold at least once every two weeks. The author's own research findings concur with that estimate.

A panel assembled by the National Institute on Alcoholism and Alcohol Abuse (NIAAA) recently recommended modifying the one-dimensional definition of binge drinking offered by Harvard to take blood alcohol concentrations (BAC) into consideration. The modified definition adds a time frame, a two-hour period, during which the 4+/5+ threshold must be reached. Theoretically, this pattern of consumption could lead the average male or female to achieve a peak BAC level of roughly 0.08%, though actual BAC readings could be much higher or lower depending on the factors discussed above.

The new definition is better than the old one, but it still falls short. Like the Harvard definition, the NIAAA definition still places all drinkers that reach a certain threshold, now 4+/5+ drinks in a two hour period, into the same category. Without further refinement, according to that definition a student that barely reaches the legal limit for operating a motor vehicle would be classified the same as a student that overdoses on alcohol and dies. The same level of risk is assigned to all students that cross the threshold regardless of how far beyond the threshold they go.

This creates a number of problems that can hold back our understanding of, and thus our ability to respond to, risky drinking. In the fall of 2004, Samantha Spady, a 19 year old student at Colorado State University, died of an alcohol overdose. She was one of at least five students around the country to do so that year. News reports sprung up overnight linking her death to "binge drinking." No doubt about it, she did engage in binge-drinking that night. But, rather than stopping at or around the four drink threshold, Samantha consumed an estimated 40 drinks during the hours leading up to her death. That's ten times the binge-threshold. Tying her death to binge-drinking over-inflates the risks posed by consuming four drinks of alcohol, and unfairly demonizes students who drink alcohol and technically fall into the binge drinker category but do not go to such extreme levels of consumption.

The author and his colleagues have long been intrigued by the fact that the standard binge definition simply lumps students into a few categories without measuring how far students go once they enter the binge category. To address this question, they analyzed survey data from over 10,000 first-semester college freshmen.[12] In the two-weeks preceding the survey, roughly one in five freshmen males actually consumed 10+ drinks and one in 10 females consumed 8+ drinks, twice the binge-threshold. This tells us that using a simple binge definition is just too simple. There is limited utility in dividing all students into two categories – binge and non-binge. Differences in how far students go once they cross the binge threshold are just too great. We need to begin looking at specific drinking levels, or at least begin dividing drinking levels more finely than just binge or non-binge. Doing so will go a long way toward identifying students at particular risk of experiencing and causing consequences and could allow schools to make better decisions about how to allocate their limited resources for dealing with alcohol misuse on their campuses.

Spring break hype

Nothing seems to conjure images of the debauchery of college drinking better than the concept of "Spring break." Over the years, spring break has become synonymous with drunken, irresponsible behavior. Every spring, the media saturate us with images of bikini clad young women and buff young men wandering around the planet's beaches with cups of beer in their hands. Add some wet t-shirt contests and spring break coverage is sure to draw in viewers.

Spring break is huge business, not just for the cities receiving students, but the travel agents sending them there and the cable channels covering the events. A quick perusal of websites for spring break trips reveals a multitude of all inclusive packages for students, many of which include unlimited drinking at a variety of clubs for the entire duration. And many of the students to whom the packages are sold are quite underage according to U.S. laws.

Unfortunately, the media always focus on the festivities that occur during spring break, not the consequences that occur during the breaks or after. Spring breakers not only do damage to their livers, they also wreak havoc in spring break hotspots. An estimated 150,000 to 200,000 students, hell bent on partying, descend on Cancun alone each year. The damage they do is noteworthy! According to one article:[13]

> "The U.S. Consulate in Merida, Mexico, whose territory includes Cancun, says that during the eight-week spring break period in 2002, U.S. students accounted for two deaths, 360 arrests, four injuries that required medical evacuations out of the area, one rape, 495 reports of lost or stolen property and 504 'general welfare inquiries' — usually from parents back in the USA who were worried about a student's whereabouts."

Those are just the crimes and consequences that the host government documents. The weeks following spring break are extremely busy for campus health centers and local doctors, who have to deal with the spike in pregnancies, abortions, and cases of sexually transmitted infections that result from all of that drunken decision-making. Exact numbers can't be known due to confidentiality concerns, but it is likely the numbers would not be comforting.

While stereotypical spring break trips do happen, and the consequences are real, much of the hype surrounding spring break is just that – hype. A few years ago, a student in one of the author's classes told him an interesting story about her spring break experience in Jamaica. She said that she walked out onto a sparsely populated beach and noticed a small group of people crammed into a small area of sand, with TV cameras focused on them. It was MTV and they were clearly trying to capture footage that American consumers wanted to see – kids going crazy on their wild spring break trip to Jamaica. Few advertisers would pay to push their products in between footage of an empty beach in Jamaica, so they were apparently trying to create the illusion of craziness as best they could. This is certainly not to suggest that spring break trips are Zen-like experiences for most students. The point of these trips is often to go to some far off place and get drunk repeatedly over a period of a week. However, the public do not see episodes of MTV's show, *Spring Break*, in which students volunteer to build homes for the homeless, deliver food aid in foreign countries, and so on. They simply see craziness, even if it has to be manufactured by the media to give the public what they want. A little digging quickly turns up plenty of alternatives to stereotypical spring break trips, like working for Habitat for Humanity, going on a backpacking trip, sight-seeing that does not include beaches and bars, or even going to beautiful spring break-like destinations that don't draw very many spring breakers.

A few years ago, the folks at MTV decided to take their *Real World* program concept and extend it to a spring break trip to Cancun. In fact, they called it *The Real Cancun*. The pseudo-documentary captures and displays many of the stereotypical spring break activities, including wet t-shirt contests, drunken club hopping, drinking on the beach, etcetera. It is referred to here as a pseudo-documentary because the footage does not capture the normal behaviors of spring breakers in their natural habitat. The producers created many of the scenarios in which the kids, all of whom were underage according to U.S. alcohol laws, acted out their hedonistic fantasies. They chose the cast, paid for the trip, and enabled their antics.

This story is mentioned because it serves as a perfect example of how the media sometimes encourage and then exploit the adventures and misadventures of kids in order to make money, regardless of the cost to the kids. In one scene, two of the characters are shown and heard, briefly, having intercourse that was captured on night-vision cameras in their rooms. Both "cast members" were intoxicated at the time. One of the characters in The Real Cancun was a reserved 18-year-old who had never had alcohol and did not plan to do so on the trip. The producers were complicit in situation after situation in which he was pressured by peers to drink until he finally caved. What if something tragic had happened as a result? What if he goes on to become an alcoholic after blowing his plans to stay alcohol-free? From an ethical standpoint, despite the fact that the kid was 18 and agreed to be on the program, the producers would have been more than a little responsible for his fate.

Do alcohol ads increase consumption?

No discussion of underage drinking would be complete without examining the role that advertising plays in shaping and molding kids' attitudes toward alcohol and their expectations about what alcohol will do for their lives. The purpose of most advertisements is to convince us that the quality of our lives will improve if we use a particular product. One of the author's personal favorites is a Hummer commercial in which a humus eating thirty-something male "reclaims his manhood" simply by buying a Hummer. Clever, yet transparent.

Many ads, including the Hummer commercial, are designed to make us feel uncomfortable with our current lives. Once that has been accomplished, the pitch is made. This involves telling us how our lives could be better if we would only buy their particular products or use their particular services. Deodorant commercials fit perfectly into this category. In the typical deodorant commercial, we are shown a character that is rejected because of his/her smell, only to find acceptance once the deodorant is applied.

Other ads, like those for alcohol, try to sell us products by telling us, or showing us, what awaits us if we use them. We are made to believe that drinking will instantly make our lives, including our romantic lives, more exciting. Alcohol ads are notorious for pairing scantily clad, attractive young women with their products. The message is not hard to decipher – we are supposed to believe that average looking males will be mobbed by attractive women if they just order the right brand of beer.

Do such ads actually cause people to drink more? Research has so far failed to reveal a clear-cut relationship between alcohol ads and alcohol use – though some studies suggest that some alcohol ads are appealing and quite familiar to children. Recently, researchers at the University of Connecticut reported a correlation between the number of alcohol ads viewed by teens and their levels of alcohol drinking.[14] A similar relationship was found between industry advertising expenditures per state and the drinking levels in those states. While these findings are suggestive, they do not establish a causal link between alcohol advertising and the amount of alcohol that people consume.

Rather than recruiting new users, it makes more financial sense for a beverage company to use ads in an effort to grab market share. Americans spend more than $120 billion on alcohol every year, $50-$70 billion of which is spent on beer. A company stands to make far more profit by stealing a few percent of the market away from a competitor than by causing a few abstainers to start drinking. For instance, gaining 0.5% of a

$50 billion market would generate an extra $250 million for a company.

If alcohol ads do not cause non-drinkers to start drinking alcohol, then what's the harm? The constant stream of ads reinforces the false perception that everyone drinks and that alcohol is so safe that it is not even considered a drug. Companies promise short-term scratches for adolescent itches. Their marketing tactics transmit and reinforce social messages that the world could do without. Beer commercials, and now new liquor commercials, promote the expectation that alcohol and sex go together perfectly, and yet society is still figuring out how to deal with sexual assault, teen pregnancy, and the spread of sexually transmitted infections. Alcohol increases the odds that all of those events will happen. The vast majority of teens and adults are unaware of the laws regarding sexual contact with females who are intoxicated. Beer commercials only serve to confuse the issue by promoting, implicitly and explicitly, the use of alcohol to attract and capture potential mates.

There is reason to be concerned that such commercials might affect how male teens view and treat women, or how young women view themselves. These would be concerns regardless of whether the ads influenced drinking choices at all. How many beer commercials have you seen that send the message that women should be treated with respect? In these ads, women are invariably shown as the prize that men will receive for drinking a particular brand of beer. All of this is done without any warnings that things could go terribly wrong. Beverage manufacturers are not required to list potential side effects, health effects, or drug interactions in their ads, despite the powerful, and often disastrous, consequences that routinely follow purchasing and consuming their products.

Beverage manufacturers should be allowed to advertise just like everyone else. But they also have a responsibility to list the potential side effects, warnings about drug interactions, and appropriate serving size information on their products. The logic is simple and the proposal seems sensible. When companies sell potentially hazardous products, they simply must do all they can to protect consumers from the harm their products may cause.

Booze in the barracks

High school and college students are not the only young people dealing with alcohol related issues. Many military men and women begin their service as adolescents, and estimates suggest that more than 25% of military personnel aged 18-25 engage in heavy drinking one or more times per week. In many ways, 18 marks the dawn of adult-like responsibilities, but it does not necessarily mark the end of adolescence – certainly not from a neurological standpoint. Healthy 18 year old recruits can follow directions well. But what about when their fingers are on the triggers and they have to decide, in a split second, whether to fire or hold fire? We have already discussed the impact that immature frontal lobes can have on impulse control and decision making. We have also seen that young brains are more likely to interpret emotional expressions on other's faces as indicating fear and other negative feelings. When the adrenaline is pumping, it is a lot to ask of an 18 year old to make split second, and accurate, decisions. Add alcohol, or hangovers, which we know cause problems with attention and can make fingers unsteady, and the possibilities are unsettling.

The amount of pressure experienced by young recruits is difficult to imagine, and many young soldiers, like their non-military peers, drink alcohol to excess. This fact simply evades public discourse about alcohol until something newsworthy happens, and then soldiers are often characterized unfairly as drunken brutes.

Soldiers represent an additional source of income for beverage manufacturers. As is the case with civilians, the cost of the damage done by alcohol abuse among soldiers is picked up by tax payers – not by the companies selling the products. Another externalized cost of the alcohol business.

How much does it cost? A 1997 report from the Office of the Inspector General of the Department of Defense concluded the following:[15]

> "In FY 1995, the military retail system generated alcoholic beverage sales of about $600 million and realized gross profits of about $164 million. However, DoD costs for health care associated with the detection, rehabilitation, and treatment of active duty, retiree, and dependent personnel with alcohol related diseases and injuries were about $557 million. The lost productivity costs for active duty personnel hospitalized for alcohol attributable disease was approximately $13 million for the same period. Non-DoD societal costs for alcohol related incidents attributable to active duty, retiree, and dependent personnel were roughly $396 million."

Note that the estimate of beverage sales does not include money spent on booze off base. As in the larger society, in the military, the cost of alcohol overshadows the amount of money spent on it.

Additional research has shown that the stress of deployment, even for non-combat missions, leads many soldiers to increase their consumption in an effort to deal with the strain.

In the past few years, the author has had the honor of visiting several military bases at home and overseas. Recreational drinking is a common means of escape and relaxation among soldiers, many of whom are fresh out of high school. This usually occurs without incident. However, as is the case in the civilian world, when rapes, murders, and other violent offenses occur, alcohol is often involved. This appears to be the case in a recent, highly publicized incident in which four soldiers stationed in Iraq drank whiskey and took pain pills before allegedly raping a 14 year old girl and killing her family.

It is important to remember that the actions of a few drunken, rogue troops do not reflect the behavior of all soldiers anymore than the actions of a few unruly college kids reflect the behavior of all college students. Further, there are certainly plenty of underage soldiers who drink and do so responsibly. In fact, at this writing, the Marine Corps has very recently opened the door to allowing marines between the ages of 18 and 21 to drink when overseas under certain conditions. The rationale behind this action, with is compelling, essentially boils down to the "old enough to fight, old enough to drink" argument. The wisdom of the decision should become clear over the next several years.

Alcohol and young brains

The social and direct health consequences of underage drinking should be sufficient to compel the conclusion that we should work hard to keep alcohol out of the hands (and brains) of our kids. A rapidly growing stack of literature suggests that alcohol affects adolescents differently, at a neurological level, than adults, adding further reasons to view alcohol as inappropriate for kids. These data are reviewed in great detail in an upcoming book from W.W. Norton and Company. However, we will briefly discuss the findings here.

Studies with both rats and humans suggest that the adolescent brain is affected differently by alcohol than the adult brain in both short-term and long-term ways. Here are some of the key findings from research on the topic, with the species studied included in parentheses:

- The brain circuitry involved in memory is more vulnerable to alcohol in adolescence than adults (rats)
- Adolescents sustain more brain damage following a four-day drinking binge than adults (rats)
- Alcohol prevents new cell birth in the brain more potently in adolescents than adults (rats)
- Alcohol impairs memory more in adolescents and young adults relative to adults (rats and humans)
- Alcohol produces less sedation, or sleepiness, in adolescents and young adults than in adults (rats and personal experience!)
- Alcohol impairs balance less in adolescents and young adults relative to adults (rats and some human work)
- Repeated alcohol exposure during adolescence alters the way that people respond to alcohol later in life (rats and humans)

Differences in how alcohol affects adolescent and adult brains could help explain why those who start drinking at young ages are more likely to become alcoholics than those who delay the onset of drinking until young adulthood.[16] Researchers at NIAAA, led by Dr. Ralph Hingson, examined data from 43,000 U.S. adults aged 18 and older. Overall, those who started drinking by the age of 14 were much more likely to become dependent on alcohol at some point in their lives (47%) compared to those who waited until they were 21 or older (9%). The study also suggests that earlier drinking is associated with a broader range, and greater severity, of alcohol related problems. The prognosis is simply poorer for those that start drinking at an early age. It seems these data provide a compelling argument that delaying the onset of drinking among kids should be an important component of any strategy aimed at reducing alcohol abuse and dependence.

The pivotal question, of course, is whether kids that start drinking early are driven to drink at a young age due to family history or some other genetic or environmental contributions, or if the early exposure itself leads to a higher propensity for alcohol abuse. Dr. Hingson's study revealed

SideNotes

Who cares about rats?

Much of the available data on the potential brain damage caused by exposure to alcohol during adolescence comes from studies done with rats. How relevant could such data could possibly be to the human condition? After all, rats and humans are not exactly the same. The truth is that most of what we know about how all drugs—prescription and illicit— affect the brain has been gleaned from research with rats. Research on Fetal Alcohol Syndrome serves as a prime example of the sometimes beneficial interplay between human and rat research. We know that women who drink during pregnancy can give birth to children with physical and/or cognitive abnormalities. Yet, there is no *proof* from the human work that alcohol *causes* the symptoms seen in Fetal Alcohol Syndrome. However, rat research, in which pregnant rats are given alcohol and their offspring are studied, provides support for the damaging effects of alcohol on the developing fetus. It is true that rats are not humans, but our brains are similar enough that insights gleaned from rat research can be used to guide hypothesis-driven research with humans.

that age of onset was a significant predictor of alcohol dependence *even after* family history and several personality variables were statistically controlled for, suggesting that the age at which the brain is first exposed to alcohol really does influence the odds of developing a problem with alcohol down the road.

Hopefully, future work will tell us more about how age of onset contributes to problems with alcohol. But, for now, we do know that the association exists, and it can be a persuasive component of alcohol education, whether such education occurs in the schools or around the dinner table. While the nature of the relationship between age of onset and alcoholism remains unclear, there can be no doubt that trying to delay the onset of drinking is a worthwhile effort.

Drinking and driving – bringing the laws in line with the science

If we held a conversation with every adult in the country simultaneously, it is unlikely that very many people would disagree that operating a motorized vehicle, any kind of motorized vehicle, after drinking is dangerous – so dangerous in fact that it shouldn't be done, people should be educated about the risks, and laws preventing it should be enacted and enforced. If only it were that easy.

In the U.S., adults are technically allowed to drive cars after drinking until their BAC levels reach 0.08%. The legal threshold has decreased over the years, thanks in part to extremely hard work by Mothers Against Drug Driving (MADD), but the limit is still out of step with the science. Some of the abilities needed to drive effectively are impaired at BAC levels as low as 0.02%, others fall off at levels around 0.04%; one-quarter to one-half of the current level at which it is legal to drive! Indeed, 0.02% is the legal limit enforced in some European nations. By the time a person, particularly a light drinker, reaches 0.08%, there aren't any driving related skills left unimpaired. Because of this, driving at or near 0.08% is extremely dangerous. It is true that most fatal accidents caused by drunk drivers occur at BAC levels higher than 0.10%, but that doesn't negate the fact that driving at 0.08% is quite dangerous.

While gearing up to do a study in which college students were administered enough alcohol to raise their BAC levels to about 0.08%, the author mixed himself the cocktail he would be giving students, ingested it, and measured his BAC level to see how impaired he felt. There is no way he could have safely operated a motor vehicle at that level, not that he's the safest driver on earth sober, either! The reader might be surprised how intoxicated they would feel at 0.08%. For a 200 pound man, reaching that limit requires consuming 4 or 5 drinks in a one-hour period. That's more than just having a drink or two at dinner with friends.

For adolescents between the ages of 15-20, motor vehicle crashes are more likely to claim their lives than anything else. While they make up only 7% of the licensed drivers in the country, people in this age range account for 20% of all traffic fatalities. Nearly a third of drivers aged 15-20 that are killed in fatal crashes were drinking at the time. The majority, 75%, had BAC levels below 0.08% - the legal limit for adults.

Every state in the country now observes zero tolerance laws for underage drinking and driving. If you aren't old enough to buy alcohol, then it is illegal to drive with any detectable amount of alcohol in your system. While the limit is technically

---

SideNotes

The tragic and inspiring story of athlete Mark Zupan

Mark Zupan is a quadriplegic wheelchair rugby, known as murderball, superstar. He was also a central focus of the compelling documentary, "Murderball." Mark began playing murderball after a surreal drunk driving crash left him completely paralyzed from the waste down and with minimal use of his arms. At 18, Mark was a college soccer player on scholarship. After drinking heavily at a bar, he stumbled into the parking lot, climbed into the back of his friend's truck, and passed out. His friend, drunk himself, later left the bar unaware that Mark was in the back. On the way home, the truck spun out on a highway and struck a tree. Mark was thrown from the bed of the truck, over the tops of some trees, and into a ravine. His neck was broken, but he somehow managed to hold on to a branch for 14 hours, covered from head to toe with red ants. Until he was spotted by an employee on his lunch break the following day, no one was aware that Mark was missing or that he had been in the back of the truck. He has made the most of his life since, accomplishing more than most people in perfect health could possibly do and he seems to have a great deal of fun doing it. He has also forgiven his friend, the driver, who is still working to forgive himself.

0.00%, some states use thresholds as high as 0.02% or 0.03% to account for error in the measuring devices. These laws are only useful if they're enforced, both in terms of arrests and in terms of sentencing.

Regardless of how stringent the laws are, and in spite of a drop in teen drunk driving fatalities over the years, a large percentage of young drinkers continue to drink and drive. This includes many students on their way to some of the best colleges in the country. In a recent study, the author examined alcohol consumption and alcohol-related consequences among college-bound students during the summer between high school graduation and their first college semester. Roughly 12% of students, both male and female, drove after drinking at least once during a two-week period. That is way too high. Perhaps if these bright and motivated students understood the true impact of alcohol on driving-related brain functions, some would re-think the decision.

With enough effort, healthy morays surrounding drinking and driving could become engrained in the culture. Indeed, there is certainly more awareness about drinking and driving now than at any time in the past, and rates of drinking and driving have declined. Much more can be done to reduce these rates even further. Modifying and enforcing the laws is one part of the process. But the rest has to do with communicating the risks and consequences to teens in a way that motivates them not to do it. As is always the case, parents are the first line of defense here, and should lead the way in teaching kids to avoid combining alcohol and things with engines.

Over the years, the alcohol industry has spent a portion of its riches promoting designated driver programs. Do they work? Sound scientific data are lacking, but the programs deserve a close look. Essentially, the message from the industry is that it's okay to go to bars or parties and get drunk, just make sure someone else drives you home. Designated driver ads do send the message that getting drunk and driving is a bad idea. However, they also imply that getting drunk is perfectly fine, as long as there isn't any driving involved. The alcohol industry, like other for-profit industries, is motivated to make money. As such, the true intentions of all voluntary endeavors, like the promotion of designated driver programs, should be considered carefully.

What can parents do about underage drinking?

It is quite easy to get lost in the data on underage drinking and lose sight of the simple fact that this is a solvable problem. Like headaches and debt, it is far easier to prevent teens from starting a drinking habit than to stop it once it starts. There is no shortage of advice available to parents, but some of it is just not very good. Having good facts is the best first step.

Parents are the very first line of defense in protecting kids from the damaging effects of alcohol. Early and honest discussions with kids about the potential impact of alcohol on the developing adolescent brain, combined with early detection of alcohol use and abuse, are central to helping avoid the damaging effects of drinking. The right balance of establishing and enforcing strict rules, encouraging teens to explore and spread their wings while making safe decisions, and establishing strategies to help get them out of dangerous situations in a hurry, can help protect their brains and allow them to reach their full potential.

Before initiating a discussion with your teen about alcohol, get prepared. The National Institute on Alcohol Abuse and Alcoholism (NIAAA) suggests that answering the following questions can help parents assess how prepared they are.

Yes___ **No**___ Do you know how to discuss alcohol use with your child and where to get information to help you?

Yes___ No___ Do you know your child's friends, and do you feel that they provide positive influences on your child's activities?

Yes___ No___ Do you know the extent of drinking by children in your neighborhood and how to find local organizations that are working on the issue?

Yes___ No___ Do you know the legal consequences if your child is caught drinking alcohol?

Yes___ No___ Do you know your State's laws about providing alcohol to anyone under 21?

If you answered no to the first question, about where to find information, the author recommends beginning at the homepages of either NIAAA (www.niaaa.nih.gov) or SAMSHA (www.samsha.gov). He is particularly fond of a SAMSHA website called "Family Guide," which can be accessed at www.family.samhsa.gov. Remember that you do not have to be an expert on these topics. If your child raises questions that you don't have the answers to, tell them you'll find the answers. Relay the information to them once you do. Alternatively, search for the answers on the Internet with your child. This strategy provides additional opportunities to discuss issues like drinking with your kids.

As we have discussed in previous sections, there is something about family dinners that serve as protective factors against teen drinking. Specifically, kids who have dinner with their families on a nightly or near nightly basis are less likely to drink and engage in other risky behaviors than kids who eat alone. Why this is, no one knows for sure, but it probably has more to do with the conversations that take place around the table than the actual eating part. If you eat dinner as a family, it's a perfect time to have conversations about your child's life and to be proactive, discussing topics that are not yet a big deal in the child's life but might be soon. This can help your child establish healthy expectations for the future and for parents to establish policies. Discussing driving in the year before the child begins the process of earning a drivers license is a good example.

Acronyms often spell cute and condescending words – but they can be helpful for remembering strategies for communicating with teens about alcohol and other pertinent issues. The U.S. Department of Health and Human Services recommends a strategy known as "WISE" to help facilitate discussions with teens about risky behaviors.

> **"W"** is for **"Welcome"**
>> Be available and treat your adolescent with trust and respect. Whether you know it or not, you are the most important resource that your child has.
>
> **"I"** is for **"Interest"**:
>> Ask your teens questions that show your interest in their opinions, friends, school, etc, and do it in a non-judgmental manner. Let your teen talk freely about his or her concerns and experiences. Remember that this is a golden opportunity to let them tell you what is on their minds.
>
> **"S"** is for **"Support Good Goals"**
>> Talk with your teen about their goals for the fu-

ture and support those that are healthy. Let them know about your hopes for them. Set high expectations for them. Data show that our teens want to know what we expect of them.

"E" is for **"Encourage, Educate and Empower"**
Give your teen the guidance, information and skills they need to be successful

Like other strategies, this one works best when healthy lines of communication already exist. Indeed, we know that children are less likely to drink or engage in other risky behaviors if they feel connected with their parents. Even if things are rocky at the moment between you and your teen, the WISE strategy can help get things on track.

Humans seem most content when we can predict the future. We would rather know that a major stressor, like an exam or surgery, is coming up rather than being hit with it out of the blue. Life for teenagers is a rollercoaster ride. Their bodies and their social worlds change so much that it can be dizzying for everyone. A structured home life with set rules and expectations might seem annoying to some teens, but it will probably help them to thrive in the long run.

It is a good idea to establish, and perhaps even post, a set of "house rules." They don't necessarily have to contain anything specific about drinking, but that can help. These rules make everyone's expectations clear, and can serve as a contract of sorts between parents and kids. Thus, if rules are broken there are no surprises. Here are some tips for creating your House Rules and strategies for disseminating and enforcing them.

1. Rules should be clear, fair and consistently enforced

2. Discuss the rules and be certain that your teen understands what you expect
3. Make consequences clear
4. Do not modify rules on the fly even if your teen complains (this is part of their job!), just keep referring them back to the list
5. Remember that rules create valuable structure and help teens feel safe, no matter how much they moan about it!

Once house rules are established, the work begins for both parents and teens. Parents must help to ensure success by structuring circumstances in ways that are consistent with the rules. For instance, if the rule regarding alcohol use is that it isn't acceptable, then we should try to guide teens away from alcohol and reinforce their decisions not to drink. This can be accomplished by following some additional suggestions, gleaned partially from the U.S. Department of Health and Human Services:

1. Encourage supervised group activities. Know and support the groups your teen participates in. If you do not approve, do not let your child go.
2. Make sure your teen is not spending too much time in unsupervised activities. Sports, tutoring, and even after-school jobs are positive ways to ensure that your teen is safe and productive during the after-school hours. Kids involved in extracurricular activities are less likely to drink, do other drugs, or engage in other risky behaviors.
3. Form a pact with your teen that you will pick him/her up if they ever find themselves in an uncomfortable or potentially dangerous situation.

If you are so inclined, agree not to ask your teen questions about their evening until the next day. This could reduce the teen's resistance to the idea of calling you for a ride.

4   Determine a set list of questions that must be addressed before you agree to let your teen leave for an outing. If they won't answer the questions, or don't answer them honestly, they can't go. Such questions could include:

- Where will you be?
- What will you be doing?
- Who will be there?
- When will you be home?
- Will adults be present?
- How can I reach you?
- When will you call to check in?

5.   Be available to talk to your teen regularly. Attempts to initiate discussions with teens can often be met with high levels of resistance. Keep trying. Good communication supports good decisions.

We all want teens to make the journey through adolescence with as little discomfort as possible for everyone involved. There are no magic recipes for success and we simply cannot protect them the way we did when they were children. We will eventually have to let them go. Adolescence is the training period – for us as well as them. The main trick seems to be using a combination of unconditional love and conditional support. Kids who know they're loved but also know the rules will fare much better than those without overt love and with no structure or consistent enforcement of rules.

Should parents let their kids drink at home?

You might be surprised how common it is for parents, particularly affluent parents, to allow teens – theirs and other people's – to drink in their homes. Prom parties and high school graduation parties are common examples of when this might happen, but typical weekends are fair game for these folks, too. Is that legal? Under most circumstances, no. At present, 32 states have laws on the books, called "social host" laws, forbidding adults from allowing people under 21 to drink in their homes. To check your state's laws, please visit this page on the Mothers Against Drunk Driving website – www.madd.org/laws. Keep in mind that, even if such laws haven't been passed at the state level, your city or community might have its own ordinances outlawing teen drinking in your home.

A recent article in the Chicago Sun Times discusses a situation that represents a worst case scenario. In October, 2006, two Chicago area parents allowed teenagers to drink in their basement to celebrate homecoming. After leaving the party, one of the teens, an 18 year old student, crashed his car into a tree near the home – killing himself and the passenger. The parents, Jeffrey and Sarah Hutsell, were charged with allowing the teens to drink in their basement. The Hutsells lived in an affluent neighborhood and were characterized by neighbors as very decent people. The guilt they feel must be overwhelming. They certainly didn't intend for the party to end that way. In a similar, equally tragic case, three teens were killed in a drunk-driving accident in Pennsylvania in

> "Not sharing alcohol with your children is a risk factor for binge drinking"
> - Stanton Peele, CNN.com Sept 28, 2007
>
> "What??"
> - Author of this book

2003 after leaving a party hosted by a parent. The parent was sentenced to 1 – 4.5 years in prison for involuntary manslaughter.

These examples should serve as strong warnings. It might seem sensible to let teens drink in your home so that they don't do it on the street, but it's a very slippery slope, and one best staying off. Even if you can prevent teens from leaving your basement and getting behind the wheel of a car, your presence upstairs cannot always prevent overdoses, vomiting, death, sexual assaults, and some of the other nasty things that can stem from teen drinking. In addition, allowing other kids to drink in your home sends very mixed messages about underage drinking, and potentially undermines the efforts of other parents. It would certainly violate their trust, and place you at risk for law suits. In short, if you're thinking about letting teens drink in your home, or at a party hosted by you for any occasion, don't! You might seem cool to the kids, but you'll seem like a criminal to the community.

One of the confusing issues that makes it difficult for parents to decide how to deal with drinking in their homes has to do with teen drinking in European countries. The general perception here in the U.S. is that parents in European countries have the adolescent drinking thing figured out. Here's the logic:

- Their teens can drink — ours cannot.
- Their teens drink in moderation — ours drink to get drunk.
- So, if we let our teens drink — at least at home — they will learn to drink in moderation like the European kids.

Even if the logic seems to work, the basic premise is flawed. First of all, the U.S. and Europe are different. Secondly, there are large differences between teen drinking habits across

European countries. And the perception that European cultures, in general, have the problem under control is simply inaccurate. Let's look at the data.

The European Union (EU) recently commissioned a report on alcohol use among its 25 member states. The report was released in June, 2006. Among EU members, the average age of first drink was 12.5 and the average age of first drunkenness was 14. In Denmark, 70% of 15 year olds were drunk at least twice in the year before the data were collected. U.S. kids look like teetotalers by comparison. In the 2005 Monitoring the Future Study, 34% of 10th graders in the U.S. reported being drunk at least once in the previous year.

What about so-called binge drinking? There is a belief that European kids drink more often, but consume less per drinking occasion, while kids in the U.S. are more likely to binge. Actually, according to a 2005 report from the U.S. Department of Justice and the Pacific Institute for Research and Evaluation, American teens (15-16 year olds in this case) were less likely to binge (5+ drinks) in a 30 day period than teens in 34 out of 35 European nations. The graph below includes data from U.S. teens and those in 14 countries examined in the EU report.

When trying to interpret data comparing drinking rates in various countries, it is important to keep in mind that what constitutes a single serving can vary tremendously. For instance, while teenagers in Spain are more likely than teenagers in the U.S. to report crossing the five drink threshold for binge drinking, their servings might be considerably smaller than those in America. As such, what appear to be large differences in rates of binge drinking in the U.S. and various countries might not be so large after all.

There do appear to be differences between how American and European teens drink that go beyond the amount of alcohol they consume. Research indicates that there is a strong placebo affect with alcohol. In laboratory settings, college students served non-alcoholic beer rather than real beer still exhibit many of the changes in thoughts and behaviors associated with alcohol. In part, this has to do with expectations regarding how people are supposed to behave when they drink. These expectations are culturally influenced. In the U.S., many kids are led to believe that anything a person does when they're drunk is excusable. "What happens in [insert city here], stays in [insert city here]." Indeed, drinking is often used as an opportunity to express pent up urges that are inappropriate to express during daily life. Vandalism, aggression, sexual promiscuity, etcetera. In some ways, this is captured by the ubiquitous utterance on college campuses – "Work hard, play hard" – though there are plenty of students that play hard harmlessly.

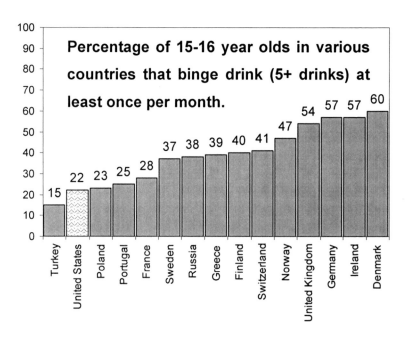

Percentage of 15-16 year olds in various countries that binge drink (5+ drinks) at least once per month.

Country	Percentage
Turkey	15
United States	22
Poland	23
Portugal	25
France	28
Sweden	37
Russia	38
Greece	39
Finland	40
Switzerland	41
Norway	47
United Kingdom	54
Germany	57
Ireland	57
Denmark	60

Kids in many other countries do not seem to share the view that anything goes when a person is drinking. While teens in many European countries out-drink teens in the U.S., becoming overly rowdy and obnoxious while drinking is simply not acceptable in many of those countries, so it doesn't happen as often. American kids might not drink as much as European kids, but they often act like they do! The good news here is that reshaping expectations about how one is supposed to express themselves when they drink could ameliorate some of the consequences of underage drinking here at home, including sexual assaults, drunk driving, vandalism and other crimes.

Here is a passage from an article in the June 25, 2007, issue of Newsweek containing the author's opinion on the issue of whether parents should allow kids to drink at home:

> "Even if they don't become alcoholics, teens who drink too much may suffer impaired memory and other learning problems, says Aaron White of Duke University Medical Center, who studies adolescent alcohol use. He says parents should think twice about offering alcohol to teens because their brains are still developing and are more susceptible to damage than adult brains. 'If you're going to do that, I suggest you teach them to roll joints, too,' he says, 'because the science is clear that alcohol is more dangerous than marijuana.' "

Each parent has to form their own opinion on this topic, and the author definitely is not suggesting that parents teach their kids to smoke marijuana. However, it is important to look at this issue honestly, and from a data-driven perspective. Most parents would not want their kids smoking marijuana, yet many see no harm in "teaching them how to drink." Why not "teach them how to have sex," or perhaps "teach them how to drive drunk." The odds are that many teenagers will do those things, too. The question is, how much more data will adults need before they're willing to do more to prevent alcohol from getting into the brains of kids and, potentially, causing problems? And when will the culture finally turn on the industry that pumps alcoholic beverages into the society with little regard for the health of future citizens?

Again, it is the author's view that there is nothing wrong with alcohol use, or even the use of some other drugs, by responsible adults. However, these things are inappropriate for developing brains, and should be unnecessary in a world where the needs of adolescents are met through other, healthier activities.

Clearly, not every adolescent will be affected negatively by a parent's decision to allow them to have an occasional glass of wine with dinner. However, the risks are many and great. The parent might have the best of all intentions, but opening the door to drinking during adolescence leaves kids vulnerable to the misleading messages coming from those who wish to prey on their desire to break the rules, fit in with other kids, and practice acting like adults. To you, it might seem like healthy life-skills training. To them, it might seem like a green light to drink alcohol. There are no guarantees they will take their single-serving drinking habit with them when they leave home.

Further, upwards of 20% of the population will, at one point in their lives, have a problematic relationship with alcohol, and drinking early increases the odds that a kid will end up on the wrong side of the equation. Do we really need to stack the deck against kids even further by intentionally giving them the drug at home?

What does it all mean?

As far as drugs go, alcohol is a pretty nasty one, even if it can be fun and relaxing. The legality of the drug and the messages conveyed through aggressive, glitzy marketing campaigns are out of step with the risks that alcohol poses. Moderate consumption (one drink per day for females, up to two for males) among adults is absolutely fine, assuming the adult in question is otherwise healthy and has no history of substance abuse. And, most importantly, can maintain a moderate level of use without it escalating and impacting one's life negatively.

If we want to do something about the underage drinking problem, changes need to be made in the way that alcohol is marketed. All alcohol ads should be closely scrutinized by independent panels of adults and community members before they are aired (the same should go for other drug ads, by the way). At present, such ads can be aired for months before being scrutinized. By then, the ads have achieved their purposes. Ads depicting alcohol-related sexual activity, or even suggesting that alcohol could lead to sexual activity, should be banned entirely. As with other drug ads, alcohol ads should contain detailed warnings about the consequences that can result – including death! If Valium has to carry a warning that it shouldn't be consumed with alcohol, why shouldn't alcohol carry a warning that it shouldn't be consumed with Valium? The fact that a commercial for alcohol would have to include 30 seconds or so of warnings should paint a compelling picture of the risks involved.

Companies selling alcohol need to take ownership of the fact that their products do great harm to many consumers and adjust their marketing strategies accordingly. Excluding the warnings simply because there are too many is entirely unacceptable. Providing consumers with accurate, and complete, information about the risks is a social responsibility that beverage manufacturers should meet voluntarily, or be forced to meet by law. Perhaps educating the public about the risks of alcohol could be part of Peter Coors' (CEO of Coors Brewing Company) community service for his recent DUI conviction! Even he is not immune to the negative effects that his products can have on one's life.

At this point, the underage drinking problem is firmly rooted in the culture in which our kids are raised. Through commercial and print ads, movies in which young people drink, and adult modeling, we make alcohol too alluring for many kids to pass up. We then blame them when they fall for the bait. Funding for education and prevention programs is lacking. The available programs can help, but it will take a much more concerted effort including parents, schools, prevention specialists, politicians, and kids themselves, to stimulate the kind of widespread change necessary to minimize teen drinking, dissuade heavy drinking among adults, and convey the message that alcohol is only safe when used in moderation, and only after the brain is finished developing. Parents are, and will always be, on the front lines in the battle to protect kids from the negative effects of alcohol and other threats and should be part of this effort.

Quick Facts:

- As is the case with adults, adolescents use and abuse alcohol more than any other drug.
- Research with both rats and humans suggests that adolescents might be more vulnerable than adults to the effects of alcohol on memory, including a type of temporary amnesia called "blackouts."
- Alcohol is well-known to be a neurotoxin capable of interfering with brain development.

- Moderate drinking (1-2 drinks per day) is relatively risk free for healthy adults. However, because the brain is still developing during adolescence, there is no known safe level of use for them.

- The earlier that one starts drinking, the greater the likelihood that they will go on to develop a problem with the drug, perhaps because the adolescent brain learns about the drug and habits surrounding it so quickly.

- Contrary to popular misperception here in the U.S., kids from European countries do not drink less than adolescents here, suggesting that allowing kids to start drinking at younger ages causes more problems than it solves.

- Beverage manufacturers have been given free reign to market their products as they see fit, which includes promoting alcohol as a drug that will instantly improve life with no health risks beyond those posed by drinking during pregnancy and driving while intoxicated. Hopefully, this will change in the near future.

- In order to diminish the problems caused by drinking during adolescence, we adults must do a better job of educating kids about the risks, debunking faulty expectations about the good things that alcohol will do for them, and modeling healthy drinking habits.

Chapter 8

Protecting kids from disease – The immune system, how it works, and how to keep it healthy

Each of our bodies is a vast community of trillions of individual cells, all working together for a common goal – to keep us alive! Toward that end, cells in the body are organized into several separate systems, each making vital contributions to our sustenance. One of the most important systems in our bodies for keeping us psychologically and physically healthy is the immune system – the collection of cells, tissues and organs that protects us from diseases and wages wars against enemies that get behind the gates. In this chapter, we will discuss the immune system, how it changes during adolescence, how it influences the way we think and feel, and how to keep it running strongly and efficiently in order to keep adolescents disease free.

Ahston Bonds was a typical, healthy adolescent. That all changed in October, 2007, when the Virginia high school student died following a week-long battle with an antibiotic resistant bacteria called Methicillin-resistant Staphylococcus aureus, or MRSA. His death triggered a media frenzy and prompted 21 schools in Virginia to be closed for cleaning. Fortunately, MRSA is rarely deadly in young healthy people, but the event, like others before and after it, brought the subject of disease prevention and treatment in adolescents to the forefront, and stimulated national discussions about how to keep kids infection free. While such discussions tend to center around the availability of drugs for various conditions, the fact is that we humans come equipped with an extraordinary system, called the immune system, capable of battling and defeating most infectious agents on its own. By maximizing the health of our kids' internal defense mechanisms, we can minimize the chances that they will become ill and succumb to potentially deadly pathogens (disease causing agents).

The immune system and how it works

You might be surprised to know that most of the symptoms you experience during a nasty cold or a bout of the flu aren't generated by the viruses running amuck in your body – they're caused by your own immune system. In response to foreign invaders, like bacteria and viruses, the body fires up its defenses in order to get rid of them. Some of the body's strategies include raising body temperature to destroy microbes by causing fevers, secreting extra mucus to flush the bad guys out (causing runny noses and coughs), and sneezing.

The immune system consists of a vast army of cells that travel throughout our bodies looking for agents that could cause disease, including viruses, bacteria, fungi, and parasites. Once found, these unwanted guests are destroyed or cornered so that the harm they cause is minimized. Cells that detect foreign invaders destroy them or send for backup. Other cells move to the area to help wage war against them. Newly created immune system cells are recruited as soldiers in the war. They are given instructions about what to pursue, how to recognize it, how to defeat it, and when to stop. This story plays itself out everyday inside of our bodies without our conscious awareness. We only become aware of the battles once they get ferocious enough to affect how we think and feel.

The immune system is made up of white blood cells, all

of which begin their lives in our bone marrow – the meaty material in the center of our bones. There are several different types of white blood cells, each with its specific function. Some, like Natural Killer cells, travel around the body making contact with other cells to see if they're friend or foe. If they're foes, they get blown up. Some cells, like macrophages, take samples of invading substances to other immune cells, called T-cells and B-cells. T-cells and B-cells then mobilize a larger immune response to eradicate the invaders. After being presented with portions of a bad guy, B-cells generate antibodies - molecules that attach to proteins on the surface of the invaders, thereby signaling them for execution. (*Antibodies* should not be mistaken for *antibiotics*, which will be discussed below)

Like the brain and the rest of the body, the immune system is still developing during adolescence.[1] Levels of white blood cells increase throughout the teen years. Adolescence is a stage of life dominated by learning, and the immune system follows suit. Like the individual adolescent, the immune system is shaped by interactions with the outside world. It has memory. Once exposed to a foreign invader, the immune system will remember it and be prepared to deal with it more quickly the next

SideNotes

Does it really matter if doctors wash their hands?

These days, we all know that tiny microbes can make us sick. None of us would even consider delivering a baby without washing our hands. In the early to mid 19th century, that was still common practice. In fact, many babies were delivered by doctors who had just performed autopsies on people who died from unknown diseases. In the late 1840s, a Hungarian physician named Ignaz Semmelweis observed that hand washing by doctors decreased rates of mortality among patients, including women delivering babies. It would be many years later before the medical establishment was willing to take his observations seriously, and hand washing became common practice. What kinds of errors and mistakes in judgment might we still be making now?

time around. This is the logical basis for vaccinations, in which some portion of a virus is injected into a person so that their immune system can learn how to deal with it and protect the body from an actual onslaught by the pathogen if it ever comes.

It is possible for the immune system to get so good at dealing with a familiar invader that you might never know that the invader even made it into your body. For instance, many of us are exposed to strains of the cold or flu viruses without becoming ill. Our immune systems are sometimes capable of recognizing and destroying the invader before it sets up shop and starts wreaking havoc. Indeed, that's really what is meant by the term "immune" – the ability of the immune system to keep an invader from making us ill.

A healthy immune system is capable of fighting threats from a wide range of invaders, including but not limited to bacteria, viruses, fungi, parasites, and something called mycobacteria – which are a little like bacteria and viruses combined. It is beyond the scope of this book to discuss all of these in detail, so we will review a few of the main ones before turning our attention to ways to help children and teens keep their immune systems prepared to deal with threats.

Some critters that threaten our health

Bacteria

Bacteria are single-celled organisms that enter the body, reproduce into colonies, and devour our resources. Some bacteria are actually good for us. Indeed, several hundred different varieties of bacteria live inside of our intestines and help us digest food and extract nutrients from it. Other bacteria, however, can do damage, often by releasing toxic chemicals. Our immune systems will have none of it. Once the unwanted bacteria are identified, our immune systems kick into high gear to eradicate them.

We live in a golden era for medicine – one in which antibiotic drugs are available to treat bacterial infections, many of which could do serious damage or even be fatal without them. It hasn't always been this way, and it might not always be this way. In 1928, in a laboratory in London, Alexander Fleming observed that a common species of mold, known as *Penicillium*, was capable of killing bacteria in Petri dishes. More specifically, because he wasn't the tidiest of researchers, his cultures of bacteria often became cultures for mold, too. Dr. Fleming noticed there were zones around the mold where no bacteria were growing. He reasoned that there was something in the mold preventing bacterial growth, and that isolating whatever it was in the mold that prevented bacterial growth could have important implications for the treatment of bacterial infections in humans. Boy was he right!

Dr. Fleming identified the component of the mold with antibacterial properties and labeled it, "penicillin." It would be another 15 years before researchers realized the full potential of penicillin and figured out how to turn Dr. Fleming's discovery into a mass producible treatment for disease. These developments ushered in a new area in medicine. One in which diseases caused by bacteria could be cured by a class of compounds we now call "antibiotics." We now know that penicillin kills bacteria by damaging their cell walls, while other antibiotics work by keeping bacteria from dividing or by interfering with their ability

> **Side***Notes*
>
> ### Bacteria and pimples
>
> For many adolescents, pimples are just part of life. As bodies grow and change, extra oil is produced and coats the skin. This oil can clog pores, allowing bacteria to thrive in the warm moist environment inside the skin. The immune system attacks these bacteria and excretes them through the infected pores. Pimples contain these bacteria – dead, dying and living. Treatments for pimples aim to dry up the oily pores and/or kill the bacteria on the skin that cause the infections.

to make necessary repairs.

Before antibiotics, people routinely died from bacterial infections that don't cause much trouble these days – diseases like strep throat and syphilis. Unfortunately, overuse and improper use of antibiotics has allowed bacteria to adapt through evolution and become resistant to some of these medicines – a prediction that was made by Dr. Fleming himself. As a result, medical science is now in a kind of race with nature. Currently, there are several bacterium that have parents and health officials concerned, including MRSA mentioned above, and bacteria that can cause deadly meningitis. Bacteria keep adapting to the antibiotics we discover, and we keep making new types of antibiotics. There are no easy answers to this escalating process, but the recent discovery of a new class of antibiotics, called *defensins*, should keep us in the race for a while longer.

Bacteria are only one type of disease-causing agents, and at least in the short term, bacteria have been easy to defeat with antibiotics. Very few otherwise healthy adolescents succumb to bacterial infection, though it does happen. Other disease causing agents can be harder to understand and much harder to defeat, medically, making them a greater concern. Viruses, for instance.

Viruses

Unlike bacteria, which are single-celled life forms, viruses are very different. They have much in common with actual, live cells – like the ability to replicate under the right conditions. However, the viruses that cause illnesses are no more alive than the viruses that cause computers to malfunction. While there is still a debate in the scientific community, viruses are generally not considered to be a part of the kingdom of living things.

A virus is essentially a strand of DNA or RNA that is wrapped in a protein coating. DNA and RNA carry instructions telling cells what to do and when to do it. Along with the DNA or RNA, these little balls of protein also carry enzymes capable of inserting instructions from the DNA or RNA into healthy cells and usurping control over what those cells do. They essentially sneak into cells and grab the steering wheels. They are untouchable by antibiotics and can often evade the efforts of the immune system for years – sometimes for life. Indeed, sometimes viruses, like HIV, actually hide inside of immune cells, making the task of finding them and getting rid of them that much harder. It would be like a shark trying to catch a pilot fish attached to its belly!

Viruses can be extremely tricky. Sometimes, we get them, we get sick, we feel better and then, in the distant future, the virus comes out of hiding and wreaks havoc again. Unlike bacteria, which the immune system can completely eradicate, it doesn't appear that viruses ever really go away. They just get beaten back into small numbers and, hopefully, stay that way.

SideNotes

Can you catch a cold from being cold?

How often have you told a child to put their coat on before going outside so that they don't get sick? Ever wondered whether that's even a legitimate thing to be concerned about? Well, it is. What better way to test this than to put people in a freezer, drip cold viruses into their nostrils, and see if they get sick? That's exactly what researchers have done. Those in the freezer are more likely to get sick than those standing outside of the freezer. Why? Perhaps because cold places stress on the body and temporarily weakens our defenses. Importantly, however, being cold can only increase the odds of catching a cold if you're exposed to a cold virus, but it is the virus that actually causes the illness.

Those infected with oral or genital herpes know that, unfortunately, viruses don't always cooperate with the game plan! In times of physical or psychological stress, injuries to the body, or the onset of other illnesses, viruses can come out of hiding and cause illness all over again.

Any parent who has taken their child to a pediatrician for a sore throat is familiar with this scenario. The doctor will say that it is either bacterial and in need of an antibiotic, or it's viral and will just need to run its course. The implication is that there are no treatments for viruses. The assumption is that the immune system will be able to successfully deal with the virus over time. This general flowchart for treatment decisions – bacteria require antibiotics while viruses require nothing – reflects a dogma that is long-standing, but may be about to change.

SideNotes

The lymphatic system? Huh?

We all know that the cardiovascular system pumps and carries blood throughout the body through a vast network of blood vessels. The lymphatic system is a second system of tubes in the body that is used to return another type of fluid back to the cardiovascular system. And it also plays a major role in fighting diseases. As blood travels throughout the cardiovascular system, fluid and nutrients leak out through gaps in tiny vessels called capillaries. The fluid that leaks out washes over cells in the body and provides them with nutrients and other molecules. The fluid, called lymph, then enters a complex drainage system called the lymphatic system. This system carries the clear fluid back to the cardiovascular system, but not before the fluid is filtered, and any foreign invaders are identified and dealt with. The points of filtration are called lymph nodes. When we are ill, we often refer to the swollen and sore points under our jaw line as swollen glands. In reality, they are actually swollen lymph nodes!

Viral ailments are usually diagnoses of exclusion. If another cause can't be found, a diagnosis of "virus" is assumed. Except in rare cases, people are not actually tested for viruses. Fortunately, the technology to detect viruses has advanced considerably in recent years, and should make the task of identifying and treating viruses easier in the future.

Understanding how the immune system works and how to help it do so can facilitate the creation of environments in which the natural immunity that our teens carry around with them can be maximized. Quite simply, if we are to avoid major, catastrophic pandemics (world-wide infections) involving potentially lethal viruses, we must do more to maximize the health of our kids' immune systems.

Mycobacteria

Mycobacteria are a fascinating cross between a virus and a regular bacterium. Technically, they are bacteria, but they lack a distinctive cell wall containing antigens that can be easily identified by immune cells. Instead, like viruses, they enter into healthy cells in the body and hide there. Both tuberculosis and Lyme disease are caused by mycobacteria. Both are also notoriously hard to treat once the mycobacteria have infested healthy cells and can cause a bewildering array of symptoms mimicking other ailments. It is likely we will be hearing much more about mycobacteria in the future.

Immune system activity and psychological health

The central nervous system - including the brain - and the immune system are intimately connected. When the immune system is engaged in a battle, the brain is affected in ways that can make the emotional state of the individual feel pretty terrible. The opposite also holds true; when the emotional state of a person is in bad shape, the immune system can be compromised.

Indeed, so deep is the connection between the two systems that our emotional states can suffer when viruses invade us, even if the immune response isn't strong enough to make us feel *physically* ill! People with chronic viral infections, say from a stubborn cold, can feel run down emotionally long after the major

Side*Notes*

Are happy people less likely to get sick?

A fascinating study by researchers at Carnegie Mellon University measured emotional characteristics in subjects and then exposed them to cold viruses. People who tended to feel positive about life were less likely to get sick than people who felt predominantly negative emotions. In a separate study, the researchers found that people who were more social were also less likely to get sick, despite the fact that being social can put you in proximity to lots of coughs and sneezes.

physical symptoms have passed.

In one recent, clever study[2] assessing the link between immune system activity and emotional well-being, researchers in Israel examined the emotional well-being of teenaged girls who had been vaccinated for the rubella virus, a common cause of illness in children. This process involves injecting portions of the virus into the body so that the immune system can learn to recognize it and protect the person against it if it is ever encountered. Following such vaccinations, the immune system can become acutely (temporarily) active, making people feel ill. In this study, girls that became slightly ill also became slightly depressed! In the words of the authors, many of the vaccinated girls,

> "showed a significant rise in several standard measures of depressed mood, as well as an increased incidence of social and attention problems and delinquent behavior... Thus, even a mild viral infection can produce a prolonged increase in depressive symptoms in vulnerable persons."

The same group of researchers took their investigations one step further.[3] They injected small portions of the cell walls from bacteria into subjects, a technique commonly used to evoke an immune response in humans in order to assess immune system health. Even though the injected material caused no physical symptoms,

> "The subjects showed a transient substantial increase in levels of anxiety and depressed mood. In addition, verbal and nonverbal memory functions were substantially impaired."

Similar findings have been observed when subjects are injected with cytokines, molecules that are released as part of the body's immune response. Some researchers argue that cytokines cause many of the symptoms of illness by acting directly on the brain:[4]

> Cytokines "act in the brain to induce common symptoms of sickness, such as loss of appetite, sleepiness, withdrawal from normal social activities, fever, aching joints and fatigue...The fact that cytokines act in the brain to induce physiological adaptations that promote survival has led to the hypothesis that inappropriate, prolonged activation of the innate immune system may be involved in a number of pathological disturbances in the brain, ranging from Alzheimer's disease to stroke...Indeed, the newest findings of cytokine actions in the brain offer some of the first clues about the pathophysiology of certain mental health disorders, including depression."

In short, activation of the immune system can make us feel bad in more ways than one. If the immune system is activated for one reason or another, we could feel slightly depressed or anxious, even if we don't have any physical symptoms of illness. Maintaining a healthy immune system capable of powerfully and quickly defending us against invaders could minimize the impact, and the length of the impact, of foreign invaders on our psychological well-being.

Indeed, as time goes by and research accrues, more and more disorders that involve psychological components are being traced to immune system health. It could be that many poorly understood diseases are either viral in nature or reflect improperly functioning immune systems, which can lead to infestation by new viruses and the re-emergence of already contracted viruses.

It is also possible, though not proven, that vaccinations could be precipitating events for many of the strange immune-related conditions that seem to be popping up these days. Let's take a brief look at vaccines and their potential to cause problems in the next section.

Vaccines – Friends or foes?

Once infected with a critter like a bacteria or virus, the immune system goes to work destroying it. During this process, the body forms a memory of the pathogen so that it can defeat it more quickly the second time around. Herein rests the logic behind vaccines. The process of vaccination involves exposing a patient, usually a child or teenager, to some portion of the pathogen of interest. Usually, the critter is deactivated, meaning that it can't cause infections. The body reacts to the deactivated pathogen and forms antibodies for it. If the pathogen ever enters the body for real, the antibodies stick to it, deactivate it, and mark it for destruction.

The following passage from an earlier work by the author describes the origin of vaccines:[5]

"In 1796, Edward Jenner, a country doctor in England, performed the first ever vaccination to protect a human against a disease – in this case, small pox. Jenner noticed that people who milked cows were less likely to get small pox. He reasoned it was because these folks were being exposed to cow pox from the cows, and that the cow pox must be similar enough to small pox that the individuals' bodies were able to learn how to protect themselves against both diseases.

To test his hypothesis, Jenner injected cow pox into an 8-year-old boy named James Phipps. A month and a half later he injected James with the small pox virus to see if his strategy worked. It did! The boy did not contract small pox, ushering in a new option for preventing disease – vaccination. (The word "vaccine" actually comes from the Latin word for cow, "vacca.")

A unique strategy was used get cow pox to America so that it could be used to inoculate colonists. Children were used to transport the virus. One would be infected before boarding ships headed for the New World. As that one began to heal, another child, and then another child, and so on, would be infected, until the voyage ended."

Vaccines have long served an important purpose in modern medicine, making it possible to prevent kids from succumbing to a litany of ailments that once wreaked widespread havoc with ease – chicken pox, flu, and even tuberculosis. Changes in rates of measles after a vaccine for it was introduced in 1963 highlight the powerful protective effects that vaccines can have against diseases. During 1962, more than 500,000 cases of measles were reported in the U.S. By the end of the 1990s, fewer than 100 cases were reported each year. Very impressive! The eradication of smallpox infections, planet wide, is perhaps the best example of how lucky we are to have vaccines in our arsenal. In 1967, the World Health Organization (WHO) launched the Smallpox Eradication Program. In 1980, the WHO announced they had succeeded in eradicating small-pox, a deadly and agonizing disease, via widespread vaccination.

In the U.S., children and adolescents now routinely receive a lengthy list of vaccinations,[6] including those for measles, mumps and rubella (MMR), hepatitis A and B, meningitis, polio, and chicken pox. It is also now recommended that kids receive a vaccine for the Human Papilloma Virus (HPV) during early adolescence (around 11 or 12 years of age). HPV is a sexually transmitted infection thought to cause upwards of 70% of cases of cervical cancer.

Without question, vaccines work. Unfortunately, their widespread and escalating use is driven in part by profits, and is out of step with what is now known about how the immune system operates. Specifically, antibody-mediated immunity, the type of immunity triggered by vaccines, is only one of the ways that the immune system learns to identify and fight infectious agents. Antibody-mediated immunity is only useful when critters are simply floating around in the body and have not climbed inside of any healthy body cells. Once inside of healthy body cells, antibodies are useless. In such cases, a different type of immune response, called the cell-mediated immune response, is needed to identify and destroy infected cells.

These two types of immune responses, antibody-mediated and cell-mediated, are related to one another in a teeter-totter type fashion. If antibody-mediated immunity is triggered, as is the case upon vaccination, cell-mediated immunity is temporarily compromised. What does this mean? Theoretically, anyway, it means that, for a period of time after a vaccination, the ability of the body to fight viruses and mycobacteria that are living inside of healthy cells in the body is compromised. Again, theoretically, this could render the individual susceptible to a wide range of infections and even cancers, which are usually kept at bay by a strong cell-mediated immune response.

For an example of why this should be a reason for concern, let's look at a recent news report regarding a failed vaccine for HIV tested by the drug company, Merck.[7] The company created a unique type of vaccine for HIV using a strain of the cold virus to carry HIV-related antigens into the body. Unfortunately, a significant number of subjects in the vaccinated group, more than the number in the non-vaccinated group, ended up contracting HIV in the weeks after being vaccinated. In other words, the HIV vaccine *increased* the chances that the subjects would contract HIV. Not exactly successful! Why might this be? The drug company itself did not offer a logical explanation. However, it is quite likely that the vaccine triggered a strong antibody-mediated immune response to the cold virus used to deliver the HIV vaccine, particularly in those who had previously been exposed to that particular strain of the cold virus. This strong antibody-mediated immune response to the cold virus could have temporarily weakened the ability of the body to protect itself from infections with viruses like HIV, which work by getting inside of healthy body cells and require a cell-mediated response to be eradicated. Thus, by pulling the body toward antibody-mediated immune activity, the vaccine could have temporarily rendered the body less capable of waging cell-mediated immune battles and protecting the person from infections with HIV.

Antibody-mediated immune activity is largely responsible for allergies, in which the immune system reacts strongly to non-threatening substances like dust and pollen, and autoimmune conditions, in which the immune system mistakes healthy cells in the body for threats and attacks them. It is possible that, in some kids, the strong antibody-mediated immune response triggered by the lengthening list of vaccines they receive could contribute to allergies and perhaps even conditions like Pediatric Autoimmune Neuropsychiatric Conditions Associated with Strep (PANDAS), in which an over-vigilant antibody-mediated immune response leads the immune system to attack brain cells involved in movement. Symptoms of PANDAS include a sudden onset of obsessive-compulsive type behaviors, like frequent hand washing, and motor tics, and seem most likely to emerge in fall as rates of strep infections increase.

Researchers have long speculated that other pediatric conditions, like autism, might have an immune-system link and that vaccinations could contribute to these conditions for many kids. At present, direct, compelling evidence that vaccines cause or contribute to autism does not exist. However, this does not mean that vaccines aren't part of the problem. Time and more data will tell.

For years, some advocacy groups have speculated that a particular ingredient, a mercury based preservative called thimerosal, in the MMR vaccine could be the culprit in many cases of autism. A recent report suggests this is not the case. Thimerosal was removed from MMR vaccines in 2001, yet rates of autism continue to climb. Discerning the cause of this increase has proven very tricky, in part because it appears that some of the increase has stemmed from changes in how kids with learning disorders are categorized. As rates of autism have climbed, diagnoses of other types of learning disorders have decreased.

At present, firm evidence that vaccines can cause health problems in kids is lacking. However, logically, the odds are very high that some kids will react negatively to vaccines and that the health of their immune systems could suffer in significant ways as a result. Arguments to the contrary would be inconsistent with the stated warnings from vaccine manufacturers. While we await further data, following the recommended vaccine schedule provided by one's pediatrician is the smartest route. To be safe, in the weeks following a vaccination, it might be best to keep kids away from people who are ill.

Keeping the immune system healthy

There is no doubt that the immune system plays very important roles in defeating and preventing infections, and that activity in the immune system influences how we think and feel. For those reasons, it is paramount that we do what we can to keep our kids' immune systems running strong.

During infancy, the health of the immune system is promoted and maintained by the constituents of breast milk. Indeed, while an infant nurses, the mother produces the appropriate antibodies and other immune factors to deal with germs to which the infant is exposed outside of the womb. This is a key reason why bottle fed babies are at greater risk than breast fed infants of contracting infections of various types.

The mother's body can no longer support a kid's immune system after nursing ends. As such, other sources of immune support, nutritional and non-nutritional, must be located. In the next few sections, we will examine some of the factors that influence immune system health at any stage of life.

Dietary supplements and immune system health

There is no substitute for living in a way that promotes healthy immune function. Eating well, exercising, getting sunlight, avoiding severe and prolonged stress are all solid and simple ways to keep the immune system functioning well. Some supplements might also help. Vitamin B6, omega 3 fatty acids, whey protein, and vitamin C have all been found to aid the functioning of the immune system. Colostrum-based products, particularly those containing "proline rich polypeptides," also known as "transfer factors," have been shown to help rebalance the immune system in cases where one end of the teeter-totter is way too high or way too low.[5] This can help the body fight viruses, bacteria, mycobacteria and cancers more effectively and diminish the severity of allergies and autoimmune conditions at the same time.

With regard to supplements, buyer beware. One of the main difficulties with the use of supplements of any kind is that they are not regulated by the Food and Drug Administration, and thus there is little if any rigorous oversight of their quality. If you are inclined to consider the use of any supplements for you or your child, it is wise to do your homework and discuss your strategy with your child's pediatrician.

Exercise and immune system health

It has long been known that exercise can boost immune system function in adults. A relatively small number of studies have examined the impact of exercise on immune system health in adolescents. Such data suggest that exercise can help to promote disease resistance in teens, as well.

A recent study assessed immune system markers in high school boys (aged 14-18.5) before and after 90 minutes of wrestling practice.[8] They observed several robust changes in immune system markers. Chief among them was a significant increase in the number of Natural Killer cells, the white blood cells that spread in the body looking for pathogens and cancer cells to destroy.

While short-term exercise seems to be good for the health of the immune system, excessive exercise is not. According to one sports medicine expert,[9]

"Risk of upper respiratory tract infections can increase when athletes push beyond normal limits. The infection risk is amplified when other factors related to immune function are present, including exposure to novel pathogens during travel, lack of sleep, severe mental stress, malnutrition, or weight loss."

This is one of those situations in which more is not necessarily better. However, unless you are an elite athlete, the odds are good that exercise will only bolster the strength of your immune system.

It is worth noting here that it is a myth that exercising helps one recover from colds and flues more quickly. Exercise benefits immune health before we get sick, not during!

Happiness and immune system health

As we have discussed, activation of the immune system during illness can have a negative impact on one's emotional state. Immune responses trigger anxiety and mild depression, among other psychological effects. Research suggests that the relationship between immune system activity and emotional well-being works in the other direction, as well. That is, our emotional states can affect our immune systems.

Several studies indicate that feeling good about life, socializing with friends, and avoiding prolonged or excessive stress can all contribute positively to the workings of our immune systems. As discussed in a text-box at the beginning of this chapter, when happy and sociable people are exposed to cold viruses, they are less likely to become ill than less-happy and less-social people. Research recently conducted in Israel indicated that exposing subjects to stimuli that caused them to feel happy, such as pleasing odors and pictures, caused improvements in key indices of immune system health and decreased levels of the stress hormone, cortisol.

In one of the most interesting studies examining the relationship between psychological factors and immune system health, researchers at Yale examined whether female AIDS patients (aged 16-55) with positive psychological characteristics (positive affect, positive outlook for treatment, finding meaning in challenging situations) lived longer than those without such characteristics. Subjects were tracked over five years. Those with positive psychological characteristics lived longer and maintained healthier immune systems during the duration of the study. This led the researchers to conclude:[10]

> "Psychological resources may protect against HIV-related mortality and immune system decline."

How, exactly, feeling good about life improves immune functioning and prolongs life in those that are ill is unclear, but research has provided some possible explanations. As we will see in the next section, expecting bad things triggers the stress response, which can be helpful to survival in the short term but can compromise our health over time. Conversely, feeling positive about the future dampens the stress response, which frees up resources to deal with other problems.

Stress and immune system health

"Under stress." "Stressed out." "I can't handle the stress." "You're on my last nerve." Ever heard comments like that? What do they mean?

"Stress" is actually two things – the thing causing us stress, called the stressor, and our reaction to it, called the stress response. The stressor can be anything – an impending math exam, loss of a loved one, squad car lights in your rear view mirror, what have you. They can even be positive things, like playing in a championship game or graduating high school.

When exposed to a stressor, the body reacts in a way that prepares us to deal with it. This is the stress response. Under appropriate circumstances – like when you're exposed to a stressor and the stress response is briefly activated so that you can do something about it – stress is a good thing. If you have an exam coming up and feel absolutely no stress about it, the odds are low you'll be motivated to study hard and do well. On the other hand, too much stress can be debilitating, both in the short-term and long-term. In the short-term, being overstressed can incapacitate us. If you have an exam coming up and are simply overwhelmed by the stress of it, the odds are low you'll be able to focus and perform, no matter how motivated you are. Each person has an optimal level of stress – one which compels action and also maintains ability.

While we all feel over-stressed from time to time, having a high stress level for an extended period of time can have negative consequences, including for our immune systems. People who care for loved ones with diseases like Alzheimer's are at a greater risk of disease themselves, in large part because of the impact of stress on their bodies. Prolonged stress weakens the body's ability to protect and heal itself. When we feel stress, the adrenal glands (located above the kidneys) release a hormone called cortisol. Cortisol helps prepare us to act and also temporarily suppresses immune responses, including inflammation. This probably allows us to keep fighting against the stressor until the mission is complete, without the immune system becoming overactive and diverting resources, at least initially. The problem comes when the stressors don't go away, the stress response stays activated, and cortisol levels stay above normal. When this happens, the immune system stays suppressed and the body becomes more susceptible to a wide variety of disease states, from colds and flues to cancers.

Prolonged stress is also bad for the brain. Cells in certain brain areas are highly sensitive to cortisol. In the hippocampus, which is critically involved in the formation of memories for facts and events, a small amount of cortisol can promote memory formation while a large amount of cortisol can actually kill the cells involved in making memories. Again, a little cortisol goes a long way, but too much is bad.

The relationship between stress and learning may have significant implications for teens in school. Many teens are under great stress when it comes to studying, getting good grades, making parents happy, and getting into selective colleges. These very factors, which are so prevalent for so many teens, might be inhibiting the very cognitive processes, like memory formation, that are so critical for success. At the same time, such stress might compromise their immune systems and leave them vulnerable to illness. When the author of the current book is sick it's usually right before a major trip or a grant deadline.

There is not much known about how the adolescent brain responds to stress, and how that might be different from adult responses. However, early research suggests that adolescents react more strongly than adults in lots of situations and to lots of stimuli, particularly threatening stimuli. They are also more likely to interpret facial expressions as negative rather than positive. Given the high levels of stress many kids are under, and the negative affects of stress on the body, it is paramount to help kids stop and smell the roses sometimes. They won't be very effective in school or in extracurricular activities if they're chronically ill from a worn down immune system! The importance of intentional relaxation for stress relief, health and well-being was discussed in Chapter 3. Meditation improves a variety of immune markers. Simply sitting quietly and breathing slowly for 15 minutes per day probably does the same.

How to avoid getting sick the old fashioned way— Flu as an example

A healthy immune system is needed to protect our bodies, and our kids' bodies, from the ravages of disease-causing viruses and microbes. Unfortunately, even the healthiest of us are susceptible to new viruses for which we lack an appropriate defense. Some viruses, like flu, mutate (change) so quickly, that it's impossible for the body to mount a rapid defense against all new strains. Indeed, one of the main fears among health officials is that a new, extremely virulent, strain of flu might emerge and quickly sweep across the globe. Fortunately, vaccines can help prevent the flu, but even they are fallible, often preventing only about 50% of infections. The vaccine for the 2007-2008 flu season was less than 50% effective.

In addition to actively maintaining a healthy immune system and getting flu shots, this is where the basics, like hand washing and avoiding exposure to pathogens, come in. Below is an excerpt from a 2006 report from the World Health Organization, called "Nonpharmaceutical interventions for pandemic influenza, international measures."

"Pandemic preparedness ideally would include pharmaceutical countermeasures (vaccine and antiviral drugs), but for the foreseeable future, such measures will not be available for the global population of >6 billion. Thus, in 2005... the World Health Organization (WHO) recommended nonpharmaceutical public health interventions in its updated global influenza preparedness plans. Such interventions, designed to reduce exposure of susceptible persons to an infectious agent, were commonly used for infection control in previous centuries."

Frequent hand washing and avoiding contact with sick people are powerful approaches to escaping the flu. Again, having a healthy immune system also helps. According to the CDC (same article as above):

"Serologic testing indicates that approximately 30%-50% of seasonal influenza infections may not result in illness."

There must be something about some exposed people that allows them to beat the virus early before it creates a problem. Of course, we are talking about the typical flu bug here, not the supervirus that world health officials now fear.

There are limits to how well we can protect ourselves. The common flu virus can be spread by infected persons 24-48 hrs before symptoms emerge. A closed-door business meeting could lead to a rapid spread of the illness before anyone even becomes ill. According to the CDC (again, same article as above):

"Influenzalike illness developed in 72% of passengers seated in an airplane that was on the ground for 3 h without ventilation and that held a person with symptomatic influenza. On a 75-seat aircraft, 15 passengers traveling with an influenza-infected person became ill. All 15 persons were seated within 5 rows of the index patient, and 9 were seated within 2 rows."

Because there are limits to how well the immune system, no matter how healthy, can protect us from highly contagious pathogens, the best gift we can give ourselves, and our communities, when our kids have the flu — whether the seasonal variety or a pandemic superbug — is to keep them at home. According to a recent report by Michael Haber from Emory University and colleagues from the CDC,[11]

> "..if persons with influenzalike symptoms and their household contacts were encouraged to stay home, then rates of illness and death might be reduced by ≈50%."

And, so, despite the lack of magic pharmaceutical bullets to prevent viral pandemics, low-tech strategies like hand washing, and avoiding contact with sick people, along with maintaining a healthy immune system, remain effective at keeping kids from coming down with ailments.

What does it all mean?

The immune system is a vast network of cells all working together to protect us from foreign microbes trying to sneak in and set up shop in our bodies, as well as body cells that have become cancerous and are now a threat to various organ systems, and perhaps the whole colony. When activated by any perceived threat, the immune system can have a palpable impact on our psychological states. Even mild activation of the immune system following vaccinations seems sufficient to cause subtle increases in depressed affect and anxiety for weeks or months to come. Most of us know that minor allergic reactions to pollen, pet hair, mold, or other common irritants can instantly put a person in a bad mood and take the fun out of a day.

Research suggests that strengthening the immune system

through exercise, laughter, and a healthy diet can stave off illness. It can also boost mood and increase the quality of life in general. Kids who are healthy miss fewer days in school and function better overall. From a socioeconomic standpoint, raising immune system status could potentially save billions each year in sick leave and lost productivity due to illness. Doing so could also slow the spread of annoying viruses like those that cause cold and flu. Not everyone gets sick. If we increase the number of those people, they could buffer the rate of transmission of certain viruses.

The immune system, like the rest of the body, undergoes changes during adolescence. Like the brain, the immune system also has the capacity to modify itself through experience. By helping kids make wise decisions around health-related issues, like exercise and hand washing, we can help them maximize the health of their immune systems and minimize the chances that illnesses will interfere with their lives.

Quick Facts:

- Our kids come equipped with an entire biological system dedicated to preventing and overcoming diseases.
- The immune system undergoes poorly understood changes during adolescence.
- When the immune system is weakened, kids are susceptible to a wide variety of diseases.
- Stress and lack of exercise weaken the immune system, while exercise and even laughter strengthen the immune system.
- When the immune system is activated people tend to feel depressed, anxious and lethargic, even if the immune activation is not strong enough to make the person feel physically ill.

- Vaccines are powerful assets in the fight against diseases, as they can actually prevent an individual from contracting diseases that can kill, like meningitis, hepatitis, polio, tuberculosis and so on.

- Many have asserted that vaccines cause health problems in some kids, and they might be correct, but strong evidence for such a position is currently lacking.

Chapter 9

Puberty and "raging hormones" – What do they have to do with adolescence?

Strange things happen on the way from childhood to adulthood. Kids start dressing differently, thinking differently, and doing things differently. Along side of the psychological metamorphosis of adolescence, a physical transformation occurs. Boys and girls start to grow into young men and women. They get taller, their shoulders get broader, girls get curvier and start their menstrual periods, boys start generating sperm and both grow hair in new places. These physical changes are all part of puberty and are designed to help prepare humans to be capable of surviving on their own and to have children should they decide to do so. In this chapter, we will explore puberty and discuss its relationship to adolescence.

If this book were written a decade ago, a chapter on puberty might have been the central focus. The text might have discussed how we can't blame our kids for acting crazy because their hormone levels are entirely out of control. We still have remnants of that general view in mainstream culture, and hormone changes do contribute to adolescent behavior. However, it is quite clear now that surging hormone levels cannot account for everything that happens during the second decade of life.

Puberty and adolescence overlap but are not one and

the same. Puberty – which stems from the Latin word *pubes* or *hair* – refers to hormone changes that result in three categories of growth:

1. The appearance of secondary sex characteristics, which refer to physical features other than reproductive organs that distinguish women and men. These include breast development in females, different patterns of pubic hair growth in males and females, differences in distribution of muscle and fat, widening of the hips in females, growth of facial hair and deepening of the voice in males, and other changes.
2. Further development of primary sex characteristics, like creating sperm in the testes and releasing eggs from the ovaries.
3. A growth spurt.

These changes prepare our bodies for reproduction and the ability to protect and care for our young. In short, the changes that occur during puberty transform the bodies of children into the bodies of adults.

Adolescence is defined more succinctly than puberty but yet less specifically. Adolescence is the transition from dependence to independence. Dr. Ron Dahl, a medical doctor and expert on adolescence, discusses his take on the juxtaposition between adolescence and puberty as follows:[1]

"Let us then provisionally define adolescence in humans as *that awkward period between sexual maturation and the attainment of adult roles and responsibilities.* This definition has proven useful in several ways. It captures the concept that adolescence begins with the physical/biological changes related to puberty, but it ends in the domain of

social roles. It encompasses the transition from the social status of a child (who requires adult monitoring) to
that of an adult (who is him- or herself responsible for
behavior)."

In some cultures, including many small towns in modern America, adolescence can be compressed such that the
transition to independence is largely completed before the end
of puberty. In contrast, it is possible for puberty to end long
before the transition to adulthood is complete. This is certainly
true for many college students.

Indeed, these two aspects of development – the physical
changes brought by puberty and the psychological and brain
changes which occur throughout adolescence – can slide over
and under one another. They always overlap and interact, but
not perfectly. The onset of puberty and events related to it (e.g.,
first menstrual cycle in females) continues to shift to earlier and
earlier ages in America while events marking the successful
transition into adulthood (e.g., first professional job and mar-
riage) come later and later. Thus, in the modern age, our bodies
begin to prepare us for adulthood long before we begin to
prepare ourselves to function as adults. Both puberty and
adolescence are moving targets – and they don't move in
concert!

Unfortunately, as sexual maturation shifts to earlier ages
and social maturation shifts to later ages, a new window of
developmental vulnerability has emerged. For most kids, there
are now several years between the completion of physical
development and the attainment of adult-like decision-making
and impulse-control skills. The fact that so many teenage
adolescents are willing to flash for those "Girls Gone Wild"
videos serves as a prime example of how this gap is often
exploited by those more interested in profits than the wellbeing
of kids. It also serves as further evidence of the need to modify

the mainstream culture to mold healthier kids and account for the fact that 18 no longer reflects young adulthood for most citizens. Just as 40 has turned into the new 30, it seems that something like 25 is turning into the new 18.

Hormones and puberty

Cascading changes in hormone levels are at the heart of puberty.[2] Hormones are chemical messengers that affect cells in the body by plugging into special receptors on those cells. Bourne by the blood, they travel long distances – throughout the body. They are released into the blood stream by glands and taken everywhere that blood goes. Any cell in the body that has special receptors for a particular hormone will respond to it once it arrives, no matter how far away it is from the gland that released the hormone. In this way, glands use hormones to shout messages to any cell that has the receptors to "listen."

The changes that happen during puberty begin deep inside of the brain. An area called the *hypothalamus* triggers an area just below it, called the *pituitary gland*, to release hormones. If you point one finger at your temple and another right between your eyes, the lines would intersect right about where your pituitary gland is. The word pituitary means "snot." Early neuroanatomists thought that's what the gland made! (Neuroanatomists also named the "mammilary bodies" in the brain "mammilary bodies" because they reminded them of breasts, another creative leap.)

Hormones released by the hypothalamus and pituitary gland travel through the blood to *endocrine glands* – special tissues that create and release their own hormones – located throughout the body. The adrenal glands, for instance. Hormones from the hypothalamus and pituitary tell the endocrine glands to increase or decrease release of their own hormones into the blood.

The hypothalamus monitors the blood to check levels

of hormones circulating around in the body. The hypothalamus and pituitary then signal the endocrine glands to increase or decrease hormone release to keep things at the desired level. In this way, the hypothalamus works like a thermostat. When the temperature gets too high, the thermostat keeps the heat from kicking on. When it gets too low, the thermostat tells the heater to release more heat. When hormone levels are too high, the hypothalamus stops sending signals to the glands telling them to release hormones. If the levels are too low, the hypothalamus sends signals telling the glands to release more hormones.

At the onset of puberty, the hypothalamus and pituitary change the signals they send to distant glands, which changes circulating hormone levels and causes the body to begin transforming itself from the body of a child to the body of an adult. At some point between the ages of 8 and 10 – usually closer to 8 for girls and 10 for boys – the hypothalamus starts to release a hormone called *gonadotropin releasing hormone* (GnRH). GnRH travels the short distance to the pituitary and triggers the release of two other hormones – *follicular stimulating hormone* (FSH) and *leutinizing hormone* (LH). These two hormones, FSH and LH, enter the bloodstream and travel throughout the body. Eventually the hormones reach the reproductive glands, or *gonads* – the *testes* in males and the *ovaries* in females. In response to FSH and LH the testes release *testosterone*, an androgen, and the ovaries release *estradiol*, an estrogen. A common misconception is that testosterone is something that only men have and estradiol (usually just called estrogen) is something only women have. In fact, males and females use both estradiol and testosterone in development, it's just that males use more testosterone than females, and females more estrogen than males.

Once the hypothalamus kicks things off, puberty begins. During the next five or six years, perhaps more, a wide variety of changes will take place within both males and females. During the first ten years of life, the external differences between males and females can be subtle. By the time puberty ends, girls will look like women and boys like men. Here is a list of changes that one would expect to see during puberty in each of the sexes.

Males: Growth spurt, appearance of pubic hair in the shape of an inverted triangle (sort of), increased muscle mass, hair growth under arms and other places, growth of facial and body hair, hair line recession begins, larynx enlarges, body odor and acne appear.

Females: Growth spurt, appearance of pubic hair in the shape of triangle, uterus grows, menstrual periods begin, body shape becomes rounded, hips widen, axillary hair appears, breasts develop, body odor and acne appear.

How is puberty measured? How do we know when it starts and ends?

The onset and progression of puberty is commonly assessed using the *Tanner scale*,[3] named for the British pediatrician that developed it. The Tanner scale rates several aspects of pubertal development in order to assess progression through puberty. In most studies using the Tanner scales, reaching Stage II is considered indicative of the onset of puberty. The scales and ratings are summarized below:

Pubic hair growth in males and females

Tanner I	Pre-pubertal state (no hair)
Tanner II	Small amount of long soft hair
Tanner III	Hair growth spreads out laterally and hair becomes more curly
Tanner IV	Adult-like, curly, coarse hair extending across pubic area but not on the inner portions of the thighs
Tanner V	Pattern of hair growth reaches inner surface of the thighs

Male genitals

Tanner I	Pre-pubertal state. Testes, scrotum and penis childlike.
Tanner II	Skin on scrotum thins, reddens and enlarges. Testes enlarge. Penis length unchanged.
Tanner III	Testes and scrotum enlarge. Penis lengthens.
Tanner IV	Skin of scrotum darkens. Testes and scrotum enlarge. Penis grows in length and width.
Tanner V	Testes, scrotum and penis reach their adult size

Female breasts

Tanner I	No breasts (pre-pubertal)
Tanner II	Breast buds forms. The areola (the reddish area around the nipples) begin to widen
Tanner III	Breasts begin to grow and are elevated
Tanner IV	Breasts continue to enlarge and become elevated. As the breast tissue becomes wider than the areola, the areola form a secondary mound on the breast
Tanner V	Breasts reach final adult size. The areola returns to contour of the surrounding breast.

As mentioned previously, the age at which kids reach Stage II of the Tanner scales is often considered the onset of puberty. The scales refer to observable changes in the individual. In reality, the hormone changes that eventually led to the observable changes must have occurred sometime earlier.

Acne and other annoying aspects of puberty

Unfortunately, pimples are often one of the clearest signs of puberty. There are few things about puberty more confusing, annoying, and embarrassing. Imagine (or remember!) that you're trying to fit in with other kids, climb to the top of the social hierarchy, attract members of the opposite sex and then....out of the blue... your face breaks out. Acne only makes the task of being a teen harder. Why does it happen? What can be done about it?

When puberty begins and androgens – namely testosterone – are released from the ovaries and testes, as well as from the adrenal glands, they produce a wide variety of effects. These hormones travel throughout the body and influence every cell with receptors for the hormone. One set of structures affected by testosterone are the sebaceous glands, which are located in the skin. These glands produce an oily substance called *sebum*, which is excreted onto the skin and helps moisten and waterproof skin and hair. Testosterone causes the sebaceous glands to produce more of this oil, which can clog the ducts, or pores, trap bacteria in them, and cause the pimples associated with acne. Pimples are actually small, local infections.

> **Side**Notes
>
> **What causes body odor?**
>
> The skin contains two categories of sweat glands. One category, apocrine glands, are found in areas where body hair grows, like the armpits. These glands can be triggered to generate sweat by strong emotions in addition to an increase in body temperature. The sweat produced by these glands is relatively odorless on its own. So what causes the odor? Bacteria. As bacteria on the skin break down sweat from the aprocrine glands, they give off the bad odor characteristic of "body odor." Deodorants cover up the smell, while antiperspirants prevent the aprocrine glands from releasing sweat.

Over the counter acne medicines help dry the oil on the skin and diminish the odds that the pores will become clogged. Antibiotic-based treatments, whether oral or topical, kill the bacteria that might normally infect the clogged pores.

Periods

The onset of the female menstrual cycle, menarche, is a major developmental milestone. The menstrual cycle usually begins a few years after the earliest signs of pubertal development, such as the appearance of breast buds. On average, females in America begin menstruating at 12. Colloquially, we often refer to menstruation as a female's "period." The word "period" can be used to describe one full completion of a cycle.

Maybe that's how it ended up becoming slang for the end of the menstrual cycle.

Why do women have periods in the first place? Each month, somewhere toward the middle of the monthly cycle, an egg is released by one of the ovaries. If reproduction were baseball, ovulation would be an underhand pitch! If it becomes fertilized by a sperm cell, the egg – called a zygote at this point – divides a few times and then implants itself into the wall of the uterus. If the egg is not fertilized and does not implant itself into the wall of the uterus, the body gets rid of the egg and the special lining in the uterus created for it. The egg and the lining are washed out of the female reproductive system in the menstrual flow.

Until the beginning of puberty, circulating levels of sex hormones (estradiol and testosterone) are roughly similar in males and females. Once puberty begins, males and females develop different patterns of hormone release throughout the day and over the course of a month. Males are relatively boring with regard to hormone changes. Because of the way the circuitry operates, hormones tend to be released in rhythmic pulses. In males, the magnitude of these pulses changes little from day to day. In females, the magnitude of these pulses depends on which day of the month it is. That is because, in females, an intricate dance of hormones occurs during a roughly 28 day cycle, culminating in the release of the egg and, if necessary, a flushing of the system to prepare for the next opportunity for impregnation.

The menstrual cycle is typically expected to complete itself in 28 days, though this can run short or long, usually long. Indeed, during the first few years after the onset of menstruation, irregular periods, and perhaps failure to release eggs when the opportunity comes, is quite common. In a previous chapter, we discussed how knowledge about the hormone cascades underlying the female menstrual cycle was used to create a pill capable of preventing impregnation.

For unknown reasons probably having to do with enhancing the ability to compete for mates at the right time, there is *some* evidence that the menstrual cycles of females living in close proximity, such as in dorm rooms, tend to become synchronized.

Antidepressants for PMS?

Prozac, the most widely used prescription psychoactive drug ever, save perhaps Valium, works well for depression in some people. It also causes severe side effects in some people and seems to be less effective for adolescents than adults. It's a drug that has made its maker, Eli Lilly, many billions of dollars. The problem for drug companies like Eli Lilly is that patents on drugs do not last forever. Once a patent expires, generic equivalents can be produced by other companies. This generally lowers the cost of the drug considerably and diverts profits from the original patent holder. This can be a huge problem for companies that make a large chunk of money off of a few drugs. Such was the case for Eli Lilly. At one point, Prozac generated more than one-third of Eli Lilly's income. In 2001, the patent was about to expire.

Faced with dwindling profits from Prozac, Eli Lilly began looking for other uses for the drug, including its potential to treat Premenstrual Dysphoric Disorder (PMDD). The disorder is recognized as an official disorder by the American Psychological Association, but many experts dispute the need to consider it an actual disorder.[4] The word "dysphoric" basically means not feeling good - the opposite of "euphoric." The word "disorder" essentially means the same thing as "syndrome" (a collection of symptoms) but sounds more frightening.

The ads for Sarafem, the same thing as Prozac (fluoxetine) but with different packaging, suggest to women that their moodiness, lack of drive, and reduced patience, are signs that something is wrong with them. For a week or two per month, they suffer from a chemical imbalance, an actual disorder that needs to be treated. Luckily for these young women, Eli Lilly can provide Sarafem. According to Eli Lilly, taking Sarafem everyday in order to minimize the impact of their periods is the first and only treatment available to the throngs suffering from PMDD. The tagline, "Sarafem – More like the woman you are," clearly suggests to women that the disorder associated with their monthly cycle can be removed from their lives, returning them to their true state, one without discomfort or moodiness associated with periods. One where they are "normal."

According to Eli Lilly's commercials, women often assume they have premenstrual syndrome (PMS) but actually have PMDD. Is there really a distinction between the two? Shortly after marketing Prozac as Sarafem, Eli Lilly was cited by the Food and Drug Administration for airing misleading advertisements. Too bad they don't have to run retractions!

So, what about the use of antidepressants to treat PMS? Does it work? It is probably safe to say that it does for some women. There are, however, a few important caveats and warnings worth mentioning. One is that the feelings associated with PMS can be similar in many ways to feelings associated with pregnancy – moodiness, nausea, fatigue, discomfort, etcetera. While there don't seem to be any major consequences of exposing unborn fetuses to Prozac (lots of women who suffer from depression take Prozac while pregnant) the drug does alter circulating hormone levels. Subtle effects on both the mother and child could be hard to detect. Prozac is listed as Category C with respect to the potential impact of the drug on developing babies during gestation, meaning that the ultimate effects are not known and the potential benefits should be carefully weighed against the potential risks. Adults that abruptly stop taking antidepressants can feel really terrible for a month or more as their brains adjust to the reduced levels of transmitters. Logically, a similar outcome awaits newborns, though exposure to the medication in breast milk likely helps wean the brain off of the drug.

The second major concern has to do with female adolescent development. Periods, and the discomfort associated with them, begin long before adulthood. In fact, as we discussed, menstruation begins early in puberty and is beginning earlier in life as time goes by. The impact of antidepressants like Prozac on adolescent development is entirely unknown. This is true even for adolescents treated with Prozac for depression, the disorder for which it was originally intended. The best course of action is to make such decisions following careful consultation with one's doctor.

Do females even need periods?

A growing number of doctors and patients are opting out of menstrual cycles altogether... sort of. In the next chapter, we will discuss female birth control pills and how they work. With regard to periods, it turns out that, if one continues taking birth control pills throughout an entire month and does not pause or take a placebo to allow for menstrual flow, periods can be skipped. Theoretically, they could be skipped forever, but those who use the pill this way typically allow for a few periods per year. One common strategy is to have a period once every three months, meaning four periods per year.

For adult patients who experience severe cramps and discomfort during menstruation, which is often accompanied by extreme psychological duress, this makes sense. It is certainly worth discussing with your doctor. But what about for teenagers? At present, there is no conclusive research on the possible developmental consequences of skipping periods. The concern would not be about skipping the bleeding, but rather the possible long-term effects of the alterations in hormone levels during adolescent development. Even things like cyst formation in the ovaries could be affected. Teenage girls have been taking birth control pills for decades now, apparently with minimal risk. However, that's when the regimen allows for periods. Unless medically indicated, the wise course of action would be to avoid altering the usual hormonal cycles any more than necessary during adolescence. The long-term consequences, if any, could emerge decades down the road. It is simply too early to tell.

Cracking voices

For males, cracking voices are a tell-tale sign of puberty. When talking to teenage boys, it's common for them to instantaneously flip from baritone to falsetto and back again. It can be embarrassing and very funny, but is utterly beyond their control. What causes this? It is related to a slackening of the vocal cords and actually comes later in puberty rather than at the very beginning. It is completely normal and generally resolves after several months as the young man grows into his elongated vocal cords.

Why is puberty starting earlier and earlier?

At the turn of the 19th century, the average American girl began having periods at about the age of 14. By the turn of the 20th century, the average age dropped to 12, perhaps a little over. Similar trends have been observed in boys. Why are American kids starting puberty earlier? Several mechanisms have been suggested – everything from too much TV to synthetic hormones that find their way from our toilets, to fish, and then to people.

One of the primary factors driving early puberty, at least for females, appears to be fat content in the body. The female body must have adequate supplies of stored nutrients in order to have babies. It seems that the brain monitors levels of a hormone called *leptin*, which is released by fat cells, to estimate how much stored energy the female has onboard. When it reaches an appropriate level, menstruation begins. At least that's the idea, and it certainly fits with the data. In countries where young females carry around less body fat than in America (which is basically everywhere), menarche starts later. When people from these countries move to the U.S. before their periods begin and adopt American eating habits, their periods begin earlier than expected.

If diet influences the timing of menarche, then kids enrolled in programs aimed at reducing obesity should begin menarche later than other kids. That is exactly what researchers at the Harvard School of Public Health have observed, and published, in 2005.[5] They selected 508 girls aged 10-13 from 10 different schools. At the onset of the study, none of the girls had started having periods. The schools were assigned to one of two conditions – control schools where the curriculum remained unchanged, and intervention schools where the curriculum was modified to include an obesity prevention program. Intervention schools utilized a program called Planet Health. The goal of the program was to reduce adolescent obesity by increasing consumption of vegetables, increasing physical activity, and decreasing TV time and the intake of high fat foods. Not a bad set of goals! The students were monitored over a period of two years.

Students at the two types of schools were similar at the beginning, but they were quite different at the end. Amazingly, it seems the intervention program altered the trajectory of pubertal development. Compared to girls at control schools, girls at intervention schools started their periods later, gained less weight and had lower percentages of body fat. As an added bonus, they also watched less TV and exercised more! The study provides compelling evidence that environmental (e.g., educational curriculum) and psychological (e.g., making the decision to exercise and eat healthier) factors play significant roles in the onset of menstruation. Education changes behavior and behavioral changes influence development.

The effectiveness of the Planet Health program shows that quality educational programming can kill lots of birds with a few stones. Girls at the intervention schools not only weighed less and started their periods later, they also seemed to adopt healthier habits in general as a result of the program. Lots of the problems that arise during adolescence – psychological disorders, risky sexual practices, drug use, and so on – share common denominators. Eating for health, exercising, and spending limited time in front of the TV are good for anyone – and the new data show that teens are no exception.

Delaying the onset of menstruation won't just save money on maxi-pads, it might also save a girl's life. By one estimate, with each year that menarche is delayed, a girl's risk of breast cancer goes down by 5% or more. The age at which adolescents attain the level of maturity necessary to function on their own and make adult decisions is occurring later and later. Delaying menarche by taking good care of oneself diminishes the number of years between the onset of fertility and the development of good decision making skills. As such, it should decrease the odds of teen, or even pre-teen, pregnancy, as well as reduce the risk of cancers.

The growing time-lag between the observable, physical changes that occur during puberty and the psychological and brain changes that occur during adolescence has wide-ranging implications. Quite simply, as the years go by, our children begin to look like adults earlier but are not prepared to function like adults until much later. The disconnection between a mature body and mature thinking creates the illusion that our teens are adults when, in fact, they are far from it. If a 16 year old looks like an adult, why can't we try them as adults for their crimes? Because they aren't adults. Legally, 18 marks the end of childhood and the beginning of adulthood. In reality, many of today's 18 year olds could probably use a few more years of practice before being released into the adult world.

Talking with kids about puberty

Regardless of how we learned about puberty, those of us that are adults had to learn about it. It doesn't take much skill to go through puberty, but the changes can be disconcerting if one is unprepared. For instance, did you know that about one in 10 males will develop swollen breast tissue, resulting in lumps behind the nipples? It can't be much fun for a boy to find lumps under his nipples without having any idea why. Taking the time to explain some of what to expect not only conveys important information, but also builds trust, opens lines of communication, and helps put the child at ease. Discussions about puberty are also a great way to lay the foundation for further discussions about adolescence – including discussions about sex, drugs, and internet privacy. If an adolescent feels comfortable coming to a parent or other adult with questions about puberty, odds are they'll be more likely to seek adult advice about other sensitive topics.

What does it all mean?

Puberty represents the unsettling physical metamorphosis that all children go through on the way to adulthood. It is not the same thing as adolescence but they overlap. Adolescence represents the psychological, social and some neurological changes that prepare humans to function in the world. It is closer to the surface than puberty and tightly tied to the culture in which one lives. Puberty and adolescence generally occur during the second decade of life, at least here in the West. Puberty begins sometime near the age of 10 and completes itself around the age of 18 or so. Adolescence begins sometime after the age of 10 and might not complete itself until the mid-20s for some people.

For both sexes, puberty means body growth, hair growth and maturation of the sexual organs. From a survival standpoint, the changes during puberty seem aimed at allowing us to reproduce and to protect our offspring so that they can one day reproduce and protect their offspring, as well. From a psychological standpoint, puberty and the changes that go with it can be confusing. After 12 or 13 years of period-free lives, females suddenly start menstruating, boys' voices start crackling, pimples sprout up, and their bodies suddenly go through a growth explosion.

The physical preparations for adulthood emerging from puberty would be useless without behavioral and psychological advances, as well. This is where adolescence comes in. Through interactions with the outside world, the developing adolescent brain organizes itself in ways that will allow the individual to function in the current society and put their newly mature bodies to good use.

Quick Facts:

- During childhood, patterns of hormone release are relatively similar for males and females. That all changes with the onset of puberty sometime late in the first decade of life.

- At the onset of puberty, a cascade of hormones are released triggering changes in physical appearance and causing males and females to differentiate further.

- Male hormone levels remain fairly consistent while female hormone levels fluctuate, following a one month cycle that culminates in menstruation, or one's "period"

- The physical changes of puberty are aimed at preparing us to be able to function like adults and procreate. Adolescence involves the learning of culturally specific behavior patterns for males and females to allow that to happen.

- Puberty is starting earlier and earlier, perhaps due to our high fat diets.
- The adolescent transition to adulthood is coming later and later.
- As such, there is now a unique window of vulnerability for kids during which their bodies are physically mature yet they remain unprepared to function as adults.

Chapter 10

Birds, bees and adolescents – The facts about teens and sex

As bodies grow and change during puberty, and social pressures shape behavior and expectations during adolescence, most people experience a sexual awakening. We suddenly realize that there are reasons why we have a reproductive system. The combination of a sexual awakening and the pressure to be physically perfect during adolescence, reviewed in an earlier chapter, puts inordinate pressure on kids to fit in. It is a very confusing time for both kids and their parents. In this chapter we will explore issues surrounding teen sexual attitudes and behaviors, and discuss some of the risks, including sexually transmitted infections. We will also discuss strategies for helping adolescents deal with the pressures and responsibilities inherent in their sexual development.

In the second half of the last century, America underwent a sexual revolution. Adolescents and young adults asserted their freedom to use their bodies as they saw fit. For some, that included having plenty of sex. Nineteen sixty-seven witnessed "The Summer of Love." In the memory banks of some of you reading this book, the Summer of Love could probably be renamed, "The Summer of Doing Psychoactive Drugs and Having Sex with People You Didn't' Know."

The sexual liberation asserted in the late 1960s quickly spread to those not involved in any kind of intellectual, civil or chemical movements. Female birth control pills emerged on the scene during that decade, giving women a sense of control over their sexuality that was previously unknown. Rates of inter-course among teens, which had been rising even before the sexual revolution, rose steeply in the years after the Summer of Love, and communicable sexual diseases spread like plagues. For some, "Make Love, Not War" quickly gave way to "Make Love, Get Sores"!

As the glory days of the sexual revolution passed, subsequent generations of adolescents found out the hard way that free love can actually be quite costly in the long-run. Let's take a look at what has transpired in the last few decades; how attitudes about sex, exposure to sex, rates of sex, and conse-quences of sex have changed. We'll discuss the role of natural adolescent development in the sexual awakening that occurs during the teen years and examine ways in which parents and communities can take advantage of the ease with which teens learn to shape healthy attitudes and behaviors around sex.

Sexual attitudes and behaviors

The first time most of us start a sentence with something like, "When I was a kid...," we are in total disbelief. That's what adults say! As kids, we can't wait to be adults. As adults, we seem to be surprised to find ourselves there, and talk about how much simpler things were back then. It's very easy for us to assume that, when we were teenagers, we knew more than the current wave of teens. It is also common to hear adults say that the moral fabric of society has decayed since we were adoles-cents, or that current teens are even farther off course than we were. That might be accurate for some issues, but when it comes to sexual attitudes and behaviors it is more complicated than that.

After the Summer of Love, rates of intercourse among teens increased during the 1970s and 80s.[1] By some estimates, in 1970, 5% of 15 yr old girls and 32% of 17 year old girls had engaged in intercourse. Those numbers increased to 26% and 51%, respectively, by 1988. Fortunately, and for reasons not immediately clear, levels of sexual involvement among teens actually decreased in the final years of the 20th century. Data from the 2005 National Youth Risk Behavior Survey[2] suggest the percentage of teens in 9th through 12th grade who engaged in intercourse decreased from 53% in 1995 to 47% in 2005. In addition, those having intercourse had fewer partners. In 1995, 18% of sexually active teens had four or more partners. This number dropped to 14% in 2005.

The drop in the number of sexual partners is a good thing. But, still, the numbers indicate that nearly 50% of kids in grades 9-12 have had intercourse. To understand why, let's take a look at some of the factors that influence the likelihood that a teen will become sexually active:

Media – Research suggests that kids who see lots of sexually suggestive content in the media (e.g., television, movies, video games) are almost twice as likely as other kids to become sexually active.

Parents – Parent-teen communication about sex also plays a prominent role in determining the likelihood that a teen will become sexually active. Kids who know that their parents would disapprove are less likely to do it. It's amazing how powerful simply talking to kids can be!

Religiosity – Teens that have parents that hold strong religious beliefs and regularly attend religious services are less likely than other kids to have intercourse before the age of 18. Similarly, teens with their own strong religious beliefs (particularly those who regularly attend services) are less likely than their peers to have sex before the age of 18.

Friends – Several studies suggest that the likelihood that an adolescent will become sexually active is strongly influenced by whether the individual's friends are sexually active.

Thus, one could argue that kids who view less sexually suggestive media content, have had conversations with their parents about sex, have religious faith, and hang out with non-promiscuous friends would be less likely than other teens to become sexually active. The relative impact of these factors is not known, but it does seem clear that parents who want their teens to hold off on sex should find non-threatening ways to express that hope, and place reasonable limits on the exposure that a teen has to sexually explicit media and sexually active peers.

It is important for parents to remember that the brain in their teen might not be on the same page as theirs, and delaying gratification can be inherently difficult for many kids. Add alcohol or other intoxicants to social situations and unplanned sexual encounters are more likely to happen. With regard to teen sexuality, effective communication and limit-setting are crucial. If parents don't help guide their teens through the minefield of sexual development, who will?

Sexually transmitted infections – Hidden consequences of promiscuity

In the spring of 1996, workers at a Sexually Transmitted Disease clinic in Atlanta, Georgia, witnessed a stream of teens coming in with concerns about their genitals. They quickly realized they were dealing with a bona fide syphilis outbreak. By the time the outbreak was contained, more than 200 teens and young adults had become infected. At the center of the outbreak was a group of Caucasian girls, the majority of whom were between the ages of 13 and 16. The boys involved tended to be older, between 17 and 21. The disease spread like wildfire at drug fueled sex parties in the Atlanta area.

Here is a description of the events in a subsequent medical report about the outbreak:[3]

> "Sex was usually public and communal; the girls would have sequential and simultaneous sex partners, experiencing vaginal, anal, and oral sex, occasionally at the same time, and occasionally with more than one partner at a particular orifice. The girls also had sex with each other, and numerous sexual encounters outside the party environment were also documented."

Given the age disparity between the females and males involved, some might think the boys had coerced the girls into having group sex, but in general that was not the case. In an interview with PBS,[4] Dr. Claire Sterk, a professor at Emory University and part of the team that investigated the outbreak, stated that "The girls certainly were running things from their point of view."

The girls were "running things"? Surely this must have been a very unusual group of girls. Not really. Again, Dr. Sterk:[4]

> "The girls that I initially met in the health department clinic looked like what I would call sweethearts, without meaning that in any negative sense. They had soft faces, soft expressions, their voices were very soft. They acted insecure. Had shy smiles. At times would blush if they were talking about the things that had been happening. The way

they dressed was basically like mainstream teenagers all over the country do. And the way they talked in some ways revealed that they felt uncomfortable talking about just the whole topic of sexuality. And so here you had the tension between the way they looked and the kinds of things that had been happening in their lives."

If the boys weren't coercing them, and there wasn't something about them that made them stand out from other teens, then why in the world would they do something like this? According to reports, disconnection from parents, boredom, and a desire to assert their independence made unique contributions to the girls' decisions to get involved, and stay involved, in the sexual escapades detailed above.

This outbreak of syphilis in the Atlanta area is not unique. This kind of thing happens frequently in towns around the country, though usually on a smaller scale. The specific infection underlying the outbreaks might be different, but risky sexual practices leading to the disease outbreaks are always present. Such outbreaks serve as reminders that, in modern America, contracting venereal diseases is a very real risk of casual sex. Drug resistant strains of bacterial infections like gonorrhea are now endemic and viral infections like HSV-1 or -2 (herpes) and HIV become baggage for life. Not all adolescents that contract genital herpes will have

SideNotes

Is oral sex sex or not?

This question is not as easy as one might think. Bill Clinton is a very smart man and even he had difficulty with this one. Regardless of what we adults think about the issue, many of today's kids are being taught, socially, that oral sex is not sex. Regardless of what one calls it, there is an array of infections that can be transmitted through mouth to genital contact. One way to help fix the problem is to establish fact-based health education courses administered by trained people. Another way is for parents to talk to their kids about this issue and to make their opinions known, whatever they might be.

recurrent outbreaks, but about 1 out of 3 will, and they can expect several flare-ups per year until their bodies get things under control. Perhaps even more frightening is the fact that upwards of 1 out of 10 females that contracts herpes will have an outbreak of viral meningitis (caused by the herpes virus) concurrent with their first genital outbreak. For some, this will be a recurring problem and could explain some cases of nasty, unpredictable, repeating bouts of headaches lasting for a week or so that respond poorly to headache medicines. Youch!

School sex education programs – Do they work?

Sex education is a touchy subject that many adults don't like to discuss. From a research standpoint, should schools teach kids about sex? To answer this question it is important to define the goals of sex education. Teaching the facts? Changing attitudes? Delaying the onset of sex? Increasing the use of birth control? Let's go for the big one. Do sex education programs decrease sexual activity among kids and/or delay the onset of sex? Some programs do and some don't.

In his 2006 review of the impact of sex education on behavior, J.J. Sabia of the Department of Housing and Consumer Economics at the University of Georgia, says the following:[5]

"Findings suggest that those on each side of the ideological debate over sex education are, in a sense, both correct and mistaken. Opponents are correct in observing that sex education is associated with adverse health outcomes, but are generally incorrect in interpreting this relationship causally. Proponents are generally correct in claiming that sex education does not encourage risky sexual activity, but are incorrect in asserting that investments in typical school-based sex education programs produce measurable health benefits."

This sobering assessment of the benefits and potential consequences of sex education suggests that we have a long way to go if we want to deliver effective sex education through public schools. Ideally, the current approaches would be improved and standardized so that all kids get similar information. Dyslexic policies have mandated standardized testing when, in fact, it is information and not testing that ought to be standardized. With regard to sex education, the information should be science-based, data-driven, and free of the moral prescriptions or judgments that characterize many programs now. Those aspects of the issue should be addressed outside of school walls, in the safe confines of homes, churches, etcetera. In other words, the component that schools provide should be approached purely from a health standpoint and based on rigorous science. It is up to parents and other adult caregivers to help kids figure out what to do with that information.

Let's look at an example. HIV is a virus that can be transmitted through sexual activity, and represents a major threat to the health of adolescents and adults. People need to know about the disease, how it is transmitted, and how to avoid contracting it. Education about HIV, which leads to the deadly condition known as AIDS, is critical. Moral perspectives and abstinence education might be useful, but they don't stop viruses from passing from person to person in moments of passion and ignorance. Educators cannot make decisions for teens, but they can equip them with the knowledge they need to think for themselves. It seems reasonable to expect that parents, not schools, should be responsible for teaching kids how to conduct themselves when it comes to sexual activity. Schools can help to inform these discussions by providing accurate health informa-tion that teens can use flexibly according to their own values;

values that should be learned and nurtured outside of school. The source and nature of those values is a personal and family matter.

What about programs that seek to reduce the risks inherent in sex by advocating for safe sex rather than, or in addition to, advocating for abstinence? School programs offering students condoms serve as an example of such efforts. Many adults are unsure how they feel about such approaches and fear that promoting *safe* sex might end up promoting *more* sex. While such fears are valid, the data should help assuage them. For instance, according to the non-profit research group, RAND, programs that make condoms available to kids in the Los Angeles area seem to promote safer sex without promoting sex in general. The researchers tracked nearly 2000 students in grades 9-12 over the course of a year following the implementation of a condom availability program. The percentage of students having sex during that year did not go up, but the percentage of males indicating that they always use condoms during intercourse increased from 37% to 50%, and the percentage reporting that they used a condom for their first experience with intercourse increased from 65% to 80%. Attitudes toward sex and condom use were unchanged or changed in ways consistent with delaying sex and using protection. In short, the program seemed to achieve its objectives – facilitating safer sex when sex happens – without increasing rates of sex or the percentage of kids initiating sex.

It is worth noting that programs geared toward promoting safer drug use rather than safer sex achieve similar objectives, even it the logic behind such initiatives is counterintuitive at first. In 2003, the government in British Columbia, Canada, opened the first ever legal "shooting gallery" in Vancouver as part of a three year pilot program. Open 18 hours per day, the legal shooting gallery provides heroin addicts with a place to inject themselves using clean needles. No matter how one might feel about giving addicts needles, sharing needles accounts for roughly ½ of new cases of HIV/AIDS in some areas. The shooting gallery approach is aimed at reducing public health costs associated with injection drug use by ensuring that clean needles are used and dirty needles are turned in. In Vancouver, the approach appears to be working. Overdose deaths are easier to prevent in such an environment, injection drug users are off the streets while they're in the facility and the clean needles minimize the spread of deadly diseases. It does not appear that the approach has increased or decreased the number of users, but this is left to be determined.

In short, sometimes the best approaches from a public health standpoint require viewing issues such as sex and drug use from pragmatic health perspectives. Nobody wants to give adolescents, or adults, the green light to have sex or shoot up with drugs. However, in the event such decisions are made, there should be mechanisms in place to minimize the damage that is done. Condoms diminish the odds of pregnancy and, like clean needles, diminish the spread of disease. Doing our best to dissuade sex during adolescence and allowing for easy access to protection should an adolescent decide to go through with it is emerging as a pragmatic approach with data behind it.

Teen pregnancies and abortions

Here is some good news for you. According to research by the Alan Guttmacher Institute, fewer teenagers are getting pregnant these days and fewer teen pregnancies are ending in abortions.[6] In 1972, 95 out of every 1000 teen girls aged 15-19 became pregnant (almost 10% or 1 in 10). In 1982, the number had grown to 110 per 1000 and remained at that level in 1992. However, in 2002, the rate was only 75 pregnancies per 1000 teens in that age range. This is more than a 25% drop in teen pregnancies between 1982 and 2002. A small increase occurred in 2007.

The percentage of teen pregnancies ending in abortions has also fallen. In 1972, 19% of teen pregnancies in girls ages 15-19 ended in abortions. The number grew to 43% in 1982, declined to 35% by 1992 and further declined to 22% by 2002. This is nearly a 50% drop in rates of abortion between 1982 and 2002.

Sexual development, orientation and gender

Puberty and adolescence is the time when most people develop a sense of themselves as sexual beings. Although sexual awareness and behavior emerge in earnest during adolescence, the groundwork for a person's sex and sexuality begin to emerge far earlier. It's beyond the scope of this book to discuss all of the issues related to sex and sexual orientation, but a cursory overview of the science involved in the study of sexual orientation and the adoption of gender roles can provide a context for thinking about these things.

There can be little doubt that both individual biology and the environment, including the environment inside of the womb before birth, contribute to sexual orientation during adolescence and beyond. The process of human development begins with the fertilization of the female's egg by the male's sperm. A normal, complete cell contains 23 pairs of chromosomes – tightly wound masses of genetic code. These chromosomes contain all of the information necessary to develop and maintain a human being. The sperm brings half of them, 23 chromosomes, to compliment the egg's 23 chromosomes. They match up with each other, making 23 pairs.

One pair of chromosomes, called the sex chromosomes, determines whether the child will be genetically male or genetically female. The egg contains an X sex chromosome. If the sperm brings an X sex chromosome, the child will be genetically female. If the sperm brings a Y sex chromosome, the child will be genetically male. This is the first step in sexual development, the determination of whether the developing baby will be genetically male or female.

Both genetically male and genetically female fetuses have the potential to develop male or female genitals. Research suggests that exposure to the hormone testosterone at critical times during development in the womb determines whether the genitals develop down male or female paths. Importantly, development of internal sex organs and the external genitalia occur at different times. As a result, it is possible for a fetus to develop the internal reproductive organs of one sex and the genitalia of the other sex. Given that the brain mechanisms underlying sexual orientation and sex-specific behavior patterns also seem to be influenced by hormones early in development, it is possible to develop complicated combinations of external genitals, internal reproductive organs, and attraction to one sex or the other.

What about the adoption of gender roles and the development of gender identity after birth? Does biology or the environment have the final say? We can't be certain, but biology generally seems to win. Despite common misconceptions about the topic, it does not seem possible to successfully turn boys into girls and vice versa just by creating environments that reward or punish particular behaviors. It might be possible to shape behavior patterns through reward and punishment, but that does not change the underlying behavioral tendencies. For instance, in the past, institutionalized schizophrenics would be tormented until they stopped expressing their psychosis. Were they cured? Absolutely not, only their external behaviors were changed. The same occurs when males are forced to behave like females and vice versa.

One of the most compelling and tragic examples is the case of a boy named David Reimer. David, whose birth name was actually "Bruce," was born genetically male and with all of the male plumbing. During the circumcision, something went wrong and David's penis was mutilated. The doctors urged David's parents to raise him as a girl instead. They renamed him "Brenda" and did just that. David was miserable. Unfortunately, the psychologist overseeing the case, John Money, wasn't forthright about the case with the public, the scientific community, or David's parents. He claimed that the gender switch was a success, while the reality was that David was suffering greatly. He was confused about his sex and gender, and often wanted to die. When David hit adolescence, he found himself attracted to females. He did not understand why he failed to fit in with other girls.

Despite the environment, the hormone supplements, and the female clothes that he wore, David felt like a boy and wanted to behave like a boy. In his mid-teens, David refused to continue seeing Dr. Money. Eventually, he was told what had happened and began living his life as a male, something he knew to be right all along. Despite loving parents who nurtured him and treated him as a girl and stubborn medical oversight, David maintained a male orientation throughout the process. He lived as a man until his death in 2004 at the age of 38. David committed suicide with a sawed-off shotgun, a patently male way to end one's life. For more about this fascinating and emotionally gripping story, check out the book, *As Nature Made Him: The Boy Who Was Raised as a Girl*, by John Calopinto.

Thus, despite widespread misunderstanding among both lay people and the medical community, simply manipulating the environment is not enough to determine whether a male or female will develop a male or female gender identity. In the womb, the process of sexual differentiation depends upon biology, in the form of genetic information contained in chromosomes and the presence or absence of testosterone at critical times. After birth, sexual development, and probably sexual orientation as well, are guided by an interplay between biology and environment, with more of the responsibility resting on the side of biology. People can choose whether to be sexually active with either sex, but the underlying drives are biological in nature and most likely beyond the control of the individual or the adults around them.

Sex and violence

In 2008, researchers in South Africa reported a study in which they followed 2360 adolescent students to assess the predictors of early initiation of sex in relationships. In the 15 months after the onset of the study, around 300 students had their first experience with intercourse. Among the chief predictors of early initiation of sex were the intention to have it and the presence of violence in romantic relationships. This fits perfectly with observations from the U.S.

Violence in adolescent relationships is far more common than is comfortable to recognize, and sex is often a key component of such relationships. Estimates suggest that as many as 1 out of 3 adolescent females will experience violence in one relationship or another, perhaps several. Indeed, women aged 16 to 24 are the most likely to experience violence in relationships. In many cases, the violence is used by young males to control their girlfriends. Many young females make the mistake of assuming that their boyfriend's hostility, jealousy and possessiveness is romantic and an indication of the depth of their love. This scenario can quickly become a true pattern, a cycle, for many developing young people. If the parties involved, both the male and the female, do not learn to handle their use of power and expressions of intimacy in different ways, unhealthy relationships are destined to become part of their adult lives. Further, the presence of violence in young relationship is predictive of other problems, such as suicidal behavior and substance abuse. Sadly, for many young people, sex, love and violence become intertwined in ways that ultimately interfere with healthy psychological development.

The realities of intimate partner violence during adolescence have compelled lawmakers to take action. Each year, Idaho Senator Mike Crapo leads a highly supported measure through the House and Senate to designate the first week of February as "National Teen Dating Violence Awareness and Prevention Week." In laying out the need for the initiative, the resolution (S. Res. 388) captures the scope of the problem nicely:[8]

- Whereas 1 in 3 female teenagers in a dating relationship has feared for her physical safety;
- Whereas 1 in 2 teenagers in a serious relationship has compromised personal beliefs to please a partner;
- Whereas 1 in 5 teenagers in a serious relationship reports having been hit, slapped, or pushed by a partner;
- Whereas 27 percent of teenagers have been in dating relationships in which their partners called them names or put them down;
- Whereas 29 percent of girls who have been in a relationship said that they have been pressured to have sex or to engage in sexual activities that they did not want;
- Whereas technologies such as cell phones and the Internet have made dating abuse both more pervasive and more hidden;
- Whereas 30 percent of teenagers who have been in a dating relationship say that they have been text-messaged between 10 and 30 times per hour by a partner seeking to find out where they are, what they are doing, or who they are with;
- Whereas 72 percent of teenagers who reported they'd been checked up on by a boyfriend or girlfriend 10 times per hour by email or text messaging did not tell their parents;

- Whereas parents are largely unaware of the cell phone and Internet harassment experienced by teenagers;
- Whereas Native American women experience higher rates of interpersonal violence than any other population group;
- Whereas violent relationships in adolescence can have serious ramifications for victims, putting them at higher risk for substance abuse, eating disorders, risky sexual behavior, suicide, and adult revictimization;
- Whereas the severity of violence among intimate partners has been shown to be greater in cases where the pattern of violence has been established in adolescence; and
- Whereas the establishment of National Teen Dating Violence Awareness and Prevention Week will benefit schools, communities, and families regardless of socio-economic status, race, or sex: Now, therefore be it

Resolved, That the Senate:
(1) designates the week of February 4 through February 8, 2008, as ``National Teen Dating Violence Awareness and Prevention Week''; and
(2) calls upon the people of the United States, high schools, law enforcement, State and local officials, and interested groups to observe National Teen Dating Violence Awareness and Prevention Week with appropriate programs and activities that promote awareness and prevention of the crime of teen dating violence in their communities.

And so, abuse in intimate adolescent relationships, many of which include sex, is a significant problem. Preventing such abuse requires talking about relationships with kids at an early age and helping them establish expectations for healthy relationships before they reach dating-age. Detecting violence in adolescent relationships requires adults to closely monitor their kids for signs that the relationships they are in are volatile. Remember that, often, the only observable bruises in abusive relationships are emotional. For more information, a good place to begin is the website for the Alabama Coalition Against Domestic Violence (www.acadv.org).

Birth control – How does "the pill" work?

As we discussed in the last chapter, sometime early in the second decade of life, most females begin menstruating. The menstrual cycle is an intricate dance of hormones and chemical feedback loops that results in the release of an egg and either impregnation or menstruation – bleeding that flushes out the female reproductive system and prepares it for the next opportunity for impregnation.

Once scientists identified the hormones involved in the menstrual cycle, it was only a matter of time before someone figured out how to disrupt the process and keep the egg from being released, thus foregoing that month's opportunity for impregnation. There are several types of birth control products capable of doing this, including pills. The most common type is actually a combination of pills. For the first 21 days of the menstrual cycle, a pill containing two synthetic hormones is taken. Synthetic estrogen and progesterone prevent an egg from being released. They also cause the mucus over the cervix (the opening to the uterus) to thicken, making it harder for sperm to swim into the uterus and fertilize an egg if one were present. From day 21 until the end of the cycle, a placebo pill is taken. During this time, the woman has her period and then the cycle starts over.

There are several health risks and benefits that should be considered before taking birth control pills. On the positive side, there is evidence that taking the pill reduces one's chances of getting ovarian cysts and cancers, non-cancerous cysts in the breasts, uterine cancer, and pelvic inflammatory disease. It might also improve acne. There is also a patch available for those who prefer to wear their birth control on the skin rather than take a pill.

While relatively safe, neither the pill nor the patch are without risks. The most common side effects include headaches and weight changes – up or down. It is a popular misconception that birth control pills cause weight gain. They might, but they might also cause weight loss. Initial side effects sometimes go away or can often be resolved by adjusting the dose. However, although rare, some individuals can be at increased risk of blood clots, strokes and heart attacks. The blood clot risk is even higher for those women using the patch. Smoking cigarettes while on the pill or patch can increase the odds of such serious side effects even more.

Below is a widely used acronym, "ACHES," that can help users of the pill or patch recognize if they are having serious side effects. In the event that an individual experiences such symptoms when taking the pill, they should call their doctor immediately or head to the emergency room.

Abdominal pains (severe)
Chest pain or shortness of breath
Headaches (severe)
Eye problems, such as blurred vision
Severe leg or arm pain or numbness

Obviously, the decision to use the pill or patch is a big one, and it is often confronted by teenage girls feeling alone and a little frightened. It is important to make this decision in an informed way, and that means with good medical advice, a full understanding of the implications of sexual activity in the overall life of the young woman and, preferably, plenty of input from parents. This topic can be a challenging one for teens and their parents to confront. But, like drug use, friends, driving, and other important decisions in adolescence, an open and scientifically-informed conversation can ease fears, build trust, and lead to smart choices.

Another kind of pill

Beside traditional birth control pills, there are other, controversial contraceptive pills on the market. These are taken after the act of intercourse to prevent a pregnancy from occurring. There are different types, but they are generically referred to as "morning after" pills. Specific brands of morning after pills might contain different levels or types of hormones. One such brand, "Plan B," contains both synthetic estrogen and progesterone in high doses. As such, it's really just a concentrated version of the birth control pills discussed above. In this case, the name, "Plan B," implies that "Plan A," presumably abstaining or having safe sex, didn't work out!

Morning after pills can decrease the odds that an egg will be released through ovulation, that it will fertilized if it is released, and that it will implant itself successfully into the lining of the uterus if it is released and fertilized. In general, the strategy is thought to be between 50-75% effective at preventing pregnancy, though the success rate will depend on several factors, including when the pill, or pills, is taken. To be optimally effective, the pill should be taken within the first 24 hr after intercourse, though research suggests that, in some cases, it can still work if taken within the first 120 hrs (5 days) after unprotected intercourse. Sperm can live for a week or so after intercourse, meaning that impregnation can come days after the actual act.

Even though they work, at least sometimes, morning after pills should not be relied on as contraceptives themselves. As a parent, keeping some around in case of unplanned emergencies is one thing, but allowing teenagers to even consider using them as a primary contraceptive is unwise to say the least. Nausea and vomiting are not uncommon, and the pills can also provide a false sense of security – remember, they are only effective between 50-75% of the time. Those are not good odds when it comes to pregnancy!

Would it be possible to make a pill for males?

Birth control pills for females take advantage of the fact that circulating levels of hormones change throughout the month in the female body. By introducing synthetic hormones at the appropriate times, ovulation can be blocked. Males, on the other hand, have relatively steady levels of circulating sex hormones. Testosterone is the key hormone involved in sperm production, as well as libido. Men generate sperm all day long. It's just one of our many skills. Preventing this from happening would require removing testosterone from the body or blocking its effects somehow. Historically, the most common way of ridding men of testosterone has been to orchidize them. "Orchidectomy" is another way of saying "castration" which is another way of saying "removing the testicles." Without testicles, testosterone levels plummet. The adrenal glands above the kidneys can make some, but not enough. After being orchidized, violent sex offenders and pedophiles have been found to lose interest in sex altogether. Others lose interest in the act itself, but retain interest in the topic. Some stay interested in the topic and are still motivated to have sex.

As discussed above, using birth control pills to prevent ovulation in females carries minimal risk. Blocking testosterone to prevent the creation of sperm would be disastrous for males, particularly during adolescence. Many orchidized subjects begin to develop feminine physical characteristics, including broader hips but less broad shoulders, breast tissue, changes in skin and voice. In short, the odds seem low that we'll have a birth control pill for males anytime soon, at least not one targeting testosterone.

Those waiting around for male birth control pills to come out shouldn't give up hope yet. Nothing would make a pharmaceutical company happier than creating a pill that makes males temporarily infertile. Adding that compound to Viagra would generate a lot of profit – and make for some very happy customers. So far, no one has figured out precisely how to do it, but it's only a matter of time. Whatever the mechanism, it will probably not be a testosterone blocker for reasons discussed above. Potential candidates include drugs that make it hard for sperm to swim, drugs that make it hard for sperm to recognize the female egg, and herbal supplements that could interfere with the process of sperm generation.

The problem with contraceptives

The science of contraception has clearly advanced, creating myriad options for consenting adults trying to avoid pregnancy. These options work for adolescents, too. However, focusing solely on how to prevent pregnancies ignores two facts. The first is that sexually transmitted diseases are often undeterred by contraception. The pill provides zero protection against diseases, and genital lice (a.k.a., "crabs") couldn't care less if a male wears a condom. The second is that teenagers really shouldn't be having sex anyway! The focus on safe and effective means of contraceptives must be balanced by efforts to minimize, delay, or prevent intercourse among adolescents that are unready to become parents – which includes just about all adolescents!

As one can imagine, there is nothing romantic about teen pregnancy. It will definitely change a person's life, but at a time when they are unlikely to be prepared for it. But pregnancy aside, there is another reason for teens to delay sexual intercourse – their brains are not yet developed in the ways that will later allow them to grapple effectively with the powerful interplay of physical pleasure, interpersonal emotion, and relationship building that sexual activity can bring. When the brain is organized and the frontal lobes are in full swing, these experiences can be very meaningful for an individual and bring maturity to a relationship. Before that, these experiences can be confusing, disorienting and can have lasting repercussions.

What does it all mean?

Today's teens seem to be more cautious when it comes to sex than the last few generations. Students in the 9th through 12th grades today are less likely to have sex, and have sex with fewer partners, than teens a few decades ago. Still, nearly ½ of all 12th graders in America have had intercourse. That seems high and raises important questions about the role that sex plays in adolescent development.

Sex education programs tend to be poorly conceived, regardless of how professionally they are administered, and agenda-driven inaccuracies and moral prescriptions too often trickle into the content – a fact that should alarm anyone, regardless of their stance on sex education in public schools. The good news is that there is good evidence that kids can be motivated to take responsibility for their behaviors and keep themselves safe if the issues are presented to them in clear, concise, data-driven, and sincere ways. This is an issue that requires in-depth and on-going dialogue between parents and kids, and the development of standardized, science-based sex education courses free from moral perspectives and aimed at arming kids with facts.

Quick Facts:

- The physical and hormonal changes of puberty trigger a sexual awakening in adolescents.
- This awakening brings with it a level of responsibility foreign to most teens.
- Despite the perceptions of many adults, and for reasons that are not clear, today's teens are actually *less* sexually active than teens from previous generations.
- Numbers of sexual partners and rates of teen pregnancy are both on the decline, but the risk of contracting sexually transmitted infections higher than ever before.
- In order to help teens make wise choices and deal with sex in a cautious and mature manner, parents and other caregivers must talk with their kids about sex and the risks and responsibilities that go with it.

Chapter 11

What happens when the road gets too bumpy? An introduction to adolescent psychological disorders

For a variety of reasons, the road to adulthood can be particularly rough for some kids. When an individual's thoughts, behaviors and emotions get in the way of their ability to function adequately, they might reach diagnostic criteria for one of a long list of psychological conditions that can emerge during the adolescent years. No cures exist for any of the major psychological disorders afflicting adolescents, though companies keep cranking out prescription drugs to treat them. In this chapter, we will examine the issue of "abnormal" behavior during adolescence and will discus several of the common disorders affecting teens.

Sometimes, development doesn't go according to plan. For a variety or reasons, as brain changes unfold, circuits don't form properly, levels of chemical messengers are not optimal, and the faulty wiring is reflected in dysfunctional behaviors, thoughts, and emotions. The causes are many, and include preexisting biology and unhealthy environments. Given the number of medications available to treat psychological disorders, one might assume that we understand the ailments – why they happen, where in the brain the problems are, and how to fix them. Unfortunately, that's not the case. Not even close. We know surprisingly little about the causes of most psychological disorders that occur during adolescence, or at any other time in life for that matter.

Psychological disorders are not like familiar bacterial or viral infections, though it appears that some conditions might be triggered or worsened by infections. There are no blood tests for depression or schizophrenia. While brain scanning technology has improved, the use of this technology in diagnosing disorders is still in its infancy. Accurate diagnoses can be made based on clinical criteria, but require careful behavioral observation and painstaking review of family and social histories. These diagnostic activities require a skilled and insightful clinician, particularly when dealing with teens, whose behavior might normally seem...well, *abnormal* relative to adults.

Early evidence suggests that many psychological disorders that emerge during the teen years might be related to faulty remodeling of brain circuits during adolescence. Recall that adolescence is the stage of development in which the frontal lobes are handed organizational control over behavior. If something goes wrong in the transition of authority to the frontal lobes, it is quite possible that problems with affect and behavior could result. We will have to await the findings of further research before the link between adolescent brain development and psychological disorders becomes clear.

> "They say they're gonna fix my brain
> Alleviate my suffering and my pain
> But by the time they fix my head
> Mentally I'll be dead"
>
> - *Institutionalized*
>   Suicidal Tendencies (1983)

In this chapter, we will take a brief tour of some of the psychological difficulties that afflict teens. We'll begin by discussing what the word "abnormal" means and putting views of normalcy in the proper historical context. Next, we will explore several of the disorders themselves, including depres-

sion, ADHD, conduct disorders, anxiety disorders and schizophrenia.

A thorough look at adolescent psychopathology and the
treatment options available would require at least one large
book volume for itself. Our investigation in this chapter will be
cursory and will serve as an introduction to the issues.

What does it mean to say someone is "abnormal"?

The simple fact that we have a category of conditions
referred to as "psychological disorders" suggests that we know
what a person who is "psychologically ordered" looks like. Sure,
we could create a long list of characteristics, like – always acts
appropriately, never lies, maintains ideal body weight, no sleep
problems, etcetera – but this just isn't consistent with reality.
The reality is that we humans have become extremely good at
controlling our behaviors so that we can keep the social machinery running smoothly. We use good manners even when
we don't feel like it, we "bite our tongues" when we are mad but
shouldn't say anything, and so forth. However, not even the
most well-groomed citizen can keep their inappropriate behavioral tendencies at bay forever. We all make mistakes and we all
have difficulty dealing with one type of situation or another. In
other words, we *all* exhibit maladaptive behavioral patterns at
some point. This seems to happen often during adolescence as a
matter of course. So when does a person's behavior spill over
from slightly maladaptive to clinically pathological?

In general, when psychologists say someone's behavior
is "abnormal" or "dysfunctional" or "pathological," the implication is that the person's current thoughts, feelings and behaviors
are interfering with their ability to lead a healthy productive life.
In addition, it is assumed that the internal emotional or cognitive state of the individual is suffering, as well. In other words,

the person isn't functioning well *or* feeling well.

As adults, our behaviors do not change that much from day to day and our roles in life are generally established and somewhat stable. This makes it relatively easy to detect departures from normalcy. In contrast, during adolescence, everything in our lives is changing, and quickly. This includes our thoughts, feelings, behaviors, and even our physical features. We are built to engage in mild conflict with authority and test the rules. This can make the task of detecting truly troublesome behavioral patterns even more difficult with teenagers.

If an adult that always parts his hair on the side and doesn't have pierced ears showed up at work one morning sporting a Mohawk and wearing earrings, people might think he had lost his mind. For adolescents, dressing like this one day, and then perhaps dressing differently the next, is commonplace, and might even earn them the reputation of being stylish. If a normally calm and collected mother of three began experiencing repeated and intense outbursts of emotion that involved making statements like, "I hate you," to loved ones, her family would have legitimate reasons for concern. But this scene is not uncommon in houses housing teenagers, including the "normal" ones. Rapid changes in weight, irritability and mood swings, and changes in sleeping patterns would be considered signs of trouble for any adult. To some extent, these are to be expected during the adolescent years.

And so, the word "abnormal," when used in the clinical sense, means that the person is not functioning in a healthy way. Clearly, there are times when perfectly healthy and well-adjusted people don't function in healthy ways, too, but abnormal behavior reaching clinical significance is different. In cases requiring treatment, the abnormal behavior is either persistent (like repeated bouts of depression or ever-present difficulties with attention) or serious enough to put the individual's health and well-being in jeopardy (like hearing voices or talking about suicide).

Detecting the problem is just the first part. The next is trying to figure out how to help get the person back on track and functioning at a high level again. In other words, to make them "normal" or "well." To put current diagnoses of disorders and current treatment options in perspective, let's take a brief tour of the history of these things. As we will see, opinions about what makes some people normal and others abnormal, and how abnormal people should be treated, are culturally bound and have changed considerably over the years.

A brief history of the diagnosis and treatment of mental disorders

It is much easier to make sense of the current uncertainty surrounding the causes and appropriate treatment strategies for mental illness when current thinking is placed in its proper historical context.[1] It turns out we have always been uncertain of the causes and appropriate treatments for psychological disorders, so our current confusion is nothing new. Fortunately, we seem to be a lot closer to understanding these conditions than we were just a few decades ago, and definitely closer than we were a few hundred years ago!

Evidence from early written history suggests that abnormal behaviors were thought to arise from supernatural forces that somehow entered the sick person's body. Fortunately, a treatment option was developed for these folks. Unfortunately, it involved knocking a hole through the skull to let the evil spirits out, a technique called *trephining*. Surprisingly, some patients actually survived this procedure.

Around 400 B.C., the famed physician, Hippocrates, proposed that behavioral disorders emerged from the brain. He believed the problem was related to the flow of four humors – yellow bile, black bile, phlegm and blood. In his view, too much phlegm can make a person sluggish and too much black bile caused depression. His ideas for the causes of these conditions might have been off target, but his ideas for treatment options were quite advanced. Exercise, bland diets, lots of rest and abstinence from sex and alcohol were part of his plan. Hippocrates firmly believed that psychological conditions should be treated like other medical conditions. A major advance!

During the middle ages in Europe, roughly 500-1350 A.D., thoughts about mental illness drifted back toward a demonic view, one that held that abnormal behavior is caused by demons that infiltrate the body. The prevailing view was that the devil caused psychological problems and that torturing the mentally ill person was the best way to drive the devil and his minions out. Religious rituals, or *exorcisms*, involved beatings, lots of prayer and starvation in an effort to the make the physical body so uninhabitable that the devil would leave.

The plight of the mentally ill improved in some ways during the European Renaissance (1400-1700 A.D.) Modern thinkers and health practitioners were returning to the general view offered by Hippocrates, that mental conditions are like other illnesses and should be treated as such. On the other hand, the early Renaissance also witnessed continued persecution of the mentally ill. At this time, Europe was ravaged by unusually chaotic weather, famine and disease. In 1486, a book entitled "Malleus Maleficarum," or "The Witch Hammer," was published, blaming witches for the problems and ushering in another era of persecution. One common test to assess whether one was a witch involved tying them to a board, throwing them in the water, and seeing if they sunk or floated. If they sunk, they weren't witches, if they floated they were witches. This appears to be the origin of the saying, "damned if you do, damned if you don't." It is estimated that, between the 14th and 17th centuries, upwards of 500,000 people, mostly women, were declared witches and hanged or burned at the stake. Twenty alleged witches were killed in Salem, MA, in the 1690s. Fortunately, witch trials were outlawed shortly thereafter.

The 18th century finally witnessed the dawn of humane care for the mentally ill. In Europe, asylums, or mental hospitals, were created to house those with apparent psychological conditions. While they opened with good intentions, many quickly became overcrowded. In some, like Bethlehem Hospital, often called "Bedlam," tickets were sold to the public who would then walk around and gawk at the chained up, feces covered patients.

Fortunately, the 18th century also witnessed strong efforts from advocates for the mentally ill, including Benjamin Rush, considered the father of American Psychiatry, and Phillipe Pinel, the head of an asylum in France. Pinel convinced the French Government to allow him to unchain many patients. He also replaced the dungeon-like quarters with well lit rooms, fresh air, and exercise, and spent countless hours talking with patients. As a result of Pinel's approach, some patients were eventually set free, an outcome all but unheard of up until this point.

In 19th century America, a New England school teacher named Dorothea Dix campaigned courageously for better treatment of the mentally ill here in the U.S. She succeeded in raising enough money to build 32 mental hospitals across the country. Sadly, many of the new asylums became overcrowded and began resembling asylums in Europe.

During the early 19th century, a man named Anton Mesmer claimed to be able to cure the mentally ill through *mesmerism*, a form of hypnotism. His work led several young thinkers and doctors, including Sigmund Freud, to look for a psychological basis for mental disorders. This gave birth to talk therapies, which remain indispensable in the treatment of some conditions today.

The historical momentum leading up to the 20th century gave birth to two somewhat divergent lines of theory and treatment for psychiatric disorders. We still operate under these two different perspectives today. One of them involves a focus on the biology underlying disordered thoughts and behaviors. This is known as the *medical model*. The other line of thought suggests that conditions emerge from inner psychological conflicts that can be resolved in non-medical ways. A view known as the *psychogenic perspective*.

The first half of the 20th century witnessed the development of three medical strategies for treating mental illness that propelled the medical model to the forefront and permanently changed the way we view and treat disorders. Electroconvulsive Shock Therapy (ECT) was introduced in the 1930s. For some reason, passing electrical current through the brains of many mentally ill patients, particularly those with severe depression, can lead to short-term improvements in behavior and affect. Indeed, the technique is still used for roughly 60,000 patients per year who suffer from treatment resistant depression. Fortunately, patients treated with ECT these days are given medications to relax their muscles first. This wasn't always the case. Early patients treated with ECT would often break bones while flailing around as the current was passed through their brains.

In the 1930s, a Portuguese researcher named Antonio de Egas Moniz, at the University of Lisbon Medical Center, learned of research examining the impact of frontal lobe damage on behavior in chimpanzees. It appeared that the chimps were made calmer by the procedure. Dr. Moniz paired himself with a neurosurgeon, Almeida Lima, and devised a technique for humans in which two holes were drilled in the skull, a surgical knife was lowered into the brain, and the connections between the frontal lobes and the rest of the brain were severed. The procedure was initially known as a leucotomy but eventually earned its current name, "lobotomy." Dr. Moniz received a Nobel Prize for his work in 1949 and was later shot and paralyzed by an angry lobotomy patient.

During the 1940s, an American physician named Walter Freeman modified Moniz' approach to lobotomies such that the procedure could be performed under local anesthesia in a physician's office. An ice pick was inserted above each of a patient's eyes, tapped into the brain by a mallet, and then swished back and

SideNotes

Ice pick lobotomy

Below is a picture of an unidentified young male in the midst of an ice pick lobotomy procedure. With a mallet, the pointy device is driven through the bony eye socket. Next, the device is swished back and forth, severing connections between the frontal lobes and the rest of the brain. The frontal lobes allow for voluntary, goal directed, intentional behaviors. If the connections are cut, the person loses many of those functions. Because the procedure makes some psychotic patients easier to deal with, the lobotomy was popular in the decades leading up to the discovery of antipsychotic medications in the 1950s. The ice pick lobotomy procedure was particularly popular here in the U.S. where it was developed by Walter Freeman.

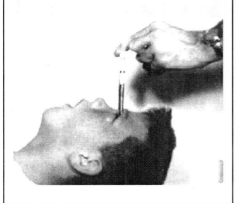

forth to sever frontal lobe connections. Without the ability to carry out plans devised by the frontal lobes, many patients became calmer, but some did not. Dr. Freeman pushed for the use of lobotomies for everything from criminal behavior to schizophrenia.

In 1952, Freeman performed 228 ice-pick-type lobotomies for the state of West Virginia in a two week period. By all accounts, Dr. Freeman took great pride in the speed with which he could complete such surgeries. He would later be banned from performing the procedure when, in 1967, he performed his third lobotomy on a long-time patient and she died during the procedure. As such, both the careers of Moniz and Freeman would end in controversy and tragedy.

In the 1950s, pharmaceutical treatment options emerged, first for schizophrenia, then for depression, and then for anxiety. This essentially ended the era of psychosurgery, at least in the U.S., and ushered in the era of pharmacotherapy in which we find ourselves now.

During the 1960s, continued overcrowding at mental facilities, combined with the advent of psychiatric medications, led to a movement known as *deinstitutionalization*. The idea was to discharge large numbers of mentally ill under the assumption that they would receive adequate treatment from community centers and local doctors. Sadly, the support mechanisms were not sufficient for most patients, creating a large wave of homeless citizens suffering from mental illnesses.

Today, we still find ourselves approaching the study and treatment of mental disorders from these two divergent perspectives – one suggesting that faulty biology gives rise to maladaptive thoughts and feelings (medical model) and the other suggesting that psychological conditions are primarily problems with thoughts and feelings and that biology need not be considered (psychogenic perspective).

Current approaches to helping kids with psychological disorders

The task of trying to decide whether a teenager's seemingly pathological behavioral patterns are simply part of normal adolescent development, or if the individual is truly having difficulty functioning in life and is in need of help, is a challenging one. Later in the chapter, readers will find the diagnostic criteria for depression according to the Diagnostic and Statistical Manual of Mental Disorders Version 4 (DSM-IV), the clinical guidebook for psychological disorders used in the U.S. In Europe, clinicians use something called the International Statistical Classification of Diseases and Related Health Problems 10th Revision (ICD-10).

While the symptoms checklist

SideNotes

What is the difference between a psychologist and a psychiatrist?

Most psychologists hold PhDs in psychology, with specialization in their areas of interest. Those with clinical training can see patients but cannot prescribe medicine. Psychiatrists, on the other hand, can see patients and prescribe medicine. Rather than receiving PhDs, psychiatrists must first complete medical school to receive an MD before completing specialized training in the biology underlying psychiatric conditions. In a very general sense, clinical psychologists tend to represent psychogenic (non-biological) perspectives to mental health while many psychiatrists view mental conditions primarily as medical conditions. While most people associate Sigmund Freud with clinical psychology, he was actually an MD.

does include some caveats about how the symptoms might be manifest in children and adolescents relative to adults, the diagnostic system is far from perfect and probably does not do depression in adolescents justice. Most adolescents pass through many of these symptoms as their normal development unfolds.

The current science of diagnosing and treating mental disorders is improving, but not as rapidly as improvements are being made in other areas of health, such as treating heart conditions or diabetes. The financial incentive to develop more effective options is certainly there. According to The John D. and Catherine T MacArthur Foundations, depression in adults costs employers more than $40 billion per year just in reduced job performance and absences. A study funded by the Foundation found that it only requires an investment of about $500 per patient for quality mental health care sufficient to reduce the time that employees spend dealing with their depression and reduce the number of depression-related absences by one month in a two-year period.

What exactly are the treatment options for kids with mental health conditions? Depending on insurance coverage and the specific disorder, a variety of options are available. Psychotherapy, or "talk" therapy, can help kids with some problems, like anxiety disorders and depression, while medications are the primary route for treating conditions like schizophrenia. Often, a mix of approaches is used, such as medications combined with therapy or in home visits from a social worker.

The limiting factor in getting help for an adolescent is usually insurance coverage. There are plenty of highly trained professionals in a variety of mental health fields who are ready and willing to help an adolescent in need. The question is which of the many options will be supported by the insurance policy that covers the kid. That is, assuming there is an insurance policy covering the kid! A staggering number of children and adolescents are not covered by health insurance policies, meaning that their options for care might be extremely limited. To find out what options are covered by your particular insurance plan, check the plan if you have it handy or call the insurance company directly.

Most early medications used to treat psychological disorders were discovered by accident, and most within the past 50 years or so. Further, while the names and chemical formulas of drugs have changed as newer generations of those compounds have emerged, most of them still have the same general mechanisms of action as those in the early generations. Despite the flashy commercials for antidepressants and other meds, we are still in the early stage of understanding psychological disorders and how to treat them medically or behaviorally, particularly as they relate to adolescent development. Researchers at pharmaceutical companies have developed some truly life saving drugs for people who suffer from psychological disorders. But drugs can only do so much.

Like drugs for depression, non-pharmaceutical therapeutic approaches have also advanced to a modest extent. In clinical trials with adults, both exercise and specific talk-therapies perform on par with antidepressants. Roughly 60% of adult patients suffering from depression benefit from exercise, cognitive behavioral therapy or medications. Such data are not yet available for adolescents.

Now that we've taken a look at the general issue of clinically abnormal behavior during adolescence, let's explore a few of the conditions that afflict teens.

Depression

Depression comes in two flavors, both of them unsavory – unipolar and bipolar.[2] In unipolar depression, people go from normal mood to depressed mood, or sometimes just stay in a depressed mood. In bipolar depression, people go from normal mood to depressed mood some of the time and from normal mood to agitated or even euphoric mood some of the time. For this discussion, we are most interested in depression of the unipolar variety.

Unipolar depression is a mood disorder characterized by many different symptoms and feelings. Some of these are sadness, despair, hopelessness, boredom with life, and feelings of worthlessness. In order for these symptoms to reach clinically diagnosable levels, they must be severe and last for at least two weeks. There is also a milder form of unipolar depression known as *dysthymia*, which is characterized by less severe symptoms of depression that just don't go away. About 50% of people who experience one episode of major depression (see the diagnostic criteria on page 369) do not experience another one. The other 50% have a greater chance of having at least one more episode. Having two or more episodes does not bode well for sufferers, and suggests that the condition will likely be a chronic problem. Among people who are depressed for a year or more, about 1/10 will attempt suicide and around 1/100 will succeed.

The causes of depression are complex. At the level of the brain, there is evidence that depressive symptoms may result from having too little activity in a few key neurotransmitter systems, including the system involving the transmitter serotonin. The putative involvement of serotonin and similar brain messengers in depression is supported by the fact that drugs that elevate the activity of serotonin in the brain – such as Prozac, Celexa, Lexapro, Effexor, Paxil and others – can elevate the moods of depressed patients. The lengthy waiting period for effectiveness (up to 12 weeks) suggests that the ultimate effects of the drugs stem from alterations in gene expression and rewiring of brain circuits rather than the initial boost in transmitter levels.

For those who begin suffering from depression during adolescence, it's possible that the disorder was always there, just below the surface, but did not reveal itself until it was triggered by something like a major life stressor. For some, trauma or loss can trigger episodes of depression that do not abate in a timely manner. General stress might also contribute, but the overall incidence of depression is not higher among those in more stressful environments. So, as with most psychological disorders, there are huge individual differences in susceptibility to depression, as well as responsiveness to treatment. As with ADHD, discussed below, the relative lack of funding for research, combined with the record profits of pharmaceutical companies, means that the search for the causes of depression has taken a backseat to the search for pharmaceutical treatments.

DSM-IV Criteria for a Major Episode of Depression

A. Five (or more) of the following symptoms have been present during the same 2-week period and represent a change from previous functioning; at least one of the symptoms is either (1) depressed mood or (2) loss of interest or pleasure. **Note:** Do not include symptoms that are clearly due to a general medical condition, or mood-incongruent delusions or hallucinations.

1. Depressed mood most of the day, nearly every day, as indicated by either subjective report (e.g., feels sad or empty) or observation made by others (e.g., appears tearful). **Note:** In children and adolescents, can be irritable mood.
2. Markedly diminished interest or pleasure in all, or almost all, activities most of the day, nearly every day (as indicated by either subjective account or observation mad by others)
3. Significant weight loss when not dieting or weight gain (e.g. a change of more than 5% of body weight in a month), or decrease or increase in appetite nearly every day. **Note:** In children, consider failure to make expected weight gains.
4. Insomnia or hypersomnia nearly every day
5. Psychomotor agitation or retardation nearly every day (observable by others, no merely subjective feelings of restlessness or being slowed down)
6. Fatigue or loss of energy nearly every day
7. Feelings of worthlessness or excessive or inappropriate guilt (which may be delusional) nearly every day (not merely self-reproach or guilt about being sick)
8. Diminished ability to think or concentrate, or indecisiveness, nearly every day (either by subjective account or as observed by others)
9. Recurrent thoughts of death (not just fear of dying), recurrent suicidal ideation without a specific plan, or a suicide attempt or a specific plan for committing suicide

B. The symptoms do not meet criteria for a Mixed Episode.
C. The symptoms cause clinically significant distress or impairment in social, occupational, or other important areas of functioning.
D. The symptoms are not due to the direct physiological effects of a substance (e.g., a drug of abuse, a medication) or a general medical condition (e.g. hypothyroidism)
E. The symptoms are not better accounted for by Bereavement, i.e., after the loss of a loved one, the symptoms persist for long than 2 months or are characterized by marked functional impairment, morbid preoccupation with worthlessness, suicidal ideation, psychotic symptoms, or psychomotor retardation.

It is important for adults to be aware of the difference between depression and mood swings in adolescents. A teen may seem to sink into the pits of despair for a day or two and then emerge one morning smiling and humming, headphones and sunglasses in place. Don't make too much of this – a few days of moroseness is probably no more an indicator of serious depression than a few days of gleefulness is an indicator of bipolar mania. But, since serious illnesses can occur in adolescence, indeed they often emerge first during adolescence, it is important to make note of transient changes in behavior for future reference. If that mood swing starts happening frequently, or the withdrawal and sadness last for weeks, rather than days, don't hesitate to consult a health professional for evaluation. A skilled clinician will know the right questions to ask, and how to interpret their answers. Contact your child's pediatrician or school counselor if you are uncertain where to begin.

Antidepressants and suicide – Should parents be concerned?

Much has been written in the past few years about the risk of suicide in adolescents taking antidepressants.[3] Science is finally beginning to catch up with the speculation. So, do antidepressants increase the risk that a teen will commit suicide? It does not appear so, but, for a variety of reasons, kids on antidepressants are more likely to think about it.

In 2004, a 27 member panel of public representatives, psychiatrists, pediatricians, statisticians and experts in several other fields convened for two days to closely examine all of the available evidence about antidepressants and teen suicides. They concluded that there was no evidence of an increased risk of actual suicides among teens treated with psychotropic medications. However, they did observe compelling evidence of an overall increase in *suicidality*, a category that includes both suicidal thoughts and suicidal behaviors, among treated teens (4% of treated teens relative to 2% of untreated teens). This finding led the FDA to issue a warning about the potential link between antidepressants and the risk of suicide in teens.

In a recent manuscript,[3] the chair of the aforementioned panel concluded that depression, and not the treatment approaches used to keep it at bay, typically leads to suicide. Indeed, the most alarming observation reported by the panel may well have been that antidepressants are far less efficacious in pediatric populations than among adults. Only three out of 15 trials suggested that antidepressants are better than placebo treatment in kids. Perhaps this shouldn't be surprising, as the brain of a teen is not exactly like that of someone in the 20s or older. Plenty of other drugs, like alcohol and anxiolytics (e.g.,

SideNotes

Do scientologists have a valid point?

In a July, 2007, interview in W magazine, John Travolta was quoted as saying:

"I still think that if you analyze most of the school shootings, it is not gun control. It is (psychotropic) drugs at the bottom of it."

Like fellow scientologists Kirstie Alley and Tom Cruise, Travolta views psychiatrists and psychiatric meds as patently harmful to kids, and the cause of many teen suicides. Do they have a point? Read through the evidence in this chapter and make an informed decision.

From the author's standpoint, it seems odd that a religion based on the belief that some kind of space entity gathered up souls from the universe and threw them into volcanoes on earth would be interested in what actual data have to say about anything! They are not completely off the mark with regard to the risks of prescription meds, but are with regard to the link between suicide and antidepressants. It now appears that drugs like Chantix, Pfizer's new quit-smoking drug, are associated with actual suicides in some people, but it is depression that kills depressed people, not the meds used to treat them.

Valium), affect kids and adults differently. While antidepressants can work for kids, they are far less likely to do so.

Keep in mind that, even when these medications don't work for kids, those that take them for any extended period of time might still have to go through the uncomfortable withdrawal syndrome that cessation of these drugs can bring. For this reason, getting off the meds, like getting on the meds, should be done with a doctor's supervision.

The good news is that we have come a long way in the past few years toward an understanding of teenage brain development and that these advances are slowly being translated into improvements in treatment modalities for depression and other ills afflicting teens.

So, why might there be a link between antidepressant use and suicidal thoughts in kids? Most antidepressants require a month or more of daily use before noticeable improvements in emotions occur. Clearly, the brain changes underlying the therapeutic effects of these meds do not depend solely on levels of transmitters, like serotonin, in the brain. If that were the case, the drugs should work immediately. Instead, the slow improvements that result from antidepressants probably stem from complicated changes in neural circuits in a wide variety of brain areas, most likely stemming from changes in gene expression (this is also why getting off of antidepressants can be such a slow and difficult process). Early in treatment, many depressed individuals find themselves with more mental energy, but no real improvement in their emotional states. It could be that the enhanced cognitive activity, when combined with poor emotional functioning, puts depressed patients in a situation where it is simply easier to mull over thoughts of suicide. The hope is that the medications will eventually take full effect and the individual will be out of this danger before it amounts to anything truly concerning.

Making sense of adolescent suicide in general

Deep depression is often a precursor for suicide, but plenty of paths lead to that end. In many cases, the only similarities between individuals who choose death by suicide is that they feel so desperate that ending life is seen as the only solution. In other cases, the deaths result from failed attempts to get close to death by suicide but not actually dying. Such acts are intended solely to tell the world one is suffering and needs help. In still other cases, the suicide isn't premeditated, but makes sense in the moment. Of course, some suicides aren't triggered by intense feelings at all, but are preplanned events driven by the utter absence of positive feelings about life.

It is impossible to explain, in this brief chapter, the ins and outs of teen suicide, the differences between how males and females go about it, and all of the things that can be done to prevent suicides from happening.[4] Keeping with the theme of adolescent development and ways in which changes in the teen brain lead to changes in behavior, let's look at the anatomy of one basic path to suicide – the one where an individual feels so desperate, emotionally, that they see no other choice but to end their young life or face a future full of certain misery.

The brain exists in a perpetual tug of war between allowing behavior to be controlled by emotions and foregoing such influences in lieu of logical, rational, socially appropriate cognitive choices. Deciding to quit smoking and dealing with the urges are two different things. Dieting is easy until you get around your favorite foods. Punching your boss might make you feel better, but more than likely is inconsistent with your long-term cognitive plans. Adult living often requires us to subjugate our emotional needs in order to play stable roles in our families and communities. As such, we must delay our emotional expressions and just cope with life as best we can, often for long periods of time.

The entirety of adolescence could be viewed as a stage of change dominated by a shifting of control over behavior from emotions to cognition. When we are children, feelings naturally drive our behaviors. As adults, we are supposed to use thought to control ourselves as we go through our days. Until the mechanisms for such cognitive control are in place, kids can find themselves having difficulty keeping their tumultuous emotions in check and using reason, logic and planning to govern behaviors. All adolescents are in training to do so and their brains are trying to work it out.

There are times in life, particularly when we are young,

when cognitive control breaks down, allowing emotions to temporarily rule the day. This isn't a bad thing at all, when the emotions driving an individual's behavior are good ones, or an appropriate outlet is chosen for expressing feelings that are negative (sports, for instance). And we could all use a good cry from time to time. However, when toxic emotions aren't given the opportunity to see the light of day, they can become overwhelming and literally usurp control over behavior. In such cases, terrible and unpredictable things can happen. These are the ingredients for situations in which a person simply "snaps." Urges bubbling to the surface build up sufficient pressure to swamp the cognitive control centers and lead people to act in ultimately unhealthy ways. For some kids, this pressure generates unruly behavior. For other, it generates self-destructive behavior.

Ask any 15 year old about their plans for the future and they will probably tell you what they are doing that night or the coming weekend. During adolescence, the future is measured in days and perhaps weeks rather than months and years. As adults, we tend to recognize that heartbreak, rejection, harassment, and conflicts with authority can sting at a deep level, but that we will probably get by somehow. This isn't as easy for adolescents, particularly if the sum total of their life experiences suggests that things will not get better for them. As irrational a choice as suicide seems to most adults, it can be the

"I want to be very clear. I don't blame Ryan's suicide on one single person or one single event. In the end, Ryan was suffering from depression. This is a form of mental illness that is brought on by biological and/or environmental factors. In Ryan's case, I feel it was the "pile on effect" of the environmental issues mentioned above that stemmed from his middle school life. Tragically, teenage depression often goes undetected against the backdrop of typical teen angst. And since most of us have never received basic education in the signs and prevention of teenage suicide at any point in our lives, young people suffering from depression are at greater risk."

Ryan's father, John Halligan
www.ryanpatrickhalligan.org

only choice that seems reasonable to a desperate kid.

In cases of suicide, it is common to try to pinpoint the specific cause and then try to understand how things could have gone differently. Indeed, the development of suicide prevention methodologies depends upon such insights. While there normally are precipitating events for suicides, such events only culminate in suicides when the right person meets the right circumstances. The ripple effects of divorce, particularly contentious divorce, can carry kids closer to suicide, but not always. Rejection by a classmate or romantic interest can be sufficient to push a kid over the edge, but only for a small portion of the adolescent population. How such events will affect a particular kid is difficult to know ahead of time.

The idea that suicides are triggered by events is true, but such acts typically follow lots of events over lots of time. Slowly, internal and external currents carry a kid to a dark psychological place where dying, and going through the steps necessary to do so, seems more palatable than living. Once in this place, any number of events could trigger the end.

The heartbreaking story of Ryan Patrick Halligan serves as a powerful example of how young lives can be brought to premature ends out of acts of desperation that follow years of emotional torment. Ryan's story also highlights the fact that malicious kids bent on hurting other kids can find them anywhere these days – in school, out of school and online.

In an eloquent online memorial to his son, John Halligan recounts Ryan's life and the events culminating in his death. Like many kids, Ryan exhibited some learning difficulties during childhood. This made academics challenging and ensured that Ryan would remain an easy target for bullies that prey on kids that are different. One kid was particularly venomous and, beginning in the 5th grade, regularly tormented Ryan. A handsome but frail young boy, Ryan struggled to fit in and make friends, and assured his loving and involved parents that he could fend for himself. Indeed, in the 7th grade, it seemed that Ryan might finally get a reprieve from being bullied. The Assistant Principal at Ryan's school had to break up a fight between Ryan and the bully, and Ryan was happy with his performance.

His parents became concerned when, a short time after, Ryan announced he had befriended the bully. At around that time, Ryan also began chatting online with a popular girl from his school. Later, in person, and in front of other kids, the girl announced to Ryan that she had just been pretending to like him and that he was a complete loser. The bully he befriended turned out not to be a friend, after all, and was responsible for a malicious cyberbullying campaign against him. It seems that these realizations drove Ryan to that place where death seemed too alluring to continue living.

Not all suicides are brought about by oppression and bullying, as the story of Taylor Hooten attests. Taylor Hooten was a healthy and popular teenager at Plano West Senior High School in Plano, Texas. He had a 3.8 GPA and, by all accounts, was a good kid. He was the nephew of major league pitcher Burt Hooten and an excellent baseball player himself. It was his quest to become the best that ultimately led to his death.

Unbeknownst to his supportive and present parents, Taylor began shooting steroids to improve his game. In retrospect, the puffiness, weight gain and bad breath served as signs of his covert activities. But what parent of an otherwise happy, healthy and well-behaved adolescent would have seen such things as warning signs? The first injection started Taylor down the path to self-destruction, but the trouble really began for him when he abruptly stopped using the supplemental hormones. The brain reads the injected hormones as a signal that there are sufficient levels of natural steroids in the body and tells the testes to stop producing testosterone, hence the shrinking of testicles that often occurs in those who choose to use anabolic steroids. If one stops too abruptly, the body finds itself in testosterone debt and remains there until the levels restabilize. The deep depression that followed was simply too much for Taylor Hooten. Like the Halligans, Gwen and Don Hooten found their son hanging in his room and now find themselves wondering how this could have happened to their family.

Suicide is too complex to reduce to a simple series of causes and effects. Even when precipitating events can be identified, their impact on the person's behavior depends on things that happened long before that. This makes the task of preventing suicide a challenging one, as it requires identifying a wide range of risk and protective factors and then figuring out how to augment the role of protective factors in kids' lives while minimizing the role of risk factors. For this reason, suicide prevention is an effort that ties together virtually all other efforts to improve the lives of kids. This holds true both at the level of an individual kid and the level of entire cultures. Kids with the right blend of healthy biology and healthy environments do not choose to take their lives. Thus, by the nature of things, any effort to promote healthy development is an effort to prevent suicide.

The state of Florida leads the country in its efforts to prevent suicide. In 2007, Florida established in law a Statewide Office of Suicide Prevention, housed in the Executive Office of the Governor. Erin MacInnes, Director of the Office, summarizes the complex nature of suicide and suicide prevention at the state level as follows:

"Suicide is a multifaceted yet preventable public health problem requiring attention from an entire community to ensure that the protection and welfare of youth is a priority. There is much we can do to ensure citizens of any age do not lose hope in their future and consider suicide as their only option. Teens suffering in silence and dying by suicide is a tragedy we can curtail by implementing collaborative, comprehensive approaches at all levels of the lifecycle. A centralized structure is necessary to integrate a statewide effort and provide a unified direction, but the opportunity to transform lives occurs at the local level. It is imperative to promote resilience and connectedness among communities, families and individuals in order to create a strong foundation from which youth can successfully face life stress."

As with other issues, like drinking and sex, it is important for parents to discuss the topic of suicide with adolescents. Most adolescents end up touched by suicide in some way, and ignoring the topic means leaving kids to wrestle with the issues on their own. It is a myth that talking to teens about suicide plants the idea in their heads and increases the odds they will take their own lives. Such discussions can help kids make sense of suicide and imbue them with confidence regarding how to proceed in the event they are ever concerned about a friend or loved one. John Halligan captures nicely the importance of talking with teens about suicide in the following passage from the website he created in memory of his son, Ryan:

"It's widely accepted that young people are more inclined to share their feelings and problems with their friends first as they enter the teenage years. Therefore, young people need to be educated in basic suicide awareness and prevention as our first line of defense against this very preventable cause of death. They need to be taught to take the suicidal comments and signs very seriously and know that it's important to seek adult help urgently for their friend."

According to suicide researchers Bearman and Moody,[5] kids who have supportive friends are less likely to commit suicide, while isolated kids with few friends, and those that know people who committed suicide, are more likely to do so. Educating young people about the myths and realities of suicide, including signs to be on the lookout for, can help create social safety nets and increase the odds that kids thinking about suicide will get help before it's too late.

The website, Kidshealth.org, has an informative section on teen suicide that can provide parents with background material and some advice for how to talk with kids about the issue. A wide range of additional resources can be found on the website for the Kristen Brooks Hope Center, www.hopeline.com, and the website for the Suicide Prevention Resource Center, www.sprc.org.

In a crisis situation, help can be found 24 hours per day, seven days per week, by calling the National Suicide Prevention Lifeline at 1-800-273-TALK, or by dialing 911. To find crisis hotlines in your area, visit the website Suicidehotlines.com.

Attention Deficit Hyperactivity Disorder

Most adolescents struggle a little bit to get through their school days and the homework that follows. It can be difficult to pay attention in class when the sun is shining outside and it is close to lunch time. Does that mean that any kid who has difficulty focusing has a disorder? Of course not. In this section, we will discuss what happens when problems with attention reach truly pathological levels. First, we will need to discuss what attention is, what it is good for, why it's bad when it doesn't work well, and how a kid's experiences can influence it.

Imagine two kids sitting in class, both matched in just about every way. Same socioeconomic status, both come from healthy homes, identical IQ scores. Yet, one earns the highest grade in the class while the other earns the lowest. How is this possible? While sitting in class, an array of sensory signals impinge on us. The brain extracts this information and uses it to learn. At the same time, our brains are conjuring up memories of past experiences and creatively combining past and present concepts into novel patterns. This is where attention comes in. Attention is the ability to process specific information to the exclusion of other information. For instance, when a teacher is teaching, attention allows students to focus on the lesson rather than intrusive stimuli coming from elsewhere in the room or from within one's own brain.

Attention is like a flashlight with three different settings. One setting allows us to focus on specific stimuli or internal states. For instance, if someone says "look at that!," attention can be focused on whatever "that" is. One allows us to focus more diffusely on a larger range of stimuli or internal states. This is what happens during a normal conversation about an issue. The third setting is the most impressive one. It allows us to divide our attention to multiple streams of information at once. Dividing attention is not easy, particularly when we are young. For example, research indicates that adolescents can drive cars perfectly well as long as they keep their attention focused on the task at hand. It is when their attention becomes divided between driving and doing things like operating cell phones or talking with friends in the back seat that things tend to go wrong.

Attention is central to learning. It allows us to amplify the signal of interest and reduce the amount of brain processing devoted to less relevant stimuli. The importance of attention for learning is not age-specific. That is, at any stage of life, attention plays an important role in learning. However, the ability to pay attention does change with development. If you have children, or have ever been around them for any length of time, you know that four-year-olds are quite capable of learning, but have difficulty focusing their attention beyond a few minutes at a time. Indeed, this is perhaps one of the reasons that young children enjoy watching fast-paced television programs and engaging in play for which a long attention span is not necessary.

The capacity to pay attention does not necessarily convey a tendency to do so. We learn to pay attention. As we progress through school, the demands to pay attention increase. At the college level, students often have to sit through two- or three-hour lectures, perhaps on subjects that they do not find inherently interesting at all. Yet, if they want to pass the courses, they must pay attention.

The voluntary paying of attention is largely a frontal lobe mediated process. The frontal lobes, brain areas right behind the forehead, are nowhere near finished developing by the end of childhood. It is during the adolescent period that we hone our abilities to use the frontal lobes to direct attention, sustain it, and even split it. It seems reasonable that, as this development unfolds, the frontal lobes might gain and lose some control, meaning that a child might exhibit an amazing capacity for attending to things one week and perhaps a diminished capacity the next week. Future research should help tell us whether the development of attention is a linear process during adolescence or follows a pattern resembling something like the stock market or climate change.

Obviously, there are environmental factors that can modulate attention. Research dating back to the mid-1970s tells us that teenagers who listen to music while studying learn less than those who study in silence. Dividing attention, no matter how much, can delay mastery of the primary task at hand. In addition to environmental distracters, attention and learning can be influenced by a students' interest in a subject. Indeed, in a recent survey of 470 high school dropouts by Civic Enterprises, the number one explanation given for dropping out was that the classes were not interesting (As a side note, 38% of dropouts also cited "too much freedom and not enough rules in my life" as a causative factor.) Whether such students would really stay in school if the lesson plans were somehow made more exciting is unclear. Obviously, teachers shouldn't feel compelled to sing and dance during class in order to increase attention, but finding ways to make the material as interesting and relevant as possible and to engage children actively in the teaching process seems a good idea. Until students master the ability to pay attention, anything we can do to help them attend is useful.

It is quite clear that the physical environment influences our ability to pay attention and our motivation to do so. A 2002 report from the National Clearinghouse for Educational Facilities (NCEF) examined the relationship between school environments, physical facilities in particular, and student achievement. The report identified several physical facets of schools that impact academic performance. One such factor is air quality. An estimated one in five kids attends schools with poor indoor air quality. Poor air quality can cause a set of symptoms referred to by the Environmental Protection Agency as "sick building syndrome." These symptoms include irritated eyes, noses and throats, nausea, dizziness, upper respiratory infections, headaches, sleepiness and fatigue. As might be expected, such symptoms make it more difficult for kids to pay attention, no matter how motivated they might be!

Lighting is yet another physical aspect of school facilities that seems to affect attention and learning. In particular, the amount of natural sunlight that students are exposed to during the course of a day has been associated with school perform-ance. A recent study examining the relationship between school lighting and classroom achievement found that students in classrooms with high amounts of natural sunlight outperformed students in classrooms with less sunlight. Similarly, students in quieter classrooms outperform those in noisier classrooms.

In summary, attention refers to the ability to direct our brain resources toward particular stimuli or internal thoughts, and to sustain our focus on those things even when other interesting stuff is going on around us. Attention isn't a yes/no thing. People have varying degrees of ability to focus attention at different times in their lives and even different times of the day. We all have difficulty with attention when life is stressful or the environment is too distracting. And so, problems paying attention in school do not always reflect organic brain abnormalities. Whether due to emotional distress or simply lack of training, many children have difficulty paying attention. For others, difficulty paying attention might just be a developmental phase. As brain development unfolds, the ability to focus and maintain attention often naturally grows stronger. Some kids, however, suffer from a very real, brain-based condition that makes paying attention in school, and thus benefiting from the learning experience, extremely difficult if not impossible.

Actual Attention Deficit Hyperactivity Disorder (ADHD), known as Hyperkinetic Disorder in Europe, is characterized by a dysfunctional level inattentiveness and/or hyperactivity and difficulty controlling impulses to do things.[6] Dysfunctional means that the symptoms are causing substantial problems for the child. Children with these symptoms often exhibit other problems as well – including poor learning capacity and difficulties judging the passage of time. Children with ADHD often have difficulty withholding the urge to execute a behavior until the appropriate time. For instance, during conversations with other people, it is customary to wait until the person is finished speaking before starting to talk. This can be difficult for many who suffer from the disorder.

Lack of interest in school work, leading to a lack of attention to instructors and materials, is not the same thing as ADHD. ADHD is a serious neuropsychological syndrome, and solid brain research is beginning to shed light on its mechanisms. For those who have ADHD, paying attention and following along with instructors can be extremely challenging, even if the motivation to learn is high. So, if your child is having difficulty in school, before heading to your primary practitioner to ask for medicine, ask yourself why the child is having difficulty. Are they *trying* to learn? Are they *trying* to stay still and wait their turn? Are there circumstances in their lives that could be leading to genuine, but temporary, problems with focusing? Could the school environment be getting in the way? If everything else seems to be okay, it's possible they have an actual disorder.

Estimates are that about 5% of all school aged children suffer from ADHD, yet only about 2-3% of children are diagnosed with ADHD and prescribed medication, suggesting that the disorder is not, in general, over diagnosed and over-medicated as many argue. That doesn't mean that kids aren't inappropriately diagnosed and treated, it just means that the overall percentage of kids being treated probably does not overshoot the number of kids in the country that have ADHD.

It is interesting to note that the rate of diagnosis and treatment of ADHD varies considerably with geography in the U.S., with the highest rates in the Northeast. There could be something in the water, the clinicians are particularly good at recognizing true cases of ADHD, or it is overdiagnosed in that particular area. No one knows at this point.

Boys are around five times more likely to be diagnosed with the disorder than girls. Comorbidity (co-occurrence of other disorders) is quite high in those with ADHD, with estimates suggesting that as many as 50% also suffer from another psychological disorder. If one identical twin has ADHD, the odds are quite high, upwards of 90%, that the other twin will develop it, too, pointing toward the organic nature of the condition.

Is ADHD a new phenomenon?

Although ADHD seems like a "new" disorder, it was first characterized around 1900 and the characterization has evolved since. In 1902, a physician named George Frederic Still studied a group of 20 children that he described as defiant, passionate, lawless, and difficult in general. The group consisted of three boys for every one girl. All of them exhibited troubling behavior by the age of eight, and they all came from solid family environments, leading Dr. Still to conclude the problems were likely to be biological, and possibly inherited. This was a particularly important observation given that, at the time, it was generally accepted that such problematic behavior always arose from bad parenting or that the children were just "rotten."

In 1934, Eugene Kahn and Louis Cohen described hyperactivity in some children who had suffered brain damage from encephalitis. Their observations led to the publication of a paper describing their "organic driveness" theory of the basis for hyperactivity.

A few years later, in 1937, a physician named Charles Bradley made the decision to give benzedrine (amphetamine) to "behaviorally disordered" pediatric patients. Why he decided to give a stimulant to these kids is not clear, but it seemed to help. And so, as far back as the 1930s, doctors have been using stimulants to treat disorders that look like what we now call ADHD.

In 1980, the diagnosis of Attention Deficit Disorder (ADD) was added to the DSM-III. The diagnosis included two categories – ADD with hyperactivity (ADD/H) and without (ADD/WO). That changed in 1987 with the release of the DSM-IIIR, the revised version of the DSM-III. At that time, the two diagnoses were combined into a single diagnosis – Attention Deficit Hyperactivity Disorder (ADHD).

Causes and treatments of ADHD

What causes the condition initially is unknown, but the brain mechanisms involved are becoming clearer. The causes seem to be present even before birth. As mentioned above, studies of monozygotic twins, those with identical genetics, suggest that if one twin develops ADHD, the odds are 90% that the other twin will develop it as well. Among children born solo, who go on to develop ADHD, between 10-35% have a parent or sibling with a history of ADHD. These findings suggest that while ADHD may not be 100% genetic in cause, heredity certainly plays a strong role. So, as with depression, if there is a family history of the disorder, it is wise to keep watch for symptoms.

It is also unclear whether people outgrow ADHD, but there is some evidence that this occurs. Some estimates suggest that the symptoms diminish in as many as 90% of patients between adolescence and adulthood, though this research is difficult to interpret. A good initial diagnosis of ADHD made during childhood or adolescence is based on in-depth interviews with parents and teachers and testing of the child. In contrast, follow-up during adulthood to determine if symptoms have improved usually involves little more than self-report assessments, which tend to be more favorable than the facts. As such, the number of patients for whom the disorder persists into adulthood is probably underestimated in these studies.

Treatment options for ADHD consist primarily of drug treatments and behavioral therapy. An ongoing multi-center study examining the effectives of various treatments suggests that medications are superior to therapy alone, and that adding therapy to medicines does little to boost effectiveness. Stimulants remain the most commonly used drugs to treat ADHD. Drugs like Ritalin (methylphenidate) and Adderall can work very well if prescribed properly after a thorough evaluation indicates sufficient symptoms to yield a confident diagnosis. Estimates are that between 75-90% of sufferers improve significantly with stimulants. Although these drugs activate, or stimulate, control subjects, they have an apparent calming effect on those with documented ADHD.

The stimulants that are used to treat ADHD are relatively safe when prescribed and used appropri-

SideNotes

The impact of major life stress during adolescence on mental health during young adulthood

In a fascinating study, researchers at the Institute for Public Health Research, University of Connecticut, interviewed high school seniors to assess the prevalence of adverse childhood experiences - like divorce, abuse, witnessing drug use in the home, etc. Two years later, they followed up with subjects by phone. Kids who experienced adverse events were more likely to exhibit depressive symptoms, drug abuse and antisocial behavior two years after high school. There was a cumulative effect of adverse experiences on the likelihood of exhibiting problems during the follow-up. So, as the negative life experiences of kids accrue, so do their chances of suffering, behavioral and psychologically, down the road.

ately. At the doses that are typically prescribed, there is little risk for tolerance, addiction, or withdrawal, and there is no evidence that taking a stimulant for ADHD while young increases the odds of substance abuse later during adolescence or young adulthood. That said, the drugs can cause uncomfortable side effects that include dizziness, jitteriness, sweating, high heart rate, and insomnia. Depending on the dose of the drug and its formulation, the therapeutic effects can last all day or can fade long before bedtime. When the effects wear off, some suffer a rebound effect that results in a worsening of symptoms. This can be a problem if, for example, the child has great difficulty concentrating on homework. In a situation like this, the prescribing physician might consider changing the dose or daily dosing pattern.

Importantly, do not fall into the trap of assuming that the effectiveness of the medications necessarily confirms the diagnosis of ADHD. Stimulants improve performance in kids with the condition, but they also tend to improve performance in anyone that takes them. Just because an adolescent's grades improve while on stimulants does not necessarily mean that they had ADHD to begin with. It is vital to have a thoughtful diagnosis before beginning pharmacological treatment to make sure than any improvements that occur during treatment reflect real improvements in the condition, not just the beneficial effects that stimulants have on the ability to learn.

It should be noted that ADHD drugs do have abuse potential. They can produce a buzz and certainly create activation and alertness that some people find pleasant. One of the newer areas of drug abuse research relates to children and teens sharing or selling their prescribed ADHD stimulants. This is a serious problem and is more prevalent than many might think. It is important that children understand that these are powerful drugs that can have unanticipated negative effects in people for whom they are not carefully prescribed. And it is obviously important for parents to be fully aware of the location and usage of their children's medications.

Healthy adolescents often take their friends' stimulants for something more than a speed rush. There is one segment of the population that abuses these drugs for reasons that have nothing to do with feeling buzzed…academic performance. It is a sad commentary, but there are many high school and college students who abuse ADHD medications as a way to enhance their academic performance by enabling them to stay awake or alert while studying or working on academic projects. This trend has become prevalent enough that some have begun to refer to Adderall as "The Ivy League Crack." Of course, driven students have been using caffeine, in various forms, for decades for the same purpose, but use of ADHD medications escalates the risks to a new level.

How do stimulants work in people with ADHD? There is no simple effect that accounts for all of the changes that these drugs can produce. But one important effect is related to the frontal lobes in the brain. The frontal lobes allow us to regulate our behaviors and plan for the future. As mentioned previously, it appears that ADHD is often related to problems with frontal lobe functioning. Stimulants increase levels of the neurotransmitter, dopamine, in the frontal lobes. The increased dopamine function allows circuits within the frontal lobes to do their job and help control impulses and guide focused behavior. Still, although stimulants can help manage the symptoms, there are no treatments available that "cure" ADHD. Before that can happen, we must first come to an understanding of what causes it. We know that increasing dopamine levels in the frontal lobes can help, but that doesn't provide an explanation for why the condition starts in the first place.

Clearly, most parents would prefer that their children and adolescents need not be treated with any medications whatsoever. In the case of treatment for ADHD and other significant psychological conditions, medications are worth it if the individual has enough difficulty functioning without them that the condition impedes healthy psychological and social growth AND if the medications really do make enough of a difference to improve functioning. The hope is that, by treating the condition and allowing the individual to function at a higher level, interactions with the environment will be healthier, and thus the brain will be molded in healthy ways not possible without the pharmaceutical help. In this way, the medications are like psychological training wheels. When it comes time to take the training wheels off, this should be done very slowly and under the supervision of the prescribing doctor.

Problems with anxiety

Anxiety is a troubling emotional state in which the individual perceives that something bad just might happen, and soon. For most of us, most of the time, anxiety is tied to a particular situation or thing. Anxiety about a dentist appointment or exam, for instance.

We all experience anxiety. At least we should. Healthy levels of anxiety help prepare us for potentially difficult events. Sometimes, however, anxiety becomes a real problem for people.[7] For some, it remains switched on permanently, something called generalized anxiety disorder. Post-Traumatic Stress Disorder (PTSD) is a learning related condition in which an individual reacts intensely to stimuli similar to those present during a traumatic event, such as a bomb explosion. Each time a loud explosion occurs, it triggers an overwhelming emotional response that was learned during the trauma. In between such events, an individual with PTSD can experience very high levels of anxiety in general.

The emotional experience of anxiety is closely associated with activation of the sympathetic nervous system, the system of nerves responsible for preparing us to fight or flee. For those who experience intense anxiety, a variety of physical symptoms often co-occur, such as agitation, flushing (blotchy reddening of the skin), trouble falling/staying asleep, sweating, lack of appetite, tremors, tachycardia (increased heart rate), dizziness and fainting, and others. Anxiety if a full-body experience.

Fortunately, several treatment options are available for those suffering from problems with anxiety. For adults with generalized anxiety disorder, newer generation antidepressants, like Effexor, have shown promise. Too little research has been conducted to know if such meds have comparable effects on adolescents. For acute episodes of anxiety, such as panic attacks, many adults take benzodiazepine-like drugs, including Valium and Xanax. While they are now often prescribed for adolescents, their impact on anxiety in teens is poorly studied.

The role of therapy in treating psychological disorders of adolescence, including anxiety disorders, should not be understated. Therapeutic approaches like cognitive behavioral therapy (CBT) have shown great promise in helping adolescents deal with anxiety, including the anxiety involved in Obsessive Compulsive Disorder, a condition in which an individual repeatedly engages in a behavioral pattern, like hand washing, to cope with the anxiety associated with a trigger, like germs.

In the chapter on diet and exercise, we discussed the health benefits of meditation and other activities that can pull the balance of nervous system activation from a strong sympathetic response to a strong parasympathetic response. Doing so essentially negates the sympathetic nervous system activity that stems from, and then contributes to, feelings of anxiety and fear. As a result, meditation, Yoga and other activities that involve focused and intentional relaxation can make all the difference in the world for adolescents and adults with normal to heightened levels of anxiety tied to daily life.

Panic disorder is another anxiety

> ### **Side**Notes
>
> #### The rise of Valium and drugs like it
>
> In 1972, the anti-anxiety (anxiolytic) drug Valium was the most widely prescribed drug of any type in the U.S. More than 85 million prescriptions were written in 1975. Doctors and patients found out the hard way that drugs like Valium, and newer compounds like Xanax, can be habit forming and difficult to stop due to physical withdrawal and dependence. This is powerfully depicted in the movie, "Valley Of The Dolls." The good news is that, with careful monitoring and wise decision making, such drugs can work wonders for those who suffer from intense anxiety. They seem to be safest and most effective when used on a *non*-daily basis.

related condition that afflicts adolescents. It involves intense overwhelming rushes of anxiety and fear that can immobilize an individual. Symptoms include dizziness, shortness of breath, sweating, choking, nausea, numbness and tingling, chest pain, fear of dying or going crazy, feelings of depersonalization or derealization. Not fun. To make matters worse, some patients develop a severe anxiety, called *anticipatory anxiety*, that an attack might happen, keeping them from engaging in daily activities for fear that they could have a panic attack.

Research at Stanford University suggests that panic disorder in adolescents develops as a result of both parental and individual psychological factors.[8] The authors reported that nearly 1/10 high school students at four California schools had a history of one or more panic attacks. Based on data collected from both students and their parents, the authors concluded that several family related factors, including a family history of panic attacks and having a chronically ill parent, were associated with panic disorder in adolescence.

The authors summarize the involvement of family genetic and environmental correlates as follows,

"Mood and anxiety disorders are highly familial. For example, estimates of the relative risk of panic disorder among first-degree relatives of probands with panic disorder range from 3 to 17."

That means that the odds of having panic attacks goes up somewhere between 3 and 17 times if you have close relatives with the condition.

Conduct disorders

Conduct disorders are problems with, well... conduct. Most kids get into trouble, but breaking a few rules isn't what conduct disorder is all about. Conduct disorder refers to a persistent pattern of violating the rights of others.[9] Chronic bullying, for instance, or frequent confrontations with parents or teachers. Children and adolescents with conduct disorder, unlike typical kids who simply get into trouble from time to time, seem to have little or no remorse for their actions. The American Academy of Child and Adolescent Psychology offers the following discussion on the topic:

"In order to diagnose a conduct disorders, a clinician will evaluate the teen for the presence of a repetitive and persistent pattern of behavior that violates the basic rights of others. Usually, teenagers with serious conduct disorders engage in a umber of unacceptable activities. Almost invariably, they seem to have little or no remorse, awareness, or concern that what they are doing is wrong.

For example, teenagers with conducts disorders might bully, threaten, and intimidate others. Routinely, they initiate physical fights, sometimes using weapons such as bats, bricks, broken bottles, knives, and guns. They get involved in muggings, purse snatching, armed robbery, sexual assault, animal torture, and rape.

Teenagers with conduct disorders might break into other people's homes, buildings, or cars. They might systematically lie to obtain goods or favors or to avoid obligations. They might con others, shoplift, or get involved in forgery. They repeatedly violate rules, break curfew, run away from home, or become truant. The severity of these negative or problem behaviors vary form youngster to youngster."

The world seems to be full of troubled kids. Determining which ones are truly in need of help and which are simply struggling to deal with normal life is difficult. In the case of conduct disorder, the condition requires repeated instances in which the individual acts in a disruptive and perhaps law-breaking manner.

Regardless of whether improper conduct constitutes a full-fledged disorder, many aspects of proper treatment are the same as those needed to guide a troubled, but still relatively healthy, kid. Support and encouragement, structure and enforced rules, reinforcement for progress, and so forth. Hopefully, they will either outgrow their disruptive behavioral tendencies or can be taught to control their behaviors more effectively and can avoid carrying such problematic behaviors with them into adulthood.

Schizophrenia – Splintering of the self

Schizophrenia is a confusing disorder, both for the person suffering from it and for those watching the person suffer.[10] We tend to take things for granted when they are stable and dependable, like the ability to walk and the relative ease with which we organize of our inner psychological worlds and voluntary behaviors. This isn't the case for those with schizophrenia, particularly with regard to making sense of thoughts and feelings and choosing behaviors that fit the situations in which we find ourselves.

Most of us are aware when an external voice gets processed by our brains, and when the voice we hear in our heads originates from the person we refer to as the "self." When hanging out with friends or family, we tend to agree on what's happening around us, who is in the room, what their intentions are, etcetera. We

> "During my first psychotic episode I was sitting in a room full of friends. Every one of them turned into demons... I closed my eyes and could hear them breathing next to me and clawing at my skin. A voice by my ear kept saying 'Bite him, Bite the Fucker!' Since then, it's not been so bad... On numerous occasions though, I fall into trances, in which I can't move but am fully conscious, just paralyzed. I feel them touching my body, sitting on me, clawing at my face, their beastly voices in my ears. I can't escape from these 'encounters'. I just have to wait for them to leave me alone."
>
> Text from an Internet chat site for people suffering from schizophrenia

watch television to be entertained or informed and recognize that the personalities on our favorite shows do not know us, are not connected to us in any significant way, and are not trying to deliver messages to us. For some developing adolescents and adults, things simply are not that simple. Their inner psychological worlds are splintered, insights are truly irrational and the world they perceive deviates in significant ways from the world that others perceive. The agony that those struggling with this condition feel is probably only overshadowed by the agony felt by those who watch them struggle.

Some symptoms of schizophrenia	
Delusions	False beliefs held in the face of substantial evidence to the contrary
of grandeur	Belief that one is an important character, such as Napoleon or Christ
of persecution	Belief that others are plotting against you
of reference	Belief that someone or something is delivering personal messages to you
Hallucinations	Sensory phenomenon not corroborated by others, usually auditory
Incoherent thoughts	Breakdown in normal thinking that often involves jumping wildly from one idea to another
Odd behavior	Long periods without movement, poor hygiene, odd speech patterns, and the like
echolalia	Repeating things that other people say
word salad	Stringing partial sentences together in an odd, often loosely associated, way
neologisms	Making up words

Schizophrenia is a broad category of psychological conditions characterized by distortions in thoughts and perceptions, and often difficulties communicating and behaving appropriately and consistently. With regard to odd behavior, schizophrenia brings that in spades.

Many people make the common error of confusing schizophrenia with split personalities, but they are quite different. In those with multiple personalities, each personality tends to have a consistent manner of behaving. It's just that one of several captains might be guiding the ship at any given time. Those with schizophrenia do not have the luxury of multiple selves, each having their lives together. They tend to have one chaotic self struggling to point the individual's behavior in the right direction amidst a truly bizarre and often frightening internal psychological landscape.

Two defining features of this type of disorder are delusions and hallucinations, both of which fall under the canopy of psychosis. Psychosis does not mean "crazy" or "insane," it means detached from reality in some significant way. Delusions are beliefs held in the face of substantial evidence to the contrary. For instance, some schizophrenics believe that they are someone extremely important, like the Messiah, or that people communicate with them through the television or household pets. Hallucinations refer to perceiving things, like sights and sounds, that aren't really there.

It was once thought that the onset of schizophrenia tended to come in the age range of about 18-25 for males and 26-45 for females. It has become clear that schizophrenia often comes much earlier, bringing the onset into the adolescent age range. It is thought to occur in between 1-2% of the population at some point. Not comforting odds given the severity of the condition. Somewhere between 25-50% of those diagnosed with schizophrenia attempt suicide and about 10% succeed. The disease has a high concordance rate, meaning that if one genetically identical twin gets it, the other has an uncomfortably high chance of getting it, too. Somewhere around 50% of people with an identical twin with schizophrenia will develop it, while upwards of 20% of those with a fraternal (non-identical) twin will develop it. As such, like most conditions, schizophrenia is partially genetic. Researchers believe that developing the condition requires a second hit, the first provided by genes, but the second coming from environmental stressors, an illness, or perhaps a single traumatic event. It is likely that most psychological disorders are like this. When the biological predisposition meets particular experiences during development, thoughts, behaviors and emotions become highly dysfunctional.

What goes wrong in the brains of those who develop schizophrenia? It appears that many are born with anatomical abnormalities, particularly in the frontal lobes, that make it hard for the brain to function. For most, it appears that the real problems begin when the frontal lobes are handed executive control over behavior during adolescence. If all goes well, the frontal lobes, which seem to give rise to the conscious self that we all hold so dear, slowly take on the task of guiding behavior in predictable ways and organizing thoughts and emotions in some kind of logical and unified manner. In those who develop schizophrenia, the transfer of authority goes wrong, and the frontal lobes are not capable of adequately managing the task of providing the individual with a unified sense of self and the ability to engage in smooth, consistent, goal-directed behaviors – the kind we need to be able to pull off in order to function in the world. In those with hallucinations, the brain creates odd thoughts and sounds and then mistakes the origin of these thoughts and sounds, believing that they come from outside of the individual rather than within the individual. In those with delusions, their beliefs, no matter how irrational to other people, seem to bring with them the kind of authority that only comes when one is right.

To understand the kinds of things that go wrong in the brains of those who develop schizophrenia, let's look briefly at auditory hallucinations. Most of us are aware of when the words in our heads are generated either in the head without vocalization or originated in our heads and then lead to vocalization. This is not the case in those with schizophrenia that are plagued by auditory hallucinations. For them, words generated in the head are confused with those coming from an outside source. It turns out that the brain is built in such a way that, when it works correctly, the generation of verbal thoughts, vocalized or not, leads signals to be sent to sensory areas basically saying, "Hey, any words that you perceive right now are being generated by

YOU." The same process, called *corollary discharge*, is used to tell us when we are about to tickle ourselves, pinch ourselves, what have you. Because of this process, we are aware of the difference between self-generated and other-generated thoughts, sounds and actions. There is evidence that the frontal lobes, which are supposed to send this kind of corollary discharge signal to auditory areas in the brain, falls down on the job and fails to send the appropriate signals. This can lead to mistakes in judging self-generated and other-generated stimuli, like the words and sounds involved in our thoughts. Having schizophrenics hum during auditory hallucinations is often sufficient to trigger sufficient corollary discharge to temporarily stop the hallucinations.

The good news is that treatments for schizophrenia have advanced significantly beyond locking people up forever or medicating them so heavily that they are left in drooling vegetative states. New antipsychotic medications remain similar to early medications, but are now able to help people hold the splinters together and actually function.

Recall that medications for ADHD work by increasing dopamine levels in key brain areas, including the frontal lobes. Medications for schizophrenia have the opposite effect, minimizing the activity of dopamine in key brain areas. This reveals how important normal levels of dopamine are in the brain, and provides insight into why drugs like methamphetamine, which increase dopamine levels in the brain, can cause the kinds of bizarre hallucinations we discussed in Chapter 6 when we looked at the case of Janelle Hornickel and Michael Wamsley. With regard to anti-schizophrenia drugs, known as antipsychotics, somehow, by diminishing the influence of dopamine in key brain circuits, particularly those involving communication between the frontal lobes and other structures, the circuits are able to function in a way that approximates normal to some degree.

In a broad sense, it appears that around 10% of schizophrenics overall fail to respond to treatment, 60% exhibit some relief but still require help in daily functioning, and 30% improve to the point that they can live and unction on their own. Unfortunately, these medications can have serious side effects, like weight gain and trouble coordinating muscles during movement. Regardless of how bad the side effects can be, the medications are a Godsend to many patients and their families. Therapy can be useful for helping patients and their loved ones cope, but medication is the key here.

Several attempts have been made to divide those with schizophrenia into different types. No one has yet done so satisfactorily, but one system is worth summarizing here. Those with *paranoid type* schizophrenia are characterized by delusions of persecution and grandeur. Those suffering from the *catatonic type* are characterized by their bizarre motor behaviors (movements) and often exhibit a phenomenon known as waxy flexibility, in which they tend to remain in whatever position you put them. *Disorganized type* schizophrenia is characterized mainly by incoherent thoughts and speech, and inappropriate, often flattened, emotional reactions. Finally, those in the *undifferentiated category* definitely have schizophrenia, but don't fit neatly into the preceding categories.

What about kids who are just having a hard time getting through life?

Mental health is a lot easier to understand if we lump sets of symptoms into categories and give them labels. In this chapter, we have examined depression, ADHD, anxiety disorders and conduct disorders. What about instances in which kids are just having a hard time?

All kids need love and support. Kids having difficulty during adolescence need extra. But love and support can be tricky issues when dealing with adolescents. As parents, most of us have the tendency to want to pull our kids onto our laps and protect them during difficult times. The problem is, during adolescence, many of the snags that kids run into are related to false starts on the pathway toward independence, such as relationships, jobs, etcetera. Often, adolescents don't want us to get as close to them as we want to be. Still, there are plenty of ways to demonstrate support and encouragement without coming on too strong. Taking them to their favorite restaurant, praising their efforts in various domains of their lives, giving them some extra TV time, to name a few.

Mentors can also play very important roles in the lives of kids who are having a hard time figuring out how they fit or struggling with daily stress. Many issues are far easier to discuss with trusted mentors than with one's parents.

What does it all mean?

Adolescence is a difficult stage of change, even when things go well. For many kids, adolescence is anything but smooth. When underlying biological factors meet toxic environments, the ease with which the brain is molded by experience can work against us, giving rise to maladaptive patterns of thoughts, emotions and behaviors. In other words, psychological disorders.

Given the often challenging nature of teenagers, it can be quite difficult to separate true psychopathology from normal, albeit troubling, adolescent psychological struggles. If you are concerned that your adolescent might be struggling with a true psychopathology, it's time to spring into action and have them assessed by a health care professional, like your pediatrician, or a clinically trained psychologist or social worker.

The good news is that advances in diagnosis and treatment are being made, albeit slowly, which increases the odds that a troubled adolescent will get the help they need.

Quick Facts:

- It is easy to tell when a previously stable adult begins suffering psychologically. This isn't the case with adolescents, who are moving targets in a variety of ways.

- Normal adolescence involves boredom, intense emotions and defiant behavior, often within the same day.

- For a variety of reasons, adolescents might feel a bit depressed, have difficulty paying attention in class, or be particularly defiant. For some kids, these problems can reach truly dysfunctional levels and interfere with daily life. In such cases, adolescents are often diagnosed with psychological disorders and treated accordingly.

- Depression involves more than feeling blue for a while. It involves pathological (dysfunctional) levels of gloominess, hopelessness and perhaps thoughts of suicide.

- Antidepressants do not work very well for adolescents, and can increase thoughts of suicide, but have their place in the arsenal of treatment options.

- ADHD involves persistent, dysfunctional difficulties in maintaining focus. The condition appears to stem from faulty activity in the brain's frontal lobes. Stimulant drugs used to treat ADHD work, and they appear to do so by increasing dopamine levels in the frontal lobes.

- Anxiety involves intense anticipatory fear that something bad is going to happen, and is well treated by drugs called anxyiolytics (e.g., Valium) which calm the brain's fear centers.

- Many kids have problems with conduct, but problems reaching truly unmanageable levels earn diagnoses.

- Schizophrenia is the most confusing of the conditions that often emerges during adolescence and is, by far, the hardest to treat.

- The disorder is characterized by difficulty creating and maintaining an inner sense of reality that parallels the reality of the outside world. This leads to big problems functioning in an adaptive way.

Chapter 12

Adolescents and the Internet – Keeping kids safe on the digital frontier

It seems like just the other day we were all writing letters on paper, commu-
nicating via telephone or snail mail, and ordering from catalogs. The
Internet has changed all of that. Mainstream culture began making its way
onto, or into, the Internet roughly 15 years ago. Anyone under the age of
about 15 was born into a world of computers and the web. Anyone 30 or
older had very different childhoods. This kind of thing can lead to big gaps
in understanding and communication between generations. Use of the
Internet has truly changed the social landscape for humans, for better and for
worse. Most parents know how to protect their kids from danger when they
are shopping together at the mall, but what about protecting them from
identity theft when they're shopping online? Traumatic experiences on the
Internet, such as being the victim of cyberbullying, can influence the psycho-
logical states of kids as much as the real thing. Keeping kids safe on the
Internet is an active process, which means that we adults have to be involved.
In this chapter, we will examine some of the pros and cons of Internet access
for adolescents, and provide suggestions for how to allow them to maximize
the benefit they get from it while minimizing the risks.

In 1969, four universities were connected via computers to provide a means of communication in case of major catastrophes, like war, thus forming the first long range network. Things advanced quickly from there. While Howard Dean is known for running a 2000 presidential campaign involving a major Internet component, Jimmy Carter actually beat him to it. In 1976, Carter and his running mate, Walter Mondale, used e-mail (yes, e-mail!) to plan campaign events. Queen Elizabeth sent an e-mail that same year.

By 1996, 45 million people were online. The number grew to 150 million in 1999 and 544 million in 2002. Clearly, the Internet now plays a major role in the daily lives of most professionals, students, teachers, politicians, and bargain shoppers. Duke University and others now view e-mail communication as an official means of getting messages to students. The Internet provides unparalleled access to information and resources. The Internet can also serve as a source of legitimate and healthy social support. Those with similar illnesses or interests, even if they are few in number and scattered across the planet, can connect and feel accepted.

Unfortunately, the Internet can also be unsafe if you don't know your way around. Personal information can be stolen, computer viruses contracted, and predators of all kinds lurk behind the digital facade. This makes understanding the Internet and the risks involved essential if we are to offer effective protection to young web surfers.

Welcome to the World Wide Web

Many parents of teens are out of touch with the Internet, often by choice. Anything can be found online. For people with patience to surf for what they need, an attention span long enough to stay on track, and the willpower to avoid going on spending sprees or getting lost in articles about celebrity gossip, the Internet can be a fantastic tool to get things done and find entertainment. However, for many, the Internet is an unknown, unexplored, or uncomfortable place. Whether you're interested in the Internet or not, it's a good bet your kids are. For this reason, it is critical to know the risks they face when they log on. This is particularly true if they have access to credit cards, yours or perhaps their own.

In addition to scams, spam, and fraud in general, we have all heard stories of things like kids being lured away by sex offenders, groups of suicidal people forming suicide pacts online, kids being tormented by fellow classmates on websites, embarrassing video clips being uploaded for the world to see, and so on. Unfortunately, these and other bad things actually do happen, and more often than one might guess.

Let's look at one particularly creepy example. In their publication, *A Parent's Guide to Internet Safety*, the FBI warns parents about two general types of sex offenders online – those who take their time and lure kids in slowly and those who attempt to exploit them quickly.[1] Here's some of what they have to say about those in the first category – patient, plotting, sex offenders.

SideNotes

Instant messaging and e-mail aren't just kid's stuff

On December 14, 2006, CNN.com ran an article entitled, "Those annoying little IMs? They cost $588B. U.S. office workers get interrupted on the job as often as 11 times an hour at a huge annual cost to business." It's hard to imagine that, just a few decades ago, our options for communication were essentially phone calls (with no call-waiting) or paper mail of some sort. These days, when we want to communicate with people, we want to do it *now*. Whereas it might have taken a few weeks to get a response to a letter in the 1970s and 80s, we expect replies to e-mails within a day or two. With instant messaging, we want responses, well, instantly! According to CNN, at the end of the day, access to electronic communication doesn't facilitate productivity, it derails it. One of the experts interviewed for the article "puts the blame on younger Generation X and Generation Y workers. 'They are the big-time abusers. If they need something or want something, they don't pick up the phone and ask for an appointment. They just barge in, and it's all about them,' he said."

"There are individuals who attempt to sexually exploit children through the use of on-line services and the Internet. Some of these individuals gradually seduce their targets through the use of attention, affection, kindness, and even gifts. These individuals are often willing to devote considerable amounts of time, money, and energy in this process. They listen to and empathize with the problems of children. They will be aware of the latest music, hobbies, and interests of children. These individuals attempt to gradually lower children's inhibitions by slowly introducing sexual context and content into their conversations."

And about the other type – those that work quickly to try take advantage of unsuspecting kids.

"There are other individuals, however, who immediately engage in sexually explicit conversation with children. Some offenders primarily collect and trade child-pornographic images, while others seek face-to-face meetings with children via on-line contacts. It is important for parents to understand that children can be indirectly victimized through conversation, i.e. 'chat,' as well as the transfer of sexually explicit information and material. Computer-sex offenders may also be evaluating children they come in contact with on-line for future face-to-face contact and direct victimization. Parents and children should remember that a computer-sex offender can be any age or sex. The person does not have to fit the caricature of a dirty, unkempt, older man wearing a raincoat to be someone who could harm a child."

As with other risks facing teens, it is important for parents and other adults to know the facts, in this case about the dangers that await kids online, and discuss them openly. Here are some suggestions for keeping your child or adolescent from being sexually harassed on the Internet and for keeping them safe online in general.

- Talk with your child about the risks involved in interacting with strangers on the Internet. Chat rooms and instant messaging provide ideal opportunities for sex offenders to communicate with your child. Just because their username is "HarmlessNiceGuy4U" doesn't mean anything!

- Spend time with your child online. This is a point that Microsoft founder Bill Gates stressed during an interview. Have them show you what they do, where they go, and with whom they interact. Odds are that your child won't like the idea, but explain to them that, as the parent, you need to know about the online world to which they are exposed. This isn't a punitive action – it is an information gathering and trust building exercise.

- If you have multiple computers in your home, rather than connecting every computer in every room of the house to the Internet, only connect one and place it in a common room, like a dining room, kitchen, or living room. It's much harder for unseemly things to take place online if the computer screen is visible to everyone. Your child will likely protest that this is an invasion of their privacy. They'll get over it. Slowly, as they age and mature, give them more space and privacy.

- Install software to help filter inappropriate Internet content prevent access to certain sites. A wide variety of options are available. The website www.safefamilies.org provides a wealth of information regarding filtering software, and provides free downloads of some programs. The site also features a training video for parents to teach them about the risks facing kids online and how to deal with them.

- This one is tricky and could be the source of some tension in your household. Many organizations, including the FBI, suggest regularly checking your child's e-mails for potentially inappropriate communication with people that you do not know. Explaining to your child that this is not a punitive measure in any way, but an effort on your part to keep them safe, might help diffuse the situation. This is a hard one, but some experts believe it's in their best interest. It is also what Bill Gates does with his own adolescents.

- Establish rules regarding Internet usage in the house and post them. These might include the amount of time a child can spend online and what activities are acceptable, and special instructions, such as never sharing personal information (name, phone number, address, school name) with strangers no matter how nice they seem, never share personal pictures, and never arrange face to face meetings with people they meet online. The website www.safefamilies.org, as well as others, contain sample family Internet pledges for printing and posting.

- Make it clear to your child that they will not be in trouble if they unknowingly fall victim to a sexual predator or scam, but that they must tell you right away so that you can take appropriate steps to protect them.

- Lead by example. Many kids gain access to Internet pornography the same way they gain access to alcohol – from parents! If your child finds your porn, or evidence that you have visited questionable sites, it will become much harder to convince them that such activities are inappropriate.

In the event that your child does fall prey to online threats – whether from bullies, sexual predators, or scam artists, contact your local law enforcement agency to report the event. Many law enforcement agencies have officers who are trained to deal with such situations, and can handle the situation in an assertive but non-threatening way.

A note about privacy

Establishing rules on Internet usage raises the broader issue of personal privacy. There are few things as important to teens as their privacy, and few things as unnerving to adults as giving kids space to live their own, private lives. It is very important to allow adolescents to have some privacy in order for them to begin moving toward independence. It's no less important to have a clear sense of when that privacy may be creating undue risk. Striking this balance requires calm, clear thinking and good communication.

In a May 3, 2006 interview with MSNBC's Donny Deutsch, Bill Gates suggested that parents should monitor everything about their kids' activities on the Internet until a certain age. Privacy should be given slowly once kids know how to be safe and make wise decisions online. He indicated that this is what they do at his house.

Posting personal information online – including profiles and video clips

The past few years have witnessed an explosion of sites aimed at allowing users, mostly young, to share personal information, video clips, gossip, and stories. Sites like MySpace.com, YouTube.com, Friendster.com, and the list goes on, all offer users an easy way to share personal thoughts, desires, plans, home movies, cell phone videos, etcetera. Many of these sites also allow users to post virtual diaries – or sometimes just virtual dribble – via web-logs (a.k.a., "blogs").

What many young users, or their parents, do not fully understand is that, if they post it, other people can see it! Lots of other people! By now, most of us have heard accounts of potential employers searching these sites for background on applicants and finding details that make them question the strength of the candidate's character or work ethic.[1] Sometimes both. It might seem cool to a college freshmen to write about how much she likes drinking Jagermeister and setting off fire alarms in the dorm. However, once it's up there, the whole world can see it, potentially for many years to come. Even if a kid gets all of those adolescent tendencies out of her system by the time graduation rolls around, potential job prospects would have no way of knowing that. All they would see are the pictures of her streaking down the hall with a bottle of Jager in tow.

If nobody visited these sites, then embarrassing pictures, videos, and rants could go unnoticed forever. But the fact is that social networking sites are wildly popular and becoming more popular every day. How popular? According to Alexa.com, a site owned by Amazon.com that ranks website popularity, the social networking site Myspace.com is currently one of the most visited websites in the world. YouTube.com, a site that allows users to post home video clips, holds a similar rank.

The take home message is not to post anything your grandmother would disapprove of or the secret service would investigate. If you put it online, chances are that someone will see it, now or sometime down the road!

Identity fraud

The Federal Trade Commission (FTC) received 246,035 complaints for identity fraud (a.k.a., identity theft) in 2006, making it the number one type of complaint received by the organization.[1] A 2003 report from the FTC estimated that a total of 27.3 million Americans were victims of identify fraud between the years of 1998-2003, and that the total dollar loss for businesses and banks was nearly $50 billion. Victims spent nearly $5 billion out of pocket to deal with the aftermath.

And so, identity fraud joins online sexual predation as yet another issue that parents and teens must anticipate. Identity fraud – pretending to be someone you're not – is nothing new, but the Internet has made the process much easier. Fortunately, the Internet has made checking one's credit easier, as well. If anyone tries to obtain credit in your name, it will show up on your credit report. All three major credit reporting entities – Equifax, Trans Union and Experian – will dispense a credit report to you at any time for a small fee. In fact, because of the Fair Credit Reporting Act, each of the three agencies is required to provide consumers with a free credit report once per year. According to the Federal Trade Commission in June 2007, you can request your credit reports online at Annualcreditreport.com or by calling 1-877-322-8228.

For additional peace of mind, you can purchase a package that gives you access to credit reports from all three agencies at any time and you will be contacted whenever an inquiry into your credit is made. That idea can be a good one, as dealing with credit problems early is far easier than cleaning up a big mess after theft has occurred. If you have a teen who shops on the Internet with your credit cards, it's probably worth this small investment to put your mind at ease. Otherwise, you could open your mailbox one day to find that your new self just purchased $4000 in services from a small "ranch" in Nevada!

Cyberbullying

Cyberbullying is covered in detail in the chapter on violence in schools. However, we will revisit this important topic here. Bullying involves the use of one's power to coerce others, often with the sole intention of making them feel terrible about themselves. The Internet provides an opportunity for malicious kids – and, sadly, some malicious adults – to torment their classmates without putting themselves at immediate risk of being identified or getting caught. Being able to hide in this way seems to embolden bullies to be even more cruel than they might be in face-to-face encounters. Online bullying, or cyberbullying, also provides an opportunity for kids that might

> "It's one thing to be bullied and humiliated in front of a few kids. It's one thing to feel rejection and have your heart crushed by a girl. But it has to be a totally different experience then a generation ago when these hurts and humiliation are now witnessed by a far larger, online adolescent audience."
>
> John Halligan writing about his son, Ryan Patrick Halligan, who ended his young life after years of torment on- and off-line
> www.ryanpatrickhalligan.org

normally stay on the sidelines to get involved in the bullying, perhaps to feed off of the bully's improper use of power.

Sadly, virtual bullying causes actual harm and inflicts the same deep psychological wounds caused by real-world bullying. The invisible nature of the threat makes cyberbullying a terrorist act in essence. The chorus of voices added by others emboldened by the anonymity does additional damage, and can push many kids who are already struggling with their awkward adolescent development to the brink. It is becoming increasingly and tragically common to hear reports of adolescents ending their lives after being tormented online.[2]

What does it all mean?

The Internet came onto the scene like a freight train, changed the way that we do just about everything, and shows no sign of slowing down. Even if you don't use the Internet, or do so sparingly, we're willing to bet your kids do. By arming yourself with information, talking with your kids about safe and acceptable surfing habits, moving the Internet-connected family computer into a common area, and establishing family policies, you can protect your kids from predators and protect yourself from identity theft.

Quick Facts:

- There is perhaps no better example of a generation gap than that caused by the dawn of the Internet age a few decades ago.

- Anything can be done or found online, making the digital frontier a place that offers great opportunities and equally great risks. Identity fraud and sexual predation are just two examples.

- Rules should be established regarding how often and for how long kids can be online each day, what kinds of activities are acceptable, and what the consequences of breaking the rules will be.

- Access to the web should be viewed as a privilege that kids earn by following the rules and demonstrating responsibility.

- It is wise to place the family computer in a place where it is easy to monitor online activity and help guide teens while they surf in order to ensure their safety.

- How much guidance and monitoring parents should provide is a personal decision, but the FBI and even Microsoft founder Bill Gates recommend close supervision that includes monitoring surfing habits and keeping track of whom kids communicate via e-mail.

- With the proper amount of supervision and the provision of longer leashes once responsible Internet use has been demonstrated, parents can help kids make full use of the Internet while staying safe at the same time.

Concluding remarks

In the preceding 12 chapters, we covered a wide range of topics related to adolescence. It is the author's sincere hope that you found the time it took to read the chapters well spent. The book represents an honest effort to capture the fascinating nature of adolescence as a stage of dynamic development and explore the nuances of several topics relevant to adolescent health.

Adolescence is the stage of human development during which we crawl out from beneath the nurturing wings of our caregivers and learn how to survive on our own. This transition is made possible by widespread, gene- and experience-driven changes in the adolescent body, including the brain. It is the job of an adolescent to absorb the rules and skills necessary to function independently in the current culture. It is the job of existing adults, and even older adolescents, to construct environments that teach kids these rules and skills.

Today's adults are the gatekeepers to violent videogames and TV content, prescription drugs with high abuse potential, alcoholic beverages and the like. They are also the gatekeepers to opportunities for exercise, healthy diets, genuine love and discipline. Except in extreme cases, it is the blend of healthy and unhealthy influences in a kid's life at any given time, rather than the presence or absence of one influence, that governs their well-being. This is good news, as it means progress toward building healthier kids can be made by making small changes in a number of basic areas rather than searching for magic bullets. As we discussed in Chapter 11 with regard to suicide prevention, anything that nudges a kid's mood and outlook on life in the right direction helps prevent suicide. The same holds for healthy adolescent development in general. Anything that promotes health and well-being at the moment promotes healthy development. The trick is to help kids build a little more resilience and positive momentum each day, rather than trying to engineer single experiences powerful enough to catapult them into the adolescent health stratosphere. The task of molding and shaping healthy kids is much more like making pottery on a pottery wheel than snapping together a whole bunch of Lego pieces.

Adolescent obesity serves as an apt example of the role that the culture plays in shaping kids, the importance of intra-kid variables like genes and psychology, and how few generations it takes for changes in the culture to manifest themselves as changes in appearances and behaviors. Today's adolescents weigh more than adolescents have ever weighed in the history of the world. Is there something different, biologically, about kids who live in the early 21st century relative to those who lived in the early 20th century? More than likely, no. The biological makeup of kids hasn't changed, but the culture responsible for molding them has changed. In the past century, each successive wave of teens has become larger and larger, culminating in the epidemic of obesity that we face now. After years of trying to fix the problem through medications, simplistic diet plans, and by pressuring the fast food industry to offer healthier foods, the culture is finally beginning to recognize how important individual choices and behavioral patterns are for determining our weights and general health. Hopefully, as the culture continues to change, this nationwide shift toward using an internal locus of control to govern eating will continue, we will begin to see decreases in the weights of our teens and adults and current problems with obesity will be largely ameliorated.

As is the case with obesity, solutions to many of the problems facing kids today involve helping young people, and adults, internalize a sense of control over their lives and make better long-term choices. In some ways, this is an easy task that simply requires teaching, recommending and modeling behaviors that imply an internal sense of control. For instance, kids who see adults searching for quick fixes to their problems in magazines, on television and in their medicine cabinets, are likely to learn that personal problems are best fixed by outside means. Those who see their parents and other caregivers approaching problems like being overweight through exercise and a truly healthy diet plan are likely to learn that most problems, though certainly not all, are best tackled from the inside out. In this way, we model an internal locus of control and teach kids the importance of developing one. This helps them maximize the amazing resilience that characterizes healthy young humans. It would not take long to get people on an internal-sense-of-control bandwagon, particularly if it could be profitable to companies. Indeed, if history is any guide to the future, we are due for a social shift in the general direction of self-responsibility.

Given the increasing length of time that we humans live and affect the culture, it is vital that we handle adolescence correctly and aim kids toward young adulthood with positive attitudes and strong cognitive faculties. We want our young people to invest themselves in the future, work hard to improve both their own lives and the health of their communities, and give at least as much as they take. Doing so requires that we value kids, create healthy pathways for them, encourage them to head down those healthy pathways, and then reinforce them for making wise decisions. We must also lead by example.

The adolescent brain will absorb whatever attitudes and behavioral patterns are valued in the culture so that the individual will be able to function in the current world, regardless of what that world is like. Before we can ask more of our kids, we adults need to demonstrate that we care enough about their futures to invest in the cultural changes needed to promote their healthy development. This might involve repairing our broken educational system and reinstituting physical education classes and electives that allow kids to explore the world and express themselves in healthy ways during the course of publicly funded schooling. It could also involve forcing the alcohol and pharmaceutical industries to change their marketing tactics and begin chipping in for the countless billions of dollars that use of their products costs taxpayers on a yearly basis. At a local level it could include building skateboard parks, community centers and the like. The point is that, if we want our kids to be healthy and make healthy choices, we need to create a world for them that values such behaviors. If we don't want our kids to bully others, obsess about their clothing, engage in starvation dieting, drink themselves into oblivion, and so on, we must create a world that devalues such activities, exacts punishment when necessary, offers alternative ways to meet one's needs, and truly rehabilitates those kids who get off track in order to get them back on track.

In short, we adults need to take the job of raising healthy adolescents more seriously, and begin taking the steps necessary to create a culture capable of doing so. It is not an understatement to say that our children are the future. That's just how it is! Investing more in their health and wellbeing is absolutely essential if we want them to be better stewards of the culture, and the planet, than we have been to date.

Before closing, it is worth mentioning a few things about this book from the perspective of its author. This book is an entirely independent project – written and edited by its author without the use of a traditional publisher. No doubt there are errors in the book and they will be fixed in subsequent revisions. The ideas in the book were shaped over many years of research and time spent in communities around the U.S. and elsewhere.

The actual manuscript was written over the course of four years in a range of countries, states, cities, hotels, airplanes and metros. However, the bulk of the writing was done in Bean Traders, a fantastic independent coffee shop in Durham, NC. I am truly indebted to the owners, David and Christy Chapman, for allowing me to become a fixture of their establishment and providing me with an endless flow of fresh roasted coffee and encouragement.

The reader might have noticed that nothing in the text was written from the first person, and that the often annoying third person was used throughout, as in "It is the author's opinion." There are several reasons for this, most notably that the book is meant to be a popular science text and not a book about the author or the author's opinions in particular.

While the book contains lots of words covering lots of topics, a long list of topics were not addressed. No doubt this frustrated many of you that made it this far and probably plenty more that didn't get to the end. There are several reasons for the missing material in this first edition. The most obvious explanation is that the author simply is not qualified to write about topics that stray too far from his own education, and doing so could have disastrous consequences! Also, a tremendous amount of material from various drafts covering myriad issues didn't make it into the final manuscript. The size of the book was getting out of hand and was showing signs of the potential to keep growing until no longer readable. As Philosophical Theologian, Stephen Joel Garver, writes about the size of a complete medieval Bible on parchment paper,[1]

> "Binding such a tome together in a single volume would produce an unusable text, too heavy to lift, and easily damaged"

In subsequent editions, the book will be expanded to address missing pieces, add resources, and review emerging topics relevant to adolescent health.

Thank you for taking your valuable time to read this book!

Notes and references

Introduction

[1] Each of these stages can be divided into several substages.

Chapter 1 - Adolescence

[1] Overview of adolescence and advice for parents for how to survive raising adolescents from KidsHealth.com http://www.kidshealth.com/parent/growth/growing/adolescence.html

[2] Casey BJ, Giedd JN and Thomas KM. Structural and functional brain development and its relation to cognitive development. Biological Psychiatry 2000;54:241-257.

Chapter 2 – Body image

[1] Media's Effects on Girls: Body Image and Gender Identity. National Institute on Media and the Family. Available online: http://www.mediafamily.org/facts/facts_mediaeffect.shtml

[2] Greenberg BS, Eastin ME, Hofschire L, Lachlan K, Brownell KD. Portrayals of overweight and obese individuals on commercial television. American Journal of Public Health 2003:93;1342-1348.

3   Cosmetic Surgery Quick Facts: 2005 ASAPS Statistics. The
    American Society for Aesthetic Plastic Surgery. Available
    online:
    http://www.surgery.org/press/procedurefacts-asqf.php
4   Available online:
    http://news.bbc.co.uk/2/hi/health/4147961.stm
5   Boodman SG. For more teenage girls, adult plastic surgery.
    The Washington Post, October 26, 2004. Available online:
    http://www.washingtonpost.com/ac2/wp-dyn/A62540-
    2004Oct25?language=printer
6   Seuol CK. Peer pressure plastics. Time Magazine, Au-
    gust 5, 2002. Available online:
    http://www.time.com/time/asia/covers/1101020805/p
    lastics.html

Chapter 3 – Diet and exercise

1   www.dietdrugsreport.com
2   FTC Stops Bogus Ads for "Bio Trim" and Other Weight-
    loss Products. Federal Trade Commission, November,
    2005.   Available   online:
    http://www.ftc.gov/opa/2005/11/biotrim.shtm
3   Brassell, B. How meditation promotes weight loss. May 17,
    2007. Available online:
    http://www.associatedcontent.com/article/244527/how
    _meditation_promotes_weight_loss.html
4   Kilgore WDS, Yurgelun-Todd DA. Developmental
    changes in functional brain responses in adolescents to im-
    ages of high and low-calorie foods. Developmental Psy-
    chobiology 2005;47:377-397.
5   A Review of the Use of Vending Machines in Public
    Schools. Office of Legislative Auditor General State of
    Utah. Report #2006-10, September, 2006.

[6] McMurray C. Junk food a staple for many teens. In Gallup, Gallup and Newport, "The Gallup Poll: Public Opinion 2004," Rowman and Littlefield, 2006.

[7] School vending machines "dispensing junk." Center for Science in the Public Interest, May 11, 2004. Available online: http://www.cspinet.org/new/200405111.html

[8] Barnes VA, Davis HC, Murzynowsk JB, Treiber FA. Impact of meditation on resting and ambulatory blood pressure and heart rate in youth. Psychosomatic Medicine 2004:66;909-914.

[9] Manjunath NK, Telles S. Spatial and verbal memory test scores following yoga and fine arts camps for school children. Indian Journal of Physiology & Pharmacology 2004:48:353-6.

[10] Lazar SW, Kerr CE, Wasserman RH, Gray JR, Greve DN, Treadway MT, McGarvey M, Quinn BT, Dusek JA, Benson H, Rauch SL, Moore CI, Fischl B. Meditation experience is associated with increased cortical thickness. Neuroreport 2005:16:1893-7.

[11] Cahn BR, Polich J. Meditation states and traits: EEG, ERP, and neuroimaging studies. Psychological Bulletin 2006:132;180-211.

[12] Orme-Johnson DW, Schneider RH, Son YD. Nidich S. Cho ZH. Neuroimaging of meditation's effect on brain reactivity to pain. Neuroreport 2006:17:1359-63

[13] Aftanas L, Golosheykin S. Impact of regular meditation practice on EEG activity at rest and during evoked negative emotions. International Journal of Neuroscience 2005:115:893-909.

Chapter 4 – Videogame violence

[1] Lurie K. Violent games. ScienCentral News. May 14, 2004. Available online: http://www.sciencentral.com/articles/view.php3?article_id=218392248&cat=1_7

[2] "Manhunt 2 - first look. Check out the schizophrenic sequel to the most violent game ever." Written by Mikel Reparaz and available online: http://www.gamesradar.com

[3] Brief amici curiae of thirty-three media scholars in *Interactive Digital Software Association et al* v *St. Louis County et al.* No. 02-3010, United States Court of Appeals for the Eighth Circuit. September 24, 2002. Available online: http://www.fepproject.org/courtbriefs/stlouis.html

[4] Mathiak K, Weber R. Toward brain correlates of natural behavior: fMRI during violent video games. Human Brain Mapping 2006;27:948-956.

[5] Carnagey NL, Anderson CA. The effects of reward and punishment in violent videogames on aggressive affect, cognition, and behavior. Psychological Science 2005:16;882-890.

[6] Brady SS, Matthews KA. Effects of media violence on health-related outcomes among young men. Arch Pediatr Adolesc Med 2006;160:341-347.

[7] Barron M. Militarism and video games: An interview with Nina Hunteman. Media Education Foundation, 2003. Available online: http://www.mediaed.org/news/articles/militarism

[8] Dietz TL. An Examination of violence and gender role portrayals in video games: Implications for gender socialization and aggressive behavior. Sex Roles 1998;38:425-442.

[9] Available online: http://www.igda.org/articles/rreynolds_ethics.php

[10] Das DA, Grimmer KA, Sparnon AL, McRae SE, Thomas BH. The efficacy of playing a virtual a virtual reality game in modulating pain for children with acute burn injuries: A randomized controlled trial. BMC Pediatrics 2005:5(1).

[11] Violent video games increase aggression and violence. Testimony by Craig Anderson, PhD, at a Senate Committee hearing on "The impact of interactive violence on children." Tuesday, March 21, 2000.

[12] Huesmann LR, Titus-Moise J, Podolski CL, Eron L. Longitudinal relations between children's exposure to TV violence and their violent behavior in young adulthood: 1977-1992. Developmental Psychology 2003;39:201-221.

[13] Geen RG, Stonner D, Shope GL. The facilitation of aggression by aggression: Evidence against the catharsis hypothesis. J Pers Soc Psychol 1975;31:721-726.

[14] Anderson CA, Carnagey NL, Eubanks J. Exposure to violent media: The effects of songs with violent lyrics on aggressive thoughts and feelings. J Pers Soc Psychol 2003;84:960-971.

[15] Robinson TN, Wilde ML, Navacruz LC, Haydel KF, Varady A. Effects of reducing children's television viewing and video game use on aggressive behavior: A randomized controlled trial. Arch Pediatr Adolesc Med 2001;155:17-23.

[16] Konrad R. Child advocates upset over violence in 'Manhunt 2' video game, even in toned-down version. Associated Press, October 30, 2007.

Chapter 5 – Bullying and school shootings

[1] Brookmeyer KA, Henrich CC, Schwab-Stone M. Adolescents who witness community violence: Can parent support and prosocial cognitions protect them from

committing violence? Child Development 2005;76:917-929.

[2] Hurt H, Malmud E, Brodsky NL, Giannetta J. Exposure to violence: Psychological and academic correlates in child witnesses. Arch Pediatr Adolesc Med 2001;155:1351-1356.

[3] Augustyn M, Groves BM. Training clinicians to identify the hidden victims: Children and adolescents who witness violence. Am J Prev Med 2005;29:272-278.

[4] Flannery, D., Singer, M. & Wester, K. (2001) Violence exposure, psychological trauma and suicide risk in a community sample of dangerously violent adolescents. Journal of the Academy of Child and Adolescent Psychiatry, 40(4), 435-442.

[5] Cillessen AHN, Mayeux L. From censure to reinforcement: Developmental changes in the association between aggression and social status. Child Development 2004;75:147-163.

[6] Presentation entitled, "Bullying Among Children & Youth." U.S. Department of Health and Human Services, 2005. Available online: http://stopbullyingnow.hrsa.gov/ppt/Bullying_Among _Youth.ppt

[7] Take action against bullying. U.S. Department of Health and Human Services, 2003. Available online: http://mentalhealth.samhsa.gov/publications/allpubs/ SVP-0056/

[8] DeRosier ME and Marcus SR. Building friendships and combating bullying: Effectiveness of S.S. Grin at one-year follow-up. J Clin Child Adolesc Psychol 2995;34:140-150.

[9] Deadly lessons: School shooters tell why. Chicago Sun-Times Special Report. October 15-16, 2000. Available online: www.suntimes.com/shoot

Chapter 6 - Drugs

[1] US Food and Drug Administration. Federal Food Drug and Cosmetic Act. Available online: http://www.fda.gov/opacom/laws/fdcact/fdctoc.htm

[2] Johnston, L. D., O'Malley, P. M., Bachman, J. G., & Schulenberg, J. E. (2007). Monitoring the Future national survey results on drug use, 1975-2006. Volume I: Secondary school students (NIH Publication No. 07-6205). Bethesda, MD: National Institute on Drug Abuse, 699 pp.

[3] Smith NT. A review of the published literature into cannabis withdrawal symptoms in human users. Addiction 2002;97(6):621-32

[4] Kouri EM, Pope HG. Abstinence symptoms during withdrawal from chronic marijuana use. Exp Clin Psychopharmacol 2000;8(4):483-92.

[5] Zickler P. Evidence accumulates that long-term marijuana users experience withdrawal. NIDA Notes 2000;15(1). Available online:
http://www.nida.nih.gov/NIDA_notes/NNVol15N1/Evidence.html

[6] Giedd et al. Brain development during childhood and adolescence: a longitudinal study. Nature Neuroscience 1999;2:861-863.

[7] National Drug Policy: United States of America, Benjamin Dolin, Law and Government Division, 24 July 2001, Library of Parliament

[8] Charles Whitebread, Professor of Law, USC Law School. The history of the non-medical use of drugs in the United States. Speech at the California Judges Association 1995 annual conference. Available online:
http://www.druglibrary.org/schaffer/History/whiteb1.htm

[9] Bonnie RJ, Whitebread CH. The forbidden fruit and the tree of knowledge: An inquiry into the legal history of American marijuana prohibition, Virginia Law Review, 1970, 56(6).

[10] Zernike K. Antidrug program says it will adopt a new strategy. The New York Times. February 1, 2001.

[11] Project Northland material can be found here: http://www.epi.umn.edu/projectnorthland/schoolba.html

[12] Above the Influence homepage: www.abovetheinfluence.com

[13] Monitoring the Future homepage: www.monitoringthefuture.org

[14] SAMSHA treatment locator page: http://findtreatment.samhsa.gov/

[15] Vaughn MG, Howard MO. Adolescents substance abuse treatment: A synthesis of controlled evaluations. Research on Social Work Practice 2004;14(5):325-335. Available online: http://rsw.sagepub.com/cgi/content/abstract/14/5/325

[16] Kadden et al. Abstinence rates following behavioral treatments for marijuana dependence. Addictive Behaviors 2007:32(6);1220-1236.

[17] Wilson DB, Mitchell O, MacKenzie DL. A systematic review of drug court effects on recidivism. Journal of Experimental Criminology 2006:2(4);459-487. Available online: http://www.springerlink.com/content/164371146v5m4736/

[18] Pitts WJ. Measuring recidivism in a juvenile drug court: Systematic outcome study of a juvenile drug court using historical information. The Southwest Journal of Criminal Justice 2006:3(1);17-34.

[19] Huddleston CW, Freeman-Wilson K, Marlowe D, Roussell A. (2005). Painting the current picture: A national report card on drug courts and other problem solving court programs in the United States. Bureau of Justice Programs, Washington, D.C.

Chapter 7 - Alcohol

[1.] http://www2.potsdam.edu/hansondj/controversies/1114796842.html

[2] http://www2.potsdam.edu/hansondj/index.html

[3] Blocker JS. Did prohibition really work? Alcohol prohibition as a public health innovation. American Journal of Public Health 2006:96(2);233-243.

[4] http://www.chooseresponsibility.org/

[5] Johnston, L. D., O'Malley, P. M., Bachman, J. G., & Schulenberg, J. E. (2007). Monitoring the Future national survey results on drug use, 1975-2006. Volume I: Secondary school students (NIH Publication No. 07-6205). Bethesda, MD: National Institute on Drug Abuse, 699 pp.

[6] http://www.securityoncampus.org

[7] http://www.hazethemovie.com/

[8] White AM. What happened? Alcohol, memory blackouts, and the brain. Alcohol Research & Health: The Journal of the National Institute on Alcohol Abuse and Alcoholism 2003:27;186-196.

[9] White AM, Swartzwelder HS. Age-related effects of alcohol on memory and memory-related brain function in adolescents and adults. Recent Dev Alcohol 2005;17:161-76.

[10] Harford TC, Wechsler H, Buthen BO. Alcohol Related Aggression and Drinking at Off-campus Parties and Bars:

A National Study of Current Drinkers at College. Journal of Studies on Alcohol. 2003; 64(5): 704-711.

[11] http://www.collegedrinkingprevention.gov/

[12] White AM, Kraus CL, Swartzwelder HS. Many college freshmen drink at levels way beyond the binge threshold. Alc Clin Exp Research 2006;30(6):1006–1010.

[13] Leinwand D. Alcohol-soaked spring break lures students abroad. USA Today, January 5, 2003. Available online: http://www.usatoday.com/news/nation/2003-01-05-spring-break-usat_x.htm

[14] Snyder LB et al. Effects of alcohol advertising exposure on drinking among youth. Archives of Pediatrics and Adolescent Medicine 2006;160(1):18-24.

[15] Office of the Inspector General of the DoD, Evaluation Report on the Economic Impact of Alcohol Misuse, Report No. 97-150, June 2, 1997

[16] Hingson R, Heeren T, Winter M. Age of drinking onset and alcohol dependence—age at onset duration and severity. Archives of Pediatrics and Adolescent Medicine. 2006; 160:739-746.

[17] Youth Drinking Rates and Problems: Comparison of European Countries and the United States. Office of Juvenile Justice and Delinquency Prevention. U.S. Department of Justice. Available online: http://www.udetc.org/documents/CompareDrinkRate.pdf

[18] Data collected through the European School Survey Project on Alcohol and other Drugs (ESPAD) can be searched according to different drugs and behaviors. Available online: http://www.espad.org/

Chapter 8 – Immune system

[1] Bartlett JA et al. Immune function in healthy adolescents. Clinical and Diagnostic Laboratory Immunology 1998;Jan:105-113.

[2] Yirmiya R. Depression in medical illness. West J Med. 2000; 173(5): 333–336.

[3] Yirmiya R, Pollak Y, Morag M, Reichenberg A, Barak O, Avitsur R, Shavit Y, Ovadia H, Weidenfeld J, Morag A, Newman ME, Pollmacher T. Illness, cytokines, and depression. Ann N Y Acad Sci. 2000;917:478-87.

[4] Dantzer R, Kelley KW. Twenty years of research on cytokine-induced sickness behavior. Brain Behav Immun. 2006 Nov 4 ahead of print

[5] White AM (2007) A Guide to Transfer Factors and Immune System Health. Charleston, South Carolina: BookSurge.

[6] Immunization of adolescents recommendations of the Advisory Committee on Immunization Practices, the American Academy of Pediatrics, the American Academy of Family Physicians, and the American Medical Association. MMWR 1996;45(RR-13):1-16.

[7] Cohen J. Did Merck's failed HIV vaccine cause harm? Science 2007;318(5853):1048-1049.

[8] Nemet D, Mills PJ, Cooper DM. Effects of intense wrestling exercise on leucocytes and adhesion molecules in adolescent boys. British Journal of Sports Medicine 2004;38(2):154-158.

[9] Nieman DC. Current perspectives on exercise immunology. Current Sports Medicine Reports 2007;2(5):239-242.

[10] Ickovics JR, Milan S, Boland R, Schoinbaum E, Schuman P, Vlahov D. Psychological resources protect health: 5-year survival and immune function among HIV-infected

women from four US cities. AIDS. 2006;20(14):1851-1860

[11] Haber MJ et al. Effectiveness of interventions to reduce contact rates during a simulated influenza pandemic. Emerging Infectious Diseases. 2007;13(4):581-589.

Chapter 9 – Puberty

[1] Dahl RE. Adolescent brain development: A period of vulnerabilities and opportunities. Annals of the New York Academy of Sciences 2004;1021:1-22.

[2] For an excellent review for lay audiences of the changes that occur during puberty please visit this site: http://www.kidshealth.org/teen/sexual_health/changing_body/puberty.html

[3] Overview of the Tanner scale and pubertal development: http://www.answers.com/topic/tanner-stages?cat=health

[4] Daw J. Is PMDD real? APA Monitor 2002;33(9):58. Available online: http://www.apa.org/monitor/oct02/pmdd.html

[5] Chavarro JE. Effects of a School-based Obesity-prevention Intervention on Menarche (United States). Cancer Causes and Control 2005;16(10):1245-1252.

Chapter 10 - Sex

[1] Abma JC, Martinez GM, Mosher WD, Dawson BS. Teen-agers in the United States: Sexual Activity, Contraceptive Use, and Childbearing, 2002. National Center for Health Statistics. Vital and Health Statistics, 23(24). December 2004.

[2] National Youth Risk Behavior Survey, 1991-2005, Trends in the Prevalence of Sexual Behaviors. US Department of

Health and Human Services. Centers for Disease Control. Available online: http://www.cdc.gov/yrbss

[3] Rothenberg RB, Sterk C, Toomey KE, Potterat JJ, Johnson D, Schrader M, Hatch S. Using social network and ethnographic tools to evaluate syphilis transmission. Sexual Transmitted Diseases 1998;25(3):154-160.

[4] PBS Frontline interview with Claire Sterk. Available online: http://www.pbs.org/wgbh/pages/frontline/shows/georgia/interviews/sterk.html

[5] Sabia JJ, Does sex education affect adolescent sexual behavior and health? J Policy Anal Management 2006;25:783-802.

[6] U.S. Teenage Pregnancy Statistics National and State Trends and Trends by Race and Ethnicity. Guttmacher Institute, 120 Wall Street, New York, NY 10005, Updated September 2006

[7] Williams TJ, Pepitone ME, Christensen SE, Cooke BM, Huberman AD, Breedlove NJ, Breedlove TJ, Jordan CL, Breedlove MS. Finger-length ratio and sexual orientation. Nature 2000;404:455-456.

[8] For more on the National Teen Dating Violence Initiative, visit the website for the initiative, http://crapo.senate.gov/issues/teen_dating_violence.cfm

Chapter 11 – Psychological disorders

[1] For an excellent overview of mental illness see the Surgeon General's report on the matter:
http://www.surgeongeneral.gov/library/mentalhealth/home.html

[2] WebMD offers an excellent section on depression:
http://www.webmd.com/depression/default.htm

[3] Goodman WK, Murphy TK, Lazoritz M. Risk of suicidality during antidepressant treatment of children and adolescents. Primary Psychiatry 2006;13(1):43-50.

[4] Warning signs of suicide and phone numbers for help from the American Association of Suicidology: http://www.suicidology.org/

[5] Bearman PS, Moody J. Suicide and friendships among American adolescents. Am J Public Health 2004;94:89-95.

[6] ADHD information and resources from the CDC: http://www.cdc.gov/ncbddd/adhd/

[7] Publication on anxiety disorders from NIMH: http://www.nimh.nih.gov/health/publications/anxiety-disorders/complete-publication.shtml

[8] Hayward C et al. Parent-reported predictors of adolescent panic attacks. J American Academy of Child and Adolescent Psychiatry 2004;43(5):613-620.

[9] Summary of conduct disorder symptoms from PsychCentral: http://psychcentral.com/disorders/sx67.htm

[10] Information on schizophrenia from NIMH: http://www.nimh.nih.gov/health/topics/schizophrenia/index.shtml

Chapter 12 – Internet

[1] A parent's guide to Internet safety. U.S. Department of Justice, Federal Bureau of Investigation. Available online: http://www.fbi.gov/publications/pguide/pguidee.htm

[2] Finder A. For some, online persona undermines a resume. The New York Times, June 11, 2006.

[3] FTC site on identity theft. Available online: http://www.ftc.gov/bcp/edu/microsites/idtheft/

[4] Willard N. Educator's guide to cyberbullying and cyberthreats. Center for Safe and Responsible Use of the Inter-

net. April, 2007. Available online:
http://www.cyberbully.org/cyberbully/docs/cbcteduca
tor.pdf

Concluding remarks

[1] Garver, J. Inventing "The Bible," Revelation, Theology,
Phenomenon and Text.
http://www.joelgarver.com/writ/phil/bible.htm

1467799

Made in the USA